Dimensions of the Sacred

University of California Press
Berkeley and Los Angeles, California

Published by arrangement with Harper Collins Publishers, UK

Copyright © Ninian Smart 1996

Ninian Smart asserts the moral right to
be identified as the author of this work

Cataloging-in-Publication data is available from the Library of Congress

ISBN 0-520-20777-7

Set in Linotron Ehrhardt
at The Spartan Press Ltd,
Lymington, Hants

Printed in the United States of America
1   2   3   4   5   6   7   8   9

To my colleagues
in Santa Barbara and Lancaster

CONTENTS

PREFACE

I am grateful to Toby Mundy and Stuart Proffitt for their help in seeing this book through to press. I also gained encouragement from my colleagues at the University of California, Santa Barbara and from my former doctoral students.

NINIAN SMART   June 1995

GLOSSARY

absolutism A philosophy or doctrine which claims that there is an absolute or impersonal force underlying the universe.

abstractification The process of replacing narratives or myths with more abstract accounts of the evolution of human affairs (such as the Marxist account of history in terms of class and material change).

Adi Granth The Sikh scriptures.

Advaita Vedanta The Hindu theology of non-dualism (see **Śankara**), asserting the identity of the human Self and the Divine Being.

agricultural rites Rituals performed in the course of agricultural work, used, for example, to enhance the fertility of crops.

alchemy A speculative system designed to change chemical and other substances for the benefit of human health and long life.

Amida Japanese name for Amitābha, the focus of devotional Buddhism.

Amitābha The Celestial Buddha in Indian Mahāyāna Buddhism and creator of the Pure Land, where the faithful will be reborn and lead a heavenly life, until the time comes for their ultimate release or nirvana.

Anabaptism A radical reformation movement which argued for 're-baptism', that is, the baptism of adults. The tradition is maintained by Mennonites, Baptists and others.

Anglicanism Those churches affiliated to the Church of England under the general leadership of the Archbishop of Canterbury: often known as episcopalianism.

aniconic religions Religions, such as Islam, which ban images or other material representations of God.

animatism The theory that material phenomena contain souls and so are animate.

animism The theory that material phenomena can be regarded as souls or as having souls.

anthropology The social science which studies human societies, usually small-scale ones.

apotropaic rituals Rituals designed to turn away evils such as disease (the Greek root *apotrop-* means 'to turn away').

Aristotle (384–322 B.C.E.)   Greek philosopher and biologist.

asceticism   The giving up of pleasures and living in austerity.

atheism   The belief that there is no God; however, some atheist systems do retain the idea of lesser gods.

audition   The hearing of divine or mysterious voices: for example, Augustine's conversion, Joan of Arc, and others.

Augustine   Saint, bishop of Hippo (354–430 C.E.) and author of *The City of God* and other works.

Avalokiteśvara   The most famous *bodhisattva* or Buddha-to-be in Mahāyāna Buddhism: changed sex and became Kuan-yin in China and Kannon in Japan.

avatar   A descent or incarnation of Viṣṇu in the Indian tradition.

Avicenna (980–1037 C.E.)   Latin name of ibn Sīnā, the famous Muslim philosopher and medical practitioner.

axis mundi   The axis of the world; the central pillar or mountain around which the cosmos is arranged and revolves.

baptism   The immersion of a Christian child or adult to initiate her or him into the Church; also used by those movements or churches which believe in adult baptism.

Baptist   An adherent of one of the churches mentioned above.

bathing, ritual   The use of immersion in water to purify or cure human beings.

behindness   The notion that the Divine is behind the cosmos.

Benedictines   Mainly Catholic monks (and nuns) who follow the rule created by St Benedict (?480–?547 C.E.).

bhakti   Devotion; devotional religion in the Indian tradition.

Bhedābhedavāda   The doctrine that the Self is both different *and* non-different from the Divine Being: this version of Vedanta foreshadows the qualified Non-Dualism of Rāmānuja (q.v.).

Bible   These are the Hebrew Bible (Old Testament) and the Christian Bible (the Hebrew Bible plus the New Testament). Even the Hebrew Bible and the Old Testament have very different interpretations, according to Jewish and Christian perspectives.

Bodhisattva   A person destined for Enlightenment, that is, to become a Buddha. In the Mahāyāna, Bodhisattvas were regarded somewhat like gods. They postponed their final liberation to help other beings reach salvation and could transfer merit from themselves to the otherwise unworthy faithful.

'born again' experience   The experience of feeling converted through immediate experience of the Lord. This is a Christian evangelical phrase but is occasionally used by people of other faiths.

brahman This neuter word in Sanskrit originally referred to the power resident in Brahmin priests, and so came to be used of the holy power in sacrifices and eventually of the Holy Power controlling and suffusing the universe.

Brahmanism A Western term referring to the doctrines and religion of Brahmins, including the idea that the holy power is Brahman (the Absolute) behind the operations of the universe.

brahmavihāras The 'abodes of holy power' in Buddhism: a term therefore for the four main Buddhist virtues, namely benevolence, compassion, joy in others' joy and equanimity.

Buddha A term used for the Buddha Gautama (Gotama) who preached the doctrine originally in human history, and for previous Buddhas, celestial Buddhas and others.

Bushido A Japanese martial art or code of phlegmatic and excellent behaviour.

Calvinism The doctrines of John (Jean) Calvin (1509–63), including the idea of predestination, viz. that an individual's destiny is already determined in advance, being within the decision of God.

cargo cults New religions in the south Pacific which saw cargoes or White goods as promised miraculously to the faithful.

caste system The Hindu or Indian system in which people are arranged in five main divisions and numerous subdivisions. The five comprise: Brahmins or priests; *kṣatriyas* or warriors, the *vaiśyas* or merchants, *śudras* or labourers, the untouchables or fifth class. These broad divisions are broken up into many subdivisions or *jātis* castes, more strictly.

celibacy The unmarried state practised by Catholic and Orthodox nuns and monks, and similar people in Buddhism, together with lone holy men and women in India.

Ch'ān The Chinese word for meditation and hence the name of the Ch'an school of Buddhism, merging Taoist and Buddhist values.

ch'i Chinese word for material energy, contrasted with *li* or 'principle'; the combination of the two constitutes things.

Christendom The domain of Christianity in the Middle Ages, as contrasted with the domain of Islam.

Chu Hsi (1130–1200 C.E.) The most influential Neo-confucian philosopher in China, whose commentaries formed the basis of the imperial examination system.

Chuang-tzu (4th Century C.E.) After Lao Tzu (assuming he existed), the most important Taoist philosopher.

civilizational religion A religion constituting in broad measure the background for a whole civilization, such as Islam or Buddhism.

combined religions Where two or more religions merge, as in the 'three religions of China'.

Communism The practical application of Marxism, as in the Soviet Union.

communitas The sense of community (Latin word) used by the anthropological theorist Victor Turner (q.v.).

comparative religion The study of the likenesses and contrasts between religious traditions, founded in the nineteenth century.

Confucianism The State ideology based on the tradition of K'ung or Confucius (the Latin rendition of his name used by Catholic missionaries to China). Sometimes Confucianism is taken to include not only ancestor-reverence, important in China since earliest time, but also folk religion.

Confucius (551–479 C.E.) Teacher and editor of traditional collections of writings, as well as founder of a scheme of values which has had a profound impact on Chinese history and education. Usually referred to as K'ung-fu-tse in traditional language and as Kong in modern pin-yin romanization (Chinese communist system).

congregationalism A movement in the Christian Church emphasizing the independence of congregations in governance that was important in the formation of American Protestantism.

contemplation A mode of self-discipline and mental focusing in various religions and movements (in Catholicism, Orthodoxy, Sufism and Indian yoga, for example).

cosmic royal religion A religious system (especially in the Ancient Near East) where the ruler is mediator between cosmic power(s) and earthly events.

cosmology Theory or theories about the composition and development of the universe.

coterminous religions A situation where a religion coincides in range or time with a nation or ethnic group (people, tribe, etc.).

covenant A pact between God and humankind (or a section thereof).

cross-cultural phenomenology The enterprise of seeing different classes of religious phenomena on a cross-cultural basis: e.g. noting similarities in kinds of sacrifice, devotionalism and so on.

curative rites Rituals of curing.

Dalai Lama The main spiritual and political ruler of Tibet, head of the Gelugpa denomination: the current occupant of the title (which means 'Ocean-like spiritual teacher') is Tenzin Gyatso, born 1935.

Dar-al-Islam The domain of Islam: roughly equivalent to the Christian notion of Christendom.

definitional function of doctrine The way doctrinal belief defines a group, rather than (say) ancestry.

deism The belief in a God as creator and source of ethics, but not as a continuously active being (this belief is theism): common among the intelligentsia in the eighteenth century in parts of Europe and America.

descriptive function of doctrine   The way doctrine describes the world and what is Transcendent (for example, God).

Devi   Indian representation of the Divine Being as female.

devic causation   The cause of events ascribed to a god (*deva* in Sanskrit). Thus, a rough sea would, in ancient Roman times, be ascribed to Neptune.

dharma   Traditional Indian word for cosmic order, or teaching about this, or proper or virtuous action, or truth.

Dharmakâya   The highest of the three bodies of the Buddha as envisaged in Mahāyāna Buddhism: it is the 'Truth Body', as distinguished from the Celestial or Bliss Body, or the Transformation-Body (incarnational aspect) of the Buddha.

dhyâna   In Pali, *jhāna*; in Chinese, *ch'ān*; in Japanese, Zen: meditation or a stage of meditation in the upward ascent of the contemplative life. Though the term is more familiar in the Buddhist context, it is also used in the Hindu tradition. In this book it is employed as a cross-cultural term for contemplation.

dialectical phenomenology   A way of analysing how the differing dimensions of religion interact.

dialogical faith   Faith which is in dialogue with other faiths.

diaspora   The membership of a religion scattered outside its principal homeland: for example, Hindus in South Africa, Jews outside Israel.

dimensions   The various aspects of belief: notably the doctrinal or philosophical; the mythic or narrative; the ethical or legal; the experiential or emotional; the ritual or practical; the social or organizational; and the material or artistic.

disciplines   Academic approaches to the study (of religion) such as history, anthropology, philology, etc.

doctrinal or philosophical dimension   The aspect in which a religion expresses itself in relatively abstract and philosophical terms, for example, the doctrine of impermanence in Buddhism, or the Trinity doctrine in Christianity.

Dualism   The Hindu system (*Dvaita*) which expresses the difference of God from souls and things.

Dvaita   Dualism (see above).

dynamic phenomenology   A way of classifying and comparing changes in religion.

Eckhart, Johannes (1260–?1307)   Notable Christian mystic, who contrasted the Divine Being as *deitas* or Godhead with the Divine Being as *deus* or personal God.

economic dimension   The economic aspect of religion.

ecumenical movements   Movements in various religions towards unity: e.g., the World Council of Churches or the World Fellowship of Buddhists.

Eleusinian cult   The rituals based in Eleusis near Athens which initiated and gave a sense of rebirth to those who particpated.

emanation   The way the world or some other entity is thought of as emerging out of the Divine Being: it has a less dramatic and willed sense than the notion of creation.

emptiness   The void or nothingness thought of as lying at the basis of reality according to mainstream Mahāyāna philosophy.

Endzeit   German word for 'end-time' contrasted with the original time or *Urzeit* in the story of the universe: for example, the Last Things or *Endzeit* in the Christian story involves the Second Coming of Christ and the judgment passed on human beings.

Enlightenment   (1) The experience of the Buddha under the Bo Tree in which he came to understand the universe; (2) The period from the mid eighteenth Century to the early nineteenth, in which reason, democracy and other values came to the fore.

Episcopalianism   The branch of Christianity linked to the Church of England, and involving leadership by bishops (Greek *episkopoi*) – hence the name.

equanimity   One of the four great virtues in Buddhism (with love, compassion and sympathetic joy).

essentialism   A belief in essences and that religious and other concepts can be clearly defined in their essence.

establishmentarianism   The belief that there should be an official or establishment religion, such as the Church of England in England.

ethical or legal dimension   The aspect of a belief which incorporates moral and legal values.

ethics   The theory or philosophy which systematizes moral values.

Eucharist   The Christian communion service, sometimes referred to as the Mass (in Catholicism) and the Liturgy (among Eastern Orthodox).

evangelism   Preaching and the attempt to convert new members.

evolutionary theory   The theory that humans evolved from other animals.

existentialism   A philosophy which emphasizes human feelings as vital in understanding the world: see, for example, the work of Søren Kierkegaard (1813–55), Jean-Paul Sartre (1905–80) and Martin Heidegger (1889–1976).

exorcism   The use of rituals to expel evil forces from a human being.

experiential dimension   The aspect of belief which involves emotion and experience: e.g., the vision of Isaiah in the Temple, the Buddha's Enlightenment.

fascism   The ideology of Mussolini and others, sometimes applied to Nazism. Typically, fascism is a hyper-nationalist and totalitarian system.

folk religions Religions of non-elite groups. In China, they can be distinguished from Confucianism and Buddhism.

Free Church Those churches which distinguished themselves both from the Church of England and Catholicism: for example, Congregationalists and Baptists.

Gandhi, Mahatma (1869–1948) Notable Indian spiritual and political leader, who emphasized non-violent action.

Gautama (Gotama) The family name in Sanskrit (Pali) of the Buddha (566–486 or 448–368).

Gītā Short for *Bhagavadgītā* or 'Song of the Lord': the most famous Hindu scripture.

globalization The way institutions and interactions of religions and other aspects of human life become part of the global, rather than the regional or local, scene.

gnosis Greek word for 'knowledge', used to refer to spiritual knowledge or vision and important in the movement known as Gnosticism, which emerged in parallel with Christianity and Judaism in the first centuries of the Common Era.

Gnosticism A philosophy or religious view emphasizing gnosis.

Gospels The part of the New Testament containing the narratives describing Christ's career.

grace The divine power which vivifies or saves the faithful.

Great Vehicle The Mahāyāna, so-called because it is a great vehicle bringing the faithful to liberation (as opposed to the 'Lesser Vehicle' of the Theravāda tradition).

guru Spirital teacher who dictates to his (or her) disciples.

Hajj The annual Muslim pilgrimage to Mecca (Makkah).

Harijans Untouchables in the Hindu context; the term was created by Gandhi who struggled on their behalf. Nowadays the word Dalit is preferred.

Heilsgeschichte German term for 'salvation history', used most in the Christian context, to refer to God's dealings with humanity and centring on the career of Christ.

henotheism Treating a given god as the only one in a certain context: for example, in a hymn to Indra, Indra is treated as supreme and unique.

Hindutva Modern word for 'Hindu-ness', often used in the 1980s and 1990s for a Hindu quality of life that Hindu nationalists seek to impose in India (rather than the pluralistic or secular regime imposed by the present Indian constitution).

Hua-yen Buddhism A form of Chinese Buddhism (with Japanese and other varieties) – originally Indian – which stresses the interconnectedness of all events in the universe.

humanism A philosophy emphasizing the centrality of human beings.

ibn 'Arabi (1165–1240)   A notable Sufi (Muslim) mystic and philosopher who, among other things, influenced Dante.

icons   Christian and particularly Orthodox pictures of Christ and the saints: more generally, the religious representation of holy figures.

ideology   A (normally secular or non-religious) worldview, such as Marxism or Fascism.

illud tempus   Latin for 'that time': used by Mircea Eliade (1905–87), to refer to how 'once upon a time' or 'in the beginning' are used in myths and stories to posit a sort of 'intermediate', undatable time.

illusionism   A philosophy like that of Advaita Vedanta which stresses the illusory character of the ordinary world of experience.

immanence   The way God or the Divine Being is operative within the world: often contrasted with transcendence of the way the Divine Being exists outside of, or beyond the cosmos.

incarnation   The way a God is manifest in a human or other being: for example Christ, or the *avatāras* of Viṣṇu, such as Rama and Krishna.

individualism   An emphasis on the importance of the individual human being.

Indra   A major god and warrior deity among the Aryans who settled in India and a chief player within the pantheon of the Vedic hymns.

indulgences   Releases from time in purgatory sold to Catholics during the period immediately before the Reformation, and a cause of popular disgruntlement.

ineffability   The notion that many religious entities (such as God) and experiences (such as, mystical ones) are wholly or in part incapable of being conveyed or described by words.

integralism   A term sometimes used to indicate modern radical movements in Islam and elsewhere.

interiority   The inwardness of religious experiences.

internalization of ritual   The way rituals can be replayed internally, such as the silent 'saying' of the Lord's prayer, or substituting yoga for sacrifice in the Hindu tradition.

Isis cult   The worship of the Egyptian goddess Isis, spouse of Osiris and mother of Horus.

Islam   Submission – generally used as a term for the Muslim religion.

Jainism   The austere religion parallel to Buddhism and re-founded by Mahāvīra (540–469 B.C.E.).

Jātaka   A Buddhist narrative describing a previous life of the Buddha and typically stressing a moral point.

Jehovah's Witnessses   A modern religion founded by Charles Taze Russell (1852–1916) which preaches the imminence of the 'Last Things' and Armageddon, when the saved will rule with Christ.

jen Chinese (Confucian) virtue of humaneness.

Jina 'Conqueror', title of Mahāvīra and other leaders of the Jaina tradition (Jaina being an adjective based on the word Jina).

joy, sympathetic One of the four great virtues of Buddhism (see **equanimity**).

judgment, final The last judgment, taking differing forms in Zoroastrianism, Christianity, and so on.

jurists Legal experts expounding the relevant law (for example in Islam or Catholicism).

Kalki The future incarnation of Viṣṇu, appearing as a kind of Messianic figure at the end of this era of history.

karma Literally 'deed'; the law governing human lives from birth to birth.

kenotic theme The theme in Christian theology of the self-emptying of God when he became incarnated in Christ (from the Greek term *kenosis* or emptying).

kokutai Japanese term for the 'national essence' of Japan.

Krishna Common spelling of Kṛṣṇa, avatar of Vishnu.

Kṛṣṇa See above.

Lao-tzu Older contemporary of Confucius and reputed founder of philosophical Taoism: later became a God in religious Taoism.

Last Things The period at the end of history when history is 'wound up' or consummated, for example, through the Second Coming of Christ.

li 'appropriate behaviour', emphasized as highly important in the Confucian tradition.

liberalism The belief in freedom, modern knowledge and progress, and often incorporated into modern forms of faith (for example, liberal Protestantism, Catholic or Islamic modernism).

liberation theology A Christian movement, prominent in Latin America, blending Marxist and Catholic values.

liberation Term often used for salvation, especially with reference to Eastern religions.

liminality The state of being betwixt and between in ritual processes.

literalism A reading of scriptures which tends to stress their literal meaning.

living dead Ancestors still remembered and animated in the imagination of the living.

Lotus Sutra The most celebrated scripture of the Mahāyāna tradition, and important in the piety of the Nichiren tradition.

Luria (1534–1572) An important Jewish mystic and exponent of the Kabbalah, with a strong messianic message.

Lutheranism That form of Christianity conforming generally to the teachings and ethos of Martin Luther (1483–1546).

Macrobius (c. 400 C.E.)   Latin writer, author of the *Saturnaliá*.

Madhyamika   The philosophy of Nāgārjuna, arguing for a position beyond views and underlining the emptiness of the ultimate.

Mahābhārata   One of the two great Indian epics, containing the *Bhagavadgītā*.

Mahāvîra   The re-founder of the Jaina tradition (540–468 B.C.E.).

Mahayana   The Great Vehicle, a major segment of Buddhism: see Great Vehicle.

Maimonides (1135–1204)   Jewish philosopher and commentator whose most famous work was *Guide of the Perplexed*.

Maitreya   The future Buddha destined to restore the Teaching at the end of the present era.

Mani (216–?277 C.E.)   The founder of the Manichean religion, which contained elements of Zoroastrian, Christian and Buddhist teaching.

Manu   The author supposedly of the *Manusmṛti* or system of Hindu law.

mantra   A formula or sacred prayer.

mantric causation   A way of influencing the world through sacred formulae.

Maoism   The Marxist philosophy of Mao Zedong (1893–1976).

Māra   The Buddhist 'Satan': summing up the forces gathered to obstruct liberation.

Marxism   The philosophy ultimately derived from the thought of Karl Marx (1818–1883).

material dimension   Those aspects of religion exhibited in material form, such as temples, paintings, special clothing and pilgrimage sites.

materialism   The theory that the world is basically or wholly material.

Mencius (?390–305 B.C.E.)   The next most important Confucian philosopher, after Confucius himself.

merit   In Indian religions and in Asian Buddhism generally, the notion that virtuous or pious action creates merit, which will help in future lives. Also merit is thought of as capable of being transferred to the otherwise unmeritorious faithful and so comes to be the equivalent of grace in the Christian tradition.

metaphysics   Another word for an overarching worldview, delineating the real nature of the world.

Methodism   A reforming movement which split from the Church of England under the leadership mainly of John Wesley (1703–1791).

millet system   The Ottoman system of giving non-Muslims, notably Orthodox Christians and Jews, a measure of independence under their own leadership and laws.

Mīmāmsā   One of the systems of orthodox Hindu thought; actually, being devoted to ritual interpretation, it is rather practical. Because it thought the scriptures were primordial it refused to acknowledge the existence of God, as then their origin would be from him. Adjective: Mimamsaka.

modern religions The thousands of new movements in all parts of the world, together with the phenomenon of old religions in new places (such as the Hare Krishna in America).

modernism Liberalism in religion, incorporating modern knowledge into older traditions.

monism The view that there is only One Being (for example, Advaita Vedanta in the Hindu tradition), which sees the ordinary multiple world as illusion.

monomyth Where the religious narrative is single, not leaving space for other myths, as in polytheistic systems of belief.

monotheism Belief in a single, all-encompassing personal God.

Mormonism The Church of Jesus Christ of the Latter-Day Saints and its offshoots, originally founded by Joseph Smith (1805–44).

Muhammad (570–632) The Prophet of Islam.

mysticism The practice of contemplation; important at various stages of religions – in Buddhism, in third-century Christianity and onwards, in the Sufi movement in Islam and so on.

Myth and Ritual School A school of scholars, mainly oriented towards ancient Near Eastern religions, stressing the close connection between myth and ritual (the former being the 'score' of the latter – 'score' in the musical sense).

mythic dimension The narrative or mythic aspect of religion – for example, the story of Christ or the stories of Krishna.

nāstika Religions in India denying the authority of Hindu revelation, such as Jainism, Buddhism and materialism.

Native American religion The religion or religions of indigenous American peoples in the United States and Canada.

Nazism The hyper-nationalist ideology animating Hitler's Germany.

Neo-Confucianism A vital renewal of Confucianism mainly from the eleventh and twelfth centuries onwards, with notable contributions from Chu Hsi (1130–1200) and Wang Yang ming (1472–1529).

Neo-Platonism A renewal of Platonism, mainly expressed by Plotinus (204–270 C.E.), a mystical synthesizer of Platonic thought. Neo-Platonism had immense influence on Christian thought and contemplative practice.

New Age Ideas, practices and movements of the 1980s and 1990s loosely based on new trends in Western thinking such as yoga, astrology, belief in rebirth and so on.

Nichiren Buddhism The kind of Buddhism following the example and teaching of Nichiren (1222–82), a nationalist leader who urged his foll-owers to reverence the Lotus Sutra: a movement now quite influential in the West.

nirvana   Liberation according to Buddhism, like the blowing out or quenching of a flame.

Non-Dualism   Advaita Vedanta: a major school of theology in Hinduism, asserting the non-duality between the Self and the Divine Being. The world from the higher monistic perspective is illusory.

non-identity theory   A theory in Indian philosophy, held by Buddhists and some Hindu schools, that cause and effect are different or non-identical. The Western parallel is with David Hume's view of causation.

non-theism   Such systems as Buddhism and Jainism, which do not believe in or take seriously the idea of a Creator God.

numinous experience   The type of religious experience delineated seriously by Rudolf Otto in his 1917 book *Das Heilige*. The experience emphasizes the otherness and tremendous and mysterious power of the Other, but is different from most mystical or contemplative experience.

occasionalism   A view (found in Islam and elsewhere) that events in the world are occasioned by God, but are not mutually causes and effects (they may be regular in sequence, but are simply phenomena directly caused by God).

Orphism   A broad movement in ancient Greek religion supposedly stemming from the teachings of the poet and divine Orpheus (sixth century B.C.E. ?). It promised liberation from reincarnation through appropriate rituals and good conduct.

pacifism   The practice and philosophy of peace, chiefly expressed in modern times by Quakers and by Gandhi (see above).

Pali Canon   The scriptures of the surviving Lesser Vehicle cult, namely the Theravada. They are composed in the Pali language, originating in North India, which stands to Sanskrit roughly as Italian does to Latin.

panenhenic experience   A dramatic experience of one's unity with the cosmos: literally an 'all in one-ish' experience.

pantheism   The belief that God and the universe are one and the same. The clearest example is Stoicism.

pan-Africanism   Commitment to the unity of all African cultures (or at least sub-Saharan African cultures).

pan-Slavism   A nineteenth- and early twentieth-century movement to unite all Slavic peoples (Russians, Poles, Serbs and so on).

paranormal   That which may be natural but is outside of the normal in human experience, (for example, telepathy).

Parsees   A word for Zoroastrians, especially those who migrated from Iran (Persia) to India.

particularism   The theory that some range of phenomena, such as Christian mysticism, has its own particular characteristics and cannot really be compared to other phenomena (for example, Islamic mysticism).

Passover   Jewish festival recalling the deliverance of the Israelites from Egypt.

phenomenology   (1) The attempt through informed empathy to present others' experiences and beliefs from their points of view, and involving the suspension of one's own values (*epochē*); (2) a morphology or classification of types of religious phenomena.

Platonism   The philosophy of Plato and his successors.

Plotinus (204–70 C.E.)   The most important Neoplatonist philosopher.

pluralism   The notion that different traditions can be accommodated together in the same culture or nation.

political dimension   The political aspect of a sacred tradition.

polymyth   A group of variegated myths in the same tradition – for example, Hindu myths.

polytheism   The belief in many gods.

polytopism   The ability of a divine or celestial being to appear in different places – such as the Virgin Mary in Guadalupe, Lourdes, and so on.

predestination   The notion that human destinies are already known and fixed in advance by God or Fate.

Presbyterianism   The Calvinist tradition in Scotland and elsewhere, involving a democratic system of church government.

presentative aspect of ritual   The way ritual presents or re-presents an event, such as the Lord's Supper or the Passover.

process theology   A movement in Christian theology which emphasizes the changing character of God as part of the continuous process of creation.

projection theory   Any theory which sees religious entities such as God as projected from basic human needs (such as Freudian theory).

psyche   The soul or deeper consciousness of a human being.

psychomantrism   The view that sacred formulae affect the soul.

Pure Land   A Buddhist heaven delineated by the so-called Pure Land schools of Buddhism, especially in China and Japan, and presided over by the Buddha Amitabha or Amida (the Japanese version of Amitabha).

Pythagoreanism   The philosophy of Pythagoras (sixth century B.C.E.), including belief in reincarnation and the view that the world is composed of numbers and geometrical forms.

Qabbala (Kabbalah)   The 'tradition' of Jewish medieval mysticism.

Quakerism   The values of the Society of Friends or Quakers, founded in the seventeenth century, stressing pacifism, the primacy of conscience and inner Christian experience.

quietism   An attitude of quietness and non-aggression.

rabbi   Jewish jurist and religious leader.

Rāma   Incarnation of Vishnu, hero of the *Rāmāyaṇa*.

Rāmānuja (?1077–1157)   Hindu theologian and chief exponent of Qualified Non-Dualism or Viśiṣṭādvaita.

Rāmāyaṇa   One of the two great Hindu epics, concerning the great deeds of Rāma.

realism   A philosophy emphasizing the reality of the world.

reconciliatory function of doctrine   Ways in which agreement in doctrine or philosophy can bring together religious groups involved in differing or conflicting practices.

redeath   The other side of rebirth: everyone reborn has died again!

reductionism   A theory which reduces religious experience and belief to a projection of underlying material or psychological causes (for example, sexual envy).

Reformation   The great movement from the early sixteenth century rejecting Roman Catholic tradition and centralism.

responsive function of doctrine   The ways which doctrines and philosophies respond to challenges.

revivalism   A movement or movements reviving a tradition, for example, through vigorous evangelism.

Ṛgveda   The main collection of the Vedic hymns in ancient India.

rites of passage   Rituals which confer a new status on a person, such as baptism, marriage, funeral rites, etc.

ritual dimension   The aspect of belief manifested in rituals and other practices, for example, the Eucharist, contemplative practice.

Romanticism   The early nineteenth-century movement emphasizing nature and human feeling.

ruralism   Being or wishing to be in country or rural settings.

sacraments   Rituals often using material means to convey substance: for example, the Christian communion uses bread and wine to convey the substance of Christ to the participants.

sage   A Confucian scholar and wise person, and by analogy other similar people in other contexts and traditions.

Śaiva Siddhānta   Śaiva Doctrine: a theological tradition, especially important in Tamil Nadu in South India and in Sri Lanka.

Śaivism, Kashmir   Another main Śaiva theological tradition flourishing originally mainly in Kashmir.

Sāmkhya   A major Hindu system of philosophy, linked to the Yoga system: it emphasizes the evolution of the cosmos and the liberation of souls or *puruṣas.*

sanctification   The way a person becomes holy or saintly, for example, through the grace of God.

Sangha   The Buddhist order of monks, nuns and holy laypersons.

Śankara (788–820)   Hindu saint and philosopher, chief founder of Non-Dualism or Advaita Vedanta.

Santeria   A Cuban Afro-Catholic religion, combining West African elements with traditional Catholicism.

scapegoat theory   A theory that makes use of the notion of the scapegoat; see the ideas of René Girard.

scholasticism   A system of scholarly philosophical commentaries and inter- pretations of a tradition: notably applied to medieval Catholic philosophy in the West.

sects   Denominations, more particularly those which tend to be 'otherworldly'.

secular worldviews   Worldviews which are not, by modern English usage, 'religious', such as Marxism, humanism or Fascism.

secularization   The move in which societies become less religious in a formal sense, and in which there is greater individualism.

self-awareness   *sati* or self-awareness is a major part of Buddhist practice, involving clarity about one's feelings, thoughts and intentions.

shamanism   The kind of belief and practice associated with the figure of the shaman, whose spiritual experience can provide cures and predictions, especially in hunting and gathering societies.

Shari'a   The system of Islamic law.

Shi'a   A major denomination of Islam, dominant in Iran and strong in Iraq and elsewhere.

Shinran (1173–1262)   A pietist Buddhist saint who emphasized Amida's grace and was founder of the Jodo Shinshu or True Pure Land School.

Shinto   The way of the gods (*kami*): the traditional Japanese religion established during the Meiji period (from 1868) as the official focus of Japanese national sentiment.

shirk   Idolatry or the elevation of any being or goal alongside obedience to God or Allah (in Islam).

Sikhism   The religious tradition created by a succession of Gurus and existing alongside Hinduism in the Punjab and elsewhere.

sky gods   Divine beings, such as Zeus, Varuṇa and Jupiter, associated with the sky: often male and conceived as all-seeing and creative.

social dimension   The aspect of belief which manifests itself in society and social organizations (for example, through a Church or Sangha).

staretz   A spiritual father in the Russian Orthodox tradition.

Stoicism   A Graeco-Roman philosophy and religious worldview, incorporating pantheism and an austere ethos.

stūpa   A Buddhist memorial mound later developing into the pagoda, usually containing relics of the Buddha or of a Buddhist saint.

Sufism   The mystical or contemplative strand in Islam.

superimposition This occurs when a value or attitude is superimposed on some activity or phenomenon: for example, seeing work as a form of prayer or seeing sunsets as the work of the Creator.

supernaturals Gods or other supernatural beings postulated in a religion or culture.

superstition A hangover from some prior religion, as with Western practices such as not walking under ladders; more generally, an irrationally held belief or one which has no spiritual meaning.

synagogue Jewish meeting place.

syncretism Where two or more traditions blend; for instance in Voodoo there are strong elements of African religion and Roman Catholicism.

taboo A sacred ban on some activity or restriction on relations with an individual, such as a chief.

T'ai-chi The Supreme Ultimate in Neoconfucian thought.

T'ai Hsü (1889–1942) Modern Chinese Buddhist reformer, emphasizing renewal of meditation.

T'ai-ping (Kingdom of Heavenly Peace) The name of a major rebellion in China in the 1850s, partly inspired by Christian ideas.

Talmud The main text of Judaism; an extensive commentary on the Mishnah, existing in two main forms, the Babylonian and the Palestinian Talmud.

Tantrism Forms of Hindu and Buddhist traditions, especially in North India, emphasizing sacramental and sometimes sexual rituals to gain liberation.

Taoism Philosophical Taoism is expressed in the *Tao-teh Ching* and subsequent writings; religious Taoism essentially dates from the first two centuries C.E., and involves an elaborate pantheon and various practices and institutions which carried the religion forward.

Tao-teh Ching The Classic of the Way and its Power – a text ascribed to Lao-tzu.

tapas Austerity as practised in the Indian tradition (literaly 'heat', since heat was engendered by austere practices).

theism Belief in a personal God.

theology A Christian term for systematic thinking about God and the world.

Thera-Therīgāthā Verses of the (early) Buddhist monks and nuns.

Theravāda Doctrine of the Elders: a major branch of Buddhism in Sri Lanka and south-east Asia.

Thomas Aquinas (1225–74) Chief Catholic philosopher of the Middle Ages and very influential on modern Catholic theology, especially before Vatican II (1962–5).

Three Aspect Doctrine In Mahāyāna Buddhism the notion that the Buddha is manifested in Three Bodies or Aspects – as the Truth, as Celestial Buddhas and as the earthly Buddha.

timelessness God or nirvana is sometimes thought of as timeless, that is, without time, as distinguished from being everlasting (of infinite time).

Tīrtham̐ kara Literally 'Ford Maker'; title given to the leaders of the Jains from time to time (Mahāvīra in this age).

Torah Jewish teaching or law, as given to Moses both in written and oral form.

transcendence The mode in which the Divine Being exists beyond the cosmos or distinct from it (also applied to nirvana).

transnational religion A religion stretching over more than one nation or ethnic group.

transphysicality The notion that consciousness lies beyond the physical stratum on which it is built.

transpolytheism The belief in an absolute or Divine Being lying beyond the gods; a belief however that does not deny the gods but may regard them as manifestations of the one Being.

transtheistic belief The belief in an Absolute which lies beyond the personal God corresponding to the idea of theism.

Trinity The belief in the ultimate Three-in-One of traditional Christianity (Father, Son and Holy Spirit).

underworlds Hells and purgatories in which humans dwell, lying 'below' this world.

Unification Church The organization founded by the Revd. Sung Myung Moon whose members are known colloquially as 'Moonies'.

Unitarianism A branch of Christianity which rejects the Trinity doctrine, stressing the Unity of God.

Upaniṣads A major philosophical section of the Vedic revelation in the Hindu tradition.

Urezeit The 'beginning times' as depicted in Christian and other myths, as opposed to the *Endzeit*.

utilitarianism The ethical view that morality and moral rules should promote the greatest happiness of the greatest number and the least suffering of the least number.

Vaiṣṇava A devotee of Viṣṇu.

Vajrayāna The 'Diamond Vehicle' in Buddhism, associated with Tibetan Buddhism.

Vatican II The reforming Second Vatican Council, 1962–5.

Veda Hindu revelation as found in the Vedic hymns and various other works.

Vedānta Literally the 'end of the Veda': Hindu systems of theology.

Vinaya   The discipline books of Buddhism, delineating the rules of the Sangha, and so on.

Viśiṣṭādvaita   Qualified Non-Dualism: the theistic philosophy of Rāmānuja and his followers.

Vodun or Voodoo   Afro-Catholic religion of Haiti.

Xenophanes (?580–?480)   Critic of religion in ancient Greece.

yoga   System of meditation in the Indian tradition.

Zarathustra (Zoroaster)   Founder of Zoroastrianism, from Persia (Iran).

Zen   Japanese meditation Buddhism.

ziggurats   Ancient Near Eastern pyramids and temples.

Zionism   The movement to create a national state in Palestine, viz. Israel.

Zoroastrianism   Religion founded by Zarathustra: found in Persia and India (among the Parsees).

INTRODUCTION

This book ranges widely over the religions and ideologies of this world. I believe that by seeing the patterns in the way religion manifests itself, we can learn to understand how it functions and vivifies the human spirit in history. In this book I consciously try to classify the elements of worldviews, both in their beliefs and in their practices. These classifications come from reflections about the varying cultures of humankind. Though I sometimes simplify, this is in the hope of clarifying perceptions. I have also fortified the text with many allusions. It might be useful for the reader to consult with some narrative on faiths and world religious history, such as my own *Religious Experience* (new edition, 1986), or my recent slim works *Asian Religions* and *Religions of the West* – but there are plenty of other fine surveys of a similar kind.

In providing a kind of physiology of spirituality and of worldviews, I hope to advance religious studies' theoretical grasp of its subject matter, namely that aspect of human life, experience and institutions in which we as human beings interact thoughtfully with the cosmos and express the exigencies of our own nature and existence. I do not here take any faith to be true or false. Judgment on such matters can come later. But I do take all views and practices seriously.

This book is in some sense a phenomenology of religion. That is, it belongs in the same genre as Gerardus van der Leeuw's famous *Religion in Essence and Manifestation* (VAN DER LEEUW, 1938). But my book, and indeed van der Leeuw's, could also be called a morphology of religion, incorporating a theory. It explores and articulates the 'grammar of symbols' – the modes and forms in which religion manifests itself.

The word 'phenomenology' derives from the philosophical tradition of Husserl. But comparative religionists (henceforth I shall simply call them religionists) use it in a different way from philosophers (SPIEGELBURG, 1960). Among religionists it means the use of *epochē* or suspension of belief, together with the use of empathy, in entering into the experiences and intentions of religious participants (WAARDENBURG, 1973). This implies that, in describing the way people behave, we do not use, so far as we can avoid them, alien categories to evoke the nature of their acts and to understand those acts (KING, WHALING, 1984). In this sense phenomenology is the attitude of informed empathy. It tries to bring out what religious acts mean to the actors.

But this book is something else: it is intended to delineate the various manifestations of religion in complex ways. It discusses a number of theories – about myths, doctrines, art, rituals, experience, organizations, ethics, law – and a certain amount of religion, politics and economics. So it is an ambitious enterprise.

Gerardus van der Leeuw used the term 'essence', which implies a definition of religion. I do not here wish to affirm a definition in the strict sense. Moreover, I believe that there are sufficient affinities between religious and secular worldviews (such as applied Marxism and nationalisms) to include the secular in the scope of this work. I hope this will make the book comprehensive. To split a category can be dangerous if it is taken too far. Because religion is separated from secular worldviews, for instance, it is assumed that East Germany was a secular state; in fact Marxism functioned in that country much as a state religion, as Lutheranism once had. If you did not adhere to the state religion you were denied opportunities in education and employment. So my enterprise here, though largely concerned with religion, can also be categorized as a version of worldview analysis (SMART, 1983).

The term 'worldview' is not the best. It suggests something too cerebral. But religions and comparable worldviews should be studied at least as much through their practices as through their beliefs. Likewise nationalism involves more than a set of myths or stories about 'our' country: it involves practical actions and acknowledgments of loyalty; it involves joy when 'we' win (at soccer or at war), the speaking of 'our' language, appreciation of the monuments and beauties of 'our' country. So when I use 'worldview' I mean incarnated worldview, where the values and beliefs are embedded in practice. That is, they are expressed in action, laws, symbols, organizations.

We tend of course to think in our own languages, and this provides canals of usage down which our intellectual barges navigate. I am not saying that other tongues are necessarily better, but sometimes they offer illuminating terms which we can incorporate into our own. So we probably need an international vocabulary.

Cross-cultural phenomenology of religion

The phenomenology (that is, the theory and morphology) of religion has usually been conducted in European languages, notably English, French, German and Italian: see the work of Eliade, Parrinder, Chantepie de la Saussaye, Heiler, Bianchi (BIANCHI, 1964; SHARPE, 1975). But it is important to make use of terms drawn from non-European traditions. Shaman, mana, totem, tabu/tapu, yoga and karma have all entered the English language, but there are other vital terms which have not and which might be most useful in cross-cultural comparisons.

The dominance of the English tongue in cross-cultural comparisons is no accident. It is largely a product of colonialism and therefore of unequal cultural power relationships. Moreover, British and American scholars played an important role in developing the subject. There was often the tacit assumption that Christianity was normal religion, and that it was against this norm that the primary comparisons were to be launched. English is fast becoming the major global tongue and is therefore a proper vehicle for such explorations, but there is no reason why we should not employ a range of cross-cultural terms to further comparisons. I shall in this book make use of a number of crucial expressions, including *bhakti* (devotion), *dhyāna* (meditation) and *li* (appropriate behaviour). Sometimes distinctions and nuances are clearer and richer in other languages than English. There may be differing ways of carving up the territory. Sometimes this may justify us in creating neologisms. In the West it has often been assumed that God and gods are normal: a system is either theistic or polytheistic. But what about the Theravada? Its Ultimate is not God or the gods, but nirvana. Should we then see Christianity and Judaism as major non-nirvanistic religions?

In affirming that phenomenology should be conducted on a cross-cultural basis, I am saying two things: that its findings should make use of cross-cultural terminology and sensitivity; and that there should be no assumption of the priority of one tradition as the norm. This is where informed empathy has another role, in creating the sensitivity to allow me (a Westerner, a Scot, a male, an Episcopalian, albeit with Buddhist leanings) to enter into other cultures' attitudes (SMART, 1973). But in thinking about the cross-cultural we need to reflect on what the boundaries of cultures are.

The boundaries of traditions, regions, cultures

The word 'cross-cultural' may be understood to refer to items belonging to broad cultural areas, such as China, South Asia and Europe. But there can of course be many traditions within areas: thus Jaina, Buddhist and Hindu traditions are important in classical India. But even here there are vital sub-traditions within each, while some scholars rightly question whether we can really treat Hinduism as a single tradition (SMART, 1993). In modern times perhaps we can, because that is how to a great degree it is perceiving itself. But what about in classical times? We have to be realistic in the study of religion and take the richness and variegations seriously.

That is often why the insider can be wrong about her tradition. When Kristensen said that the insider is always right, he meant that she is right about herself (KRISTENSEN, 1960). That is, she has certain feelings and beliefs and they are an important part of the data we as religionists are set to explore. But an insider can be terribly wrong about her tradition, ignorant about or insensitive to the variety of her religious heritage. I once heard a Baptist minister give a lecture on Christianity which was, phenomenologically speaking, absurd. What he identified as true Christianity would not be accepted by great swathes of Catholicism, Orthodoxy, Episcopalianism, Methodism and so on. Indeed, one major use of the word 'phenomenology' is to mark off what we as religionists are trying to do from those committed interpretations which essentially are part of preaching (MACQUAR-RIE, 1981).

Thus we must distinguish between descriptive and normative uses of such terms as 'Buddhism' and 'Christianity'. But the most important point here is that traditions are plural. Moreover, they may vary regionally as well as by lineage or tradition. The Episcopal church in Fiji may vary greatly from its counterpart in Scotland; Theravada Buddhism may differ markedly in Thailand and Burma; the Unification Church in Korea and England may have great differences.

While the comparative study of religion is usually conceived in macro terms, it could equally well be construed as dealing with micro or intra-tradition comparisons.

Questions of comparison: platform and context

The expression 'comparative religion' or 'comparative study of religion' (I would prefer 'comparative study of worldviews') has met with some disfavour in differing eras. In a backlash against missionary colonialism the word 'comparative' has been taken to express a certain arrogance – comparisons, as the saying goes, being odious. It has sometimes been under suspicion for an opposed reason, it being thought that comparativists love likenesses excessively, thus blurring the uniqueness of the preferred religion (some form of Christianity) (JORDAN, 1905). But there is no need at all for comparison to stand on a superior platform, and comparing traditions, sub-traditions or whatever involves the discerning not only of likenesses but of differences.

It might be thought that my present ambitious project has its own platform, maybe not that of the certain and confident missionary, but that of the Western 'scientist' who wishes to look at religions and worldviews from a platform of analysis and superior understanding. It is true that in a sense I do start from a platform of 'science'. I believe that religious studies can be, within the limits of recognition that it is a human enterprise (being by and about human beings), scientific (SMART, 1973). But I cannot believe that by itself this claim is arrogant. Arrogance arises rather from the manner in which a method is pursued. If the anthropologist visits a village simply to get material for a doctorate, without consideration for the villagers as fellow human beings with their own sensitivities and concerns, that is arrogant and heartless. But the enterprise of advancing knowledge by itself is not arrogant. Yet what of knowledge and power relations? What if the whole structure of knowledge displays a certain arrogance?

I would defend the comparative study of religion on a number of grounds. First, it has often acted as counterpoise to cultural tribalism, such as often prevails in Western universities and, especially, in theological schools. Second, it often raises fruitful questions for contemplation by religions and more generally worldviews: any real similarity betweeen the piety of one tradition and that of another poses obvious questions for each. Third, because of ideological prejudices, religious studies is too often neglected among the social sciences, where projection theories seem to be fashionable: the comparative study of worldviews can be a source of insights, as Weber well knew.

The deeper challenge to cross-cultural studies concerns context. The point was most incisively made by Hendrik Kraemer (KRAEMER, 1938). Even if we think that we have made a valid comparison, for instance between Luther's and Shinran's account of 'grace', the divergence of context between the two may invalidate the comparison, in the sense of alike-claiming. The details of context give quite diverse flavours to the two phenomena.

The problem with this thesis is that everything becomes so particularized as to be incommensurable with anything else. This is self-defeating in a number of ways. It means that there is no vocabulary which can properly describe the offerings of different cultures. Besides, while we know that each individual human being is unique, implying that each person has a divergent set of flavours drenching her experience, it does not follow that we have no common feelings and perspectives. It does not follow that we cannot study medicine, which depends upon a range of alike-claims. We all have noses, even if each one is subtly different from all others. Anyway the proof is in the actualities: and we shall see how well the theoretical and descriptive similarities laid forth in this book stand up to the necessary contextualities. Part of my way of dealing with the problem is the use of dynamic and dialectical phenomenology.

Dynamic patterns and dialectical relations in phenomenology

Because of essentialism (the view that a given type of phenomenon has a common essence) and other factors, earlier phenomenology tends to by synchronic and static. There is no harm in this within certain limits. Alike-claims and unalike-claims can be of this character. But we may also want to see if there are patterns of change. Do new religions tend to get institutionalized in certain ways? And, if so, what other effects does this have? Do certain forms of religious experience release creative or organizational behaviour in their recipients? And so on. If we can discern patterns, that is what I call dynamic phenomenology (PYE, 1972; SMART, 1983). Now obviously patterns of change in human history tend to be synergistic, so that they combine. Alternatively, a pattern of change in one context leads to different results in another context.

By dialectical phenomenology I mean more particularly the relationship between different dimensions of religion and worldviews. In general we can say about any system or scheme that one element in it is in principle affected by all others. An organism functions as a whole, so that an injury to one part affects the whole to a greater or lesser degree. A set of religious doctrines, for instance the teachings of Eastern Orthodoxy, is a sort of loose organism. It is not necessarily a consistent whole, but one doctrine, such as the creation, is affected by others, such as the incarnation of Christ (so Christ becomes Creator) or the definition of the sacraments (so the created world is viewed as sacramental). We can therefore see items in this field in the context of the scheme in which they are embedded (SMART, 1958). But more than this, we can view the items in one dimension (in this case the doctrinal dimension) in their interaction with items in other dimensions, for instance the practical (or ritual) dimension. The idea that the world is created out of nothing should be seen in the light of the intensity of Christian worship: no limitation should be set on the glory of God. The idea that there is an ineffable aspect of God or Brahman should be related to the mystical path, as well as to other factors, such as the performative analysis of indescribability in the context of supreme praise (in other words, seeing how the language of ineffability actually performs the act of praising: you get something like this in 'I cannot say how grateful I am' which conveys how grateful I am).

Again we can see dialectical phenomenology at work in relation to a secular worldview. It is part of the doctrine of the United States that it favours and incarnates democratic values: this in turn has effects on the style of the Presidency. Its rituals include the practice of the President's going out and about among the people and being populist in his actions (displaying himself as a 'man of the people').

The dimensional analysis of worldviews

To flesh all this out I need to give a more detailed account of what I mean by the dimensions of religion (SMART, 1989). The pattern which I put forward is primarily directed towards what traditionally in English are called religions (I will not at this juncture go into a comparison of other concepts such as *dharma, magga, tao, chiao, dīn* and *religio*). But the schema also applies to worldviews other than religious ones.

The schema has a double purpose. One is to provide a realistic checklist of aspects of a religion so that a description of that religion or a theory about it is not lopsided. There is a tendency in older histories of Christianity for instance to emphasize the history of doctrines and organizational matters: you can pick up church histories (so called, for the title already makes some assumptions) which say very little about the spiritual and practical life, or about ethical and legal matters, or about the social dimension on the ground, other than the organizational side. Some treatments of the Hindu tradition concentrate on myth and social organization, and say very little about the philosophical side or about patterns of experience and feeling.

So one purpose is to achieve balance. The other is to give a kind of functional delineation of religions in lieu of a strict definition. I also avoid defining religion in terms of its foci or content. That is, I am not saying that religion involves some belief, such as belief in God or gods, because in some religions, notably in Theravada Buddhism and Jainism and in phases of the Confucian tradition, such beliefs are secondary, to say the least. As we shall see, two of my dimensions can concern the gods most lavishly – namely, the doctrinal and mythic dimensions – so it seems better not to try to define religion by content. The best we could do is use a phrase like 'ultimate concern' (TILLICH, 1969), yet this is rather empty and too wide-ranging. Or we could trot out the 'transcendent': a useful place-holder, open to as many ambiguities as 'religion' itself.

I do not deny that there is a role for place-holders. We need a term to stand for the phenomenological object of religious practice and experience. I prefer 'focus', in part because it has a plural ('foci'), whereas 'the ultimate' cannot be very naturally plural and in part be-cause it does not carry any ontological baggage (SMART, 1973). It does not matter whether Vishnu exists or not – that is, it does not matter for our purposes, though for the faithful of course it matters – or whether there is a transcendent ultimate; but we can still recognize that Vishnu is the focus of the Vaishnava's dreams and worship, as Christ is the focus of the Eucharist. But it does not define religion to say that it has a focus.

The notion of a focus enables us to talk about worship and other activities in meaningful ways without having to comment on their validity, without having to comment on whether there is a Vishnu or a Christ. But it does enable us to think of Vishnu as focus entering into the believer's life, dynamizing his feelings, commanding his loyalty and so on. This is an advantage in discussing a controversial subject like religion. For a believer the focus is real, and we can accept this even if we do not want to say that it (or she or he) exists. I thus distinguish between 'real' and 'existent' as adjectives. The former I use, in this context, to refer to what is phenomenologically real in the experience of the believer. Whether the real in this sense exists is an altogether different question.

To return to the dimensions: in each case I give them a double name, which helps to elucidate them and sometimes to widen them. The list of seven in the first instance is drawn from the catalogue in my book *The World's Religions* (SMART, 1989). I first enunciated the idea in 1969 (SMART, 1969), but had a slightly smaller list. I add two to the seven which are in my view the most basic. The extra two are the political and economic dimensions of religion. The seven are as follows (the order is rather random).

1. The ritual or practical dimension. This is the aspect of religion which involves such activities as worship, meditation, pilgrimage, sacrifice, sacramental rites and healing activities. We may note that meditation is often not regarded as a ritual, though it is often strictly patterned. This is partly why I also call this dimension the practical (EVANS-PRITCHARD, 1965).

2. The doctrinal or philosophical dimension. For different reasons religions evolve doctrines and philosophies. Thus the doctrine of impermanence is central to Buddhism. It also interacts dialectically with the ritual or practical dimension, since philosophical reflection of a certain kind aids meditation, and meditation in turn helps the individual to see existentially the force of the doctrine. Some traditions are keener on doctrinal rectitude than others: Catholicism more than Quakerism, Buddhism more than traditional African religions, Theravada more than Zen. We may note that diverse traditions put differing weights on the differing dimensions. Religions are by no means equidimensional.

3. The mythic or narrative dimension. Every religion has its stories. The story of Christ's life, death and resurrection is clearly central to the Christian faith. The story of the Buddha's life, though somewhat less central to Buddhism, is still vital to Buddhist piety. In the case of secular worldviews and to an important degree in modernizing traditions, history is the narrative which takes the place of myth elsewhere. So the version of history taught in a nation's schools is not only a major ingredient in the national sense of identity, but enhances pride in 'our' ancestors, 'our' national heroes and heroines.

4. The experiential or emotional dimension. It is obvious that certain experiences can be important in religious history – the enlightenment

of the Buddha, the prophetic visions of Muhammad, the conversion
of Paul and so on. Again there are variations in the importance
attached to visionary and meditative experiences: they are obviously
vital to Zen and Native American classical religion (the vision quest);
they are less important in Scottish Calvinism. But they or associated
emotional reactions to the world and to ritual are everywhere more or
less dynamic, and have been studied extensively (e.g. OTTO,
1917/1923).

5. The ethical or legal dimensions. A religious tradition or sub-
tradition affirms not only a number of doctrines and myths but some
ethical and often legal imperatives. The Torah as a set of injunctions
is central to orthodox Judaism; the Shari'a is integral to Islam;
Buddhism affirms the four great virtues (*brahmavihāras*); Confucianism lays down the desired attitudes of the gentleman; and so on.
Again, the degree of investment in ideal human behaviour varies: it is
central to Quakerism, less important in the Shinto tradition (though
Shinto ritual was tied to the notion of the *kokutai* or national essence
during the Meiji era and into the between-wars period). In modern
national states certain norms of civil behaviour tend to be prescribed
in schools.

6. The organizational or social component. Any tradition will
manifest itself in society, either as a separate organization with priests
or other religious specialists (gurus, lawyers, pastors, rabbis, imams,
shamans and so on), or as coterminous with society. Embedded in a
social context, a tradition will take on aspects of that context (thus the
Church of England cleric begins to play a part in the English class
system).

7. The material or artistic dimension. A religion or worldview will
express itself typically in material creations, from chapels to cathedrals to temples to mosques, from icons and divine statuary to books
and pulpits. Such concrete expressions are important in varying ways.
If you only have to carry around a book (like an evangelical preacher
in Communist Eastern Europe) you are freer than if you have a great
monastery or convent to occupy.

Let me sketch out, for a couple of worldviews, how these dimensions operate. I shall take classical Christianity first (namely Catholic and Orthodox Christianity in the centuries not long after Constantine) (*Oxford Dictionary*, 1983).

1. Ritually the Church had evolved more or less elaborate patterns for celebrating the mass, liturgy or eucharist. It had various other sacramental rites, ranging from baptism to marriage to consigning the dead to the next world. It was also evolving the cult of saints, pilgrimages and so on. In practical terms there was a growing emphasis on the life of meditation. This helped to enhance doctrines relating to the ineffability of the Divine Being (especially the assumption in the liturgy and myths that God was male).

2. The religion had succeeded in fusing together motifs from the Jewish tradition and from Neo-Platonism (that is, the worldview of Plotinus and other religious followers of Plato during the 3rd and 4th centuries C.E.). Those charged with settling its doctrines tackled many current intellectual problems (assisted by thinkers such as Augustine and the Eastern Fathers) and grappled with matters arising from the narrative dimension. If, as the Biblical stories affirmed, God was successively creator, incarnate Jesus and mysterious inspirer, how could all this be reconciled with monotheistic Judaism? The answer was the Trinity doctrine, generator of heresies but gradually settling down as the norm within the two great churches.

3. The main narratives came to derive from the Old and New Testaments, though the church had to explain itself historically from those times up to the present – hence that great interpretation of history in Augustine's *The City of God*. The myths were wedded to ritual: for instance, in the eucharist's re-enactment of the story of the Last Supper, or in the evolution of a church calendar that re-enacted other parts of the story through the year and celebrated the saints, the heroines and heroes of the salvation history.

4. The creation of networks of monasticism favoured the cultivation of mysticism, which was reinforced by the absorption of Neo-Platonist ideals. In addition, the development of colourful, even

glorious ritual enhanced the more ordinary emotions of the devotional life.

5. The settling of the church into more defined ecclesiastical organizations helped the formation of a legal system, while Christian ethics was already well established through the Ten Commandments and the definitions of Paul and others in the epistles.

6. Organizationally, the two halves of the church eventually drifted apart, though each retained a fairly well-defined structure in alliance with the secular power. Most notable was the growth of monasteries, reflecting new ways of being Christian after the religion became fashionable, which in turn gave rise to a need to strengthen the spiritual life.

7. Meanwhile the churches had taken over many of the glorious buildings of the old Roman Empire and went on to construct new ones, giving Christianity a formidable material dimension reinforced by techniques of painting which encouraged the decoration of churches. Icons in the East performed an important ritual function, despite the largely aniconic traditions of Judaism, out of which Christianity had evolved.

These then are brief illustrations of the dimensional analysis of Christianity. A parallel inventory of a secular worldview can be drawn up (BELLAH and HAMMOND, 1980). In running through the dimensions I shall select the case of United States nationalism, starting with the mythic dimension.

1. The mythic dimension of the United States is contained largely in the received history – how the Union came into being, arising out of the rebellion against the British (pre-revolutionary history, including a slice of British history, to some extent serves as a sort of Old Testament). In subsequent history, certain items have a significant ritual role, especially the Civil War and its reflected depths as expressed on Memorial Day.

2. The doctrinal or philosophical dimension is expressed in the constitution as enshrining the values of a democratic society, and

loyalty to these values is an important mark of a genuine American citizen. It was notable that in the McCarthy years a counter-doctrine (communism) came to be seen as the central heresy (GELLNER, 1983).

3. The ritual of the United States is seen in various activities: saluting the flag, singing the national anthem on important occasions such as baseball games, the ceremonial duties of the President, pilgrimages to celebrate national monuments and, more informally, the beauties of the American landscape, wearing uniforms where appropriate, the honouring of past heroes such as presidents, poets, musicians and writers.

4. The emotional dimension is found in reactions to moving national occasions, to celebrations of patriotism, to the singing of significant songs and so on.

5. The ethical dimension is evident in puritan ideals, democratic values and patriotic values.

6. Organizationally, there is the deployment of the nation's institutions, in which certain functionaries play a key part. The priesthood of the nation are perhaps the schoolteachers, who induct the young into the national myth; the saints are the heroines and heroes; other sacred people (in a way) are the military. There are some tensions: people are often and necessarily critical of the President as a political figure; but as ceremonial leader of the nation he should command 'our' loyalty. And often a person's particular religion may run counter to the religion of the nation.

7. Finally, the nation incarnates itself in its material dimension: above all in the landscape, with its marvels and its familiarity; but also in the memorials and buildings of Washington and other sacred spots, including the battlefields of the Revolution and of the Civil War.

The relationship of the dimensions to disciplines

These various dimensions are not set in concrete. It is obvious that other ways of looking at worldviews are possible. The question is not whether my approach is the only one, it is whether it is fruitful. Clearly there can be more than one fruitful way of analysing religions and, more generally, worldviews. But it is worth considering how the dimensions relate to various disciplines within the academic marketplace. Indeed we may relate those disciplines to religious studies, which incorporate the exploration of various traditions and regions.

Textual and philological studies. Broadly, language studies have played a great part in the history of religions, for two main reasons: first, they are the key to texts which constitute the scriptural authorities of so many traditions (DENNY and TAYLOR, 1985). Second, they are the key to texts which are the chief sources of our knowledge of ancient and not so ancient religious traditions. We shall later examine the phenomenology of sacred books (and by contrast of oral traditions). We shall also advert to the social significance of the specialists who created and looked after such books (mainly males, mainly elite). Languages are also important for fieldwork. The sacred scriptures are often sources of a major part of the mythic dimension. They can also be vital (as in the case of the *Upaniṣads*) in the evolution of the doctrinal or philosophical dimension.

Anthropology and sociology. It can be argued that these two supposedly separate disciplines are really the same subject. As the joke has it: sociology is about us and anthropology is about them. Actually it is more complicated. Classically anthropology has concerned itself with small-scale and largely non-urban cultures. Non-Western societies which are not small-scale have sometimes fallen between the two stools. It seems logical that we should include all social studies under the same umbrella. Be that as it may, both have most to do with what I have called the social or organizational dimension, but it turns out too that anthropologists have helped to pioneer studies in ritual and myth, while sociologists have laid foundations for the exploration of secular worldviews. Many of the most prominent theorists concerning religions and ideologies have been sociologists or anthropologists

(BANTON, 1966); these include thinkers such as Durkheim (DURKHEIM, 1965), Lévi-Strauss (LÉVI-STRAUSS, 1966), Douglas (DOUGLAS, 1966) and Geertz (GEERTZ, 1973), while a number of prominent recent writers have dealt in a fecund way with new religious movements, such as Wilson, Robertson, Lanternari (LANTERNARI, 1963), Martin and others (YINGER, 1970). Naturally I shall draw on much of this theoretical and empirical work in later chapters (SKORUPSKY, 1976).

Psychology and psychoanalysis. The psychology of religion is no doubt less flourishing today than it was, particularly in America under the influence of William James. But we now have much greater resources to draw on, both tradition-oriented and cross-cultural studies of mysticism for instance (with much work on Sufism, Buddhist meditation, Chinese and Japanese mystical traditions, Christian contemplation and Qabbala; and some parallel work on shamanism in various societies in Siberia, Africa, Korea and among Native Americans, for example). It is important to work up our knowledge of mysticism into systematic shape, and this will be one of the aims of this book.

Psychology obviously concerns itself with what I have called the experiential dimension (STRUNK, 1971). In addition, psychoanalysis, in part because of its incorrectness, has much to do with the mythic dimension and the way human symbols operate, while theories of the unconscious can clearly be important in theorizing about religion. Of course, psychoanalysis has a strong theoretical structure, which we do not need to accept at face value. One of the reasons for using phenomenology is that it enables us to judge whether the empirical results of our descriptive work really do confirm or disconfirm theories, but it cannot do this if the theoretical structure is already built into the very descriptions which are supposed to test the theory (HOMANS, 1979). So our phenomenological approach to the descriptive (and evocative) task should not be taken as a rejection of theories of the unconscious and the like, so much as a way of clearing the ground for the testing of those theories. Obviously, we separate out pastoral psychology from phenomenology: it is a kind of committed practice generative of spirituality, and as such is part of our subject matter (TILLICH, 1952).

History. Obviously the history of the religious and other traditions is simply part of general history, but one may then enquire whether religious history plays a formative or less than formative role at a given time in a given context (this, by the way, is the issue embraced by reductionism: reductionism implies that religion always has a secondary part to play). Issues concerning history are nevertheless complicated by the fact that history itself may be viewed religiously in ways that come into conflict with scientific history – for instance, in relation to the supposed historical facts recounted in the New Testament (RUDOLPH, 1962). A similar kind of conflict can occur in secular history (so called), for a society may view a piece of history in a certain way, only for later research to show that the real facts were rather different. Our phenomenological approach gives some status to perceived history as one of the causative factors at work in a given context. Because scientific history is critical of sources and received opinions, it can clash severely with religiously interpreted history: so it is necessary to be clear at a given juncture whether we are talking about phenomenological or actual history. There is another complication. The word 'history' refers sometimes to the story and sometimes to the method. When I referred to scientific history, what I meant was the method of doing history in as scientific (and impartial) a way as possible (BREISACH, 1983). Naturally the notion of what counts as scientific is controversial: the Marxian and the non-Marxian historians might debate the matter. But, leaving that aside for the moment, one meaning of 'history' is the method. Another meaning is the history or *story* of what is arrived at by doing history. We might talk about the history of the Second World War, referring to the story of that war. In this book I shall on the whole use 'story' to refer to the relevant flow of events, and 'history' to refer to the methods (MESLIN, 1973). It is sometimes important for us to refer to the process of delineating the story from a phenomenological point of view. There is an advantage in my using 'story' in the way described, for story is also a general category of which one subdivision is myth (which after all means 'story' in Greek); and in this way I assimilate myth and history. I believe this is phenomenologically realistic, since (historically arrived at) national stories do function as identity myths.

Ethics and law. The ethical dimension of worldviews is important, and part of what is customarily called ethics relates to its analysis. But only part: for much of what is undertaken under the head of 'ethics' is either normative ethics (not our prime concern in this analytic and phenomenological work) or metaethics. But the history of ethics, and of law, is vital to our understanding of how worldviews operate. And a central part of our concern here is comparative ethics, that is the comparative study of ethics. This is a subject not much undertaken in recent times (but see CHIDESTER, 1987).

Philosophy. Much of philosophy is concerned with debating and proposing solutions to problems. In short it has to do with building worldviews, rather than simply with analysis. Though an intellectual exercise, it is also value-laden. It is not as such part of the history of ideas or, more broadly, of the descriptive study of worldviews and religions. And yet the philosophy of religion is frequently viewed as part of religious studies (LONG, 1980). It is well to pause and consider here what part reflection may play in religious studies.

Classical philosophy of religion, which should in my view be regarded as the philosophy of worldviews (SMART, 1983), concerns itself with certain of the principal topics in Western religion, such as the supposed proofs of the existence of God, the problem of evil and the question of immortality (SWINBURNE, 1977). Its scope should be widened so that it becomes cross-cultural and includes discussion of the criteria of truth in religions. In its most general form, perhaps, it should be seen as reflecting about the truth, value and relationship of the world's worldviews. But obviously reflection about is different from description of, and even from theorizing about. The descriptive task has a certain priority: unless we know what it is we are reflecting about, how can we reflect appropriately? Some exponents of religious studies, wishing to stick rather strictly to the empirical and scientific study of the subject, are not happy with including philosophical-type reflection in the discipline. They are often motivated by a suspicion of the way in which (Christian) theology has dominated and perhaps infected the field (RAMSEY, 1957). There are academic and institutional dangers here, I do not doubt. Still, it seems inevitable that some reflection will arise out of the study of religions and, more generally, of worldviews (HICK, 1966). Is it better to keep such reflection inside or outside the academy?

Whatever the answer to such a question, the reflective mode, about truth and value in worldviews, is not strictly relevant to my approach in this book, even if this book is highly relevant to the reflective mode. It is not so relevant because our purpose here is not to judge worldviews or to worry about their truth or otherwise. I shall not pretend that my conclusions will be beyond debate: my varied theories will doubtless be open to question. But in trying also to present features of religions and slices of history I shall hope as far as possible to be appropriately descriptive. My tasks will not be part of the philosophy of religion.

There is, however, an aspect of the philosophy of religion which is something other than reflection about truth, consistency and so on: namely, the delineation of and debate about method in the study of religion. Obviously such methodological thinking is highly relevant to my task. It is part of a more general discussion of the philosophy of the social and human sciences. The present chapter is much taken up with this. No less obviously the history of philosophy concerns us here: it is in large measure the history of worldviews. Once constructed a worldview becomes history (EDWARDS, 1967)!

The history of philosophy can play a leading role in the delineation of the doctrinal and philosophical dimension. Certain aspects of philosophy may contribute to some understanding of other dimensions: for instance, the concept of performatives is highly relevant to the analysis of ritual.

Art history and the material dimension. 'Art' is a somewhat loaded concept, and so it is that art history tends to cover only a slice of religious art: Buddha statues at Sarnath; Leonardo da Vinci; Raphael and Rouault; West African bronzes; the Mughal monuments of north India – in short the high-quality products of religion. But the material dimension just as often incorporates the kitsch and the aesthetically deficient: plain chapels in Bradford; posters in the streets of Banaras; ex-voto paintings in Mexico; and so on. In this respect the study of the material dimension goes beyond the more conventional art history (HERMEREN, 1969).

I might add that the history of music too has this wider swathe to cover. How we should classify it I am not sure, but I shall include it primarily under the ritual dimension. It is a most important area of religious studies, but very little developed.

Theology. Though the term 'theology' is used of an academic discipline in the West, its assumptions are very much open to question. I believe it should be characterized as Christian, Islamic, Jewish and so forth, since it is typically tied to a view of where authoritative doctrines and scriptures come from. But much of what goes on under the rubric of theology is descriptive, for example the history of Western religious thought or the probing of texts in a quest for history. But constructive theology, which is a branch of worldview-construction, is more a part of the *data* of the descriptive and phenomenological treatment of religions.

At the level of worldview-construction and debate about worldviews, theology belongs to reflection about religions and worldviews. It should be conceived as plural in scope: there is a place neither in mainstream academic life nor in a global culture for restrictions on the positions explored. But again such religious reflection has little to do with my principal purpose here. This does not imply that methodological or other insights may not be yielded by primarily theological works – for instance, there is something important being claimed on this front in Kraemer's *The Christian Message in a Non-Christian World* (KRAEMER, 1938), in his estimate of the importance of context. But the task of constructing a worldview on the basis of cross-cultural facts is quite different from the kind of analysis and theorizing which I am undertaking here.

Political science. I shall later on be adding to my regular dimensions in referring to the political and economic aspects. Sometimes the political significance has been underplayed, partly because of an over-spiritual and ideal treatment of religion, and partly because of a predilection for reductionist theories. But the 1979 Iranian revolution, especially, has altered perceptions about the importance of religion in human affairs. If the dimensions sketch out what worldviews are in themselves, then the relation between them and political factors in a given society gives us some handle on the empirical question of reductionism: if the dimensional factors have a potent effect on the political process, then religion is a vital factor in that bit of history; but if the political process strongly affects the dimensions, then politics is a dominant factor in that bit of history. More dialectically, both effects may be working together. These more empirical ways of looking at reductionism should also help to avoid the fallacy of supposing that because a given position is not true it cannot have a potent effect on its society. Moreover we can see already that there is a whole cluster of factors within worldviews which are relevant to politics: loyalty to one's nationalism as incorporating a certain world-view; divine kingship; Anabaptism and incipient individualism; the status of the Sangha in Theravadin monarchies; Confucianism as a state ideology among the Chinese bureaucracy; the concept of the caliph in Islam; religious convictions in Israel and the question of the occupied territories; and so on (MERKL and SMART, 1983).

Economics and various exchanges. Although religionists have not much interested themselves in economics, it is a fruitful subject in relation to worldviews, ranging from such expansive theses as Weber's concerning Protestantism and the rise of capitalism to current thinking about Confucian values in the East Asian economic upsurge. But it also embraces deeper questions of exchange: for example, consider ways in which lay Buddhists give material goods such as robes and food to monks in exchange for moral instruction and enhancement of their own merit. I shall therefore devote some space to the study of the worldview dimensions in relation to economic attitude.

So much then for a brief account of major disciplines as they stand in regard to religious studies. There are some areas I have not explicitly written about: Indology, classical studies, Chinese studies, African studies and so on. Needless to say, these subjects have a place within the embrace of religious studies, and religious studies in turn have a role within these subjects. The same can be said of women's studies (DOUGLAS, 1977). This is illuminating above all because it brings new perspectives and questions into the academy, which needs continuous stirring. One of the liveliest and most transforming areas since the mid-1970s has been that of women's studies (OCHS-HORN, 1981).

Questions of ancient and modern

I turn now to consider the distribution of the religious material in the subsequent discussion. A great deal of van der Leeuw's material was ancient. I would prefer to have more of it modern. The reasons for this judgment are several. First, the only kind of religion we are actually going to meet is a modern one. We might meet the Dalai Lama, but not Paul or Buddhaghosa. Those modern religions have all passed through a certain fire, that of the colonial and industrial periods. Second, I would like this book to give people an understanding of our world, and, while I would not have them ignorant of the deep past, I would like them to resonate with the lessons provided for modern times.

Traditions have of course been greatly changed by modernity. Take the colonial period. Many cultures underwent profound disturbances as a result of European, and to some extent American and Japanese, colonial domination. Indian culture, previously seesawing between Muslim and Hindu rulers and cultural motifs, came to be dominated by the British. The sub-continent experienced a whole slew of challenges in a short period – conquest itself, the building of the railway system, industrialization and the impact of British exports, missionary endeavour and with it criticism of the indigenous heritage, especially the Hindu, new patterns in school and higher education, the English language, a new access to and appreciation of Indian history, and ideas of democracy. To an extent modern Hinduism was formed in response to such challenges. The concept of a unified whole called Hinduism, which burst forth from the pages of thinkers like Swami Vivekananda, was in some ways a new idea – certainly as expressed and forged into a modern Hindu ideology. The beauty of it was that it left so many things in place: the numerous cults and practices and pilgrimages and villages and temples and gurus and so forth could remain the same, but they could have an overarching umbrella. The new Hindu ideology favoured democracy, independence for India, moderate reform, English-speaking education, a new humanism (seeking human satisfaction within the depths of the eternal soul), a philosophy of toleration and a return to the classical texts of the tradition. In all such matters Hinduism took on some new shapes and gave itself a strong and modern air (CRAWFORD, 1986).

Other traditions took somewhat different paths. Japan, anticipating trouble, modernized on its own, and in the process reshaped to some degree its complex religious structures, containing Shinto, Buddhist and other elements. It also created some new religions. We could go on to list the ways Islamic, African, Chinese and other cultures responded to the impact of the modern. But they were all to a greater or lesser degree transformed, and it is the resultant set of religions that we have to deal with today. This is why, without being exclusively bound to them, my treatment will incorporate examples from modern religions and worldviews. So far, though, I have mentioned the non-Western cultural areas. But what about the effects of modern change upon Christianity and Judaism? And what of the modern ideologies?

Christianity did not have to undergo colonialism, as many other religions and cultures did, but there were other challenges which needed to be met: the whole traumatic process of industrialization, the rise of new scientific knowledge, the creation of the national idea and so on. While one major part of Christianity, Orthodoxy, has remained remarkably intact, Protestantism (above all) and the Catholic church have undergone numerous reforms and changes, as they tried to adapt themselves to the new world of the last 200 years. Judaism has been transformed in not too dissimilar ways, though with a notable addition – the creation of the Jewish state in Israel has had all kinds of dynamic effects on the practice of Judaism.

The ideologies will also attract our attention, since in differing ways they express alternatives to the modernized religions. Marxism was especially important after the Second World War in providing a worldview which, while purporting to be modern, was also anti-colonial. It could promise a theory for rallying Russia, China and other countries in their struggle against the imperial powers. As worldviews incarnated in national arrangements they supply a rich source of symbols. Parallel to them, as we have previously indicated, there are the nationalisms.

We may draw on another, less formal source. There are elements of worldviews scattered through daily life: items in music, sports, educational practice, literature, television and the movies which may have relevance to our exploration in this book, and I shall make occasional use of these resources (BELLAH, 1970).

Attempts at correlation, and networks

In making use of my analysis of the dimensions of religion I shall attempt to supply correlations. That is, I shall try to show that items in one dimension may be correlated to others, offering incipient explanatory theses. I do not want to exaggerate: one cannot make worldviews tidier than they are. But they are sometimes better patterned than at first sight appears. For instance, I think it can be shown that some typical patterns of doctrine or philosophy flow from the attempt to join the religion of *bhakti* with that of the contemplative path or *dhyāna*; or that notions like grace grow out of a certain practical soil and not out of others. Certain patterns of social behaviour can stem from the prevalence of printed books. There are sometimes circumstances which tend to transform myths into doctrines, or if you like into metaphysical ballets.

But enough wider networks can be traced, for in one way or another all the dimensions are connected. I hope therefore to provide as articulate a picture as is possible given the complexity and untidiness of the data. But because of the intertwining of items from the dimensions it is not easy to deal with them separately, that is chapter by chapter. So I shall take detours through some other dimensions in each chapter. This may justify my beginning the discussion at what may seem to some scholars an unusual point, the doctrinal dimension. I am nervous of doing so for fear of the accusation that I am being too intellectual in thinking about religions and worldviews. But there are nevertheless some advantages in this procedure. One is that some of the key expressions which are to be used in the analysis will occur in my working with the philosophical dimension. Another is that, in handling the relations between certain intellectual and philosophical notions on the one hand and rituals and other practical activities on the other, it will be possible to exhibit the practical nature of doctrines in religion.

So I shall start by exploring mainly the doctrinal or philosophical dimension, with suitable excursions. This will give us an opening on the whole field. This book is meant to delineate a kind of taxonomy through which we can better understand the structures of worldviews. Since the mid-1960s so many fine studies of the religions of the world have been published that it now seems a propitious time to weave some of the results together.

CHAPTER ONE

Doctrine, Philosophy and Some Dimensions

Thoughts on the non-theistic

Because the comparative study of religion started in the West, it is common to begin one's examination with the assumption that theism is the norm. But that is not the view of many Buddhists, and theirs is after all one of the great missionary religions of the world. Buddhist culture has spread through Asia, from India (CONZE, 1962) to Japan and into South-east Asia. There are a number of ways in which Buddhism expresses itself in a manner strongly reminiscent of theism. A Christian could easily appreciate the appeal to grace in Shinran's Buddhism. The delineation of the Pure Land is indeed heavenly and you could think that Pure Land piety is rather like Methodism, but with diverse cultural symbolisms. Nevertheless, two varieties at least of Buddhism are very different from theism: the Theravada (HAZRA, 1982) and Madhyamika, one of the mainstream forms of Mahayana Buddhism (STRENG, 1967). It was not for nothing that the Dalai Lama declared in my presence, at a large meeting in the spring of 1991 in Santa Barbara, California, 'We Buddhists are atheists.'

Now such atheism is not unspiritual. Some Western atheists are highly negative on the spiritual side of life, but Buddhism has its other spiritual resources and goals. It looks to nirvana. It relies on the Sangha. It has deep spiritual books and philosophies. But it is still atheist: it rejects the notion of a creator God who will help out with our troubles (GOMBRICH, 1971).

Again there is a qualification to be made. While the Theravada is much more strictly atheistic, the Mahayana does have some substitute for God and the gods. It conceives the role of the Buddha and the Buddha-to-be or Bodhisattva as heavenly. Buddhas become lords. They can be the foci of *bhakti* or devotion. People worship them as saviours. So there is no doubt (and we shall return to this point) that there are gods of a kind in the Mahayana. Even so, at base there is no *iśvara* or Lord in much of the Great Vehicle, and none in the Theravada (HOPKINS, 1983). Thus, although the position is a little messy, I think one can still state that in much (and in much of the early phases of) Buddhism there is no Lord, no God.

The same is true of the Jain tradition (JAINI, 1979), more clearly so because it never had a Mahayana sub-tradition. And elsewhere, in India and non-Indian systems, theism is likewise absent. But let us take the Theravada case. It is a noble and widespread faith, stretching from Sri Lanka to Vietnam, via Burma (Myanmar), Cambodia, Laos and Thailand. Its non-theistic character may enable it to act as a counter-example against certain theories in religion – indeed against most of the well-known ones. It would be useful to examine this point, for what I am saying is theoretically important, to put it no more strongly.

A glance at some theories

The Theravada raises a number of questions about the theories, for example, of Freud, Otto and Eliade. I wish at this point only to put questions, since there will be ample opportunity later to consider certain of the ideas contained in these and other theories. First, there can be no doubt that Freud's seminal notions on the unconscious and on the hidden ballet within the psyche are fecund, in general terms, for those wishing to interpret myths (consider the work of DONIGER, e.g. 1973). Nevertheless the framework of his interpretations was nineteenth-century theism, both Christian (FREUD, 1927) and Jewish (1939). It is baffling to apply Freudian theory to the Theravada, from which both Mother and Father seem to be puzzlingly absent. Some writers in the Sri Lankan tradition, notably Padmasiri de Silva (1974), have used Freud in a surprising way, essentially as undermining Western theism but not Theravadin non-theism. If Freudian theory is to be retained it would have to be expanded to take account of non-theism. There is of course a lot of mythic or narrative material in Buddhism, but it does not seem to have, in the Theravada at least, the same density and mysteriousness as Hindu myth, which has often therefore seemed a wonderful hunting ground of Freudian interpretation. By 'myth' in the Buddhist case I am thinking primarily of the Jataka stories and the narratives of the Buddha himself. In general the ritual dimension is less important in the Theravada than in so much of the Hindu tradition, which, with the Brahmins, has always retained within it an elite of ritual specialists. The emphasis in the Theravada has been on the psychological and merit-producing significance of public rites, rather than on their inner power. But more of that anon.

Otto's famous book (OTTO, 1917/1923) on the holy delineates an important strand of religious experience which is for him the central one. His formula for describing the holy as the *mysterium tremendum et fascinans* is an apt one, and I shall make extensive use of it. But it does not seem aptly to cover experience in the Theravadin case, where practice focuses on concentration; which in turn aims at a kind of purified consciousness. The ascent of the *jhānas* (stages of meditation) grows ever more subtle (BUDDHAGHOSA, 1964), culminating in the realization of certain formulae such as 'There is nothing.' There is no creature-feeling, or sense of awe, or fascination with any phenomenological object. It is true, as Otto himself said, that there is a way in which a Theravadin monk will find nirvana fascinating, but he will not do so, I think, in the required manner. The contemplative experience, as it is often described elsewhere, abolishes the distinction between subject and object: most comprehensively in the Theravada. But the numinous experience postulates an Other. There is no reason at all why there should not be more than one sort of basic experience in religion. I take Otto's to be one of them. But his desire to make it universally central rests perhaps on an essentialist yearning. Moreover, if all religious experiences are somehow at heart the same, the differences between religions become more difficult to explain. I shall attempt to show that my hypothesis of two (or more) strands of basic religious experience has much greater explanatory power.

As a young man Eliade went to India and did some marvellous things. His books on yoga (1958b) and shamanism (1964) are fine creations, most useful to scholars, and reflect his judgments on certain aspects of religious experience. Yet Buddhism does not seem to figure deeply in his mature thinking. His consciousness was perhaps more Eastern Orthodox and Hindu than Buddhist. He was interested in symbols, so his predilection is understandable. But the schema which he worked out, comprising important materials and concepts from the history of religions, has a Jungian resonance, though it scarcely fits the non-substantiality of mainstream Buddhism and has a concealed Divine Being lying behind it. I am thinking of such items in his cosmology as the hierophany, the coincidence of opposites, the *axis mundi* and *homo religiosus*. The Eliadean interpretative scheme has more to do with god-directed (including 'archaic') religions than it has to do with the emptiness and insubstantiality of the Theravada and of mainstream Mahayana. We shall return to these points later.

So much for my brief excursus into three theories. It is designed to show among other things that beginning with the Theravada does make a difference. But let me add a footnote. The Theravada does of course incorporate gods, spirits and the like (MARASINGHE, 1974). The cosmos as seen in the Pali canon does seem to crawl with *devatās* and *devas*. The religion blesses pilgrimages, merit-making, slicing coconuts for the gods in temple shrines. It has even taken over Mahayana practice in having statues of the Buddha. But, though it has a lot of the paraphernalia of popular religion, it is nevertheless clear about the secondary nature of these phenomena: they are, as it were, hollowed out, as the cosmos itself is hollowed out.

The ultimate in the context of the non-theistic

There is no creator or supreme object of worship in the Theravada, unless you count the Buddha, but this is not strictly recognized by the religion itself. I shall come back to this in considering whether we can talk about *bhakti* in this context. But I am proceeding on the principle that, strictly speaking, such worship is not to be found in the Theravada. As for creation *and* salvation, this is not the task of the gods. The great God Brahma, seen as creator by the Brahmins, falsely supposes that he made the world, for as the first being to come into existence during a cosmic epoch he falsely infers that other beings came into being because of him: *post me*, he reasons, *propter me* (VON GLASENAPP, 1966). The illusions of God do not entail that there is no ultimate: there is ultimate liberation, *nibbāna*. But it is neither an ultimate Being lying within or beyond the cosmos, nor some kind of divine being. There is no use in Theravadin language for such locutions as 'Nirvana is all-pervasive or supports the world or is omnipresent'. Nirvana is transcendent in the sense that it is not part of the *loka* or cosmos. Everything in the *loka* is impermanent and indeed subject to the three marks of existence – not just impermanent but without self (*attā*) and suffused with illfare (*dukkha*) as opposed to welfare (*sukha*). Later the Mahayana were to alter the status of nirvana, so that it could in a sense pervade everything, being identified paradoxically with *saṃsāra*, the impermanent round, the round of rebirth. But, as far as the Theravada goes, nirvana is transcendent but not immanent. I would say that nirvana is known as transcendent in the intuitive experience of and subsequent reflection upon inner liberation. Hence various metaphors which are used of nirvana: the other shore, the highest security, the matchless island and so on. But although nirvana is the ultimate it is not the ultimate Being or God, but rather the ultimate state, to be classified ordinarily in the Indian tradition as *mokṣa*, or salvation or liberation (COLLINS, 1982).

A theist might want to say that nirvana is simply the ineffable side of God, but that would not be a phenomenological judgment. It would be bringing in one tradition to interpret another (we see how 'interpret' is a weasel word). There is nothing wrong with doing this: if you are a theist you need to make sense of nirvana from the standpoint of theism. But it is not natural for a Theravadin to identify nirvana with God. The nirvanist of course needs conversely to make sense of theism: so far with not much success, in my view, but perhaps it is early days. Buddhists might want to take a hard line and simply carry on rejecting theism (though in this case they might need to say more about the experiences and rituals which feed theism: the numinous and *bhakti*) (WELBON, 1968). At any rate, from the standpoint of orthodox Theravada, the highest goal is nirvana, and that becomes the ultimate. Matters are a little different among the Jains. By analogy the equivalent is *kevala* or whole liberation. But the Jain cosmology and metaphysics are somewhat different. The cosmos is a unified whole: the top of the universe, or rather the top of the universe conceived as a material entity, for around it lies infinite space, contains the perfected ones or liberated souls in a region which contains no medium of motion. In other words the souls of the liberated ones cannot move: they can arrive there but they cannot leave, nor can they have any truck with the rest of the cosmos. And so, like the Buddhas, but for a different reason, they cannot enter into *bhakti* relations with the denizens of the world. But, strictly, the perfected ones are not transcendent, while the Buddhas are not of this *loka*, even if we cannot say that they belong to some other *loka*. What are we to say of the difference? Perhaps that while the Jain liberation is not metaphysically it is psychologically transcendent.

The gods in non-theistic systems, and others

The gods can play varying roles. For instance in Olympus gods may have different ranks, and in much of Greek religion Zeus and Hera are chief, in the sense that they are first among equals (roughly). There are also lower spirits and lesser beings such as heroes, who still rank above humans. Many societies have a whole continuum of spirits and beings, ranging from high gods down to ghosts. We shall consider these hierarchies later.

Another variety is what may be called refracted gods, that is to say gods and goddesses who are lower manifestations of the Supreme Deity: we see this most notably in the Hindu tradition, where (especially in recent times, though the motif is found way back in the *Ṛgveda*) the many gods are perceived as so many manifestations of the One Reality.

The word 'god', as it is used in English, refers to the superhuman (ELIADE, 1958a). Sometimes the term 'supernaturals' is used in anthropological literature to point to this class of beings. It is worth noting that the Indian word *deva* is used over a wider range, referring not only to the superhuman but also to a king or a husband, and in the feminine to a queen or lady. For some purposes of course a king or queen can function as god or goddess, acting as a conduit of power between the higher sphere and the lower. There is a hierarchy of lesser forms in which the All-Highest may seek to express himself. These forms can be either servants or incarnations, depending on which model of godship is chosen by the relevant schema of belief and practice.

Typically, the lesser gods do what the Highest wishes or commands. But this is not exactly so with the Buddhist gods. They may from time to time co-operate with the Buddha, but they are far from seeing it as their destiny to fulfil his commands. Gods function as powers in the material *loka*; and *devatās* are lesser powers, with whom we may need to engage, at building sites for instance, for they have views about the propriety of places selected for erecting structures. This is much like dealing with local bureaucracies. But the gods are pretty independent, so that various ritual and magical means may have to be employed to keep them in a beneficent mood. The gods in the Theravadin case are, then, forces to be reckoned with, though they have no intrinsic importance as far as salvation is concerned. Indeed, from the standpoint of the higher values of the world, it is the path to nirvana which is the high road. The gods are to the side, off the beaten track, useful but not otherwise significant.

So there is a sense in which the gods are 'loose'. They are not really integrated into the system, from the functional point of view. They represent a certain level in a hierarchy of beings. Perhaps this is their chief significance, given that the cosmos considered as a whole has differing levels, sometimes matched with different heights of achievement in the scale of *jhānas*. The upper levels are heavens (where gods exist), the lower purgatories. We shall later have occasion to dwell upon the function of cosmologies.

Likewise there are gods, divided into four classes, who dwell in the cosmos as delineated by the Jains. But, as Buddhists also believe, the supreme leaders (*tīrthaṃkaras*) can be born only as humans, not as gods. That places humans above the gods. One of the epithets of the Buddha is *devātideva*, god above gods. But the first 'god' in the compound is not to be taken literally, for obvious reasons.

So let us make a provisional conclusion about the gods. First, when there is a supreme God, Goddess or Couple, the rest of the gods exist more or less as servants of the supreme, or as substitutes (people go to the lesser gods for fear of disturbing the higher ones unnecessarily). But in the case of non-theistic religions there is not a supreme God, but rather a set of supreme teachers and an ultimate liberation. So the gods are 'loose' in the system. They function as powers, but are not spiritually important.

A new nomenclature for dealing with the problem

Western authors have tended to think of religions as monotheistic or polytheistic or animistic or whatever. But in the case of non-theistic religions the occurrence of gods is by no means the most important thing about them: the gods are incidentals sucked into the doctrinal scheme with a certain cosmology. There are modern Buddhists who essentially dispense with the gods, seeing them as mythological accretions. If one seeks an encapsulating name, one might call such belief-systems 'transpolytheistic' (SMART, 1993), reacting against Zimmer's locution 'transtheistic' (ZIMMER, 1972). What 'transpolytheistic' means is that there are many gods, but the higher goal transcends them.

I would prefer to use 'transtheistic' for systems of belief which stress that there is a *brahman* or non-personal X lying beyond (transcending) the personal Lord or *īśvara*, a *deitas* lying beyond *deus*. Where the Supreme is conceived non-personally it is quite common to perceive the personal God as intermediate, lying as it were 'below' the non-personal. We shall return to consider such cases later. A transtheistic system may also be transpolytheistic, treating the lesser gods and goddesses as servants or refractions of the supreme Lord. So we have three decks, so to speak: the top deck is the X; the second deck the Lord; the third deck is the gods.

Many societies have had a not very well defined sense of the Supreme Being. There is often what has been called the High God (and we shall return to this theme in our later treatment of the mythic dimension). But the gods are relevant to differing spheres of life and may be only loosely integrated. Their independence of one another means that they are not necessarily in their collectivity a coherent force. So as far as gods go, there are diverse models: a non-theistic transpolytheism; a theistic transpolytheism; a transtheistic transpolytheism; a polytheism. And then of course you can in the modern style have no gods at all.

Gods and other supernaturals

One might define a god as a being who is or can be worshipped appropriately. There are various other invisible or supernatural beings who are not in this way gods; thus evil beings may have the same sort of powers as gods, but may be inappropriate to worship because they are on the 'other side': they are evil beings. In the Buddhist context there is Māra, the great adversary, the death-dealer, a sort of Satan. He has large numbers of followers, moreover. Then there are ancestors, who up to a point may be cultivated like gods, but essentially belong simply to society, conceived more widely than modern positivism demands. Then there are, relatedly, ghosts, often unhappy ancestors in effect, and a whole spectrum of lesser spirits.

Gods are associated often with natural forces, of course, though they often represent social forces and may also be built up through complex stories. Krishna for instance as a god is defined by the stories told about him, and these are elaborated by the commentaries on those narratives (to cite a well-known case: his love of the gopis is taken to express the divine love of individual human souls). But it may be worth briefly reflecting on the gods and natural forces. A schema for understanding the relation between them introduces the topic of the behaviour to be directed towards the gods.

In societies which believe in gods a network tends to be built up around some significant power, such as fire. This network embraces first all the particular fires which we encounter. By extension the network threads in lightning, and the substance of the sun, seen as a fierce ball of fire out there, engaged moreover in a strange ballet with the moon, perhaps a lesser fire, and against the background of the possibly fiery stars. Anyway, sun, lightning and earthly fire are networked together. If fire is used for disposing the dead, this adds an extra existential aspect to the collage of fires. All these fires are seen as modes of behaviour of the one substance Fire. (To this extent there is a slight plausibility in the 'gods as a disease of language' theory, MUELLER, 1873). In dealing with sacred fire people treat its manifestations as pieces of behaviour, and the whole network is so to speak the body of the god. Lightning might be highly symptomatic of the feelings and purposes of the god. So the whole pattern of ritual activity becomes a way of responding to the god, communicating with him, influencing his actions.

Provided we have a sufficiently flexible view of the body, then it becomes reasonable to look on gods as persons. Hence one can enter into personal relationships with the gods through rituals, which are in part at least formalized versions of human interchanges. There is also the problem of the definition of magic. Older discussions reflected a lot about the societies which formulated the questions. For Victorians the issue of the distinction between religion and magic was important. This reflected varying strands in late Victorian values: the triumphant virtue of science; the spiritual superiority of Protestantism (and to some degree respectable Catholicism); the degeneracy of savages, etc. Magic might be defined as formulaic performative procedures undertaken in order directly to influence the world. It represents an impersonalization of performatives to change the world, not through personal relations, but through manipulations.

In general the use of formulaic performative procedures has turned out to be ineffective. Slowly scientific methods have grown in strength and authority. But we should not exaggerate: there remains a ritual aspect to hospital and other medical procedures. The magic remains a little in medicine: but it has been there more abundantly in the past – and has often turned out to be disastrously ineffective. The use of leeches for instance had no genuine medical basis, as we now see. Still, magic is discredited because it is not paradigmatic science. It was not absurd; but it depended on a theory about the world, that performative action could be effective outside of human spheres of conduct, which turned out to be wrong.

It is of course obvious that modern physics, often resting secretly on the absolute division between living and non-living matter, helped to destroy the whole magical worldview. But it also helped to destroy the notion that performative actions towards living beings, namely gods, were useful, since essentially physical reality *is not living*. And it certainly is not conscious. The unliving world of the sun, the moon, lightning and fires could be explored better through physical (dead) principles. Physics joined forces with Western monotheism to banish the gods. Or at least up to a point: it is surprising that India, for instance, which is a highly scientific country, well developed in all sorts of ways, yet maintains its millions, billions, of gods below God. Still, maybe the gods are changing nature. Be that as it may, in the west the gods were in part banished by Yahweh and in part by physics.

Yet, to return to the gods: we can interpret ritual directed towards them as reflections of social behaviour. Perhaps at an analogical level: for we often forget that it is not only words which exist in analogical relations to one another, but actions too, and symbols, and items from other dimensions. Let me sketch some examples.

A god can be addressed as a king. He is by analogy to an earthly king: so there are analogues to courtly behaviour used in divine rituals. Where art is used, then the god is depicted with a crown or other symbols of royal status. The expressions of loyalty to a monarch are reflected in those to a god. The mythic paeans have a resemblance to the chants and songs addressed in honour of a god. Just as the Byzantine rites in Eastern Orthodoxy are not unlike the court etiquette of the Byzantine monarchy, there are analogues between earthly and heavenly manners of addressing the powerful. As it is possible, moreover, to combine motifs in new ways, for instance by joining the male and the female in the depiction of a god, or by assigning her or him varying symbolic decorations and tools or weapons, so it is possible to string different performatives together, to create imaginative and complex rites. There are similarities of structure running through the artistic, mythic and ritual dimensions.

Monomyth and polymyth

It is not often noted that a pluralism similar to that registered among the gods, is to be found in the mythic dimension. A plural scene is sketched by the relative independence of differing myths. For instance, there is no holistically conceived corpus of Greek or Hindu myths. They have arisen separately and live side by side. This reflects the plurality of the gods. It is true that the higher gods may be unified in a general doctrinal scheme and so become what I have called refracted, but there is a relative independence about how they behave. This can become one of the strengths of a refracted system: different characters in the mythic empyrean can interact. It is not possible for differing epithets of the One to interact, though on occasion hypothesized alternates of God may be mistaken for gods by taking on a certain independence.

In a monotheistic system, it is not just the doctrinal dimension that has a unified focus. The mythic too is woven into a single whole. So the whole history of the creation and its aftermath, together with the story of salvation, culminating in the *Endzeit*, develops as a single story. It may have its byways, but in principle it has a unitary theme. It is what I here call a monomyth. It takes the form of a single *Heilsgeschichte*.

Some modern tendencies

In modern times, there has been a trend towards taking polytheism less seriously. It is true that attempts to revive small-scale religions, such as those of Native Americans, and to unify African religion (RANGER and KIMAMBO, 1972), have imparted new life to traditional pantheons, or at least to the conception of such pantheons. But modernist Buddhists have played the gods down, seeing them as a manifestation of popular or mass religion, but not of the essence of the faith. Only when backed by theory, on the whole, is polytheism acceptable: for example, in transpolytheistic modes, where the many gods are seen as the refracted modes of the One. While it is reasonable (people often think) to react to the cosmos as if it exhibits

God's behaviour towards us, that is to look on the whole cosmos somehow as God's body, the notion that there are separate deities controlling fire or the earth or what-have-you is seen as somewhat primitive. God may be localized in the sense that she may have manifested herself specially at a certain place, but this is different from the function-particularity of a specialized god. (Gods can thus be polytopic, as distinguished from omnipresent, and are often both. The Virgin Mary is polytopic (WARNER, 1976), perhaps not in a strong sense omnipresent, though it is never inappropriate, wherever you are, to call upon her. The Christian God is omnipresent and polytopic. But more of this anon.)

The emptying out of the cosmos of spirits and gods represents a certain 'secularizing' of the universe. But we should notice that the original Buddhist refusal to deny the gods made way for what proved to be a fruitful symbiosis between Buddhism and indigenous, agriculturally based religions throughout Asia, and helped to merge the three religions of China during the last thousand years. Probably its most important 'grammatical' lesson is that the contemplative life is not necessarily conceived, as is often claimed, as a sort of union. Because the study of mysticism in modern times started in the West, it has been assumed that its aim is union with God, with the One. But this is misleading. Since mysticism involves, by virtually universal testimony, the disappearance of the subject–object distinction, then if an Other is postulated a kind of merging or union is envisaged, often expressed in terms of the image of love, of the two-in-one (SMART, 1958; KATZ, 1993). But if an Other is not postulated, the image of union does not arise. This is the case with the Theravada. So Theravada Buddhism is an important example not just for the numinous but for mysticism as well.

Another issue, to which we shall return, is the belief which accompanies and helps to define liberation in the Indian non-theistic systems, namely belief in reincarnation or rebirth. Since 'reincarnation' suggests that some entity is incarnated again and again, and since in the Theravadin analysis there is no such entity, I prefer to use the term 'rebirth'. It is only one, of course, among a number of models of life after death. It has important modificatory effects on other beliefs: it generates a relatively relaxed educational theory, while belief in one chance only against the backcloth of the awful choice between heaven and everlasting torment makes salvation a deeply dramatic matter.

Also important in the Theravadin philosophical economy are various analyses of the cosmos: the three marks of existence, namely impermanence, selflessness, suffering; the chain of dependent origination; the five groups or factors or types of events which go to make up human life; the steps to be taken in treading the eightfold path.

The three marks, while philosophical in shape, are also deeply practical: it is not enough to understand that everything is impermanent, you must feel it too, absorb it into your existential attitude. This lesson is repeated in such works as the *Therīgāthā* and *Theragāthā* (*Songs of the Nuns and Monks*: Pali Text Society, 1966). It cannot be too strongly emphasized that, particularly in Buddhism, abstract-sounding doctrines have powerful salvific significance. Abstractions have human meaning. (It may be noted that there is an analogue in Marxism, with its abstract ballet of the dialectic of history which has at the same time a practical significance.) One of the major functions of timeless nirvana is to act as a contrast to impermanent cosmic life. There is a not dissimilar contrast in substance-bound accounts of the transcendent: this world is evanescent in contrast to the eternity of the divine Substance. This perhaps has its strongest expression in Islamic occasionalism.

Forms of theism, and its inner complexities

So far we have looked at non-theism and polytheistic pantheons. Usually there is a continuum of spirits embracing both gods and lesser beings, but notable kinds of theism may also repudiate gods. Judaism, Christianity and Islam scorn alternative gods. It may be that they embrace at differing times other spirits, such as angels, saints and djinns, devils, ghosts and so on. In some respects saints are similar to lesser gods in types of refracted theism. If you deal with a saint in relation to thunderstorms or illness it is not so very different from dealing with a god or goddess. Such systems as Voodoo (Vodun) develop the similarities. This is one reason why the Catholic cult of saints is repudiated by the severer kinds of Protestantism.

Refracted theism allows of much greater myth flexibility, not merely because a system may be theistic and polymythic but because mythic entities, such as a god and a goddess, can have mutual relations: they can, say, make love, which a single deity cannot do without mythic grotesquerie. Moreover a single God has to be female or male at a certain time at least, at least in regard to the language used about her or him. This has, as we know, led to severe problems of imagery.

One function of philosophical reflection is to diminish literalism. It is obvious that if God is described as a spirit and lives in a transcendent sphere he cannot have a chest, literally: therefore he cannot have hair on his chest, and in no normal way can he be conceived as literally male. At most you can say that a certain rather truncated masculine language is used about him, which yet has to be interpreted. So a modicum of reflection leads to the conclusion that God is neither literally male nor literally female. This reflective function of philosophy has a spiritual function in that it helps to elevate the terminology and spirit of religion.

There are intermediate states between polytheism and theism – for instance henotheism, the addressing of a given God as sole God, even when (outside the frame of a given ritual) other gods may be recognized (GONDA, 1970). This is most developed in Hinduism, where there are alternative representations of the One. The major doctrinal systems are forms of Vedanta, such as Non-Dualism and Dualism, together with such other schemes as Saiva Siddhanta, Kashmir Saivism and Lingayata.

The shape of such systems is determined greatly by the differing pulls of *bhakti*, which implies some degree of difference between God and the worshipper, and mysticism, which implies union (HARDY, 1983). A major model for signalling the presence of the Divine within the created cosmos is that of panentheism, and in particular the analogy of soul–body and God–cosmos. The cosmos is God's body, over which he or she has perfect control (while we have only imperfect control over our own bodies).

Mostly we think of theism as involving some creation or emanation. But what do we say about supreme foci of *bhakti* who are not in the strict sense creators, though they may function in other ways like gods?

Thus Mahayana Buddhism has for instance Amitabha (Amida) and the great Bodhisattva Avalokiteśvara (Kuanyin, Kannon), who not only are foci of *bhakti* but, because of that, are saviours. This arises from the logic of *bhakti* and the numinous. A brief excursus on this theme seems appropriate.

Grace and the logic of bhakti

The numinous experience contains within it the seeds of *bhakti*, for it reveals the *mysterium tremendum et fascinans*. The awe-inspiring overwhelming character of the Other can seem alienating: it reflects itself perhaps in those African myths of how God withdraws upwards, or raises the sky, leaving the first man and woman down here on earth. But the appropriate reaction of humans in their feeling of creatureliness or relative insignificance is to worship the *mysterium*. In attributing holiness to the Other, humans naturally come to conceive the Other as the sole source of holiness (sole at least within a given frame, hence the henotheistic pattern). In having ritual contact with the Other the worshipper expects transmittal of the holy substance. The Other becomes the source of holiness: he or she transmits a blessing to the worshipper. In this way, the focus of worship naturally (so to speak) becomes a benefactor. The way is prepared for the formation of mutual love between the worshipper and the focus. So *bhakti* springs forth for numerous religions (OTTO, 1917). We see the logic of *bhakti* expressed in diverse ways: as grace, as the transfer of merit (in Buddhism) as mercy (in Islam), as predestination (in Calvinism and in Islam), and so on. This helps to explain the difference between self- help and other-help (*tariki* and *jiriki*) religion (EARHART, 1982).

Inner complexities in the Divine Being

While the Lord is personal, albeit typically in an analogical sense, there is frequently some sense that the Divine Being is also non-personal. This is the most basic complexity in the Divine: the contrast between the persona and the impersona (HICK, 1987). While there appear to be subsidiary reasons for the contrast, such as the reflection that the Divine exists independently of the cosmos and of worship and so should not be reduced to relational attributes including personhood, the basic reason is to do with styles of religious practice. The practice of worship and *bhakti* supposes the personhood of the focus, but the direction towards which the contemplative life is steered is a sort of pure consciousness in which recognizable attributes are absent. The goal becomes indescribable. And so that dark and dazzling side of the ultimate is seen as an impersona. The Divine may have more than one reason for being indescribable. It may be because she is at the summit of contemplative experience; but it may be because she is beyond words of praise (SMART, 1958). The latter is a more raw performative: to say that words fail is to use words to convey something beyond ordinary words. But to say that the mystical experience is indescribable is to say something about what ordinary description amounts to and to affirm that it does not apply here. There may be a third kind of ineffability – it is sheer bliss. In other words, you can have three forms of indescribability which could be crudely summed up as 'You are greater than words; you are not to be depicted by ordinary descriptive adjectives; you are sheer bliss' (SMART, 1958).

Anyway, the two sides of God reflect two kinds of religion: the religion of *bhakti* and the religion of *dhyāna*. They can coexist equally: this is one model. Or the one or the other may be posited as superior – *deitas* over *deus* in Eckhart; *brahman* over *īśvara* in Sankara; and conversely *īśvara* over *brahman* in Ramanuja (SÖDERBLOM, 1933).

There are other complexities, where for instance divine attributes become partly hypostatized, as in the Zoroastrian concept of the *amesha spentas* and the Qabbala notion of the Sefirot. Some inner complexities arise in part from the mythic dimension, notably the Trinity doctrine and the *trikāya* or Three Aspect (Three Body) doctrine in Mahayana Buddhism.

The Trinity and the narrative dimension

The structure of the Divine in Christianity has to reflect the narrative of the faith. That narrative postulates certain crucial episodes – the creation of the cosmos, the covenant with Israel, the life of Christ, the coming of the Holy Spirit at Pentecost, the second coming, and so on. As far as the Hebrew Bible and the New Testament go, it is as though God manifests as three beings – the Father, the Son and the Spirit. Since the early Christians found themselves worshipping God in these differing forms, and since the faith sprang from a strictly monotheistic religion (whose aniconic practices were in part intended to reinforce this strictness, making Judaism such an especially numinous religion), it was necessary to devise a formula which could accommodate both the narrative assumptions and the purist view. That the formula is framed in Greek philosophical terms gives it too abstract an air, given that the Trinity doctrine is supposed to have a spiritual and ethical meaning too. The intimacy of the relationship between the three Persons is meant to express the perfect love which is internal to the divine nature and a wonderful model for Christians to reflect on, and to follow in their ethical life. At any rate, the complication in the inner life of the Trinity is essentially due to the outer events of the narrative dimension, taken as revealed.

The narrative is, of course, different in Buddhism, and so the pressures towards the Three Aspect doctrine are different.

The Three Aspect doctrine in Mahayana Buddhism

The exigencies behind the *trikāya* are more philosophical, though the narrative side has its importance. At the philosophical level there was the need to unify three 'decks' of focus and practice. At the bottom deck there is the world of rebirth, and within that the life of the Buddha Gautama, not to mention preceding Buddhas. He taught the *dharma* or truth, also identified with ultimate reality (or, if you like, unreality). His appearance on earth is a kind of transformation of *dharma* into human form, a sort of incarnation, though one should use the comparison most cautiously. Magically, truth takes on a form in which it can be preached. Then at the next deck there are those Buddhas who are like gods: celestial 'beings' who can create paradises, to help those who call upon them with faith. Such great Buddhas as Amitabha manifest the bliss or *sambhoga kāya* of Buddhahood. Finally at the uppermost deck there is the *dharmakāya* or truth body of the Buddhas. This last is fundamental, but identified too with emptiness or *śūnyatā* (NAKAMURA, 1977). In this threefold nature the truth is unified. The elements of myth come in on two levels. First, they are brought in by the narratives of the earthly Buddhas. This is the underlying pulse of the basic narrative of the Buddhist tradition. Much of the rest of the story is appended to this – the previous lives of the Buddhas, the autobiographies of monks and nuns who recount their conversion and salvation, even the chronicles of the island of Sri Lanka. Second, the myths come in because of the narratives and symbols associated with the high Buddhas and Bodhisattvas who form the foci of *bhakti*. Doctrine enters as well as myth in order to indicate that the differing strands of religion are really unified: the ethics and analysis of the Buddha's original path, the *bhakti* religion and the moral path of the Bodhisattva, the obliteration of subject and object and of all concepts in the ultimate emptiness taught by the *dharma* – all these are brought together. One can look at the matter in a different way by considering the various identities of experience.

Thus the emptiness of everything is what the *dharma* is all about: it is the *dharma*. The *dharma* is the essential nature of the Buddha. It is the Buddha, so the truth body of the Buddha is also the manifest bodies of the Buddhas. It is ultimately identical with the enjoyment or bliss body of the Buddhas and the transformation bodies of the earthly Buddhas.

Other variations of inner arrangements

Other structures are also found, such as the emanationist ballet of Neo-Platonism and the mysterious developments within the Great Ultimate or T'ai-chi. In the case of Neo-Platonism we have a schema which is predominantly contemplative, but which weds the mystical One to forces that help to explain the creation and governance of the world. Emanation, being less personal and wilful than creation, fits

the picture of the impersona better. We shall return later to the
imageries of the origin of the cosmos.

The question of the Lord and of creation

In equating the Lords of the Mahayana with the supreme Beings of
the Hindu and other traditions I have not treated the doctrine of
creation with as much seriousness as might have been wished. In fact
creation is taken in many traditions to be crucial because it makes
individuals ontologically dependent as well as soteriologically dependent on the Lord. So despite the warmth and intensity of *bhakti*
religion in mainstream Mahayana it does not as fully integrate the
worshipper with the cosmos as does regular theism. Moreover, we
have to take into account other factors in the Mahayana, notably that
it is not a religion of substance, of being. Perhaps emptiness functions
as a kind of shadow-substance, or has a substantive film over it,
disguising its hollowness. But in essence it is not a substance: it is not,
like typical theism, a system contrasting impermanent events with a
permanent reality. If anything, impermanent events are seen against
the background of insubstantiality. So although the Mahayana in its
Pure Land variety has an analogy to theism, it is not truly a form of
theism. It is, however, a well-developed form of *bhakti*.

Typically doctrines of creation imply the reality of both poles: that
is, the creative pole and the created pole. Hence the Biblical saying
that God saw that the created world was good. Ontology gets suffused
with value overtones. For much of the Buddhist tradition the unreality of interdependent things is affirmed. But there are more
positive or realistic versions, notably Hua-yen. In affirming the
interpenetration of all events it takes a much more positive attitude
towards events than mainstream Mahayana schools. Moreover the
notion of the Buddha-nature gives a stronger analogy with regular
theism, in that the inner principle shining in each living being and
indeed in each event shows some analogy to the way God is conceived
as inner controller in Vaisnava theism or as guiding spirit within the
world in the Christian tradition (COOK, 1977). Some forms of
esoteric Buddhism or Tantric Buddhism are much more substantia-

list in tone, having taken over flavours of Hindu ritualism, with its atmosphere of the transformations of substance.

The strong sense in Hua-yen of the interconnectedness of creation chimed in with existing Chinese conceptions of a harmonious *tao* or nature. This parallels the Greek notion of an orderly whole or cosmos. It is notable that these ideas of order do not stem from the belief in a rational Creator. Theism itself of course militates against a piecemeal universe. It supposes that the universe is a single product of a single Lord.

One source of the cosmos idea is reasoning: it is reasonable to think of the universe as a single whole. But another source is the panenhenic experience (ZAEHNER, 1957) – that is, when a person senses a profound solidarity with the whole. It is probable that this is the main root of the sense of the *tao* in the anthology known as the *Tao-teh Ching* (LAU, 1982). It was in later times easy to blend the panenhenic experience with Buddhist practice. It is very possible that the panenhenic gave vigour to Hua-yen.

Idealism and realism

We have noted that creation doctrines are realistic. There are two or three reasons why mystical doctrines are idealistic. One is illustrated from Advaita Vedanta. Since it is built on the notion of being or substance (in accordance with the main trend of orthodox Brahmanical thinking), and since the identity between the *ātman* or self and the one Being, Brahman, is observed strictly, the world of appearance with its multiplicity is regarded as magical illusion. Second, Buddhist *vijñānavāda* takes consciousness to be a crucial ingredient in ultimate reality, since it is by purity of consciousness that you reach liberation.

Ramanuja held that the illusionism of Sankara's school utterly undermined the meaning of *bhakti*: how can there be reverence and love for the Other if there is no Other? The *bhakti* mode of faith becomes merely fictive on the Advaitin account.

All this has implications for the role of the transcendent. The notion that the Other or the ultimate is timeless and beyond space is a philosophical doctrine which helps to demarcate it from the worldly.

It is compatible with a certain interpretation of immanence, in which the immanent is 'within' all things, but not literally – it represents another way of being outside literal spatial characterizations. Usually both a transcendent Creator of the world and an immanent sustainer have their timelessness registered as everlastingness rather than as strict timelessness, since the creative and sustaining process is continuous. But the numinous Other is seen as creating a real though dependent world. Being changeable and dependent, the world is inferior to the Other. Somewhat similarly the transcendence of nirvana in the Theravada demarcates it as spiritual: concerns with the real but changeable world of flux are worldly, even when they relate to the gods.

So we have here in the Theravada a mystical or contemplative religion which is not idealistic. Why the difference? Because the Mahayana schools represent a kind of shadow monism. They assert not a monism of being, but a kind of monism of consciousness, and plurality is thus something which needs to be explained away. Because the Theravada has no need to explain away the plurality of the world, and nirvana is not an underlying or all-pervasive being or thing, there is a natural acceptance of the reality of the impermanent.

Monism as an alternative to theism

We have noted how early Taoism (namely philosophical Taoism) expresses a monism, of a single world under the control of the *tao*. It is probable that the philosophy of the *Brahmasūtra* is a variety of identity-in-difference theory, that is the doctrine that the cosmos and souls are both identical with and different from the *brahman*. Such a 'realistic' monism was developed by ibn ʿArabi to express his Sufi belief. Both his view and that of the *Brahmasūtra* keep a balance between the impersonal and the personal God (DASGUPTA, 1975).

So we have various possibilities, which can be set out as follows:

(1) Non-theistic liberationism with a continuum between the world and the liberated state – Jainism.

(2) Non-theistic (and atheistic) liberationism with transcendent nirvana – Theravada Buddhism.

(3) Idealistic quasi-monism – mainstream Mahayana schools. I say 'quasi-monism' because what passes for an absolute is not a substance.

(4) Realistic quasi-monism: Hua-yen Buddhism. It is quasi-monism in so far as there is a single interpenetrative system, the cosmos.

(5) Idealistic monism – Advaita Vedanta.

(6) Theistic monism: that is, systems such as those of Eckhart and ibn ʿArabi which make the impersonal One primary and the personal God secondary.

(7) Realistic monism, such as philosophical Taoism.

(8) Personalistic theism, such as Ramanuja's system, Jewish, Christian and most Islamic theologies. But note that such theism can be (a) non-polytheistic and (b) transpolytheistic.

The varied systems can of course take very diverse mythic clothing. Generally speaking the more theistic a school is, the greater the attention paid to *bhakti* and the numinous experience; while the less theistic it is, the more attention paid to the contemplative life and to the mystical experience. There are also the following systems to consider:

(9) Polytheistic systems or pantheons.

(10) Secular atheism.

Polytheistic systems most frequently incorporate shamanism, with its attendant inner experience of divine powers. Secular atheism involves the rejection of all forms of traditional religious experience, though religious emotions may surface in such contexts as nationalism.

Human gods and other beings

So far we have been looking towards the transcendent. But it is also common for human beings to be looked on as divine or quasi-divine. Divine status has often been accorded to kings and queens, such as the pharaohs and in a limited way the Roman emperors. More important is the holiness accorded to spiritual teachers. This leads to the notion that some humans are themselves in some degree divine, not because of their function so much as because of their intrinsic holy power. In the case of the avatars of Viṣṇu there are varying mythic reasons for ascribing divinity to them. Where there is a supreme God, the divine human is often perceived as an incarnation or avatar of the one God. But if there is no supreme Being, the situation is more complicated: in some way the human incorporates the ultimate or the essence of the truth. Thus in Mahayana Buddhism the rough equivalents of avatars are the great Buddhas-to-be or simply the earthly Buddhas. Buddhahood becomes an analogue to divinity. But what is present in the 'divine' human is what is there in the transcendent − emptiness, for instance, or the *dharma*. Emptiness, as we have said earlier, is a quasi-substance, and this filmy 'nothing' is found in the sacred human being (STRENG, 1967).

There is once again a contrast between the monomyth and the polymyth. The single narrative of Christ's death and resurrection, flanked by the unified narrative of Israel and the corresponding story of the new Israel, that is the church, contrasts with the multiple myths of the avatars and the many iconographies of the various Buddhas and Bodhisattvas.

In general we may refer to the human gods as avatars: those who 'descend' from the heavenly sphere. This will provide a category for Buddhas who are not strictly gods or incarnations, though recipients of *bhakti*. They have the outer aspect of gods, but they are, so to speak, internally hollow. They do not possess the substance of gods.

Human gods perform various functions. They can as kings or queens channel power and fertility from heaven to earth. They can give out saving teachings. They can save by certain acts. They can set an example and, as recipients of *bhakti*, can function as moral ideals or heroes and heroines. Or they can perform two or more of these functions.

It becomes easy to think of how a human ascends to become a god, especially in the theory of rebirth. Co-ordinated with this is the image of a heaven in which gods dwell. This leads us on to contemplate the cosmologies which go with the differing doctrinal pictures of the ultimate.

Heavens and the question of the beyond

There is virtually universal agreement among diverse cultures about cosmology: there is the heavenly sphere (which may consist in various decks of heaven), there is the intermediate region between heaven and earth, in which meteorological phenomena occur; beneath the high heaven, there is the earthly sphere, and there is what goes on beneath the earth. Usually all these decks are seen as a single cosmos. But some systems, notably the major Indian ones under the influence of Buddhism and the other sramanic schools, have envisaged a vast or infinite number of *lokas* or world systems, each with its own major monomyth. Every sub-universe has its decks of heavens and its underworlds or purgatories beneath. In such heavens beings can be reborn so long as they remain gods or goddesses.

But there is often an ambivalence about heavens. From some angles they look like upper compartments of this cosmos; from other angles they look like the dwelling place of God. If they or the one heaven is where the supreme God dwells, it is somehow transcendent. It is beyond the cosmic heavens.

There are certain characteristics of heavens which have heavy symbolic meaning. The most basic, woven very deeply into all our languages, is the association of height with value. Supreme value seems to imply being at the top of the universe. So it is that the Tirthaṃkara or Jain liberator and saint rises to the top of the universe. There are of course some opposite but less thrustful tendencies, expressed in such terms as 'deep' and 'profound'. This imagery was exploited by Tillich (1952) and Robinson (1963). But mostly height is good: consider 'supreme', 'top', 'high praise', 'soaring achievement', 'super', 'reached a peak', 'towering', 'summit of his career', 'the sky's the limit' and so on.

But other symbols blend in with height: up there is the sky, and the sky is where the sun and moon are, so there is light. And light is a symbol of insight. It figures in illumination and enlightenment, in flashes of insight and understanding, and it dispels the darkness of ignorance. Nearly everywhere it comes into the symbolism of mysticism – the inner life, the purification of consciousness, the meeting of the divine within. So not surprisingly the heavens are symbolically potent, and they are the place where the top God or gods dwell. But how literally is the sky to be taken? This is where the ambivalence lies, for religions often want to have it both ways. The supreme God is often identified at least for some purposes with the Sky God, throughout the ancient Near East, and from there through into the great monotheisms of the Western world. It is not for nothing that the ideogram for God becomes in China the word for heaven.

Heaven also lies at or beyond the meteorological world, and so the sky is God's and sends down rain. By contrast the earth is female, to the sky's male character. Rain easily becomes a kind of sperm falling into the fecund womb of Mother Earth.

Yet such literalism is only part of the story. While it provides the rationale of various rituals in which human societies beseech the God up there for rain and fecundity, it does not quite reach where God on reflection must be. As Creator of the cosmos, he or she must exist outside the cosmos, beyond the heavens which we can see. The transcendent sphere is the true heaven if heaven indeed is where God dwells.

We shall revert to some of the issues of deep symbolism, surveying such items as water, space, air, height, depth, male, female, light and childhood under the head of the mythic dimension. It may be noted that changes in scientific knowledge, altering our literal cosmology, have their effects on symbolism. With the disappearance of a vertical model, in which the cosmos is thought to be built around and indeed to revolve around an *axis mundi* (a vast sacred mountain like Mount Meru), it is not easy to take symbolism literally. Symbols can slide into metaphors, and cosmology into analogy (SCOTT, 1985).

Questions of scale: time and space

Most cultures have envisaged the universe as rather small, the bulk of it taken up with the planetary system (typically seen as revolving round the earth). But there are some grander pictures. Above all, Indian cosmology, greatly under the influence of Buddhism, sees time as virtually infinite, partly because there is the belief in rebirth, which has living beings perpetually on the go. The division of time into huge ages or *kalpas* and beyond them into *mahakalpas* brings enormous numbers into play; and the cycle of universes alternating between quiescence and activity (and of God too, alternating between sleeping and waking, passive and active), is deeply impressive, and different in spirit from the rather short duration of the Jewish and Christian universes as traditionally depicted. And this sub-universe is matched by numberless other sub-universes. In a way it would seem not to matter how large the universe is, yet the vast numbers of Indian cosmology do mean something. They indicate our comparative in-significance. In the West perhaps God's supreme power humbles us sufficiently.

Since the 1930s there has been a tremendous expansion of *our* universe, where *we* are all who believe in science. We have yet to digest the effects upon us of vast numbers (even vaster than those of ancient India). Since the development of the Hubble telescope, we have seen the universe expand; we have seen galaxies multiply almost infinitely; and we have seen distances extend beyond the reach of our imagination. Because we have also digested during the last hundred years or more the impact of evolutionary theory, we are beginning to grow accustomed to the thought that there may be life in other galaxies, perhaps even in our own. Meanwhile the numbers are ever more overwhelming, increasing the likelihood that there is life else-where in the cosmos. If there is, we shall probably never encounter it, so in one way it does not concern us. Nevertheless it does concern us spiritually, mainly because belief in the uniqueness of this planet is the last stirring of the *axis mundi*. We are not at the centre.

To some extent this 'destruction of the centre' seemed evident in evolutionary theory (DARWIN, 1859). Here we see a different aspect of cosmology.

Living and non-living beings

In the Western religions – that is, in Judaism, Christianity and Islam – a sharp distinction is made between human and other living beings. Largely owing to the influence of Buddhism, Asia has not developed that division. Although many small-scale (e.g. hunting and gathering) societies have found something special in humans, it has been more normal for emphasis to be placed on human solidarity with animals and other living beings. The distinction between humans and other animals is a good example of the way a doctrinal or philosophical division has practical and existential consequences. It would seem that it was partly for existential reasons that it was difficult for many Victorians (by no means all, and as many of them were scientists as were churchmen) to accept evolutionary theory. Of course, it conflicted with a literal interpretation of the Bible, but there appeared to be deeper reasons, later uncovered by Freud. Animals had been deemed to be without souls, and this rather stringent separation from humans must be taken into account. (No such strict divide is to be found outside Western – in the broad sense, including Islamic – culture.) But there is more to it than that: sexuality was often associated with being an animal. Even the Book of Common Prayer suggests that the marriage ceremony and estate should be a way of fighting against a merely animal condition. So the distinction between animals and humans had to do with sexuality: to blur the condition was dangerous. From this perspective, cosmology was not at all neutral. It could be emotionally connected to human life.

The philosophical dimension of the distinction could also exhibit changes, for example in the way we see the universe. A function of doctrine is to bring unity to a group's worldview, in this case to blend religion and science. Leaving aside the emotional aspect of evolutionary theory, it was not difficult to rewrite the mythic history of the world in a manner which would co-ordinate science and Biblical history, excluding the First Things or *Urzeit*. You could see evolution as the means through which God brought humans into this world, an extended mechanism through which our planet was populated and given free and reasoning beings like ourselves. This picture of evolution into history has been drawn by a number of writers (PAUL, 1962), perhaps most spectacularly by Teilhard de Chardin in his *The Phenomenon of Man* (1955). De Chardin went further, contemplating the *Endzeit*, the ultimate unification of the whole planet and all humanity, sharing in the nature of Christ.

Such a cosmology has to be deemed religious or metaphysical. That is, talk of Christ cannot be deduced from science, though science can be incorporated into it. The notion that God guides events cannot be shown from the scientific evidence alone, but spiritual meaning can be projected on to the scientific facts. I call this process 'superimposition'. It is important in a number of contexts, for example in the treating of farm work and the like as a mode of prayer, an approach expressed in the Benedictine tag *laborare est orare*.

The way living beings and humans are categorized is significant in other ways. The Jains posit that the major contrast is that between *jīva* and *ajīva*, living and non-living beings, the former including powdery forms of microlife. Similarly for Buddhism and later for the Hindu tradition the basic in-group comprises not just humans but all forms of living being. The Hindu case is complicated by caste or *jāti*, which places humans in differing categories, treating them in effect as belonging to different species: this produces a whole hierarchy of beings draped across the cosmos from Brahmins and above down to humble insects and the like.

Where the in-group comprises all living beings, certain conditions may be imposed for the achievement of liberation. Thus it is a condition in Buddhism that nirvana is open only to humans, so that even a god needs to be reborn as a man if he is to achieve liberation. Nevertheless, if the inclusiveness covers all living beings and is coupled with a hope of liberation, a belief in rebirth is reinforced.

Clearly, category distinctions bear on ethics. The inclusive world-views of India dictate a different attitude to animals. If the Western religions create a climate in which living beings are managed for the good of humanity, greater concern for the rights of animals is traditional in Indian religions. We shall pursue such issues in the chapter on the ethical and legal dimension.

Philosophical ideas and history

The de Chardinesque superimposition of divine and evolutionary meaning on human history is an example of a kind of metaphysics of history. There are other cases: Indian theories of history, for instance, which describe successive declines from the time of the appearance of great teachers and avatars. Elaborated was the theory of *mo-fa* (in China) and *mappō* (in Japan), a dramatic period of history since the time of the Buddha. In the West the metaphysics of history was prominent from the time of Hegel (TAYLOR, 1975), with his brilliant conceptions of the operation of the dialectic in history. The ballet of class relationships in Marx's historical dialectic also took a grip on the imagination of many intellectuals and political activists. While abstractions like classes could have a powerful role to play, mythic stories – too concrete, too fanciful, manifestly non-empirical – tended to fade in the dominant imagination of the West.

Patterns of change in the doctrinal dimension

Up to this point we have largely treated of doctrines and philosophical themes in a static way. But we can also begin to see some types of change. To introduce this topic more thoroughly it is as well first of all to delineate some of the functions of doctrines in religions.

(1) Buddhist analysis has a part intellectual and part spiritual function. Thus the proposition that everything is impermanent has an existential message, an attempt to induce a certain way of looking at the world. This may be called the attitudinal function.

(2) It may be implied by the attitudinal function that a doctrine describes the relation between the transcendent and the world, or some general feature within the world, as it is. Doctrines have a descriptive function, in other words.

(3) Doctrines may give an explanation reconciling some apparent contradiction: this is the function of the Trinity doctrine, dealing with differing and perhaps conflicting aspects of the monomyth.

(4) Doctrines can help to define the community, in laying down what is orthodox. This is a particularly prominent function in the Christian tradition. Because Judaism is defined by descent and rituality, there is much less urgency in such a function in that tradition (CHRISTIAN, 1972).

(5) Doctrines (or philosophical schemes) can perform a vital apologetic function, or what may be called a responsive function. This is evident in modern Hindu philosophy, and in the reshaping of

Buddhist philosophy in response to colonial and Western thought.

(6) Doctrines can settle external contradictions created by changes in knowledge, for example following developments in modern biology and cosmology.

We can call these functions the attitudinal, the descriptive, the reconciliatory, the definitional, the responsive and the scientific respectively. They already hint at patterns of change.

One kind of development on the attitudinal front is the creation of a philosophy which helps to bridge the distance between a mythic account and daily life. For instance, the recreation of the world after a period of world-sleep is a Vaisnava story. Ramanuja's analogy suggesting that the relation between the Lord and the cosmos is like the relation between the soul and the body helps to vivify the sense of the presence of the Lord throughout his creation. This then is a development which adds force to the narrative of creation.

Cultural changes may give traditions new analytic tools for the description of what they take to be reality. Sometimes we can see such new developments as the blending of two traditions, as when Taoist concepts are used in the evolution of Chinese Buddhism, or Greek philosophical terminology is used to expound Islamic theology.

Pressures in favour of doctrinal orthodoxy are especially strong when the issues are also political. It was no accident that Christianity's councils charged with defining orthodoxy in the face of various controversies occurred during the first major period after the religion became imperial. One can see a definitional impulse asserted from time to time in the Confucian examination system.

The responsive function is most important in modern times. The Chinese responses to the West and to Christian mission – that is, the attempts to respond by the three old traditions of China – were rather weak. The Buddhist innovator, Tai Hsu, was too spiritual for national reconstruction. Taoism was too wrapped in alchemy and other non-scientific modes of thought, at least from the standpoint of a modern interpretation of science (SCHIPPER, 1982). Confucianism was over-committed to a literary and religious point of view, drawing on very ancient classics, but facing demands for a thoroughly new educational system. On the other hand, the response of the Hindu elite was highly successful, while the new Japanese nationalism, blending in Shinto ritual, also proved farsighted and successful. China eventually abandoned the three religions and substituted Marxism, or more precisely Maoism: excellent for national re-fortification and the fighting of guerrilla war, though fairly useless in economic rebuilding, until the more pragmatic thinking of Deng Xiaoping.

There are other responses to consider. Liberal Protestantism was successful in rebuilding Christian thought in the face of the new cosmologies, the application of historical method to the scriptures, and the challenges of modern society. The Roman Catholic response was much slower until Vatican II (1962–5). Even so its liberal response has been in part inhibited since John Paul II became pope in 1978. In general we can see the liberal response challenged by conservative backlashes, notably by so-called fundamentalism, which rejects not only modern historical methods but relevant slices of science as well. So there is a tendency for a bifurcated reaction to modern knowledge. Indeed much more generally one can discern a double reaction to things – in broad terms, for example, in Christianity (the favourable reaction to Greek philosophy and the unfavourable: Augustine versus Tertullian).

It may be noted that both the positive and the negative responses are 'modern' in character: neither leaves the tradition in the same place. The conservative reaction (as we tend to see it) also has its innovatory aspect: in washing away older forms of theology, in using innovatory methods of evangelism and education, and so on. These syndromes are true whether we look to integralist or fundamentalist forms of Christianity, Judaism, Islam or Hinduism. It is easier to be integralist with a written scripture, incidentally: integralism has a clear given to go back to, namely the written scripture. Of course the same manoeuvre can be undertaken in relation to orally transmitted texts, but they need to be in the custody of an expert class (books have a wider distribution). The traditionalists in charge of an oral tradition are less likely to venture into the novelties of integralism. For, although integralism generally appears to be conservative, it has a new class of exponents, different from those of controlled traditions. In short we can look on both modernism and integralism from a social point of view, as different classes of literati struggle to achieve authority. Generally modernists belong to educated classes who, thanks to their social status, can afford to be relaxed; integralists feel more threatened by social and economic conditions.

Modernism can be seen from another perspective as a form of syncretism or, as I would prefer to call it, blending. In short it blends a modern worldview with traditional Christian (or other) worldviews. This is why it is appropriate to speak of Buddhist modernism, Hindu modernism, Confucian modernism as well as Western forms of modernism. In brief, modern liberal and scientific thought is blended in with traditional worldviews such as Advaita Vedanta and Theravada Buddhism. There are variations of course in the relative ease of blends: because the Bible has such complex origins, discovered by the application of modern scientific historical methods, there is a special problem about blending revelation and reason in modern Protestant and other variations of modernism. The tendency for Christianity in the past to be fairly literalist about the Bible is an obstacle to a smooth blend. On the other hand, the relatively short period during which the Qur'an was composed is an advantage. Traditional Jewish views of the Hebrew Bible cannot be held in a modernist framework. On the other hand, Advaita as a system has an easy compatibility with a scientific worldview, and the long history of Hindu commentarial literature gives the tradition an advantage in the reinterpretation of its sources. The sophisticated nature, generally speaking, of Buddhist philosophy from fairly early times allows it to integrate modern science quite smoothly.

But perhaps the major problem with modernism is its susceptibility to fashion and opinion. It means the abandonment in large measure of any strict adherence to the verbal record of the supposed revelation. Admittedly the histories of all traditions indicate how at least in the long haul differences of interpretation seem to be subjectively based. The subjectivity may be collective, but that does not make for a difference in principle. It may be that Dvaitins have a well-established community which will agree to interpret key texts in a given way, but it is still startling to see that they take *tat tvam asi* to read *atat tvam asi*, so 'That art thou' becomes 'That thou art not' (SHARMA, 1981). Given the very wide divergences in interpretation among varying traditions, one can be sceptical of the importance given to a particular text. Even so, the existence of texts is something of a barrier to differing interpretations; and this barrier is greatly eroded in modernism. For modernism also coincides with a high degree of individualism. As usual with benefits, it starts with the elite, and so is heavily represented in the intellectual elite. But in colonial situations there is an extra complication, since the traditional intellectual elite (mullahs, pandits, *ju*) tend to get left behind by the newly educated Westernized elite (unless a given class makes special efforts, as the Brahmins did, to join the Westernized elite). This split between traditional and modern intellectual elites creates a new dynamic.

Abstractification as a phenomenon

Another phenomenon of modern times may be identified by the rather ugly term 'abstractification'. What is meant here is a transition from the mythic and the narrative dimension towards a more doctrinal account. It can take various forms. One is the superimposition of abstract categories on to the historical account, for instance *Heilsgeschichte*, or a Marxist dialectical interpretation of history, or a depth or structural way of treating myth (the whole Freudian and Jungian projects help to give a rather more metaphysical or existential slant to the corpus of myths). Again, some overarching concept such as Negritude or Africanness may be brought to bear in the interpretation of a great body of religious myth and practice in order to give the latter a place in the wider debates of the modern world. A similar phenomenon occurred in the history of major religions during the early classical period. Christianity developed a philosophical dimension as it made its way among the elite of the Graeco-Roman world, partly because myths had to be interpreted in universalistic ways, and so needed to be seen through the filter of supposedly universal philosophies. Likewise when Islam penetrated large parts of the Eastern empire it came into contact with the universal questions of Hellenistic philosophy. Judaism was less prone to abstractification, because it settled into becoming a religion for a given people.

Although the whole system was not at root (NEUSNER, 1975) unphilosophical, abstract philosophy did not occupy such a significant part of its surface as it did in other religions. The methods of Talmudic analysis and commentary kept alive both the ethical–legal dimension of the religion and the narrative dimension – so the story continued to be the central mode of illustrating and vivifying the teachings. In the Hindu tradition, the ritual texts of the Vedas were supplemented by the more abstract *Upaniṣads*, and in turn the mysterious texts of the *Brahmasūtras* needed Vedantin commentarial literature of an intensely abstract kind. Yet at the same time there were compiled extensive Puranic materials to refresh the mythic dimension, not to mention the great epics. And so in all religions there is a drift to abstractification, culminating often in strong scholasticism. In Buddhism, which started with a powerful abstract content, there grew an impressive scholastic literature in the Theravada, and in the Mahayana a very dense literature of *Prajñāpāramitā* texts, as well as of new and longer *sutras*. In the Confucian tradition the challenge of Buddhist literature in due course brought about the metaphysics of Neo-Confucianism.

Concepts of the soul

Various doctrines have emerged in diverse traditions concerning the self or soul (BRANDON, 1967). These ideas relate to the way humans deal with gods and with the ultimate. They range from atheistic materialism, in which the self is in effect identified with an aspect of the body (conscious states are identified with brain processes), through Buddhist non-self doctrine to various ideas of an immortal or changeless self (HOLCK, 1974). In the Samkhya system, which itself became a very influential ingredient of Vaisnava cosmologies, the *puruṣa* or personal soul is unchanging, but conscious. It becomes attached to a congeries of subtle matter, namely the subtle body which transmigrates from body to body. This represents a feature of much Indian metaphysics, that there is a sharp ontological divide between the soul and the subtle body. The soul is like a light illumining the material processes, which represent what

Westerners look on as mental processes. In short much of what is seen as mental in the West is (subtly) physical in India. Even here, though, the distinctions may run differently: for instance, the distinction between the soul and the body can hardly exist in the Buddhist tradition, since there is no soul or self. What takes its place is the possibility of nirvana or liberation, and the individual who attains liberation disappears as an individual – though it is wrong to suppose that annihilation occurs. So there is an ineffable X which is the saint or the Tathagata after death. The big ontological distinction is between the timeless and the impermanent (a parallel divide to that found in Samkhya). The potentiality of nirvana functions as a substitute for a soul: it more colourfully becomes the Buddha-nature in Mahayana thought, and in the Chinese and Far Eastern context generally has much of the feel of the soul in Western thought.

Most Indian systems work with the idea of many transmigrating souls or selves. In Ramanuja's qualified Non-Dualism God not only is the soul of the cosmos, but also functions as the soul of each soul: the inner controller, a concept not so far from classical ideas of the Spirit. In the Dvaitin system, as well as in Saiva Siddhanta and other non-Vedic forms of theism, there is an infinite number of souls. In Dvaita each soul is conceived as having its own particular and inevitable destiny (not dissimilar to the Calvinist picture of predestination and analogous Islamic notions).

Running through all Indian systems other than materialism is a belief in karma, with the difference that the theisms view God as the ultimate controller. And all systems postulate an ultimate end to karma's operation, as the soul or non-self in Buddhism achieves liberation or *mokṣa*. This is sometimes thought of as an all-pervasive state, or an ineffable condition, or as life in a heaven close to the Divine Being. Such a final liberation does not preclude (notably in the non-theistic systems) a period in heaven, highly blissful or luxurious. This goal may psychologically displace the conception of ultimate release, notably in the Pure Land schools, where the Pure Land displaces nirvana in popular imagination.

The last principal variation in conceptions of the self in the Indian tradition is that of the single *ātman*. The famous saying *tat tvam asi* could be taken literally: if the soul is Brahman, the one Divine Being, then there is of course only one soul. This view bears strong resemblances to the Buddhist outlook, since it implies that no individual has her own separate soul: what transmigrates is the individual subtle body. Liberation is achieved when one realizes existentially that *tat tvam asi*. It is as if epistemology and soteriology fuse.

In Chinese religion notions of immortality and salvation were of course much affected by Buddhist doctrines, especially because this religious tradition catered very effectively for individual strivings. It brought home to persons the ultimate meaning of their own lives. More traditional ideas were somewhat different: the Taoist tradition in particular looked to the task of lengthening life, through methods of alchemy and various kinds of yoga. The individual could hope to achieve immortality.

The radical distinction between the permanent soul and the body, both subtle and gross, which is characteristic of Indian philosophy, is alien to the Chinese mentality, which sees both a continuity and a polarity between forces at work in the cosmos. *Ch'i* is the ethereal cosmic power which infuses the whole of the cosmos and its separate parts: it is thus evident in rocks and the moon, as well as in foxes and human beings. If humans have a special place it is because they have very refined *ch'i*. This enables them to play a key part in the communication system of the universe, between heaven and earth.

The soul has had a different part to play in the Western systems of doctrine (CAVENDISH, 1977). For one thing, there was a tug of war between substantial and eschatological notions that ultimately derived from differing civilizations. The eschatological pictures entered from Persian civilization into Jewish religious life (NICKELSBERG, 1972). The more essentialist ideas of a soul derived from Greek civilization. The twin ideas affected not only Christianity but Islam as well. They indicated differing destinies for humankind, which came to be rather uneasily conciliated.

The Greek notion of the *psyche* itself had a double background, one mythic and the other philosophical. On the one hand the *psyche* or *psuche* (a better way of rendering the Greek) is that which goes on after death, often reflecting the appearance of the living (the idea of the *eidolon* or image was often used), and typically though not universally goes on to Hades, depicted usually as an underworld, the rather shadowy realm of the dead – a world not greatly attractive to the Greeks (similar conceptions were found in ancient Rome). The soul as conceived in philosophy and especially in Plato was more impressive. It underwent reincarnation, an idea derived from preceding religions such as Orphism and Pythagoreanism, and then infiltrated into the Greek philosophical world (CUMONT, 1959).

In the Jewish and Christian connection the impact of Zoroastrianism was strong. It is probably the most important influence on the way human beings have thought of history, as having an *Urzeit*, a main, middle period, and an *Endzeit*. This last incorporated not only a consummation of the whole of history but also a judgment of the human race. The idea was developed that human beings would be resuscitated and then judged. In short here was an organic concept of survival, and a holistic concept of the human being. This was the more mythic derivation of the idea of the soul. By contrast there was the philosophical idea of the everlasting soul, which did not have to await divine resurrection, but went on existing anyway. In the first case there was a waiting period till the end of the world; in the second, there was the natural persistence of the *psuche*. The two ideas could be reconciled, for instance by St Thomas Aquinas (COPLE-STON, 1961; CHENU, 1964), by looking to psychic persistence as incomplete without a body. For it was embodied existence that displays the full human being; and so it was only when the body was resurrected and rejoined to the individual soul that the full human being could be present for final judgment.

There were tensions between the resurrection and eternal models, needless to say (HICK, 1976). These became just as evident in Jewish thought. The great medieval theoretician Maimonides (d. 1204) (HARMAN, 1976) considered that the full soul is coextensive with bodily existence, comprising varying functions – the nutritive, the perceptual, the imaginative, the desirous and the rational. The last deals with ethical judgments, practical and intellectual decisions. The upper level of the rational soul is capable of receiving concepts from the Divine Being, and, though the lower parts of the soul die, the actualized intellect, infused thus with divine aspects, lives on and returns to its divine source. Obviously this more intellectual and philosophical account of life after death is rather different from the more mythic, eschatological picture derived from the Zoroastrian tradition (GROF and GROF, 1980).

Jewish mysticism or Qabbala not surprisingly has its own delineation of psychic forces. The basic conception of the soul is the spirit of *nefesh*, which enters the individual at birth. But beyond this are two further forces, developed through self-control and study. The *ruah* is developed through ethical practice. Beyond that the *neshamah* is cultivated through study of the Law (Torah) and the higher life of following the commandments, and so on. Later Qabbala, especially in the teachings of Luria (1534–72) (GREEN, 1986), incorporated the tradition of reincarnation into Jewish belief. This increased the opportunities for souls to collect the divine sparks that enabled them to return to the Divine (Qabbala included many Neo-Platonist and Gnostic notions) (SCHOLEM, 1961; GUTTMANN, 1964).

Islam also contained a tension between the ideals of a final judgment and of the automatic persistence of an eternal soul (SMITH and HADDAD, 1981). There was, as elsewhere, the problem of reconciling the notion of bodily resurrection with that of the eternal soul. Probably the most influential of theories about the soul and the afterlife is that of Avicenna (Ibn Sina) (MOREWEDGE, 1973). The soul is a non-material substance which is individual and belongs with a given human body. After death it persists. If it has been virtuous it will be rewarded: it will live in a state of bliss contemplating God and other celestial beings. But if it has not been involved in the virtuous and rational life, it will exist for ever in torment. The way these matters are described in scripture is not to be taken literally.

Small-scale societies and some ancient cultures believe in multiple souls, typically associated with different organs (for example, the brain and the heart) (BRANDON, 1963). There is also widespread belief that the soul can wander, for instance during dreams. The survival of the self in some form for some time is associated of course with the cult of ancestors: in effect such societies have a more expansive view of their scope than typical Western societies today, which tend to identify themselves with the living. But the idea of the communion of saints in Christianity is a mode of recognizing spiritual ancestors. There is also the somewhat unresolved question of how far successors ought to be recognized (NEWELL, 1976).

There is sometimes a degree of tension between the idea of an eternal soul considered to be intrinsic to the individual and belief in God. Given that a strongly numinous God will be thought to dispense grace, the eternal soul seems to give excessive independence to the individual. This is a reason in the Western religions for giving preference to the mythic concept of the resurrection of the dead, which stresses the miraculous and so grace-laden activity of God.

Doctrine, philosophy and the spiritual community

In looking at varied patterns of belief we have so far not said much about the relation of doctrines to a given community (CHRISTIAN, 1972). Something clearly depends on whether a religion regards itself in principle as coterminous with some widely conceived political entity. It has been common in the West to adhere in one way or another to the tag *cuius regio eius religio*, a post-Reformation slogan that in effect carried into a plural world of princely states a notion operative from the time of Constantine. The common practice in India and South-east Asia and from time to time in China, as well as in Islamic states and in preceding Persia, was somewhat similar. But within such similarities among official religions there is a large choice of authorities, including the monarchical system which evolved with the Western papacy, the patriarchal system in regions of Orthodoxy, the system of evolved learned persons, notably jurisprudents in Islam, senior monks and commentators in Buddhism, spiritual lineage in the Hindu environment, and senior scholars in the Confucian tradition. There is usually a way in which doctrines emerge as official or dominant, and various methods are used in order to mould public opinion within the community, for example through controlling appointments in university faculties. But the development of liberal institutions in the late nineteenth and twentieth centuries has eroded such control (WACH, 1964).

We shall return to these issues in dealing with the social dimension.

Other sorts of religious institution, such as sects and new religions, show different patterns both of doctrinal creation and of control.

The fact that religious or philosophical conformity is so vital in so many societies, both ancient and modern, is itself intriguing. It indicates ways in which right thinking is itself regarded as something which both gives power and is to be enforced by power. Consequently some of exactly the same moves which have been made traditionally in religious societies have been made by ideological movements.

Some conclusions about the doctrinal dimension

I have sketched some major features of the doctrinal dimension and described some issues to which we need later to return. I have highlighted the fact that a major religious tradition, namely Theravada Buddhism, can on no account be thought to be theistic, even if we adopt a generous interpretation of this term. I have argued that this religion has a contemplative or mystical core, bound up with the practice of *dhyāna* (as also, for instance, has Zen Buddhism, converging as it were from the other end of the Buddhist empire in Asia). It happens too that Buddhism is an intrinsically philosophical religion, so that the doctrinal dimension is especially important in it. But in Western terms we (and since I write in English I say 'we') are more used to theism. Hence we look on mysticism for instance from a theistic, and misleading angle. Some of the most influential writers have been Westerners in this colonial or post-colonial situation in which we find ourselves. One or two others have projected Sufism (NASR, 1972; SCHIMMEL, 1964). Others have projected Hindu neo-Vedanta (VIVEKANANDA, 1964; HUXLEY, 1954). But few have looked on the contemplative practice taking into account the Buddhist experience. Nonetheless, in our survey of doctrines we have started there.

We have suggested that there are two or three major forms of religious experience which help to account for differences in doctrines. One is *dhyāna* and the 'empty' experiences of purified consciousness; another is the experience of the numinous Other, not only exhibited in particular kinds of religious experience as delineated by

Otto, but also expressed in *bhakti*. The combinations or non-combinations of these kinds of experience help to explain differing patterns of philosophy. Non-theism expresses *dhyāna* without *bhakti*. Theism expresses *bhakti*. Theism with a strong emphasis on the ineffable and impersonal side of God combines *bhakti* and *dhyāna* in some degree of balance; while absolutism or quasi-absolutism with a Lord as lower manifestation shows *dhyāna* to be dominant and *bhakti* secondary.

Advanced and complex theologies, dependent as they are on a class of literati, may also incorporate elements arising from shamanism. This kind of religious experience is common among systems of belief which incorporate pantheons of gods and goddesses. It may be that shamanism is itself the ancestor so to speak both of *dhyana* and of *bhakti*. But, be that as it may, shamanism incorporates the perception of gods and goddesses or other spiritual powers in the process of visionary experience which may be relevant both to healing and to the prediction of fruitful areas for hunting and so on. From this perspective the miracle recorded when Jesus tells the fishing brethren (James and John, the sons of Zebedee) where to look for fish has a shamanistic air.

At any rate, we ascribe some patterns of doctrine or philosophy to differing kinds of experience and their combination. Apart from the types just mentioned there is so-called panenhenic experience, also vital and perhaps central to the early doctrine of the Tao. The blending of Buddhist *dhyāna* with the panenhenic experience can help to account for Ch'an and Zen. The merging of Taoist and Buddhist philosophy was also of considerable help in the new creative blends found in Chinese, Korean and Japanese Buddhism.

While there are mythic themes (such as that of sexuality) (DASGUPTA, 1969) which occur within mystical literature, where the notion of union is stressed because there is a Being to be united with, much of mystical writing is technical and somewhat abstract. On the other hand mythic themes, also involving love, are very frequent in the language of *bhakti*. The stories of saviours such as Krishna and Siva and Christ and Amida are important. They help too to provide a counterweight to the more abstract language which tends to dominate as theology becomes dominant. Some of the themes are vital for illustrating the ethical demands of a religion: for instance, the story of the Bodhisattva illumines the bodhisattva ideal so central in the morality of the Mahayana. We shall be exploring some further connections between the doctrinal dimension and the others as we go along.

CHAPTER TWO

The Ritual Dimension

An interactional triangle to begin with

I have already hinted at a triangle, perhaps a quadrangle, which we need to take seriously. The practice of worship supposes a superior, indeed awe-inspiring, personal Being (or Beings). So the practice implies a doctrine. But the doctrine itself, in supposing a *personal* Being (though such a Being can easily have, as we have already noted, an impersonal or non-personal aspect), also supposes a Being about whom stories or narratives can be said: in short such a Being has a mythic dimension. And so in talking of worship we speak of something about whom or which three dimensions come into play. If we want to go beyond the triangle to the quadrangle we only have to notice that worship, as we have said, is typically directed at a superior, indeed awe-inspiring, Being. By this of course I do not mean that the Being actually is superior. This is a matter of judgment. I myself hold that many devotees of new gods, such as the Guru Maharaj Ji, are actually a good deal superior to their gods (I may be wrong in this, but I just wish to indicate that the judgmental option is open to us). No: a Being does not really have to be superior but has to be *taken to be superior* by her or his devotee. And it is apt to use the expression 'awe-inspiring': there is a quality of feeling directed by the devotee to her or his superior which we should take into account. This is why Otto coined the term 'numinous'. In short, worship implies a Being towards whom the devotee is liable to direct a kind of feeling and from whom he or she may derive a kind of experience. So the experiential dimension, as well as the other three, comes rapidly into play. What happens when they do not register?

What if the devotee says: I worship that Being but he does not exist? Or: I have devotion towards him but there are no stories to be told of him, for he is not at all a person? Or: I worship him, but the prostrations actually mean nothing to me – I feel nothing, no awe, nothing? These would all be paradoxical and self-destroying utterances.

It might be possible to rescue them: the Being I worship might be held to be beyond ordinary existence and so not exist in a typical way, like a tomato. Refined non-existence could be worked at by a philosopher (like FINDLAY: 1961). But such a struggle is largely beside my point, that in a direct sense the dimensions are engaged in ritual, and we cannot in a relatively straightforward sense elude this thesis. The conclusion is that ritual studies have to be co-ordinated to other dimensional investigations.

Questions of the definition of ritual

The conclusion of the previous section is that we cannot treat ritual except intentionally: less pretentiously we cannot treat it except in relation to neighbouring aspects of religion (or more generally of human life: for there are rites of other aspects of human life, such as sport and the law). In short, ritual can merge into social ceremony. Moreover, since in this book I am concerned to extend analysis across the whole spectrum of human value-systems, I would like as wide and embracing a definition as possible. There are those who wish to confine ritual to religious activities, keeping the concept of ceremony for secular performances. That I would resist, as it repeats earlier errors of ways in which ideologies, myths and so on have been defined, incorporating value or truth judgments. So I am more sympathetic to the approach of Grimes (1982), who sees ceremony as a level rather than a genre of ritual activity (contrast MOORE and MEYERHOFF, 1977). But on the whole I prefer a more linguistic treatment. Ritual is a more general category because it can be engaged in by an individual; but a ceremony, even a private one, is a collective act. In general a ritual is an act involving performative uses of language (for example, in blessing, praising, cursing, consecrating, purifying) (AUSTIN, 1975; SEARLE, 1969) and a formal pattern of behaviour either closely or more loosely followed. Religious ritual has as one of its major forms what may be called focused ritual, in which the ritual activity is addressed to sacred beings, such as gods or ancestors. Another major form of religious ritual is what may be called harnessing ritual or yogic ritual in which patterns of behaviour are used as part of a process of self-control that seeks attainment of higher states of consciousness. Methods analogous to religious ritual which are used to control forces in the world on behalf of human goals are typically referred to as magic. Among forms of focused ritual the most important perhaps are those addressed to gods, and within this genre the central activity is that of worship. But others have been vital in the history of religions, such as sacrifices of various kinds.

To complicate the analysis of ritual there are two factors which are crucial to the way religions or more generally worldviews operate. One is superimposition, the other is internalization.

The transcendence or internalization of rituals

Generally speaking, ritual is a behavioural or bodily activity. It is not for nothing that the physical postures of Islamic prayer are laid down, for example. But, still, it is generally thought that interior attitudes also count. Worship for instance is supposed to be sincere. Moreover, the interior meaning of the activity gives it greater flexibility, so much so that it is possible to divorce the inner acts from bodily postures altogether. I can worship God while walking along a road and nobody would know. So ritual involves a kind of internalization which can in principle go the whole distance to the inside. We can thus think of a scale of exteriority and interiority. At one end a ritual is largely made up of external acts: the inner sense counts for little (though I do not think that it can count for absolutely nothing since the practitioners need at least to be intending to perform the ritual). At the other end of the spectrum the exterior requirements disappear, provided the practitioner rehearses the ritual in her head. Where acts are communal, however, there needs to be some exteriority, for obvious reasons, as mutual signals of participation. To indicate the transcendence of the bodily in rituals, I shall refer to this aspect as the 'transphysical' side of rituals.

The fact of transphysicality is connected with but different from the problematic of the meaningfulness of ritual. Certainly in the broad sweep which we are now surveying rituals have meaning, and sacred practitioners are often eager to try to elucidate them, for instance in sermons and discourses to educate the laity. But it has to be admitted that sometimes there are restrictions on meaning, which arise from the following sources.

1. Traditionalist practitioners may be tightfisted in explanation since it may be thought to redound to their advantage to keep sacred lore secret. (This does not just apply to the meaning of rituals but can affect doctrines: consider the intentional obscurity of *sutras* in the Hindu tradition; by contrast consider the claim by the Buddha in the Theravadin canon that he did not have *acariyamuṭṭhi* or the closed fist of the teacher.)

2. Rituals are often held to be rendered efficacious by exact repetition. Over a long period exact repetition will exhibit verses and the like which have become unintelligible. So it will not be surprising if an increasing content of rituals in these circumstances becomes meaningless. However, it ought to be noted that the requirement of exact repetition gives great prominence to formulae, and gradually to the notion that the formulae become effective in themselves. This imparts a manipulative character to ritual. But many religious traditions resist the manipulative mode, because there are built-in dialectical forces which act in the opposite direction.

We consider the general thesis that rituals are essentially meaningless (STAAL, 1983) to be nicely stirring but analytically inadequate. At best it is a mode of so restricting the definition of ritual as to render it sterile. We would still have to invent a term for all those performances which we here count as rituals but which exhibit both interiority and meaning.

The process of superimposition

Another complication in the defining of ritual is the fact of superimposition: that is, treating as rituals activities not originally of ritual
significance. The most famous instance is the Benedictine tag
laborare est orare; and as the hymn says 'A servant with this
clause / Makes drudgery divine'. Taken in the right spirit any
activity can become a ritual activity: study of the Torah can itself
become a fulfilment of the Torah, just as yoga can become a form of
sacrifice, and so forth.

This means that the scope of ritual activity is without limit.
Nevertheless the original example has to be there. Without literal
prayer, how can growing carrots in the monastery garden become
prayer? So in a general way superimposition is parasitic on the literal
case. But again we do not need to take this in too wooden a way, for
we have to recognize the migration of the literal via the analogical.
For instance, in Christianity there is today (except perhaps in some
marginal new versions) no sacrifice. Nevertheless the mass is regarded as a sacrifice. In the literal sense, of course, it is not a
sacrifice, but the analogical sense has risen to become the dominant
one. The literal performance of sacrifice in the tradition perished
with the destruction of the Temple in Jerusalem. And in Judaism
studying sacrifice became a substitute for the real thing.

But to return to our main concern here: the fact of superimposition (SMART, 1958) both enriches and complicates the analysis of
ritual behaviour. We can understand its meaning: an activity, for
instance, can be seen as a way of worshipping God, and so can stand
in for 'pure' worship. What is pure worship? Typically it is the
utterance of a certain sort of formula of words, together if necessary
with the relevant bodily postures. This is well expressed in the
opening section of the Qur'an, repeated thirty times a day by the
observant Muslim in the course of the cycles of prayer-performance
or *salāt*:

> In the name of God, the merciful lord of mercy. Praise be
> to God, lord of the worlds, the merciful lord of mercy,

disposer of the judgment day. Thee it is we worship, thee
it is to whom we come for help. Guide us in the straight
path, the path of those to whom thou art gracious, not of
those on whom there is wrath, nor of those who are in
error. (RAHMAN, 1979)

Parts of this can be seen to be pure worship – 'Praise be to God . . .
Thee it is we worship.' The act of the faithful here is one of pure
praise: praising is itself a ritual act of intrinsic significance, which
does not itself need any outside justification, except perhaps to show
that the focus of worship is a worthy one. Of course in a version of
theism or of transtheistic monism it is imperative that a person's life
be integrated: or, to put it another way, the supreme focus of
worship is also the Being who created the cosmos, so that worship
should not be divorced from the rest of life. So it is that daily life
and moral attitudes become woven into the life of worship – worldly
activities come to have a spiritual significance and worship of a good
God becomes integrated into the pursuit of the good life. This is
where the activity of superimposition becomes irresistible. The
moral action becomes a sort of self-sacrifice. More mythically it
becomes taking up the cross (if you are a Christian) or it becomes
perhaps a form of yoga or a pattern of following the Bodhisattva.

This does not mean that all worship becomes so integrated.
There are polytheisms, as we have noted. On the other hand in
practice it may turn out that even in theisms when people's lives
should be integrated they aren't. Indeed this is typical. Such disin-
tegration may be the easier the more a ritual is interiorized. One of
the practical functions of law is to remind people of the necessity of
daily performances. People cannot, as it were, hide in their heads.

One of the functions of the doctrinal dimension is to vivify the
cosmos in ways which will stimulate appropriate worship or other
major forms of ritual. For instance, the notion in Ramanuja that the
cosmos is God's body helps to give people a living sense of his
presence. One of the problems of deism (from a spiritual point of
view) is that it makes God seem so distant. In brief, the philosophical dimension is by no means theoretical. Part of its function is to
stimulate ritual activity.

Similarly the doctrine of the three marks of existence in Buddhism, emphasizing above all the impermanence of events in the round of existence, generates a form of meditative practice: it helps to alert us to the need for self-awareness in which we come to be empirically aware of our transitory states. Again, it is artificial to divorce doctrinal from ritual aspects of religion (RAHULA, 1962).

Another important process is the extension of the ritual dimension into ordinary language, so that the very use of language will contribute to ritual. At a secular level there is the old communist practice of referring to fellow citizens as 'Comrade', a perpetual reminder of bonding in the dialectic of history. A similar effect was attained non-linguistically in Nazi Germany by the use of the Hitler salute. But in traditional religions there are similar incorporations of religious factors into daily language through formulae such as 'God willing'.

The concept of ritual and the concept of li

In brief, my attitude to the concept of ritual is to treat it very broadly. But should it cover any repetitious or stylized performative? What about 'Good morning' and 'You're welcome'? I do not think it is absurd to count such utterances as ritual; but we no doubt need to make a concession to ordinary usage. It would not be quite normal to refer to these as ritual. Still, they do belong to right behaviour. There is perhaps advantage in adopting a Chinese notion, that of *li*, or right behaviour, and using it in the widest reference to the fulfilment of an appropriate pattern of conduct. So by this usage we have a general field of *li*, and within that a rather smaller field of ritual, and within that the narrower categories which we have listed above (SMITH, 1968; FINGARETTE, 1972).

Is there something very special about religious ritual?

Religionists often seek something *sui generis* to focus on. Because it seems best to treat of religion in a broadly functional way it is very unlikely that we should find some single *sui generis* item to become a marker of genuine religion. This is not to say that there are not some special items which some or many religions will exhibit. It seems to me that, while there can in the nature of the case be no absolute boundary between the numinous and the impressive, the experience of the numinous is something chiefly associated with religions and religious foci.

Religious rituals are often associated with God and gods, and these in turn are bathed in the feel of the numinous. But, since it is realistic to take a wider-than-theism perspective on religion, there are bound to be rituals which are less awe-inspiring, though nonetheless valid as objects of our study.

It is worth pausing there to consider some of the characteristics and connections of rituals focused on the gods. While gods may be numinous and superior to their worshippers, they are also personal beings. Rituals therefore express personal communications, and as such they belong of course to a much wider swathe of human discourse. But gods are also peculiar beings, and have an embodiment, typically, in nature. Their bodies are not quite like our bodies. For one thing, their spatial configuration can be strange: the Fire God appears wherever there is fire, perhaps wherever there is light. Jupiter may live on the sacred mountain, but he appears wherever there is lightning and thunder. Lightning is his work, a kind of extension of his fingertips (DETIENNE and VERNANT, 1978). The old theory of animism had its merits, for it brought out the way in which for the believer in 'polytheism' the world of nature in its varied aspects is animated, haunted and controlled by spirits (JAMES, 1950). These spirits are personal, but they manifest in networks of natural phenomena. All this supposes a certain attitude to the world, which most of us, not being polytheists, do not relate to. This attitude sees the world as a patterned crowd, with the various types of phenomena as animated. Perhaps we are beginning to recapture something of that sense of animation through modern ecological thinking. Even so, we are not inclined to sacrifice bulls beside the wine-dark sea, or to address hymns to the sun. Such hymns are at best poetry.

But when I say 'we', am I right?' After all, there are plenty of Hindus who have their particular gods, and we may after all be Hindus. But even here the situation is a little different from that of the pre-scientific ancient world: the modern Hindu, especially if she be educated, will not quite see the gods and goddesses as separate. They may be in motion, one with another, as they swim in the mythic dimension. They are refractions of the One. They exist in a kind of higher harmony. They are therefore less closely pinned to natural and other phenomena than they might have been in olden days (CRAW-FORD, 1982).

Once upon a time communication with a goddess or god was communication with an independent spirit, whose body was a linked network of natural or other phenomena (MARINGER, 1960). Our gods and goddesses used to go beyond the natural and have biographies of their own, not altogether tied up with particular phenomena. For the gods and goddesses were the subjects of myths, wherein they mated and fought and contrived and wielded their powers amid the heroes and humans who were their underlings and indeed often slaves (HOOKE, 1933). So a god or goddess would move in his or her own time, in the mythic dimension, and be stitched together in diverse parts of space. In imagining them, human beings drew on their particular traditions. They could add to the gods' bodies by creating statues, and to their lives by elaborating more myths (GUTHRIE, 1950). The statues expressed the nature of the gods and goddesses and were themselves conceived as ritual objects. Sometimes these representations might appear alarming, and at other times sublimely natural. The statues were, as I have said, extensions of the gods' bodies, and so became 'real presences'.

The ritual transactions had to cross a divide between the visible and the invisible. This divide was also typically one between superior and inferior power. However, we should note at this point that while a typical form of such transactions was sacrifice, some traditions have been strongly anti-sacrificial, at least in so far as sacrifice might dictate the killing of animals. But let us for the moment think about sacrifice as a means of ritual communication with the gods.

Communication can obviously have differing purposes: for instance, worship as such, giving thanks, supplication and expiation. These purposes can flow into one another. Obviously the person or group worshipping a spirit can wish to be on his or her 'right side' and this will (it is hoped) reap later benefits. So praise and supplication merge: moreover thanksgiving is *ex post facto* supplication. We give something to the god to thank him: we could easily have supplicated him in advance. There is a connection between all this and expiation (which need not be thought of in too moral a way: I may just be wanting to get rid of some blot which I fear could infuriate the spirit, who may not be particularly ethical in judgment or action). There is a common logic of pleasing the god which runs through the various intentions.

We can conceive of communication as creating a flow of power in each direction: the animal (let us say) sacrificed has its own inherent, perhaps unblemished substance, and that substance is transferred to the Other. From the Other is hoped fertility, or knowledge of the future, or forgiveness, or whatever. There is a question about the mode of transfer: this depends upon the deities concerned. Heavenly gods are typically addressed through fire, since fire causes the essence of what is sacrificed to ascend in the form of smoke, meanwhile disappearing from this middle world. But burying what is sacrificed may convey a being to the underworld. Although a sacrifice may sometimes involve a thing's being set aside for a god, such as an animal in a temple compound, mostly sacrifice involves destruction, not we would suppose *per se*, but as a means to making the essence invisible and so transferable to the invisible world lying about us.

The above reflections indicate that the gift theory of sacrifice is broadly correct, provided we see the idea of a gift to the social world in which sacrifices are a natural part. For in such a world the potency of things is important, including the potency of gifts (VAN DER LEEUW, 1974).

Although an element of mystery and potent substance should be kept in play in analysing these matters, the general attitudes lying behind sacrifice are rather straightforward. The gods and spirits are themselves typically embodied networks of natural phenomena which have their effects on human and more generally cosmic existence. Sacrifices establish communication with these powers and help to influence their conduct for the better, as far as we humans are concerned. And so ritual activity is normal enough, given a certain theory about the forces in the world.

So far I have been looking at forces within the world – at gods, for instance – as embodied networks with mythic biographies. But of course the more prevalent kind of religion in the modern world is theistic: here ritual is directed not towards particular networks but towards the one great network, the cosmos, over which the one Spirit is supposed to preside. That Spirit presides generally, but of course has a more particular presence and efficacy – in the case of the three great Western religions he (or she?) has a particular presence in the relevant salvation history, different for each of the great religions. The salvation histories to some extent overlap, and this is a comfort, seeing that in so many ways the three faiths have been so bitterly divided.

At any rate, each has a defined focus towards which to direct worship and more generally other aspects of ritual. In principle too there is a defined focus in Hindu theism, even if the question of what that focus might be is answered differently according to diverse sub-traditions. We shall return to contemplate these and other examples later. Suffice it to say that according to our analysis the interpretation of ritual is relatively straightforward. Before we press on, however, I would like to pause to dispose of one theory of sacrifice, largely because it illustrates how unwise it is to devise, or to take seriously, a theory which is based on a wider ignorance of the history of religions (indeed this is a general trouble: some of the most influential figures such as Marx, Freud and Durkheim were by modern standards rather ignorant of the facts of religion).

A note on the side: Girard and the scapegoat

A theory of sacrifice which has had quite a vogue in the period since the late 1970s has been that of René Girard (1977). Rivalry in human groups, he argues, is endemic, and so the peaceful order of society cannot be assured. Tensions can, however, be mitigated if aggressive impulses are directed towards a scapegoat. The scapegoat is treated as sacred: indeed this is the origin of the sacred. The sacrifice of such a marginal being draws hostility from the group, and the being sacrificed becomes in its own way a saviour. A special twist to all this is given by Jesus' taking on the role of scapegoat voluntarily. Girard's evidence for his thesis is the widespread existence of blood sacrifices, and the stories of fratricidal and other forms of violence attested by both myth and history.

One could not of course deny that sometimes scapegoat-sacrifice might function to diminish social violence. (But sometimes sacrifice may increase it, as in ancient Aztec culture, where it was a potent cause of war.) However, as a general theory Girard's has some evidential defects. First, there are major cultural religious traditions which have been strongly anti-sacrificial – Theravada and other forms of Buddhism, for instance, and to a lesser degree Islam. There are smaller-scale societies also where sacrifice is absent, for instance among the Australian aborigines. Second, ideas of the sacred can be attested outside the scope of sacrificial religion. Third, what if sacrifice is not real or literal, but merely analogical, as in the Jewish tradition and the major traditional forms of Christianity? Again, how violent is a sacrifice intended to be? Naturally, killing involves some violence, but one would expect, on the theory, a more widespread manifestation of really violent rites, such as the tearing apart of the animal (compare *The Bacchae*). Basically the trouble with Girard's thesis is that it is very Western and imperfectly comparative in its scope.

Sacrifice as a model of world-creation

The model of sacrificial power as the force accounting for the creation of the cosmos is most prominent among world texts in the *Upaniṣads*. Indeed, the sacred power inherent in the ritual and in the priesthood administering the ritual becomes identified as the Holy Power sustaining the universe: *brahman*. It may be noted that sacrifice typically involves the notion of transformation, for instance the change of status of the animal or other offering into something sacred, within the domain of the god, and its transfer to another sphere, for instance through the agency of Fire or Agni (BAILEY, 1983).

The notion of transformation serves as the basis of one of the two major theories of causation in Indian philosophy. It is interesting that the non-identity theory, its rival, is espoused by the Buddhists, one of the major anti-sacrificial strands in the culture of the sub-continent. The 'primitive' idea of substance lies beneath many ritual acts, which are regarded as transformative of substance. The rites may also involve the transfer of substance. Rites of passage bring about trans-substantiation of a person from one kind of being to another. The idea of participating in a collective substance, as *brahman* and its equivalents mix with the other *varṇas*, became intrinsic to the class and later the *jāti* or caste system in India. Substance not only has a certain adhesive weight: it can be represented as appearing in discrete forms, so that the mixing of *jātis* becomes a mingling of substances. While the idea of substance in this 'primitive' sense does not need to be made philosophically precise, it can be: and the evolution of the idea in Indian philosophy, and the refinement of *brahman*, helped to shape differing schools of Vedanta (SMART, 1993).

One reason, oddly enough, for the importance of the idea of transformation and of the transfer of substance within the ritual mode is that rituals exhibit a personalistic view of the cosmos, while the non-identity theory leads towards a more empirical and proto-scientific approach to the world. Personalistic approaches to the thunder and lightning, the war god, the sky and so forth imply a certain sharing of life. Such sharing is expressed in the figure of the transfer of substance. This is reflected in some religious experience. Admittedly the numinous displays the Other (though the *fascinating* side indicates a drawing together: moreover, there is a general 'logic of the numinous' that explains the motifs that the god loves us and bestows his or her grace upon us): but shamanic experience involves the sense of possession. The god enters into us and becomes part of us and we part of him or her.

Ritual and the abolition of space and time

Moving beyond sacrifice, we can now begin to appreciate another aspect of ritual behaviour, its link with myth or narrative. It is widely attested that myths are scripts for performances, though it does not follow that all narratives have to be understood as rite-scripts, of course. Some narratives become so extended that they may serve as texts for dramatic performances which have some of the functions of rituals, but whose scope goes beyond the more determinate goals of particular rituals. Again, other narratives can become detached from any ritual context they may have had and live a life of their own. This becomes increasingly possible with the reduction of stories to written form; here the control exercised by the skilled performer disappears. Moreover, the same story may have a double role: sometimes used as the script for a ritual and sometimes as some other kind of narrative. For example, you can read an historical account of President Lincoln's speech after the Battle of Gettysburg, and the same story can be used as the script during the Memorial Day ceremonies which form part of American national religion.

One of the most important aspects of ritual is the way in which it may abolish space and time (ELIADE, 1959b). Now the reasons why a place may be sacred are various – in some cases we do not really know the origin of sacrality, though mythic explanations will doubtless be forthcoming. For whatever reason, rivers such as the Jordan and the Ganga have become sacred, but the ritual of sacred bathing is not confined to such rivers. So the rite of bathing at the Minakshi Temple in Madurai counts as bathing in the Ganges. And any stream in which baptism occurs 'becomes' the Jordan. So the space between the distant holy river and the one present here and now is abolished.

Even more striking is the abolition of time (ELIADE, 1959a). The ritual scripted by a given myth, let us say the story of Easter, abolishes the gap between the then and the now. 'Jesus Christ is risen today,' the faithful cry. Note the *is* and the *today* (not 'Jesus Christ rose nearly two thousand years ago').

The abolition of time and space is what may be called the presentative aspect of much ritual. I have already referred to ways in which doctrine can make presences vivid: the role is even more striking in the ritual dimension.

This presentative role is enhanced by a calendrical disposition of events. This may or may not be closely tied to the natural cycle of the year. But by organizing holy days throughout the year a religious tradition presents itself in a balanced way and will hope to give people a vivid sense of the whole faith. Natural cycles also enable a religion to have a practical role in enhancing, or attempting to enhance, the fertility of the spring season, to stave off death and darkness as winter draws on, to give thanks for the harvest and so on.

In alluding to Gettysburg I am implying that it does not matter much or at all whether a narrative is historical. That is, pieces of history can themselves function as relevant narratives. The distinction between history and myth is an unreal one from a phenomenological point of view: in the celebration of events the faithful think that those things 'really happened'. Moreover, within a functioning modern state the teaching of history in high schools fulfils the function of presenting myths, since the history is usually value-laden, celebrating the good things and heroes of the nation's past. Early Christians, in castigating pagan narratives as myths while presenting their own story as having really happened, pioneered what is a not quite natural division of stories. It is true of course that modern methods try to establish the truth of narratives so far as this is possible, and so modern consciousness has in this way passed beyond the mythic. This has led to debates about demythologization and the like, to which we shall in due course return.

Although, as I have argued, there is a certain abolition of space and time achieved by rituals, there may still be recognition of primary and secondary space and time. Though a new Jerusalem might be built in New England, there can still be consciousness that the original Jerusalem is not there. And while a secondary Easter occurs each year (or even each day), there will still be acceptance that the primary Easter happened *then*. These are literal places and times, these ur-locations; things are a little different with events supposedly occurring – as Eliade (1973) put it – in *illud tempus*, that sacred 'once upon a time'. What are we to make of that indeterminate time and for that matter indeterminate space (SMITH, J. Z., 1978)?

I shall return to discuss these ideas in the context of the mythic dimension, but indeterminacy of location in space and time is a natural accompaniment of ritual practice, since it is so often focused on the invisible world conceived as lying beyond the literal location of action: for instance, the God may be thought of as lying invisibly beyond the altar screen or wherever, perhaps vaguely in the circum-ambulatory air and the forest canopy. In due course, no doubt, participants in rituals will come to reflect that God is everywhere, but even so presence here suggests a sort of indeterminate 'being here'. Some myths, moreover, occur at the temporal margins of the world and somehow refer to what is at the edge of the universe. People have not always had clear ideas about such limiting and liminal situations, so space and time easily become indeterminate.

Pilgrimage: overcoming space in another way

It is not possible except imaginatively to travel through time, but it is eminently what we do and must do through space. Since space tends to be spiritually bumpy, some parts of space are more sacred than others. These are typically places where sacred power or light may be found. They are places which have come to be associated one way or another with a given sacred tradition. If we use the image of a 'sacred charge', as of electricity, differing locations are more or less highly charged. It may be that a given tradition, like some 'left-wing' Protestant traditions, may wish to dispense with the notion of charged places and times, and concentrate sacrality on people: persons are more or less highly charged with holiness. But it is fairly typical for religions to nominate some places as relatively highly charged. It is good for the faithful in such a case to trek to where the sacred power is. Pilgrimage belongs to the larger-scale religions, and is prevalent in such areas as China, Korea, Japan, the Islamic world, Europe and to some extent in South America. It is not prevalent yet in Africa, and North America and north Europe, as predominantly Protestant regions, do not see much of the practice. Protestant disapproval of pilgrimage arises out of the pilgrim's belief that such ritual practices might earn merit. Such *punya* is in opposition to the Protestant emphasis on grace, that is God's activity: it is inappropriate, to put it mildly, for a person to suppose that she is saved at all by her own efforts. So *punya* is banished in high Protestantism and various rituals were banned, including the practice of pilgrimage.

Nonetheless, in the other regions mentioned pilgrimage remains popular (even, within limits, in communist China, where Marxism has its own pilgrimages, notably to Tiananmen Square and the mausoleum of Mao Zedong). A typical destination is the centre of the religion, most obviously Mecca. Classical Christianity has Jerusalem, important for both Catholics and Orthodox. Judaism has had a collective pilgrimage back to the land of Israel achieved through the Zionist movement. But this has its ambiguity: born in the days of secular nationalism, it is not religious in cast, though many of those who migrate to Israel do so for pious reasons. Israel thus has a split personality – rather like Italy, where secular, liberal nationalism was superimposed on an intensely Catholic country whose religious leadership opposed the unification of Italy *et tout celà*.

Pilgrimage typically involves individuals journeying in an arduous fashion to the sacred place, from which they derive *puṇya* (TURNER, 1974). The arduousness of the journey increases the merit, though in modern times there has been an inflationary trend with jumbo jets taking pilgrims to Mecca from say Indonesia. Imagine that journey in the past: months of voyaging, perils of shipwreck, dangers of robbers, sandstorms, thirst, the great luck involved in completing the long trip home. That is a different scenario from the modern trip to the airport, the flight in the Boeing, the car from the airport at the other end, the worthy hostel, the mingling with other pilgrims, the short trip back. In India and Sri Lanka and elsewhere the bus has multiplied pious opportunities. A group can visit thirty temples in two weeks, gaining some merit from each. The temples benefit, for the coins left by pilgrims grow ever more numerous. While efforts are less, thus no doubt diminishing the merit, the opportunities multiply as the pilgrim can embark on more journeys.

The logic of pilgrimage is to go to one of the high sacral bumps in space, draw on its merit and convey that to the periphery. There may be other goals in addition. The sacred place may have gained its sacredness not just from long custom, or from a vision seen there, or from the association with an important sacred narrative. There may also be healing, for very often the merit congeals into something else: the power of making people well.

A religion very keen on pilgrimages, though it does not wield a theory of divine power, is Buddhism. Pilgrimages occur or abound not only in Theravadin countries such as Sri Lanka and in North India, the 'home country' of Buddhism, but also in regions such as

China and Japan. But the shrines which came to be destinations of pilgrimage were not precisely locations of theophanies, except in an extended sense. Moreover, the philosophy of Buddhism is against the notion of divine substance, or even perhaps power. The Hindu tradition by contrast is quite at home with such ideas. In theory, moreover, the faithful person would not normally gain any power from the Buddha, for the Buddha is comprehensively absent. His statue is just a reminder. The *puṇya* accruing to the pilgrim should, if we stick to classical doctrine, accumulate through his action, with no input from the power of the shrine or of its associations. The merit is a psychological matter. So in some important sense there is no power accruing to the target of piety. Now things may change in the high Mahayana, where saviours and divine-seeming Buddhas emerge. In the classical epoch, the pilgrim earns his own merit: visiting a shrine that commemorates a great thing, such as the site of the bodhi tree, is a means of improving a person's virtue and so of helping him or her along the path towards nirvana. Thus in any strict sense no power is exuded from Buddhist shrines. I have called it light instead: what obtains is not so much a kratophany as a photophany.

In its own small way going to a temple is a pilgrimage, a mini-pilgrimage. This indeed is a good model for what happens in many Asian cultures, where congregational worship, though not unknown, is nevertheless not the norm. Nevertheless, there is often a congregational aspect to pilgrimage. For instance during the Edo period (1600–1868) it was common for pilgrims in Japan to travel in groups. It was also common, and indeed still is, in Catholic Europe.

The reasons for the sacredness of pilgrimage places are many. In some case a sacred place belonging to another tradition is taken over, as happened with Mount T'ai in China (originally Taoist). Sometimes the pilgrimage place is laid down in the law from the start, as in the case of the elaborate rites associated with Mecca. Mecca, of course, is central because it is the primary place of revelation in Islam, as well as being tied to Abraham (Ibrahim), not to mention Adam (KAMAL, 1961). Many Jewish and Sufi points of pilgrimage are so because they possess the tombs of holy men. Very often lesser places of pilgrimage spring up because of the difficulty in times past of getting to the main centres. In Christianity a fertile source is places where there have been visions of the Virgin Mary, such as Lourdes.

In marking where religious traditions have had their centres and points of spiritual boosting, pilgrimage centres help to vivify faith. This is most marked in Islam, where in principle the Hajj has a remarkably unifying effect. In secular religions national monuments are probably the most prominent, sometimes combining with religious ones (Westminster Abbey is a prominent example).

The pilgrimage typically has three symbolic phases. There is the setting forth, and here normally the pilgrim feels himself or herself separated from ordinary social obligations; then there is the journey itself to the sacred site; then there is the homecoming. Because of the release from social ties there is a liminality and some would say sense of *communitas* in the journey. This view was most vigorously expressed by Turner (1974). What is more obvious is that the pilgrim is set apart somewhat and therefore belongs, so to speak, to the 'other world', whose power-manifestation and light-manifestation she is *en route* to visit and partake in.

Turner's theory about *communitas* as being a property of liminality seems to me defective and unsupported by empirical evidence. The more natural occasions of *communitas* are congregational (for instance, in modern secular life football games and the like mobilize loyalties). The point about liminality, at least in rites of passage, is that it effects a kind of Gnostic transition between one substance and the other. That is, the transformation of the person from one status (being lay, let us say) to another (being a priest), and so possessing a different status, can be presumed to lie through a state of being neither this nor that. Whether a pilgrim is strictly in a liminal condition is open to question. She is in a condition which belongs outside the sphere of the ordinary world – in the divine domain, one might say. As such, she leaves behind her worldly categories. But this is not of itself a condition of being in *communitas*.

As well as literal pilgrimage there is pilgrimage by analogy: the voyage of the Pilgrim Fathers, off to find and settle a new land. This founding of new centres is an alternative to seeking old ones. Then there is the moral and spiritual sense of pilgrimage: seeing this life as a pilgrimage, a journey from here to the heavenly kingdom, as in *Pilgrim's Progress*. In a rather weak sense tourism is a sort of pilgrimage. But, directed in a certain way, it is real, for example going to Washington to touch base with the symbolic sources of the nation, and so on.

The symbolism of the future life can be integrated into the language of pilgrimage. Thus in Buddhism there is a voyage to the Pure Land as well as to Sarnath and other sites of literal pilgrimage.

Worship as a main form of the ritual dimension

So far we have contemplated certain types of ritual – sacrifice, pilgrimage, briefly rites of passage. But probably the core of ritual in religion, or at least one core, is the practice of worship, that is praise or homage rendered to a God. Pure worship lies at the heart of a number of the major religions – pure, that is, in the sense that worship is given because worship is due. It is usually mixed in with other activities, such as petitions and expiations. Nevertheless, despite such admixtures there is to be discerned a pure worship. Often it comes trailing clouds of ethics: in praising a good Lord one commits oneself to the good life. Because the Lord is Creator, worship implies certain consequences. It has to be contextualized, for its Focus has a certain shape. That shape is supplied by doctrine and myth, and, as we have noted, by the ethical dimension. So a person in worshipping a given God is also affirming acceptance of and solemn acknowledgment of that God's qualities – as Creator, as saviour, as a character in certain stories, and so on. But that does not mean that the act of worship in itself is not pure, since its principal meaning is to express praise or homage.

We need to draw a line between worship and other activities that shade into it or have an analogy. For instance, when the Catholic says an *Ave Maria* he is hailing the Virgin, but he does not strictly regard this as an act of worship: for it is proper to worship only the Divine, and the Virgin is not divine (though close to God). It might be objected that I am here just drawing on a theological distinction and not a phenomenological one. It is true that we might in the history of religions wish to compare ritual activity directed at the Virgin with that directed at Christ, for instance: we might wish to make closer comparisons than orthodox theologians would be comfortable with. Nevertheless, the theological distinction between worship and veneration, if it is observed by the participant, becomes a phenomenological one. It is part of the person's state of mind in addressing ritual activity towards different foci.

Further down the level of beings it becomes increasingly inappropriate to talk of worship. It is unfortunate, for instance, that the phrase 'ancestor worship' has entered into common currency (NEWELL, 1976). Though ancestors are invisible, one might say spiritual, entities which persist like a penumbra around living society, they are not gods. And so what we are typically dealing with in so-called ancestor worship is invisible converse with the departed. It goes beyond the cult of the dead in an Italian cemetery, shall we say, because there is much less sense of real converse with the departed in the latter context (though I do know those who go and talk to their dead relatives), which often represents a well-developed system of maintaining one's duties to the departed rather than transactional discourse with them. Ancestor exchange, on the other hand, is a much livelier felt interchange with the dead. And so we might think of a spectrum of ritual interchanges, at the apex of which lies the practice of worshipping gods and God.

To analyse this case I shall take the Anglican communion service, which of course includes important elements, especially the communion itself, that go beyond pure worship. But it is useful to take a living and detailed example.

Those who attend a service accept it as a particular token of a type: it is an instance of a patterned type which spreads throughout the Anglican community and which is, more broadly, Christian. They intend their actions, then, to operate within the context of the Christian faith. Such an account is not always true – or not always true in the same way – in other religious traditions, but it is broadly so, notably in modern, self-conscious times. Things are somewhat different in small-scale societies, though even here they are changing, as wider groups become more self-conscious. So a first piece of contextuality about worship concerns the question: in which wider framework is it conceived? (Note that some worshippers may think of their activity more widely than is orthodox within a given tradition – they may perceive all religions as worshipping the same God, for instance.)

The Anglican communion involves pure worship at various points, for example at the beginning of the Lord's Prayer and at the end of psalms (the doxology). Other prayers involve supplications, expiations and so on. The main action involves consecration of the bread and wine and its transformation into the body and blood of Christ, all this re-enacted according to the mythic script of the Gospel, the replay of the Last Supper. But it is all conducted within the framework of worship, fixed on the Focus of God conceived as Trinity. Though Christ is the more prominent focus in the communion, and though there is a tendency for a lively sense of the Spirit to fade, thus giving a slightly unbalanced sense of the Trinity, it is indeed the Trinity that in principle is praised throughout. That Trinity is conceived as transcendent, as operative 'behind' the cosmos, but also as immanent and active within particularities, above all in the action of the Last Supper (JONES, WAINWRIGHT and YARNOLD, 1978).

This action, incidentally, provides a potent means (according to the mainstream Christian tradition) of salvation: the participant shares in Christ's life and in his victory over death, in which he expiates the sin of humanity, reconciling humankind with the Divine Being. These are ideas which do not just use ritual but are framed in the conceptual apparatus of ritual – for instance, expiation or at-one-ment. The central narrative of Christianity is heavily laced with ritual notions.

The sense that God is to be worshipped and adored is conveyed by various scriptural passages: the Divine Majesty as it appears to Isaiah and to Job; Christ's transfiguration in the presense of the inner core of his disciples; God's majesty as the lord of creation, indeed creating the world by fiat out of nothing; the power and thunder exhibited at Sinai; and so on. In short the object of worship appears as a numinous Being, holy, terrible, fascinating.

The logic of the numinous and God's grace and mercy

The 'natural' Focus of worship is a holy, numinous Being. This is evident in the simple homage to power. This acknowledgment of pure power is evident in Job, in Krishna's theophany in the *Gītā* and in numerous other examples. But it is typical of supreme Beings in the world religions to represent not just power, but mercy, love, goodness as well. There is an experiential logic which brings this about, apart from the fact that theisms try to synthesize the ethical dimension with the others. Or, to put it another way, moral intuitions are taken seriously alongside religious ones, so that in the long run God has to be good (the Buddha has to be compassionate, Allah has to be merciful, the Great Ultimate has to conform to the Confucian ethos, and so on). But, as I say, there is already a kind of 'logic of goodness' inherent in the acknowledgment of the numinous, which lies at the root of what I have here called pure worship.

The power or holiness of the Focus of worship is something which the pure worshipper prizes in itself. The more you concentrate on that holiness the more logical it seems to suppose that it is the only source of holiness. This is already apparent in kathenotheistic phenomena – the God seen within the frame of a ceremony expands to fill the mental space available. Eventually the purity of worship gives rise to the notion of the inappropriateness of trying to work out one's own salvation by one's own efforts (DHAVAMONY, 1971). If there is only one fount of holiness, that fount is the Focus. Hence it follows that salvation, that is acquiring holiness, must issue from the Focus and from no other source. This idea is found in the *bhakti* religion of the Hindu tradition, in the notion of grace or its equivalent in Pure Land Buddhism, in the Christian doctrine of grace, in Islamic condemnations of *shirk* (roughly, idolatry), in orthodox Jewish piety and elsewhere (HAIGHT, 1979). In short the purification of worship leads to the exclusivity of the holiness of the Focus, and this in turn leads to the idea of human holiness as having its source in the Divine Being. This talk of exclusivity helps to account for the intolerant attitudes to other faiths often found in Western theisms, but such intolerance is a necessary consequence. For phenomenological exclusivity within the context of worship is compatible with tolerant feelings towards other myths, and such compatibilty stems from a doctrine about the relation between religions in general.

While it is not essential that there should be a holiness transfer from the Focus of worship to the worshipper, the notion is natural. This is so for a number of reasons. First, ritual itself, including worship, operates as a gate for the transfer of substance. It is part of the general theory of ritual observance that this should be so. The pilgrim, for example, approaches the source of power or light so that she can acquire some of that power or light. The main reason for propinquity to the sacred relic is to be at the gate, so that the merit of the relic can flow through to the pilgrim. So it would be natural to suppose that the worshipper opens up a channel of communication with the Focus. And along that channel flows holiness. Since in theory the Focus is either infinitely holy (being God) or virtually so (being a Buddha), there is no diminution in the power of the Focus through her or his beneficent outpouring. Since, too, the worshipper looks upon the Focus as a personal Being, it is easy to begin to translate the power flow into something exhibiting moral qualities.

Another reason for the worshipper to conceive the reality of the holiness flow is that the Focus may be thought of as Creator and, as such, may have a motivation in his work of putting living beings into the world – such a reason would be salvation, itself implying the holiness flow from the Divine to the human. As we have noted, the worshipper may also wish to align his moral and religious intuitions, and it would be natural to think that the supremely holy or powerful is also the supremely ethical, anxious to share her glory with her creatures.

But the main part of the argument is the first. It gives rise to the reflection that the Divine as a personal Being does not just open up, mechanically as it were, the gate which allows the holiness flow through it into the human worshipper. He displays by this act moral qualities, such as mercy, love, grace, compassion. So it is natural, beginning from pure power, to arrive at a God who is warm. Although the fear of the Lord is the beginning of wisdom, the conclusion is that God loves us or is merciful and compassionate towards us.

Thus there is a natural drift in differing traditions towards a religion of devotion or *bhakti*. This is why I put forward *bhakti* as a chief type of pure worship, one core at least of the ritual dimension. While no doubt it was not absent from earlier phases of Indian religion, it emerges startlingly in the *Gītā* and in the colourful *sūtras* of the Mahayana. It came to be expressed not just in Chinese Buddhism but in Taoist religion. It lies at the heart of Islam, even if Islam is always keen to underline the numinous side of the religion, in its austere heart. It is of course at the centre of Paul's religion, and we can see renewals of devotion in differing phases and circumstances of the Christian tradition. It is there at the heart of the Pharisee and orthodox line of Jewish piety.

In brief, for all the terror in the numinous, it lays down the logic of salvation and moves towards a religion of devotion and love. Moreover, the logic which we have sketched here also helps to make sense of a type of experience which is very widespread in religions, and which has its relationship to the numinous. I refer to shamanism.

The shamanistic experience and rituals of resurrection

The occurrence of dreams and visions is highly significant throughout the history of religion. They suggest to individuals who undergo them (and who may employ techniques to put themselves in the way of them, such as sweat-lodges and eremitical episodes, especially as part of rites of passage) that divine spirits are entering them. They feel the god within. Such a power source gives the individual a vigour and perception which may help the community, for instance in discerning where the animals are. A figure here is a god as Lord of the Animals, important in various cultural contexts. While the shaman is prominent in the cultures of North Asia and throughout the Americas and Africa, the figure occurs too throughout the larger-scale cultures (HARNER, 1982).

It is typical of the shaman to feel that he or she is dismembered, perhaps by ancestors or by wild animals or by other supernatural spirits. His flesh is cut off, and he is reduced to a skeletal state. But he rises up from death and travels to supernal worlds, to heavens to see god, to infernal lands to find the dead. Through such voyages he becomes in some ways pure spirit and he can travel through the air and perform wonderful deeds. As the wounded healer he can heal; as one who has known death he can overcome death and help those in states of dire sickness. Having celestial knowledge, he can advise his community. He is eminently qualified to keep its lore. His whole understanding can enrich wider religions, as in Tibetan Buddhism, which contains powerful shamanic elements (EDSMAN, 1962; HULTKRANTZ, 1973).

Prophecy and the vision of the numinous

It is notable in the Hebrew Bible that the prophets combine two characteristics. On the one hand, they have a vision of the Holy One, a numinous experience. On the other, they produce a social and ethical critique of the society and politics of their day. As in a number of other cultures they feel that they are the mouthpieces of God. Shamanistic and prophetic motifs run through the calls of modern founders of religion, such as the Rev. Moon, Isaiah Shembe, Simon Kimbangu and Joseph Smith. Prophecy has a certain dialectical ambivalence. On the one hand, the vision perceives the numinous as the Other. On the other hand, the prophet experiences possession, hence his 'Thus speaks the Lord' or other inspired utterance. So the Prophet Muhammad could give the most inspired poetical utterances celebrating the Otherness of Allah, and at the same time perceive himself as the channel through which God speaks to the human race. To a lesser extent this is the mode in which most ordinary worshippers operate: God is out there, yet I am specially chosen to do his will.

This dialectical motif helps to reinforce the sense of *bhakti*. We both worship God and partake in her. Nonetheless, it is vital to note the dialectic. Union is not easy with God, for God's Otherness is also expressed in the defects (sin, ignorance, folly) of the worshipper. The gap between the human being and God is necessary within the ambit of the numinous style and the religion of worship. By contrast the contemplative mode is different. There is no numinious Other in the Theravada; at most there is the god Kataragama or whoever, a feeble rival at the higher level to the Lord Buddha. If there is some slight air of numinosity clinging to the statues of the Buddha, there is also a vivid awareness that the Buddha is not truly available to us, so that *bhakti* is not practicable (DE SILVA, 1980).

At any rate the dialectic of worship implies the Otherness of the God, and for this reason all religions which focus centrally on worship, whatever else they may do, emphasize Dualism. Mystical or contemplative religion homes in on an experience in which duality is abolished, and so has a tendency within the ambience of theism to stress a kind of union. For this reason it is liable to conflict with the purer religion of worship.

The logic of the *bhakti* ritual is different from that of meditation or interior contemplation in so far as the religion of *bhakti* emphasizes the activity of the Divine. The mere worshipper cannot create her own salvation. Only God can achieve that. Hence the development of the cat and monkey schools of South India, interpreting in different ways Ramanuja's doctrine of grace or the activity of the Divine in bringing about human liberation. The religion of *bhakti* is that of other-help. But the religion of *dhyāna* or meditation is that of self-help (that is, unless it has already merged with other-help: here superimposition comes into play). The Theravadin saint has to work out his own liberation with earnestness.

Meditation: another core of the ritual mode

If worship represents one core or epicentre of the ritual mode, the practice of meditation represents another. In other words, there is an inventory of contemplative practices which can be summed up as *dhyāna* or yoga, important in religion but having a rather different ambience from that of worship. The term 'ritual' may not seem apt for this mode of activity, and it is true that ritual typically has a transactional character, which meditation does not have. However, meditation does have a patterned character, and it is usually associated with religion. Thus yoga is at the heart of a number of spiritual traditions, notably Theravada Buddhism, Zen Buddhism and Advaita Vedanta. There are forms of religiosity, such as the Qabbala, Sufism and Christian mysticism, where meditation is central, though occurring within a context of worship: here the concept of worship is in effect superimposed upon the practice of meditation (SMART, 1958).

There are various reasons why worship and mystical practice can coalesce, though they need not do so. For example, the worship of God leads to the abasement of the worshipper, and this in turn encourages commitment to austerities, which are often part of the surrounding practice of meditation. Again, the love of God can lead to an intense desire for union, and the contemplative life may be seen as an avenue to this. Or again, worship intensifies the sense of the invisible world 'beyond', and this may be conceived as coinciding with the invisible world 'within' (consider the *tat tvam asi* formula). Although worship and meditation do not in any way entail each other, they do have echoes of each other, allowing a sort of coalescence. Nevertheless it is clear that a religion can have one without the other. Scottish Calvinism in the past has had nothing to do with meditation in the core sense, while Theravada, especially before receiving influence from Mahayana practice, had little of the religion of worship in it. The definition of *dhyāna* needs, however, to be clarified. It has been common enough in English to translate this term as 'meditation'. This is correct enough, but there is an ambiguity. Sometimes 'meditation' is used in English to refer to a kind of inner musing on Christian myth, for instance on the last sayings of Jesus upon the cross. Or it might be used to describe what goes on at Passover, a kind of meditation on the escape of the children of Israel from Egypt. It refers in these cases to a discursive process related to the narrative dimension. But this is not how I am using the term here. For yoga or *dhyāna* essentially involves a purification of consciousness. In the end it quells the discursive mode. The same applies to theistic mysticism. By quelling the discursive, these ways of self-discipline allow the inner light to shine. Perhaps the term 'contemplation' would be more satisfactory, as a means of avoiding this ambiguity. This is not to say that discursive meditation is unimportant. In fact it is a common feature of ritual activity (in the broad sense), which serves to interiorize the mythic dimension.

Contemplative practice exhibits a number of different yogic techniques, often pursued in a communal manner, usually under the guidance of a spiritual master. It is often accompanied by austerities, and typically though not universally the organizations nurturing it (monasteries, convents and so on) practise celibacy – though Islam and Judaism are opposed to this. The ritual practice of austerities is most intensely followed in the Indian tradition and may in some contexts be thought more important than contemplation (as in the Jain tradition).

Classical Christianity emerged in the fourth century of the Common Era out of a blend of Judaism and Neo-Platonism. (The Christian tradition was up to that point a new religion developed from within Judaism. Indeed it was one of the many varieties of Judaism on offer, including rabbinic Judaism, which turned out to be dominant.) The Neo-Platonic motifs within Christianity deeply affected the theology of the Patristic period, but more than that they supplied a hardening of Christianity during a period when it was also undergoing softening, for, having become the official religion of the empire, it was attractive to place-seekers and those wishing for a comfortable existence. The austerity of the contemplative life reinforced the whole monastic movement, which gave renunciation and martyrdom new meanings. It thus became an integral part of the Christian tradition, which could thus – to put it crudely – combine a sort of Jewish worship with a Neo-Platonist mystical or contemplative element. A dissimilar pattern was evident in the emergence of Sufism in Islam, where Christian contemplative motifs could appear in new form within the fabric of Islamic worship. So worship was superimposed not just upon labour but upon contemplation too. *Contemplare est orare* (BUTLER, 1961). The Quest for the Holy God 'out there' could also be the quest for the Light 'in here'.

Already a similar sort of integration could occur within the ambit of Upanisadic thought, where the sacrifical ritual of the Brahmanical religion could be merged with the interior yoga probably derived from sramanic cults, and so inner yoga itself could be viewed as a sort of sacrifice. And pure consciousness or *ātman* could be seen to be *brahman*, the Holy Power. From this point of view the merging of rituals could have profound doctrinal or philosophical consequences.

Monastic Christianity could integrate ritual further, since the daily life of the monks or nuns revolved round the liturgy or mass. Here pure worship and the life of contemplation were blended into the communion ritual, with its complex mode of communication with Christ and the Trinity. In so far as monasteries also promoted both agriculture and study – study was itself seen as a pious activity and a kind of ritual (there were important echoes of rabbinical Judaism here) – the monastic rhythm was a fivefold one. Contemplation, agriculture and study could all be seen as forms of worship. The whole system further involved a kind of economic transaction, in that the laity – including the monarch and other feudal lords – could contribute to the upkeep and beautification of the monastery, while in return they could reap merit and moral instruction, and in general access to God.

The contemplative life tends in differing cultures to generate holy persons, who in turn generate a popular religion of veneration. In the context of Sufism the tombs of holy men (and women) are magnets of piety and devotion. Mystical adepts proved to be an important means of transmitting Islam in South Asia and Indonesia.

The conversion of emptiness into power

Part of the secret of the holy person lies in the fact that her or his mastery of the inner life itself creates both light and power on the outside. The saint or fakir or tzaddik practises inner control and austerity and is thereby thought to gain power; but how does this work? First, at one level the holy person is thought to have acquired merit. In theism his or her meditation is a gate for power, so God's power flows into him or her. In non-theistic religions the meditation and austerity themselves create merit. And so the holy person becomes charged, somewhat like a sacred place: the ordinary person by proximity can acquire some of the merit. By reverencing the holy person the ordinary person opens up a gate of power and merit, through which those qualities will flow. And after the holy one dies some relic or tomb or other material manifestation will retain some at least of the desirable power and itself become an object or target of veneration. We may note that in Buddhism all these transactions can be explained in a somewhat psychologistic manner: by treating the holy person as merit-laden the individual increases his own merit because he is in a psychologically better frame of mind from having reverenced an ideal person. It sets before him a target of moral endeavour, and by encouraging ethical behaviour actually improves his state.

Second, there is a plainer sense in which the saint gains power. In overcoming desires she is in a superior position to the ordinary person, who struggles to gain power in order, she hopes, to satisfy desires, whether psychic in gaining control over other people or material in getting the means to fulfil desires of a fleshly kind. But the saint is above all that in theory or in the perception of his devotees, and so in terms of desire-fulfilment is more powerful than the powerful (DONIGER, 1973).

This position of the saint connects with the idea of wisdom. Meditation brings him to perceive the light, and the ordinary person thinks that this gives him special advantages in insight – even into mundane matters, for instance marriage problems. So a holy monk may be sought out for advice, though sometimes paradoxically the celibate holy person has no direct experience of marriage or sex at all. This notion of wisdom or insight or *prajñā* is not the same as theoretical or factual knowledge. I shall explore it in Chapter 4 on the experiential dimension. But of course wisdom is a power. It is thus connected up with the notion that the yogi has special powers, such as levitation (in Christianity), the capacity to fly (in the Indian tradition) or to control age (in China).

Because in many cultures the holy person is regarded as different from 'normal' people, sometimes because of eccentricity, like the holy fool, but more because of her superior practice, it is easy for her to take over the mantle of the Other. The contemplative may not possess the numinous within, but begins to wear its aspect externally. So the saint comes to be reverenced, even worshipped. Within the fluidity of the concept of god in the Indian tradition she may come to be worshipped. So the person who practises mysticism arrives at a kind of numinous holiness which he imparts both to people and to objects around him. This was particularly marked in Sufism, so that saints' tombs ended up as places of pilgrimage. Modern Islamic revivalists, attributing Islam's less than happy state (because of Western incursions and conquest) to past corruption, are often eager to eradicate such a practice of reverence of holy persons, liable to manifest the deadly sin of *shirk*. This is a primary reason for the drive against Sufism in modern times.

Blending worship and meditation

While, as we have argued, it is possible to have a religion of relatively pure contemplation without serious attention to pure worship, it is common for both strands of practice to arise within a tradition. Then the values of one practice can be superimposed on the other. For instance, the practice of yoga can be seen as a form of interior worship. Or it can be seen as a kind of self-sacrifice: the restraint of desires is itself a sacrificial form parallel to external sacrifice. This was the path mainly trodden by the authors of the *Upaniṣads* (RADHAKRISHNAN, 1953). So there are analogies between meditation and worship which can be set out as follows.

1. By analogy, self-restraint is a kind of sacrifice, for you give up something precious to your ego. This works out especially well in Christianity, where the self-sacrifice of the individual parallels Jesus' sacrifice on the cross. But there are plenty of examples elsewhere.

2. The contemplative abolishes the distinction between subject and object. Now this, as I have noted, may cause alarm since it creates the tendency to talk of union, which is blasphemous in a highly charged numinous religion of worship. But it can be taken on the hither side as the destruction of the individual ego, which is the ultimate in humility and self-effacement. Humility is important because it is an attitude reflecting the deep inferiority of the worshipper to the target of worship.

3. The contemplative in exploring the inner world is in contact with the invisible, but worship in being directed outwards also goes beyond the visible world to its invisible source or sources. It becomes easy to have such models as these: that God is found within or behind human consciousness, as the inner light or controller; or that God is the soul or pure consciousness.

Ritual and the ethical dimension: some observations

This last discussion brings us to the edge of the question of the relation between ritual and ethical behaviour. We have touched on this at various junctures, but it is useful here to look at the matter more systematically.

First, the target of worship easily becomes a model, to be used with discrimination. So if God is merciful – and we have seen some of the logic in this – the human ought to be merciful too. In Buddhism the bodhisattva comes to be an object of worship: but he is also a model (or she, in China and Japan, through Kuanyin or Kannon) of compassionate action. Also by a paradox the worshipper is actually reverencing his own future state (DAYAL, 1970).

Second, worship, sacraments and meditation open up a gate to the eternal. This contact should make a person fearless – hence the role of ritual in preparing the ground for critical attitudes to society where the latter is for whatever reason perceived as corrupt (HARAKA, 1983).

Third, the target of worship is often regarded as lawgiver, telling people what their duties are. An interesting case is orthodox Judaism, where the Divine Being is the source of the law, which controls both ritual and ethical behaviour (GINZBURG, 1928). Despite the efforts of commentators down the years to rationalize this code (for instance, to treat the ban on pig's meat as a hygienic precaution in the ancient Near East), it has a certain positive, non-rational facticity which by its very non-rational character imposes a separate shape of life on the pious Jew, who is constantly reminded in the nitty-gritty of day-to-day existence of the demands on her made by God. This in turn is a very effective way of reinforcing the practice of the presence of God. (Such reinforcement is achieved by superimposition in some other theisms: that is, by seeing daily chores and activities as themselves a mode of worshipping God.) At any rate, God is regarded as the source of the law, whether this be conceived as demanding a complex of ritual and ethical duties, or as requiring a general obedience to the divine (BERMAN, 1974).

Naturally, all this may have deep social implications. Where the ritual is integrated into state or national rites, local laws may be justified by appeal to divine authority. This is an important reason why rulers and ruling elites have liked the connection between religion and political power. This is a topic which we shall come back to in Chapter 8, but examples might be such rituals as coronations, ancient spring festivals and horse-sacrifices. In each of these the ruler's status is confirmed by the Divine in a ritual way, but he also becomes a conduit of divine power and through that – he hopes – of fertility. The divine king is hedged about by rituals which place him, in the cosmological context, between heaven and earth, passing down heavenly power, and acting as the chief agent of sacrifices and other performances on behalf of his people.

While the connection between worship and mercy or compassion is relatively clear (because of the logic of the numinous), the connection between contemplation and compassion or love is less so. And yet there is a solidity in the Mahayana tradition linking these two sides which is very important.

In passing, it is worth noting the role of love in relation to theistic mysticism. It is clear in a number of traditions that sexual union becomes a model for mystical union, for obvious reasons: the union between the individual and God is a case of 'two in one', of which the best earthly analogue is sexual union. So it is that making love becomes a signal of heavenly love. This also encourages those ritual uses of sex in China and India to promote mystical union. Given a romantic interpretation of sex, contemplative union can be said to promote genuine love.

However, when we have a more purely contemplative mode of religious life, why should meditation encourage compassion? The failure to perceive the connection, and the perception indeed that meditative salvation might well be a form of higher selfishness, formed the basis of the Mahayana critique of the lesser vehicle.

It would seem that two motifs help to promote contemplative compassion, the first being the selflessness which the restraint and taming of desires promote, and the second being the insight that differing swarms of causally linked events mingle, so that according at least to the Buddhist analysis one begins to see that there is no 'mine' but only 'ours'. The four *brahmavihāras* or great virtues are suggestive: they are friendship or benevolence; compassion: joy in others' joy; and equanimity. The last named has an obvious connection with self-restraint (KING, 1964).

There is also an element of exchange, which is important in looking at the moral attitudes in a society where the contemplative ascetic life is taken seriously. The monk or nun or mendicant recluse depends on society at large for support. So it is that the giving of alms to such holy persons is part of the fabric of daily life. Such material contributions are matched by what the lay folk receive from the holy ones. First they receive moral teaching and guidance. Second they receive, by proximity, merit. So there is an exchange of visible goods (food, robes, perhaps land) for invisible ones, which help to promote the further happiness of lay people. Such an exchange is just one step removed from a sacramental transaction, where the visible becomes the vehicle of the invisible.

Generally speaking contemplative religion has a peaceful air. The monk, nun or recluse is a withdrawn person, 'unworldly'. The monastery or the hermitage or homelessness can become symbols of belonging to the 'other' world, that is the spiritual life. It is true that, like worship, meditation can become superimposed upon daily activities, as in medieval Japan, where archery or flower arrangement could become vehicles of interior training. So it was that the mystical life could be a warrior life. Part of the whole point of Zen was to overcome the rift between contemplation and ordinary life in 'this world'.

Ritual and the enhancement of the experiential dimension

It is clear that the practice of meditation is an activity intended to produce ultimately advanced states of consciousness, but worship and other kinds of ritual can also enhance the sense of the numinous. Both modes of ritual use varied adjuncts. For some Sufis dance and measured music enter into the techniques for the purification of consciousness. Music is very often a powerful ingredient in worship since it both heightens emotions, for instance of devotion, and creates a sense of awe and numinosity. Not all that we might take to be music, according to Western canons, may be classified as such in traditions outside the West. For instance, *al-mūsīqi* in the Muslim world refers to secular music, and the chanting of the Qur'an is not included in this. Since some music is essentially vocal it is hard to draw a line between the 'musical' and the stylized performance of ritual, as in the vocalization of Brahminical texts or the chanting of Taoist monks. But the reverberation of the sounds and the enchantment of the ear are factors in creating a numinous environment.

In any event the nature and circumstances of worship and sacramental ritual, including in many cases the material environment, provide a setting for the numinous experience or at least of emotions such as awe. So a ritual may both express and stimulate awe. But the more elaborate a rite the more it will depend on resources and priesthood, and often reform brings a cutback in these, and a simplification.

Developments of ritual

In varying ways rituals develop or become detached from their original contexts. A case in point is Mimamsa interpretation of Brahmanical rites. By the time this exegesis is undertaken the Vedic gods are no longer addressed but merely mentioned. The mantras become effective in themselves. Indeed if by magic we mean impersonally acting mantric techniques of changing the natural and human world, we would say that Mimamsa rituals are magical. There is some basis for looking on Buddhist *pirit* in the same way, and on a whole range of curative and other practices. The development of Brahmin rites from those surrounding the Vedic hymns (we presume) to an impersonal Brahmin operation is no doubt the result of increased concentration on the notion of *brahman* or sacred power within the mantric process and within the priests. Of course, the idea of *brahman* was used speculatively in the *Upaniṣads* as the force powering and guiding the cosmos as a whole, and this does not have a magical connotation as such, since it is a doctrinal or philosophical extension of a sacrificial idea.

There are other notable extensions and detachments. For instance, original agricultural rites could become mysteries of deep personal initiatory meaning, such as the Eleusinian mysteries. Again, the performance of myths at festivals in ancient Greece developed into drama, which, while it retained mostly religious meaning, could detach itself as an art form. Likewise the transition from oral culture to literate culture can have profound effects. The oral recital can be a ritual and ceremonial occasion, but a book can be digested in private. Of course, such digestion itself may linger on as a personal and individual ritual performance, as with people who read the *Gītā* or some other text to themselves out of a sense of ritual duty or in the hope of spiritual improvement. But often books simply escape from the original meaning of the texts which they embody. This has sociological significance too, for they can also elude the control of a priestly class.

The same applies to music or sacred sounds. There is a group of Tibetan monks who perform chants in Western concert halls: the event becomes more of an aesthetic performance than a sacred rite. But the whole history of Western music from the middle ages on represents a kind of escape from the cloister. Perhaps secular music itself becomes akin to a religious performance, generating feelings and experiences of a sublime kind. Certainly Wagner imposed a church-like orderliness and reverence upon Bayreuth Opera House, and provided a musical enactment of myths of a mysterious and moving kind, with nationalist overtones. But at any rate the secularization of music, both classical and popular, represents something of a detachment of originally sacred marshallings of sound (LANG, 1941). Something similar can be said for the visual arts. Nearly all Western art was religiously iconic, but became, from the Renaissance onwards, more and more detached from its sacred origins. To this we shall return in our discussion of the material dimension in Chapter 7.

But secularization is not a straightforward matter. For in so far as art or music comes to serve ideological purposes – for instance, socialist realist art depicting glowing pig-farms or noble leaders – it is doing much the same as it ever did in traditional religion.

It is possible to formalize ritual to serve national or political purposes. Under the Meiji constitution, Shinto came to be considered something both essentially Japanese and a kind of universal duty of citizens of the country: Shinto priests were not supposed to make doctrinal or similar pronouncements, since these might be divisive. Shinto was to become 'pure ritual'. This was in some degree a distortion of the meanings imparted to rites connected with the kami earlier. It also involved a drastic separation of Shinto shrines and practice from Buddhist temples. There was division between religion and the state, and Shinto simply was not a religion. It was just ceremonial. This foreshadowed the way the freedom of religion was enshrined in Marxist constitutions, though everyone was taught and had to respect Marxism (it did not count as a religion). There was a similar formalism about late Roman performance of state cults and ceremonies. People's private beliefs could vary as long as they performed the requisite acts. Christian and Jewish refusals to do this were regarded as fanatical and literal.

The question of the extension of rituals also obliquely raises the issue of magic, to which I now turn.

The old debate about magic and religion

John Middleton (MIDDLETON, E R) simplifies the main debate among anthropologists and others by presenting it as a contest between literalists and symbolists. The former perceive magic as instrumental, and try to achieve a cause-and-effect relationship in events. For the symbolists literalism misses the point since it does not take into account the symbolic, that is the mythopoeic and pre-logical system of cultural concepts surrounding it. There is vast scope for confusion in such a debate, but a few basic distinctions may be made.

First, a large number of human societies have had a worldview incorporating what I shall call devic causation, from *deva*. I use the term to get away from possibly misleading associations in such traditional ideas as polytheism, animism and animatism (PENUMAN, 1974). The first of these I have already used and it has a valid employment, but for the moment I want a more general term to cover the existence of gods, demons, kami and so forth. A devic-causation view differs from modern scientific worldviews, for the latter do not see physical nature as controlled by psychic forces. Or, if there is such a force, it is God and so universal: it thus leaves all scientific laws in place (monotheism is one route to rendering religion and modern science friendly sisters).

Now devic-causation theory is not pre-logical or logical either. It is natural enough and on it are brought to bear logical operations, if they are brought at all. Devic causation models our own immediate experience, which is why it is natural. That it turns out to be wrong does not make it unscientific, even if modern science has rejected it. Anyway, devic causation implies the possibility of communication. Sacrificing a bull to Neptune is in light of devism quite rational, an attempt to please the god and calm the sea before a voyage. If you believe in monotheism the dynamics of sacrifice will alter, no doubt. But for the moment let us look upon the notion that the universe is a congeries of semi-independent but interacting devic forces. One need not attribute magic to rituals which are supposed to open up paths of power and communication with the *devas*.

Let us contrast this with some mantric ceremony intended to bring rain, not by dealing with the rain-*deva*; but rather simply through the causative or transformative power of the rite itself. Let us imagine Mimamsa Brahmins doing this (though usually the ceremonies occur in a more complex setting: the person who hires the Brahmins to perform the ritual may believe in the rain-god, thus complicating the intentions). Suppose, then, we have pure mantric ceremonial. The theory is that the mantras will bring the rain, and the rain-god is a mere name. This might be regarded as a purely magical operation. But since 'magic' itself is a somewhat pejorative expression, let us use another term. I shall call the theory underlying the ritual in question 'mantric causation'. Another example can be derived from Evans-Pritchard's research among the Azande (EVANS-PRITCHARD, 1958). Here the mantric element is important in rousing the mysterious properties residing in the herbal substances used by the specialists as medicines for warding off evil or promoting good. Evans-Pritchard argues that on the whole mantric causation is used by the Azande for dealing with counter-mantras of other human beings, with the result that it is more integrated into the cultural nexus of the society and cannot be considered as influencing nature as such. That may be so, but mantric causation still occurs. The fact that I use a shield to fend off an arrow or a falling rock shows I attend to natural causation whatever the proximate origin of the natural event. I do not think

Evans-Pritchard succeeds in drawing a clear line between the so-called symbolic position and that of the literalists.

Mantric-causation theory is a halfway house towards devic causation, for it supposes not that the events influenced by the mantra are powered by a spirit but that natural objects may jump to our commands as human beings and some animals do. It is a sergeant-major's view of nature! Over time of course both the devic and the mantric theories have been replaced by scientific reflection and testing. Yet they may persist in some sort of way, no doubt because of the uncertainty present in matters of considerable import to human beings. During a drought, people pray for rain. In war, they pray for victory. And mantric causation too may be evident, as in sportsmen's superstitions. Perhaps the most developed among these are found among batsmen in cricket. They may feel the need to perform certain rites before going out to bat or to wear particular gloves or to carry some magic item in their pocket, or whatever. They believe that these things will have an effect, and in a way they do. To a significant degree success at sport depends on confidence, and these mantras and rituals may give the individual that confidence. Such collective psychological explanations may account for mantric causation continuing in circumstances of uncertainty (HUBERT and MAUSS, 1972). Yet the theory may already have been overlaid or replaced by newer views on, for example, fertility, as something achieved by the proper use of fertilizers and the preparation of crops in certain ways or the use of improved seed.

The hangover use of mantras for psychological reasons (that is, use after the worldview suggesting it is abandoned) we can perhaps see as the psychomantric attitude. Oddly enough it has a wide application in modern life in areas related to the social sciences. As human control increases, more and more of life is dominated by forces of production and economics. The most effective system appears to be a devolved one, dependent substantially on market forces. But a devolved system is unpredictable, and morale is a factor: so psychomantric utterances are not at all unusual in the sphere of economics.

Mantric-causation theory may itself draw upon symbolic analogies, so that we have the phenomenon of 'sympathetic' magic. Similarities and coincidences may suggest causal connections, say between lunar changes and menstruation.

It may be noted that mantric-causation theory as well as the notion of devic causation may become highly integrated into a cultural group's worldview. From this perspective the initial impact of a better-equipped technological society (in the form of a colonial army, for example) may be somewhat unintelligible, because the home society's viewpoint is imbued with its own cultural assumptions. That is why in various parts of the world (the American plains, Burma, Africa, China and elsewhere) similar mantric means were at first adopted to ward off bullets. Rituals were supposed to protect the warriors by turning bullets into water and so forth. Such rituals of course did not work. In less certain methods of warfare perhaps a degree of psychomantrism was effective in building confidence. But it miserably and tragically failed in unequal combat. This led to the abandonment of parts or all of the worldviews that nurtured them. Systems of thought with a high degree of magical pervasion, that is of pervasion by rites derived either from devic-causation theory or from mantric theory, have tended to 'purify' themselves and become more doctrinal and spiritual (such as Taoism and Buddhist modernism).

For various reasons magical rituals have favoured a view of the world which emphasizes potencies and substances. The notion of transformation is compelling, though some systems which have played down ritual in general, notably Buddhism, get away from substance-theory. Transformation ideas relating to causation do not in the same way stress regularities, but often use examples of mysterious changes, say from a non-alcoholic brew to an alcoholic one, or from milk to curds. Nonetheless, even within an identity or transformation philosophy, scientific speculation, as with *guṇa*-theory in Samkhya, may well occur. The whole theory of substances has been highly central in Western philosophy, as a legacy from Aristotle, and from Plato before him, despite the emergence of scientific thinking stressing regularities rather than transformations.

My conclusion about magical practices is that they depend on worldviews which are rational enough, but which have largely been superseded. There is no need to speak of pre-logical thought in the style of Lévy-Bruhl (1926). But small-scale and isolated societies, which mostly possess neither writing with the possibilities it offers of philosophizing nor the surging dialectic of ideas found among differing large-scale civilizations, did not have much opportunity to develop modern science, even though their practical rationality is often of a very high order and well adapted to very harsh conditions.

One reason why it is difficult to draw a line between societies as though they have differing concepts of rationality is that conflicts are likely to arise at the level of applied rationality. We might aver that in some contexts two plus two equals one: for example, when we combine drops of water – two drops and two drops make one large drop. Here 'plus' refers to some meaningful combination in an applied way – merging drops. A person who in such a connection affirms that two plus two makes one is not being contradictory or irrational. In general therefore it is reasonable to count so-called pre-logical thought as rational, though it is applied within a worldview or web of concepts and beliefs which we in the modern era might consider to be superseded.

Within mantric endeavours some societies or individuals may be open or experimental (HORTON and FINNEGAN, 1973) and so pertaining to early science. In other words 'open' magic tests the potencies of the means it uses. We may also note that in advanced scientific circles inherent closedness may occur. I attended a meeting of distinguished astronomers in 1947 which by a majority concluded that it would always be impossible to put a man on the moon. History is littered with examples of conservatism and resistance to new ideas in science.

Moreover, as we have already seen, it is possible for a ritual which was originally magical or at least on the edge of it to be adapted later for some spiritual purposes – for instance, the Eleusinian rituals, originally designed to promote agricultural fertility (but in so far as they embodied belief in gods they belong to the devic theory of causation, which is not strictly mantric), but which emerge in Graeco-Roman culture as a mystery religion of deep existential purport to the initiates.

Types of rituals

We have so far dealt with pure worship and meditation or contemplation. We may summarize these in Indian terms as *bhakti* and yoga in recognition of their intended inner and experiential accompaniments.

Within the ambit of worship there are activities such as petition, expiation, sacrifice, blessing, cursing. Other rituals such as rites of passage occur within that context, but can also occur within the contemplative life. Let us begin with some comments on our first list.

Naturally, they may overlap: sacrifice can be expiatory or in some other way penitentiary or purificatory. Purification arises because often it is held that the worshipper, to approach God, needs to be pure (and so undergoes rites such as washing, as in Islam, which symbolize moral purity in the face of God). It may be held that purity is necessary if there is to be communication in both directions through the gate opened by the worship.

Petition is important in one form or another, since the logic of devic causation and more generally holistic theistic causation implies that our worship of a god and perhaps sacrifice to him or her will influence divine action and therefore the course of natural or human events. Also there are varying weights assigned to the efficacy of the ritual in influencing or compelling the god. Clearly the nearer you get to the idea of compulsion the more the rite approximates to a mantric one.

Petitions lie at the heart, then, of the devic or theistic theory of the way the world works. Its scope can extend to the next world, as in masses for the dead, and prayers for a good end. Rituals of thanksgiving fit into the same schema. Ex-voto offerings, national thanksgiving and so forth assume that the god has performed or assisted in some task (such as victory in war). It is not petitioning, but it reflects a similar sentiment of 'being nice' to the Other, as also in human affairs. You ask someone to do you a favour and when he does it you thank him. Involved here too is some exchange. Worship is addressed to the god, which feeds her status and power, and afterwards gratitude likewise nourishes the god. For her part the god grants the boon, which helps the individual or group that petitions. The general schema of petition relates to and fits in with penance and expiation.

This is because an individual or group wishes to purify himself or itself for fear of some wrath or hostility on the part of the god (STEINER, 1956). Perhaps that anger has already been displayed through a natural disaster, a plague or other misfortune. As moral sensitivity develops, the fault of the person or group is perceived as ethical. Sodom and Gomorrah would have done well to look to their moral condition. At any rate, some weakness on the part of the worshippers is diagnosed as being relevant to the disaster. From this point of view it is appropriate to offer up something which will be seen as both ethical and ritual. A person may pledge herself to undertake some arduous task, such as going on a pilgrimage. In making some sacrifice to the god the sacrificer tries to restore communication, and to ease the divine wrath.

Clearly the notion that a god can be wrathful already connects up with the idea of the numinous. The fearful aspect of the god is part of the holiness of the god. This may not as yet be moralized. But by giving an offering to the god the sacrificer hopes to moderate the god's numinosity and help the operation of what I have earlier called the 'logic of the numinous'. Grace and favour may emerge out of anger and fierceness.

Worship can also have a more or less participatory emphasis. For as well as the natural benefit which a god, like the sea-god, can confers there are some spiritual ones. Gods are often thought to be immortal, so that in sharing in the divine substance the individual shares somewhat in everlasting life. It may turn out that the gods do not like this: they need to defend their status, hence the concept of *hybris*, where the individual is punished for presuming to have some divine attribute. Even so, sacramental rituals often invite the participants to share in the story and substance of the god.

There are complications to this picture in the Hindu caste system, which is of considerable interest in illuminating the complex relations between divine rituals and social order. At the top of the system is the priesthood, which has a special role in carrying on the daily life of the god, through ceremonies of waking, bathing, dressing and so on directed to the images of the divine being and consort. Such rites in part enact the myth of the god – the mythic biography as it were. The image is more than a representation of the god: the god is 'really present' in it. The Brahmin, because he is directly in contact with it, belongs to the purest species of human being. The various taboos surrounding daily life and varying from caste to caste help to produce a graduation away from super-purity to the essentially impure castes (who are therefore traditionally excluded from temples). We shall return to this topic in discussing the social dimension in Chapter 6, but we can at this stage note the general relation of the ritual and social aspects of life (BABB, 1975).

That the image in the Hindu context is not inert but in motion through the actions of the priest (and sometimes at great festivals carried with pomp around the village or town, as is the image of the Virgin in many a Catholic country) gives an impression of sacramental vitality. But it implies too that the priesthood is itself a necessary channel of access to the power of the god. One may add an historical note here. Originally the religion of the Brahmins was aniconic, as in the Vedic context. But the drive towards material representation from whatever sources in the early period was powerful enough to create a fashion for temple buildings whose chief function was to house an image. In so far as such images were of gods (rather than Buddhas and Jinas, say) the task of looking after them was for the most part captured by the Brahmins, who thus took on a new role. They may have been helped by their superior literary knowledge, which helped with their appropriation of the multitudinous mythic heritage. Eventually of course they also helped to formulate the doctrines and philosophies which defined the nature of ultimate reality and God (DUMONT, 1980).

The participatory emphasis of some worship provides us with a dialectic. On the one hand it is necessary to maintain the distance between the worshipper and the god; on the other hand the worshipper in approaching the god hopes to gain something of the substance of the divine. The doctrine of grace helps to sustain this dialectic. For on the one hand the god exudes the holy substance in some measure; on the other hand the worshipper needs to recognize that his participatory actions have nothing to do with the transfer of the exuded substance. This is entirely due to the action of the god. This attitude rules out manipulatory models of dealing with the god, which is why theisms transcend the mantic causation theory, at least in relation to God. But there are problems with an extreme doctrine of grace, since the piety or action of the worshipper does have to have *something* to do with the transfer of the substance, and ultimately with salvation. Hence the dispute between the cat and monkey schools of grace in South India among the followers of Ramanuja (LOTT, 1976).

Blessing and cursing typically fall into the same framework of communication with the gods. Often a blessing is conveyed by someone authorized in some way to do it, such as a father or mother, whose seniority gives them a special power. But a divine blessing may need some initiatory authorization: for example, a priest who by initiation is specially empowered to speak on behalf of the god, or a prophet whose initiatory vision allows him to speak in the name of his lord or lady god. In such a case a blessing can be more than optative, though it still can be merely optative. 'May the peace of God . . .' is framed in the optative mode. We cannot presume to manipulate our god.

Blessing and cursing are after all positive and negative acts. Their magical opposite numbers are destructive and constructive performances of a mantric kind. It is interesting that a mother's or father's curse, without recourse to a divine being, but simply in itself, is not regarded as magic, though its chances of success are based on the mantric principle.

Given that in certain societies magical mantras are in widespread use the fear of bad effects from other people's mantric endeavours contributes to the phenomenon of apotropaic rituals, which are designed to avert enemy influences (EVANS-PRITCHARD, 1958). Again, these can have a devic or mantric base. On the former supposition this means that the prayers against the evil or damaging influences are devic and optatively petitionary; or alternatively they are mantric and rely on 'laws' governing the world in relation to such evil or damaging forces. But even at this point the rituals associated with such rites are ambiguous. The gods too can be positive or negative. There are deities who are with you and there are deities who are against you. A ritual might be positive because directed towards a positive god but negative because it is designed to turn away some force; we might of course think of this as a positive–negative ritual.

Rituals which ward off evil forces are related, for obvious reasons, to rituals involved in the curing of disease. Some of these involve the transfer to a healthy power, through the laying on of hands or other similar procedures. In some societies, notably in Africa, health is seen as a collective, more particularly a family, affair. Therefore rites of healing involve more than the individual sick person. As we have already noted, the healer may use various medicines, such as herbs, which he or she stimulates into action mantrically by the recitation of varied formulae. Curative rites are a sub-species of positive as opposed to apotropaic rites.

In all these cases rituals have to be performed by qualified persons, that is by persons who are either formally priests, who have been trained by a traditional operative (as in the case of healing) or who are otherwise appropriate, for example because they have experienced a powerful vision. In traditional societies there are equivalents to more formal rites in modern societies.

Rites of passage

In societies which take traditional ritual seriously, and even among those Theravadin countries which while not treating ritual as very important nevertheless adhere to some traditional modes of ordering society, the categorization of people at different stages of life is of great significance. Therefore rituals which effect transitions from one category to another are a vital ingredient in social cohesion and perception. Even in societies where less formality reigns some of these rites of passage remain popular and important (VAN GENNEP, 1980).

Such rites are: welcoming a newcomer into society; dealing with a mother's uncleanness; reaching adulthood or puberty; marriage, death; and becoming a priest or adept, for example a monk or nun. Much has been written about such transitions, and a connection has been alleged between liminality and *communitas* (TURNER, 1969). These are related to individuals, but there have also been collective rituals such as dealing with the transition from peace to war. Some public ceremonials have a broader community significance than those listed above, such as the coronation of a king or queen or the installation of a president. Even the more individual cases have their public side, for they make a proclamation – for instance, 'Such a person has left the community, is dead and gone to another realm.'

The significance of a rite of passage can be explained in the following way. A person belongs to category A. Later she should belong to category B. The reason for the change is probably to do with age or some other natural transition, but it could be a matter of choice, for example to become a priest or whatever. The rite effects the transformation. Because the categories are charged, that is of sacred or deep social importance, the person cannot just move from one to the other; a special ritual is required, which proclaims the replacement of one category by another (GONDA, 1955). The in-between state which the individual should travel through is one of liminality. But in some rites it does not seem important. In fact there is a sense in which rites of passage try to eliminate the in-between condition. The society which has a well-demarcated rite of passage from child to adult does not create that 'awkward age' between the two that can plague persons caught in it, as happens in many Western societies. Turner and others have mistaken liminality for another more transcendental condition – where the pilgrim, say, is out of the usual categories. It is true that people between categories can in some sense transcend them, but that is rather different. For instance, the person who belongs to a nation and yet also does not can be perceived as super-national: Bonaparte the Italian leader of the French; Stalin the Georgian who came to be a Russian nationalist; Hitler the Austrian who became German Führer. But if we turn back to the pilgrim, we see an important distinction. She, while a pilgrim, is often conceived as no longer an ordinary citizen. She may dress differently. She is outside the usual pleasures and duties of daily life. She is in a temporary transcendental condition. If she is with a group of others in like condition this may intensify a sense of new community. But she will return to daily life in due course, with an enhanced sense of the sacred, to which she will have been more directly and powerfully exposed. If there is liminality it should exist where she passes into and out of the condition of being a pilgrim (TURNER and TURNER, 1978).

Van Gennep (1980) defined three stages in rites of passage: rites of separation, rites which are marginal or liminal, and rites of aggregation. He thought that the phases have differing importance in differing ceremonies – separation in the case of birth, aggregation in marriage, and so on. But it may depend on doctrine: if a society believes in ancestors, then death is a transition from one group, the living, to another, the ancestors. But in some societies it could simply mark the exit of the individual from society. As I observed earlier, the liminal phase may be quite minimal, where the object of a rite is simply to mark a transition, for instance in the circumcision ritual in the Jewish context. On the other hand there are situations in which individuals have a long liminality, as in the vision quest of the young person among Native Americans. But in part this is because solitude and being out of this world are typical conditions of acquiring gnosis or special knowledge through visions. Other groups, for example among Australian peoples, may have what is in effect a long period of secret education, necessitating, again, being away from the ordinary world.

Generally it seems simpler to look upon rites of passage as transitions from one substance or state into another. Consider the Hindu, and indeed Vedic, *dikṣā* which transforms an intending sacrificer. In a way it seems to suggest the theme of liminality. The sacrificer in the rite is ritually born again into a new and purified state in which he is assimilated to the gods. During this time he is hedged about by various taboos, and is treated as dangerous – indeed as numinous. His name is not to be uttered. In this dangerous state (dangerous, that is, to other human beings) he can approach the gods. After the sacrifice or other rites – we would say rites of passage – he is turned back into his usual self. The point of all this is not to make him liminal, though he may be marginalized from the standpoint of ordinary social activities, but to give him at least semi-divine prop-erties so that he is fit company for the gods.

An important function of rites of passage is to preserve categories in the face of natural or ineluctable change (HUNTINGDON and METCALF, 1979). A person dies: he is a corpse and also hauntingly a spirit, but he is not functioning any more within society. He must be dealt with ritually so that in his new condition he is placed in a new category, as dead or as an ancestor. We can see adaptations of such rites in the contemporary world. For instance, churches are being pressed to adapt the marriage ceremony for gays wishing to pledge themselves to living together. What has happened is that a new 'respectable' category of gays has been created. There should be a way of publicly recognizing and sanctioning gay faithfulness. Before that, homosexuality was abhorred by 'respectable' society: it represented a category monstrosity, between the sexes, which had been carefully defined by various taboos and quasi-ritual marks, including the wearing of different sorts of clothes. We may recall how traditionalists abhorred and still sometimes abhor women in trousers. Until fifteen years ago a notice at the start of a long sacred road up to a local shrine in Italy, which purported to be speaking for the Madonna, forbade entry to women and even young girls wearing trousers. The purpose was to prevent mixed signals. Men do not yet wear skirts (unless you count Greek and Scottish kilts) in western countries. So you 'tame' liminality by creating a category for the previous betwixt-and-between. Modern society has invented a number of these, including adolescence (a concept invented near the beginning of the twentieth century).

We have noted in the case of the *dikṣita* in the Vedic ritual context that a person is assimilated to the gods. This is a main motif of the rituals of consecration, which can on occasion be rites of passage for things as well as persons.

Consecration and purification

It is a common enough ritual perception that to approach a god or something powerfully holy a person needs to be assimilated to some degree. But the dialectic of the numinous comes into play, since she or he cannot be the equal of the god: similarity and distance both have to be represented. A priest has to be endowed with sacred substance because he is always closely involved with handling the things of the god (ELIADE, 1976). This may involve some kind of moral purification. The celibate priest for instance renounces sex, which is regarded as polluting, though in some religions marriage is believed to complete the human being, as in Judaism, Islam and Hinduism. But a would-be priest typically has a long period of training, often under a master-priest, since he needs to imbibe the knowledge and skills which his occupation will demand. The consecration is a ceremony which marks his transition to a new substance, as qualified priest, capable of handling the affairs of the god. He may or may not have other functions, such as counselling, judging or being a scholar. A

Taoist priest has to master a number of skills, including ritual dancing, exorcism techniques, the esoteric understanding of the devic hierarchy in and beyond the cosmos, and curative procedures. At the end of his long training he typically secludes himself for a period of self-purification, and ultimately is ordained during a three-day festival.

The atmosphere of Buddhist ordination is somewhat different. The novice will have trained over a number of years – twelve customarily – and the ceremony of higher ordination consists in the admission of the new monk to the assembly of monks gathered together. He will have to affirm that he is of sound mind, has parental consent and so on, and he will pledge his adherence to the monastic rule covering conduct. He will have shaved his hair as a sign of renunciation. But there is no ritual or sacramental transfer of substance as such. The monks by their silence will signify their acceptance of their new colleague. Since there is no god to approach, sanctification is not important. But admission to the order implies a high moral state of purity. In general Theravadin theories of ritual look on it instrumentally as of psychological rather than of ontological importance.

The sanctification of priests who are to handle the intimate rituals of the god is paralleled in many cases by the sanctification of things, especially buildings. The church or temple is a place apart, reserved for the god, so that secular activities are usually excluded from it. If it be turned back to secular use there is likely to be a ceremony of desanctification. The same is true of burial places, which have a numinous significance as being at the intersection of this world and the other. Implements for use in ceremonials also need purification through a rite of transition, whereby they are endowed with sacred efficacy. If for any reason the building or its contents become polluted, there are rites for dealing with that.

In the case of statues of the god in the Hindu context, something more than sanctification is involved, since the image itself contains the divine being in some sense, so that the rite of passage is much more significant – the actual endowing of the image with power. This has as an analogue the ritual of consecration of the bread and wine in 'high' Christianity, which phenomenalizes the Real Presence of the Saviour in the material elements. The doctrine of transsubstantiation in the Roman Catholic church is the most vivid and precise mode of explaining the ontology of the ritual – though the modern notion of transsignification is a much weaker notion, moving between ontology and psychology.

Sometimes the sacred space used by priests is temporary, as in the Vedic rites: originally the religion was both aniconic and templeless (GONDA, 1965). But similar principles apply. The space has to be set apart and made sacred if it is to be a suitable locale for the performance of the ritual.

Some spaces and places of course become sacred by means other than deliberate consecration. They may be sites of theophanies or hierophanies, say a place where the Virgin Mary has appeared or where a saint is buried. The visionary cases are interesting: they give rise to rituals but do not, at least not directly, arise out of them. There may be sacred places and rites, such as sweat-lodges, which help to induce visions (sacred substances such as peyote may perform the same role). The visionary component, moreover, has a ritual and mythic structure, as in the shamanistic theme of sickness, death, skeletalization and recomposition leading to resurrection.

Sometimes visions dictate sacredness, which in turn dictates rituals, such as those of pilgrimage; the counterpart of this is that sometimes practical and ritual activities themselves give rise to visions or the purification of consciousness. So it is clear that the various dimensions have varying impacts. Sometimes the boot is on one foot, sometimes on another. It is useless in general to try to deal with all religions as if basically they arise from one dimension rather than another. Nor should we always go to origins, that is to early times, as if traditions simply unfold from primary beginnings and sources. It is unwise to hold an evolutionary view. While ritual is vitally important in religion, it is not always as pervasive as it may be in some other epoch. What I have in mind here is that religions blend and change. Perhaps for early Christianity ritual was less vital than it came to be in Byzantine Orthodoxy. Then again the monastic life encouraged a new resurgence of the experiential dimension, for the mystical, that is to say the contemplative, life became prominent through the absorption of Neo-Platonism. Much later the ritual life came to be devalued in Protestantism, especially in Calvinism, but a new emphasis upon ethics emerged (paradoxically because doctrine was suffused with predestination and grace). Among Quakers ritual was rather minimized, though daily life supplied a certain amount, such as not doffing your hat because the ethos held that all human beings are equal. At different times the emphases vary, but this is not especially to be explained on any evolutionary model. There may be drifts, though most of the changes come about through the interplay of ideas, practices and traditions, and new creativities.

Does this mean that there are not changes brought about by the modern style and secularization? Is there not a movement away from ritual, partly because of social changes, such as the opportunity for new public professions other than the priesthood? Yes, but such changes are not particularly evolutionary, and they could turn out to be reversible. Naturally, mantric theories of causation are beginning to lose out. Devic styles are also becoming increasingly passé (MARTIN, 1978). The crushing of much traditional religious practice in Marxist countries cannot be ignored. The general growth in Western countries of informality in interpersonal relationships, partly in consequence of democracy, cannot fail to have an impact. The decay of authority consequent on pluralism has its effects on ritual too. It is noteworthy that neo-conservative backlashes against the above changes, while they often favour the experiential dimension (being 'born again'), may produce renewals of ritual, as has happened with modern Islamic revivalism.

Some reflections about the ritual dimension

I have presented a picture which has two pure nodes of ritual. The first is the *bhakti* or sincere worship, which addresses a supreme Being, and perhaps others lower down the hierarchy, such as saints, or the gods of refracted theism (as I have called it). I have argued that while devic causation has been a widespread theory among human beings it is less so today, now that the emphasis has switched to a more holistic model, namely theism. But the two theories, through refracted theism, can be held together. Devic theory suggests that the universe is a congeries of personal powers, and it is rational to address them through rituals such as sacrifice, pleasing them in advance or thanking them *ex post facto*. But, though the devic theory is fading, this does not by itself affect the theistic view, which means that we should worship God, who has total control over the universe and so in principle can indulge our petitions.

Gods and especially avatars have biographies: these can be tapped into through various sacramental rituals. We have later to see how myths arise and how gods acquire their reputations. Meanwhile let us note that myths often serve as the scripts for ritual activities. But the scripts can break loose and become independent mythic entities.

The second node is *dhyāna* or contemplative practice, which has its forms and formulae. Such practice causes the individual to rise higher in the hierarchy of inner consciousness in order to achieve a purification which is salvific. In non-theistic faiths there is no 'interference', but in theism it is typical to regard mystical experience as a kind of union or communion. If the mystic talks too much of union he or she becomes heretical; otherwise it is orthodox to suggest a more than hair's breadth distinction between the human soul, purified to its limits according to contemplative theory, and the Divine Being. But as we have already observed there is no need of any doctrine of union or communion where there is nothing 'out there' to be united with. This is the case with the Buddhist goal of nirvana.

But pure worship and pure meditation, while important, need to be seen in their contexts. God is worshipped not just because of his or her glory, but because he or she is supposed to hold the key to salvation – how the human soul graduates under God's guidance and or causation to a sublime condition in which he or she is in the holy presence of the Divine Being (BRANDON, 1980). But if God is saviour he or she is praised for more than his or her pure praiseworthiness. He or she is praised for being salvific. Also, as creator he or she is praised for the marvels of his or her creation (despite the pains and evils associated with life in this world). At any rate, God is praised for favours, and this means that we are no longer contemplating pure worship, which expresses deference and loyalty to God just because he or she is God.

Factors which reinforce pure worship and pure meditation are doctrines or philosophies which vivify the targets: for instance, the sense of the presence of the Divine Being or of the splendour or *mokṣa* over against the impermanence of the world. Experience is stimulative too – say, the experience of conversion or of the early stages of the mystic's progress. As we have noted, material entities can also be vital, through the creation of majesty and sublimity in icons, churches, mosques, images, temples, music and so on. By contrast the austerity of Protestant chapels and kirks is a reminder to the faithful of the auditory side of religion, of how the words of God are to be revered. In such ways various of the dimensions come in to vivify rites. We have also noted how simplicity and richness of ritual appear at different ends of the spectrum. Relative simplicity reflects, as in Islam, the sense that nothing stands between the worshipper and God, so there is no need of a priestly class.

Over the last two or three centuries, there has been in the West a diminution in the complexity of rituals. This is sometimes seen as a sign of secularization. There have been various factors at work. One was the Reformation itself, which set the scene for simplification, and in some cases the dismantling of the calendrical attention to a whole series of church festivals. Thus in Scotland even Christmas came to be viewed askance: festivals were popish and associated with a practical endorsement of the idea of salvation by works. Second, magic declined, as did mantric rites, partly because of advances in scientific thinking and their successful application. Non-mantric technology did a better job. Third, the early 1960s saw *aggiornamento* among Catholics accompanied by a simplification of ritual and greater directness of expression. Fourth, urbanization meant a demographic shake-up and with it desertion from traditional parishes and ways of life anchored in smaller agglomerations of people. Mobility is an enemy of old customs. The backlash against this breeds a neo-traditionalism (such as evangelical Christian revival), but you need emotion to glue together new faith-based communities, and so the emphasis shifts more to the experiential dimension and the phenomenon of being 'born again'. This neo-traditionalism tends to give a new role to scriptures.

Scriptures and ritual

In the traditions the tendency is for scriptures themselves to be used not just as a source of philosophical, mythic or other material, in other words as carrying authority as the word of God or as the record of the Master, but as a vital ingredient in rites (BRUCE and RUPP, 1968). Thus the Gospel is carried in procession at high-church ceremonies; the Adi Granth is the central 'icon' in Sikh gurdwaras; the Qur'an is as much an oral as a written document; and so on. The Jewish scriptures including the Talmud, a record as it were of the oral Torah, become new fields of ritual. Since the demise of the old Temple system the ancient rituals have been in effect carried on by study of the Torah, so that Torah study becomes an important part of the ritual life of the Jew (the Jewish man in particular). There is some resemblance here to the Confucian tradition, since the classics which the would-be sage studies also embody the ancient rituals and procedures, overlaid in K'ung's own teaching with the harmonious requirements of *li*. Sub-scriptures, including the *Mahābhārata*, also provide dramatic scripts, shaping performances which have an important role in the calendar of Hindus.

In Protestantism the Bible came to play an important part (which by and large it no longer does) in the domestic rituals of the faithful: households would gather to listen to daily readings from it. As we shall see in the discussion of the mythic dimension in Chapter 3, modernist critiques of scriptures, especially of the Christian Bible, have rather undermined the authoritativeness of scriptures, while the printing and translation of Hindu scriptures have removed them from control by Brahmins, which enhanced their sacrality. On the other hand the editing and translation of Buddhist scriptures, especially the Pali Canon, has greatly enhanced the vividness of Buddhist values and activity and has been a substantial ingredient in the modern Buddhist revival. Meanwhile the abolition of the imperial examination system in China in 1905 involved the removal of a central prop of traditional Confucianism. If there is something of a revival, in the 1970s and onward, of Confucianism it is due to scholarly effort and a reinterpretation of the classics, but in a very different milieu from that which prized the old idea of the sage. In societies without a previous written language the compilation of traditional myths, the written expression of new forms of religion and the numinous quality of sacred texts from incoming religions have changed the old dynamics of authority.

Sacred texts have often been used in a mantric manner or as ritual objects expressing certain values in the tradition. Sometimes the sacred text is identified with its subject. So in the Mahayana texts can take the place of relics of the Buddha; and in Nichiren Buddhism the Lotus Sutra becomes an object of faith and reverence on which the faithful can call in the hope of salvation.

Scriptures with a high mythic or narrative content naturally become scripts for calendrical performances. The Christian year is a case in point, combining the advantages of cyclical and one-way time. The story is one-way (all stories are), but it is recapitulated in a cyclical manner. The repetitiousness of ritual here is used to some advantage. In Chapter 3 on narrative and myth, we shall have occasion to discuss more extensively the whole notion of cyclical time in religion and worldview.

The sacred character of scriptures varies: in Theravada Buddhism it does not amount to much, at least in theory. The Buddha wanted his teachings understood, and no vast ritual. Om was supposed to lie behind Vedic texts (and later in the Mahayana and Vajrayana some of the characteristics of Hindu scriptures came to enter the fabric of piety). Some texts even so are used mantrically – in the ceremony of *pirit* which wards off evil. So we can see a continuum of relative sacredness, with the Theravadin texts near the bottom and Hindu ones near the top, in the way scriptures function ritually. A hyper-ritual interpretation of sacred texts was – as we have mentioned before – undertaken by the Mimamsaka school. The words are purely ritual, and contain nothing but injunctions on how to perform rites: it is a purely mantric view of texts, bypassing the gods and God. As a pure expression of priestly ideology it is interesting: Brahminical acts hereby become utterly self-sufficient. Spirituality, divine co-operation, moral improvement – none of these means anything within the sacred system (STAAL, 1983).

Ritual and the wider world of li

Religious and worldview rituals imperceptibly merge into the wider scope of *li* or appropriate behaviour both in daily life and on public occasions. Partly because of the suffusion of society by an ideology, many daily greetings and the like in many societies have a religious form, and activities such as swearing often express a traditionally religious culture. For these and other reasons it is not easy to draw a line round religious rituals. And secular worldviews create their own rituals, such as the use of proper Marxist language or of the Hitler salute. Any serious or solemn occasion takes on deep ritual aspects: the opening of a baseball game or soccer cup final; an opera performance; the start of the school year; the anniversary of the gaining of independence; the commemoration of the dead in battle; the sentencing of a prisoner; the installation of a president; a marriage; the naming of a child; the start of the new year; and so forth. On all such occasions inappropriate behaviour, like laughing at a commemoration of the dead, seems menacing and disruptive, almost blasphemous.

Yet too much formality in the inculcation of *li* perpetually breeds moves towards informality. This is reinforced in modern times by the vogue for democracy: leaders must not seem too distant; ordinary folk should have their say; traditions are subject to scrutiny and criticism. So it is that daily rituals change, though often what makes them change are themselves rituals. Thus, as we have noted, a new use of language (the word 'gay', particularly) creates a *li* which accommodates homosexuals as a respectable new category. The introduction of inclusive language, including modes of greeting, helps to install a *li* of gender equality.

These moves also have their religious counterparts, as the traditions seek to modernize their rituals and teachings, to adapt to the changing world. Even neo-traditionalism, though often conservative in relation to scripture, is highly innovative in organization and sometimes in rituals – for instance in the fashioning of new rituals for television.

Some conclusions about the ritual dimension

Some broad distinctions concerning ritual have been made. I have also emphasized varying ways in which the ritual dimension interlocks with other dimensions – for example, the way certain doctrines vivify the sense of the presence of God, which in turn helps to enliven prayer. As for the distinctions, I have noted two cores of ritual: pure praise or *bhakti*, involving humility before God; and pure contemplation, involving a series of steps towards the achievement of pure consciousness. I have noted the relation of shamanism to these modes. Moreover, the world of many gods and other beings has been explicated as involving the idea of devic causation, which makes sense of such rites as sacrifice (here the disappearance or modification of the offering is seen as a way of transferring its substance to the invisible world of the gods). Parallel to devic-causation theory is mantric causation, as I have called it, where a performance occurs which is meant to bring something about or ward off some evil independently of the gods or of God. Generally speaking, mantric causation is waning in the face of scientific and technological advancement, though it still has a role in uncontrollable and unpredictable situations. Generally too devic causation wanes in the face of theism, which has a more holistic view of cosmic processes. But the two theories can be combined through refracted theism, as with Hinduism, though a pale reflection of a similar scene is effected where saints and the like act as subsidiary beings under the one God.

We have noted that rituals are sometimes more ontologically conceived and sometimes more psychologically or instrumentally. Hence some rituals involve a transformation of substances or some manipulation of substances, while others are designed more to change the inner life of the person who performs the ritual. Rites of passage are seen as assisting primarily the transfer of some person or thing from one state to another, where the categories are important and contrasting: from being unmarried to being married; or from being alive in this world to existing somehow in the next or being an ancestor; and so on. We have also noted that many such rites involve the abolition of liminality, though liminality can on occasion give the being which is liminal special power and numinosity. We also noted how many rituals may be scripted by the myths or narratives of the tradition: such scripting becomes vivid and socially alive through the calendrical system, in which the year (for example) forms the framework for the cyclical celebration of the stories of the tradition. Similar remarks apply to secular worldview rituals, for instance in the re-enactment of key episodes in the history of the nation. The celebration of a past event can abolish time and also space. We noted too that more formal religious rituals may be diminished under modern conditions, for example by demographic mobility. And rituals of a traditionally religious kind have to be seen as belonging to the wider world of socially appropriate behaviour or *li* (SMART, 1958).

In general *li* is a necessity for human existence because courtesies and correct behaviour are in some measure a condition of being social at all. Given that some existential issues remain vital whatever the shape of human society, such as questions of birth, sex, hunger and death, there will always be some rites of deeper significance in human life. But, as we have seen, differing theories of the world – theism, devic causation and so forth – account for the traditional religious rituals which have characterized human history.

CHAPTER THREE

The Mythic or Narrative Dimension

The meaning of 'myth'

The term 'myth' has its use, though it can also lead people astray. It has become widely used in the history of religions and in other social sciences, so I continue to employ it (LANGER, 1957). It leads people astray in varying ways. An Encyclopedia of Mythology may well not include the main Christian stories, notably the life, death and resurrection of Christ (MCINTIRE, 1977). That is a leftover from Christian (and Jewish and Muslim, be it said) tendencies to treat their own stories as true and historical and other people's stories as unhistorical and untrue (JAMES, 1933). But all stories which involve the invisible, divine or sacred world are beyond being straight history. They are what I have elsewhere called 'parahistorical' (SMART, 1968). And apart from this point – which arises from the consideration that without the added invisible ingredient the history does not have its religious meaning – the historicity of quite a number of sacred stories is open to question under the scrutiny of modern historians. In any case, it is an *assumption* that an historically true story is better than one which is not. Does *Anna Karenina* suffer from being fictional, over against a biography of Brezhnev? Edward Conze once suggested to me that Mahayana Buddhism was superior to Christian faith because the stories of Bodhisattvas owed themselves to fertile spiritual imagination rather than to dull history as was the case of Jesus (Christianity's Bodhisattva). It is important to include historical and parahistorical stories in our inventory, however, for several reasons: first, so that differing religions may be treated equally – for scholars to use categories based on missionary ideas and apologetics is usually a mistake; and second, because histories have come to be the identity-supplying memories of modern ideologies, notably nationalism. The horsed Mannerheim adorns Helsinki not Rome, for obvious reasons.

There is a parallel to parahistory in Marxist history (MERKL and SMART, 1983): the dialectic plays an unseen role behind the scenes and unfolds a metaphysical pattern which gives the Marxist adherent both insight and hope. And so the ballet of forces and contradictions plays a role rather similar to that of God in theistic accounts of history.

We could if we wished simply refer to myths as stories. We would have to note that while all myths are stories, not all stories are myths. Jokes, for instance, are stories, and usually have an existential point – virtually all jokes are serious, save for a few pun-based ones and shaggy-dog stories. They deal with death, gender, sex, war and so forth. Religious jokes are an important category. Then there are other non-mythic stories: the interconnected stories in *The Scramble for Africa* (PAKENHAM, 1992) might become ingredients in other more mythic stories related to national identity, but we can take them at their face value as telling about various important sequences of events. The lines are hard to draw, though. Moreover, there are other stories, such as dramas and fictions, not to mention so-called fairy-stories, which may overlap in import with those tales which we recognize more centrally as religious myths (DUNDES, 1984). Biographies and autobiographies verge on myths too, for they bring a kind of order to lives, which helps to define identity.

Given this wider view of myths or sacred stories I do not think any one theory of myth will work (MARANDA, 1972). Certainly some notions appear simply false, for instance the idea that all myths deal with a special sort of time. Some do and some do not.

Why is the narrative dimension important?

It is characteristic of religions to have stories. On the whole they play a necessary role in the fabric of a tradition, though perhaps for differing reasons (BOMAN, 1960). One major reason is that memory of the collective past keeps it in being. And that sense of a collective past gives identity to a group, just as memory gives us individual humans an identity. Consider someone with Alzheimer's disease. Let us suppose that he has no memory and no real recognition of other people from his past. You might think this to be a blessed condition. After all, Zen adepts spend years training to live in the present. A Theravadin monk once explained to my wife that monks have glowing complexions because they live in the present. But the Alzheimer's sufferer is nonetheless regarded as a sufferer, for we think that without memory of who he is and who his dear friends and family are he has lost his identity: he is a body in an empty career, merely an outward successor to the person he once was. So memory is important to identity (but more needs to be said about the meaning of 'identity', to which I shall come). The same applies to a collective identity. A people or group becomes the more significant because it discovers or even invents its collective past. We do not think of random groups as significant: say an ice-cream van crashes and forty people in the street gather round it to contemplate the accident, and perhaps help the driver. Such a randomly assembled group has no particular significance. If they were to meet once a year to memorialize the event and engage in some common activities they would begin to acquire significance and an identity. The first thing to say about the narrative, therefore, is that it is part of the way in which identity is achieved. We are assuming in the case of a religious tradition that the group engages together (not necessarily congregational, however) in sacred activities – going to the temple, addressing the god, indulging in street festivals, initiating their daughters and sons, marrying according to certain rites, sharing certain books as important, having a collective ethos and so on. The stories of the gods help to shape the past, and to throw light on the way the group sees itself (GUSDORF, 1953; LÉVI-STRAUSS, 1964).

We have noted in Chapter 2 on ritual that gods have not only bodies but, in their own way, biographies. The bodies are often manifested natural phenomena. The biographies come through congeries of stories about them – the stories about Indra, for instance, or about Lao-tzu.

So narratives are important because they help to define both groups and sacred entities and persons. But we need to be a bit clearer about 'identity'. What does it mean in the case of persons and groups? I would say it means two things. First, it affirms continuity, which gives a group greater importance since it is no longer seen as a random collection of persons, like the gathering of spectators after the crash of the ice-cream van. Second, by implication the person connects to aspects of her past which she values. Even disasters are often good news in retrospect since they testify that the person has overcome them: one can take pleasure from an old wound. In other words, an autobiography (scripted of course by oneself) can affirm certain achievements and values. It enhances dignity.

But apart from these very basic observations about narratives we may note a number of functions of stories in the religious and secular worldview context.

Some functions of narratives in the religious context

As already noted, one function of stories is to serve as the script for ritual action: the story of the Last Supper, the Exodus from Egypt, the Christmas story, the story of Demeter and Persephone, the death of Husayn at Karbala, the myth of Isis and Osiris, and so on. But the character of the ritual actions varies widely, and this 'script' function overlaps with others (PETTAZZONI, 1954).

Another function is to explain origins, whether of the cosmos as we now know it, or of certain features of human society, or of death and other problematic features of human life, or of the immediate environment. Such myths may gear into others which depict the way of salvation or of overcoming problems.

A further area of mythic thinking is in regard to the Last Things – stories which depict how things will be at the finish of the world as we know it. This may well go with a framework which tells of different ages of the world. The whole sequence from origins to last things represents a kind of salvation and damnation history depicting the fates of those who please and alienate the God (PETTAZZONI, 1948–59).

Myths may also depict how God acts in order to deal with humanity, by for instance becoming a human incarnation. A number of these themes are summed up in the stories of the incarnations of Viṣṇu (DIMMITT and VAN BUITENEN, 1978). Thus in his first appearance Viṣṇu takes the form of a huge fish who saves the first human being when the latter is being overwhelmed in a cosmic deluge at the beginning of history. He tells Manu Vaivasvata to gather the seeds of all living beings and transports both them and him to safety. Here we can see chaos represented by the waters: God is the being who brings order to a cosmos threatened by turbulence. Next, the kidnapped Pṛthivi, or the earth, is plunged into the waters of chaos (again) by a demon; God as the boar rescues her after overcoming the demon and, placing her on his vast tusk, raises her above the waters.

In the third *avatāra* Viṣṇu is a giant tortoise. The gods and demons are trying to use Mount Meru, the *axis mundi*, to churn the waters of the great ocean in order to extract the nectar of everlasting life. Viṣṇu provides himself as a foundation on which to rest the churning stick. So far there is a theme of order and stability in these stories.

In the fourth incarnation Viṣṇu is a betwixt-and-between figure, a man–lion. He defends Prahlada, a faithful follower, from his oppressive and demonic father Hiranyakasipu. The latter is supposed to be incapable of harm from human or beast, but Viṣṇu eludes the categories by being both.

The next incarnation continues the theme of the conflict between good and evil. Bali, a member of the asuras or counter-gods, has come to dominate the world. Viṣṇu appears as a dwarf and asks for the favour of taking over that which he could cover with three strides. Miraculously he covers the whole cosmos, which he then gives back to the gods.

The sixth incarnation is as Parasu Rama or Rama of the Axe, in which form he fights against the *kṣatriyas* or warrior class, who are stuck up and have wrongly established dominance over the Brahmins. Humbled by Viṣṇu they have to yield the superiority in society to the Brahmins. Here Viṣṇu establishes order in the human hierarchy.

The seventh *avatāra* is as Rama, who of course became the central figure in the great epic, the *Rāmāyaṇa*. Rama is the ideal king; after many vicissitudes he defeats the evil Ravana, who dominates the world, and establishes a reign of peace and justice.

A not dissimilar theme pervades the story of Krsna, who is an important figure in the other great epic, the *Mahābhārata*, and who struggles against the evil Kamsa. He also assists in the civil war between the Pandavas and the Kauravas. But there are many other facets of his story, especially his adventures as a young person in Brindavan, including his numerous amorous exploits, spiritualized as expressing the love of God towards human souls (symbolized by the cowherds or *gopis*).

The most paradoxical of Viṣṇu's incarnations is his appearance as the Buddha. Mostly his function is to delude those who deserve to suffer because of their evil deeds and ignorance. By preaching the Buddhist methods he seduces them into renouncing the Vedas and orthodox Brahminical tradition. On a brighter note, he teaches non-violence, itself a partly incongruent motif in a general Hindu tradition which incorporates the necessity of force and warfare.

Finally Viṣṇu will come in the future as Kalki. On his white steed he will punish the evil and reward the virtuous, bringing this whole phase of human history to an end (GONDA, 1954).

It can be seen that there are a number of general mythic motifs woven into this collection of stories. There is the first human; there is the flood and Noah motif (in that Manu in effect saves all living things). There is the motif of cosmic stability and the possibility of immortality. There is the theme of overcoming evil, mysteriously as always entering or infecting the universe. There is the trickster or betwixt-and-between motif. There is the theme, important in the later tradition and in ritual, of the three steps to cover the cosmos. There is the notion that order implies the *varṇa* system, which introduces the hierarchical cosmos. There is the theme of the ideal monarch, and that of the spirited lover and the importance of love in the world. There is the deceptiveness of the Divine Being in dealing with wicked creatures. And there is the consummation of history and the victory ultimately of good over evil.

To all this we may add that earlier myths incorporate symbolic themes. So it is important for us to contemplate them not just as stories but as presenting themes (JUNG and KERENYI, 1969). It is probably this symbolic aspect of mythology which makes it fascinating to people in today's world, even where myths are eclectically considered rather than established authoritatively within a modern society.

The authority of narrative in traditional and modern culture

Typically myths can be considered to be relative to a given group or tradition. That is, they are the authoritative stories of such entities. They are recited as part of traditional lore, and in this way have a breathless authority, as I shall figuratively call it. The stories in this category are foundational for the group in question. This is easiest to achieve in relatively small-scale societies, but large-scale traditions are also capable of surrounding a sufficient segment of the population to give their proclaimed narratives unquestioned authority within that segment.

While critiques of myths are not unknown even in ancient societies, as witness parts of the early Indian heritage (*Upaniṣads* and Buddhism) and the writings of Xenophanes as well as a gentle scepticism in the mood of K'ung (Confucius), the modern period has introduced new dynamics in the treatment of traditionally authoritative stories (VRIES, 1977). For one thing, there is the growth, mainly in the nineteenth and twentieth centuries, of critical scholarship about scriptures, particularly the Bible, both Jewish and Christian, which itself powerfully helps to generate liberal forms of Judaism and Christianity. For another thing, the comparative study of religion has burgeoned in the same period, leading towards a certain anthologization of narratives, which gives the 'consumer' of myth choices which are quite different from traditional ones (BOLLE, 1968). Third, there are notable depth-psychological and other theories about myth and its symbolic themes, which create quite a new way of regarding the spiritual vitality of myth. Fourth, as we have noticed, other narratives have come in to replace to some extent or at least to supplement traditional stories: most notably histories of nations and of the world, which create new perspectives and new memories. Fifth, some of the pervasive convictions as to the reality of the metaphysical or unseen component in myths are less convincing in modern times than they used to be. And so there is less certitude in the approach to myths even of one's own tradition. Sixth, the pluralism of modern societies takes away some of the normalcy and persuasiveness of the myths of a once dominant religious culture. For all these and other reasons there is in recent times a fading of the 'natural' conviction of the once-authoritative narratives.

This may lead to certain changes in the way beliefs are held. Often certitude is supplied by emotional experience. That is, people may believe a myth because they have been 'born again' – converted to the faith of which the myth is part. We shall return to this theme later in discussing the experiential or emotional dimension. There may be a drive by some groups to create their own societies within society at large: part of this may be the setting up of separate schools. Groups seek to restore control over their symbols (CHIDESTER, 1991). But this often has to take the form of schools confined to their own group within the wider frontiers of a society which is up to a point pluralistic. In brief, attempts are sometimes made to create non-pluralistic societies within wider society.

The worry of challenge to one's received myths can help to explain some phenomena of persecution. It was a factor in the persistence of European anti-Semitism. Once the Church in the West had established control over the symbols of virtually a whole civilization, it nevertheless felt in some manner threatened by the continued persistence of the Jews within the fabric of Western culture. Did they not, by their very existence, supply a challenge to the absolute normality and authority of the dominant Christian myth? This epistemology, carried on in a differing way by Luther and other Reformers, laid down the absolute obviousness of the truth of the myth, given too the revealed character of the Bible, both Old and New Testaments. But the Jews did not regard the myth as interpreted and extended by Christians to be at all obvious. It was easy to accuse them (still given the epistemology) of being wilfully blind.

It is also worth noting that it is only a restricted part of belief which was thought to be capable of rational defence or, more strongly,

proof. That God exists and is Creator of the cosmos were proposi-
tions thought by natural theology to be capable of demonstration. But
the greater part of the mythic content of belief has to be taken on
faith.

Of course, it may be countered that where a significant component
of myth is historical, we simply have to accept that part at any rate as
something like a 'brute fact'. Caesar crossed the Rubicon: we can
hardly reject this claim, so well fortified by historical evidence. This
sort of sentiment may lie behind recent trends towards 'hardening' up
myths by supposing them in suitable cases to refer to historical times
and places, as with the supposed historical connection of Rama with
Ayodhya.

All this seems to indicate that we are moving out of the age of what
may be called 'fanciful' myth into that of 'factual' myth. I do not mean
by this that the more fanciful myths have not been believed in some
sense to be factual: describing reality. But now there is a more earth-
bound understanding of what is factual. So Adam and Eve have to be
real persons: or if they are not they have to be symbolic representations of a real human condition that can be described metaphysically
or existentially. This shift can be illustrated by what I call 'slitting the
fish of history'. Consider the Crucifixion: according to the story
Christ died for our sins. Now few historians doubt that Jesus died on
a cross. But from a parahistorical perspective Jesus is identified with
the Christ; and his death is seen as an atonement for the sins of
humanity ultimately deriving from Adam and Eve. Christ is the
second Adam: a whole shoal of symbolic fishes swim around him. So
all this is summed up in our original formula: and yet modern folk
latch on to the historical fact, namely that Jesus was crucified, and
separately give it a transcendental or metaphysical significance. By
separating significance from mere actuality we tend to slit the fish of
history. I am not saying this is right (or wrong): but I am observing the
nisus of modern thinking. Similar events of understanding occur or
are likely in due course to occur outside the Christian tradition. So
two directions are being taken: on the one hand myth becomes
history; on the other hand myth is being slit between history and
doctrine. This reinforces then the drift from history to metaphysics;
and indeed the drift from myth to metaphysics. It is not a coincidence

that Teilhard de Chardin became so popular: he produced a meta-physical history culminating in wonderful things – and so produced a new more deeply felt and philosophically attractive (as his devotees might have thought) eschatology.

But let us leave these abstractions for the time being and turn to the vital themes of myths – or at least a few of them; for we could not hope to produce here an inventory of them all. Let us begin with the themes of space: this is surely basic enough.

The themes of space

Recent writings in the field of religious studies have been keen to look on the symbolism of space. Let us here begin with the most basic one, that of height.

It is quite obvious that height plays an amazingly large part in the symbolism of value, just for a start. We use height unthinkingly: high value; high price; high office; high reputation; high score; the meta-phor of height is pervasive. And what about low value: low price; low official; low reputation; low score? We have the High God, and 'Praise to the holiest in the height' from Cardinal Newman. God tends to be 'up there' and heaven is of course above us, not below us. It is true that occasionally the depths do not do badly: deep thought, deep feelings and so forth are usually well regarded. Tillich went for depth; but you do not see churches built with depth. Usually the spire soars upwards, a signal that God is up there.

Consequently a number of African myths postulate that originally the sky, where God dwells, was low down and so God and the human race were not distant. But because of some wickedness or error or trickery God withdrew upwards and the gap between humans and God became greater. We may note that space enters into our symbolism of friendship – being close, being intimate and so on. Distance is implied in the symbolism of the Other, and dualism (that is distance and difference) between God and humanity is an impor-tant theme in all theistic religions.

Height is important symbolically in other ways. Since God is often pictured as 'up there' it follows that the sky becomes the symbol of heaven: where God is, but also replete with joys for lesser beings. We find heavens in a large number of cultures. Also salvation is sometimes conceived as rising to the top of the cosmos as in Jainism. But in Buddhist mystical practices too, as well as many others, the life of contemplation involves rising upward in a series of levels or steps: eventually you will get to the summit of consciousness and with luck will attain liberation. Not surprisingly the saint in Jainism rests motionless at the top of the universe as a liberated soul, not capable of further movement and not indeed able to communicate with or be communicated with by beings in the rest of the cosmic community. Anyway the symbol of heaven is almost universal, and points to the desires of human beings to reach the highest goal, the top, the supreme (and so on with more spatial metaphors).

You are not likely, faced with the upper realms, to prefer the lower ones. Of course, Earth is fecund, and there are lots of themes concerning the low ones, even if they are not hellish. More appositely for the moment, let us note some other sub-themes. One has to do with sky-gods. They are vital because they are up there, but not too distant. Mostly sky-gods are male; but the Japanese have a major activator, called Amaterasu, the goddess of the Sun and ancestress of the Imperial Family.

Another theme is that one might wish to approach the Deity. Hence the popularity in the Ancient Near East of being a pilgrim to Babylon, where a high temple could let the emperor, himself regarded as high, ascend to be 'near' the God. Similar ziggurats (so to say) are found in Aztec Mexico (and in Mayan areas to the south). There walking up steep, steep steps, others than the king could reach the top of the sacred structure and so make offerings to the God or Goddess. So there are plenty of cases where the temple structure emphasizes approach and access. All this, again, involves the symbolism of height.

Height goes with size. This again is a common theme, especially as it happens in Buddhist countries, where very large statues show the spiritual greatness of the Buddha. Though households can entertain small stupas and tiny Buddha statues, on the whole huge size is a recurrent theme of Buddhist iconography in Sri Lanka (and elsewhere).

Apart from height, centrality is another vital theme, about which there are disturbing modern implications. The centre may be conceived as the *axis mundi* around which turns the cosmos, or perhaps just the sky. It is often located at a sacred or ritual centre, such as the ancient Chinese model of the city as described by Wheaton (1971), or Jerusalem. But modern cosmology gets away from the notion that any particular place is the centre of the universe. Relatively speaking, every place is equal. This breaks up traditional pictures and casts doubt on claims to unique centrality. It is disturbing for Christians, for instance, who have seen Christ's life as being at the centre.

Usually centrality is relative to a division of space on the basis of directions from the centre: either the four conventional ones of East, South, West and North, or these plus Upwards and Downwards. Most societies are in the northern hemisphere, where North and South have special meanings: for instance North points towards the polestar. East is everywhere perceived as where the sun rises, the sun being the potent source of warmth and growth on earth. The West is reposeful, where the sun sinks, and so is sometimes identified with the life after death.

The notion of the Centre of the World is also the notion of the place where the diverse parts of the universe are in communication with one another. The *axis mundi* is depicted in varying ways, as a pole or a tree or a sacred mountain, for instance. Rituals conducted there have special communicative powers; moreover, the place where powerful rituals arc conducted may itself be seen as the centre. In short, it is the communicative ritual which confers centrality. In Tantric Yoga this idea is internalized, so that the centre lies within the yogi's body. But while the axis symbolism works with a certain cosmology, that of a flat earth, with the axis penetrating it like the upright part of a top, it hardly works with the post-Copernican imagery of the spherical earth. Of course, for quite a time astronomers continued to think of the solar system as somehow central to the universe. But even this vision has faded.

Many visions of our immediate earth environment suggest that there is a series of heavens rising above us and a series of underworlds or hells beneath us. The heavens are, as in Buddhist cosmology, sometimes matched with stages of progression in the hierarchy of meditation. There are corresponding levels of gods, while beneath there is a match between depth and severity of punishment or suffering.

More generally, as we have noted before, sacred space is actually rather bumpy, for differing places have differing degrees of potency or sacred power. Such bumpiness applies too to secular potency, so that a nation has differing degrees of sacrality in differing places. So the capital becomes the most potent place, since so much national power emanates from there. But there are other sacred locations: in Britain for instance central London is most potent, but Stratford too is vital, as are various other locations, including certain mountains, battlefields and cathedrals. In the United States there is most potently Washington DC, but also the Statue of Liberty, Mount Rushmore, Gettysburg and so on. Peoria and downtown Los Angeles are less sacred.

Transcendence and transcending space

Another important aspect of the figuration of space has to do with transcendence, which has a quasi-spatial significance (SMART, 1983). It is also an important point of intersection between doctrinal and mythic notions. There are two vital applications of the idea of transcendence. One has to do with God, and the other with liberation. God is not always thought of explicitly as transcending the universe (the primary meaning of 'transcendence'). Some kinds of piety and traditional thinking are vague on this front: God is 'up there', but where? In most religions which have time for God, he or she is regarded, however, as transcendent. That is, he or she is beyond the cosmos. But what does this mean? After all, in most cosmologies the universe and space are coterminous. Whether the cosmos is looked on as finite or as infinite (or as ineffably neither this nor that, as in Buddhism), God – existing outside the universe – is outside space. But 'outside' is itself a spatial word; so are the alternatives, such as 'beyond' or 'behind.'

Consequently these expressions are analogical or metaphorical: in other words, they are not meant in a literal way. The very word 'transcendent' is after all only Latin for 'going beyond'. 'Immanent', the term often used as an opposite, is really nothing of the kind, mainly because it only means 'being inside'. Being within is equally analogical or metaphorical. Cut open a bit of cheese and you do not see God. God is not literally within everything; but she is no doubt (if she exists) metaphorically. Now when 'within' and 'outside' (the cosmos) are both analogical 'places', who is to tell whether they are different? In most respects they are the same (though there is one implication of being within that I want to come back to, for it implies a small distinction from transcendence).

In saying that God is transcendent we are using analogical metaphors or whatever to depict where God is. It is obvious that being outside space is not being in a bit of space. It is being non-spatial. But there is also the implication that God is 'behind' this world. This metaphor suggests that she is the creator and conserver: keeping things going from behind.

There are, however, other resonances of 'behindness'. It suggests that the cosmos is a kind of screen, behind which God is found. He is invisible, holy, occasionally intervening in certain ways to make himself visible and present to humans. The metaphor of the screen ties in with the notion of the numinous and the idea of the holy. As an expression of holiness, the Divine Being is concealed, yet of course powerful, not easily seen, but emanating a *mysterium tremendum*. He is moreover other than the cosmos, other than human beings. He may reside within the cosmos and be the soul of souls within humans (the Spirit perhaps, but religions other than Christianity in taking up the same idea have differing ways of expressing it), but he is still apart from our world. Present she is also absent, like a dreaming bride.

And so behindness suggests two things at least: that God is a numinous, mysterious Being behind everything, concealed by the cosmos, though not totally, and that she is also operative behind the cosmos, keeping it going.

Now the basic difference between transcendence and immanence in this sense whereby God is 'within' all things is that immanence implies a lot of beings or the cosmos to be within: God as transcendent might exist – would exist – even if the cosmos did not. William Temple used the formulae: God minus the cosmos equals God, but the cosmos minus God equals nothing. That helps to express a central notion usually contained in the idea of transcendence in the theistic context. So, putting matters very crudely, transcendence encapsulates the idea of creation; immanence does not. But apart from this the two ideas amount to the same thing. Why should different analogical directions point in differing ways?

In brief: God is supposed to be non-spatial, creative and numinous.

But as I have already stated, transcendence can have a lesser meaning, though highly important for all that. This concerns the non-theistic religions. I am thinking here of notions such as nirvana. In nirvana you are beyond the cosmos. Or rather 'you' have disappeared but what supervenes on that individual conventionally called Gunapala is beyond the round of rebirth and of worldly constitutions. Nirvana is outside the round of rebirth. It is a state beyond states, ineffable, but outside the known network of ordinary causation. So once again we have the notion of non-spatiality. Nirvana, however, is not causative and 'behind'. It is not numinous either. Nonetheless, it does represent a condition which is not of this world. (Things in the Mahayana need somewhat differing analysis.) At any rate, the notion of transcendence in such systems as the Theravada does differ from theistic transcendence, which has another context altogether.

Sometimes there is a kind of inward transcendence, as in much orthodox Hindu philosophy where the soul or *ātman* or *puruṣa* is seen as lying 'beyond' the empirical changes going on in the self. Everything in the individual other than the soul or self is thought of as material, though made for the most part from 'subtle' matter rather than from gross matter which makes up things, including the individual body. So impulses, feelings and the senses are of this world, but the eternal and unchanging soul belongs to the world beyond. In this way there is a deep inwardness which corresponds to transcendence and indeed immanence (SMART, 1958).

To sum up: the important notions of transcendence and immanence often amount to the same thing, though 'immanence' does not quite in the same way imply the creative and supportive aspects of the Divine Being which 'transcendence' does. But these are two different analogical directions which may turn out to be the same direction. We may add two points. First, nirvana's transcendence has to be interpreted differently from divine transcendence, since nirvana in the Theravada does not have any creative or supportive context. Second, it should be realized that some Christian theological writers use 'immanence' in a less austere sense than that which we have here depicted. They mean that God is immanent when manifesting herself or himself in this world in a special way. So a secondary sense of immanence refers to the particular acts of Divine Being. This obviously has a different significance from the more basic and metaphysical sense of the term.

There are other spatial flavours to the two terms, for there is the psychologically or phenomenologically vital distinction between the notions of far and near. We have already noted here and there that some cultures emphasize the way God distances himself from humanity during the 'first days', when some indiscretion or disobedience by the first humans causes him to withdraw from their presence or propinquity and so become 'distant'. This idea links to the sense that God is numinous and Other. Yet, as in the *Īśa Upaniṣad*, he is both far and near.

Nearness has two applications. In one (that intended by the *Īśa*) it involves God being *within*, because identical with or present within the self or soul. This is a common theme of mystical religions. The other sense is that God is present to us. That is, he or she is present within the world around us as its preserver or continuous Creator. In other words even when there are no literal indications God is always present through his or her creative activity.

This notion of the continuous presence of God (I am speaking of theistic systems of belief) helps to underpin the modes through which the Divine evidences herself in the world through hierophanies or theophanies. Such events of divine manifestation form part of the fabric of myth, the stories of God which give him 'body' in history. For the rest, it links in with the notion of 'experiencing the world as' (to use Hick's phrase, going back to 'seeing as', in Wisdom's celebrated article) (HICK, 1979). In other words, we perceive the world as divinely made, preserved and animated. This is itself a mode of what I have called 'superimposition'.

The metaphysical space of the transcendent and of the immanent is an important ingredient in the understanding of many theisms and other systems. It also helps to show ways in which scientific and religious thinking differ, for science deals exclusively with what lies 'within' the cosmos. It does not go outside, to use a metaphor. On the other hand, religion tends to have a transcendental or metaphysical reference point. This is figured as belonging to a kind of hyperspace. Not all worldviews make a sharp distinction, however, between such a hyperspace and space, and there is always this floating in-between – the space or quasi-space, vaguely conceived, where the gods are. It is in some Olympian location, but no one has been there. It is the *illud spatium* corresponding to *illud tempus* (ELIADE, 1958). But as thought develops there is a drift towards a differentiation between metaphysical hyperspace and ordinary space, and this is what lies behind the notions of the transcendent and the immanent, as I have explicated them above.

A few remarks on illud tempus *and time in general*

It is sometimes remarked that time is viewed as cyclical in many cultures. People are often gripped by Eliade's *Cosmos and History* (ELIADE, 1959a) and the construction of a cyclical view of time.

Strictly speaking it is not, in certain cultures, that *time* repeats itself but that change does. Let us take a simple example. The sun rises every morning and we determine what the day is by this repetitiousness of the sun. We divide time by repeating days, months and years. But it does not follow from this that 20 October, 1992 will repeat itself. Conventionally of course 20 October will repeat itself, because that is how we have rigged our calendar. So some cultures hold that certain changes will repeat themselves – for instance, that every so often the universe and its creator Visnu will go to sleep (as in the Indian case).

However, something else does occur, as we have already had occasion to point out. Ritual can cause a kind of time travel, making an event in past time really present today. For instance, the resurrection of Christ is made present at Easter through the ritual process (including the preaching process). Strictly this is a cyclical representation of an event.

There is here a figuring in action of an important notion in many religions: namely, the manifestation of the timeless through the temporal. 'Timeless' here has to be taken a bit loosely, since the Divine Being may be seen as everlasting rather than strictly outside time – that is, going on for ever rather than being 'all at once' or *totum simul.*

There is also that betwixt-and-between concept which Eliade dubs *illud tempus.* This is a time which is not clocked, a dream time (to borrow the Australian native notion): it is the 'Once upon a time' of many folk tales.

The relative quality of time varies. As with space, time can be bumpy, some events being more sacred than others. This can be re-manifested calendrically: the year will exhibit more or less holy days and periods. This is pretty well universal among annual-calendrical societies, even if there were determined attempts in some areas of the Protestant revolution, such as Scotland, to wipe out the ritually differentiated year (though Sundays remained holy days, abstinence from secular activities being reinforced). Some modern societies have rather 'flattened' the year, since much work may be done on Sundays, stores will remain open on holidays, and so on. But at the same time the year's bumpiness may be enhanced by national holidays of a non-traditionally religious nature such as Memorial Day and Thanksgiving (which yet has traditionally religious overtones).

But there are wider ways in which the quality of time exhibits variations. Many worldviews incorporate some idea of degeneration, since they look back to a golden age from which things degenerated suddenly, as in the Jewish and Christian traditions. After this there may be improvements, with divine intervention helping the world in varying ways. Or it may be just transcendental intervention, as in the case of the Buddha or the Jina. So history has a rhythm of renewal when its quality is 'jacked up' by intervention, only of course to continue on its downward path. There is a bit of eschatology of course with Kalki and Maitreya to consider, or the T'ai-ping harmony of the future in Chinese thought. There is also creative use made, both in Chinese and more especially in Japanese Buddhism, of the concept of degeneration. History since the Buddha was usually divided into three periods: 500 years of the True Dharma (sometimes reckoned as 1000 years); 500, or sometimes 1000 years, of the

Counterfeit Dharma; and then the period of the Latter Days of the Law (Jap. *mappō*, Chin. *mofa*). This third period is normally calculated at 10,000 years, in the course of which the more regular forms of Buddhism no longer function. This is because only the teachings remain, and they are not heeded, the Sangha is degenerate, and no one attains enlightenment. In such an age salvation is possible, but under a newly conceived dispensation: it is the great era of faith, as all are afflicted by defilement and yet can, by calling on the Buddha, gain rebirth in the Pure Land and so on (TAKEUCHI, 1983).

But while Hinduism and Buddhism think of the world as running down in each age, with injections of goodness and truth by avatars and teachers, the Western religions are more optimistic. After all, God makes a covenant with the Jews and before that with the human race, although modern theologians of the Holocaust cannot really give the covenant an optimistic cast. In the Christian tradition God spoke through the prophets and produced the Son to restore good relations between humans and the Divine. The Church will lead people on until the second coming, which will be a dramatic consummation of history, though not without its black side. At any rate, the direction of historical change is not seen as degenerative. Similarly Islam has retained an optimistic attitude, even if over the last 300 or 400 years some depression has set in because of the bad state of Islam after the Western conquest of most Islamic lands, which theoretically should not have happened.

An optimistic view of temporal quality was also characteristic of the main periods of European, Asian and African nationalism. The attainment of national liberty itself became a most powerful expression of secular eschatology. After freedom was attained, things would greatly improve. Sometimes such eschatology was reinforced with that inherent in Marxist socialism, which gives an intense eschatological role to the revolution. This was an added reason for the popularity of Marxist ideas among nationalists, especially in the Third World – that is, it was additional to the advantage already cited, that on the principle that one's enemy's enemy is one's friend (a most unsafe principle as it happens) Marxism was a good modern theory to adopt since it was against both colonialism and capitalism. The combination of nationalism and Marx could thus express a very strong eschatology and sense of national salvation. This was no doubt helped by the ambiguity of the concept of 'the people'. It ought to mean the proletariat plus favourable members of the bourgeoisie, but almost inevitably it was identified with the Romanian or Polish or Chinese people – in other words an aspect of the national entity. In this way socialism could be looked on as national, rather than transnational.

Not all issues about time are to do with history, though it is with history and quasi-historical myth that we have here chiefly been concerned. There is also the question of time as dissolver of persons and things, because it is accompanied by a great flux of events. The notion that the world is impermanent is a central item in the Buddhist perception of the cosmos. It is the heart of Buddhist analysis of the world, and it does away with persisting substances, selves and divine beings. Even the longest-lived congeries of states ultimately comes apart. Even living in heaven or hell, usually no short matter, in due course finishes, dissolved by the impermanence in the very fabric of the cosmos. But the theme of impermanence is not absent from theistic religions, which mostly look on the Divine Being as everlasting or timeless and usually (though not always) as changeless.

The timeless or everlasting quality of God contrasts with the impermanence of the world. As the hymn-writer has it, 'Change and decay in all around I see.' Just as nirvana is by contrast eternal, timeless, deathless, so by contrast the crumbling world, always menaced by death, stands under and over against the shining immortality of the Creator. This of course abuts on a closely connected theme in myth and symbolism: death.

Different ways of looking on death

Let us begin with Buddhist attitudes, since they pose some interesting questions to Western and other conceptions of the span of life. South Asian thought usually envisages rebirth or redeath as the norm, so in that region of the world death has less of a final import than in the West. Yet its destructive and menacing power is not at all underplayed. A Buddhist meditation envisages the adept as seated in a charnel-ground, where dead people are either incinerated or exposed for wild animals to devour. Sitting amid the gruesome evidence of death gives the meditator a sense of impermanence and decay which is highly existential. The power of death is personalized as the mythic figure of Mara. It is interesting that Buddhism thus incorporates two rather different ways of analysing death. Doctrinally it sees decay as inherent in the 'glued-together' nature of the individual. Differing factors or events, from bodily events through to conscious states, when woven or stuck together constitute the individual, but they are inherently likely sooner or later to come apart. That is the 'metaphysical' description of death. But there is in Mara the Death-maker, the Satan of the Buddhist tradition, a mythic way of looking on death (LING, 1962). Mara not only deals death; he is by the same token the tempter, for had the Buddha yielded to temptation, and Mara sorely tried him, he would not have overcome death and provided the possibilty of liberation, beyond death. That 'beyond' is of course no ordinary beyond. The saint or *arhat* who attains nirvana is neither correctly described as surviving death, nor as not surviving, nor as both nor as neither. Nirvana is neither spatial nor time-bound. Buddhism, then, has two alternative ways of depicting death. It also has its own demythologization method (LING, 1962).

The theme of rebirth encompasses too the theme of everlasting life, not in that heavenly and glorious context which is wielded in the West, but rather in the sense that never-ending life is not a blessing. I sometimes get students to think about the disasters of both finitude and its opposite by imagining a wager with the Devil in which he promises you that if you are good, which is to say bad, he will give you a million years' life. Would I not be tempted? But after 20,000 marriages and as many careers, would I not be wearied? A similar theme is sometimes met with in Indian myth. There is also creative use made of the repetitiousness: a column of ants is figured to be all the Indras that have been (ZIMMER, 1972).

We may note that on the whole the theme of everlasting redeath forces ultimate liberation out of the universe. It is thus one of the seeds of the idea of the transcendent soul: for, if it be the soul or self which persists in the 'beyond', that beyond is somehow on a different plane from the world of rebirth, however heavenly and refined it can get. It is therefore a seed of the different division of materiality from the spiritual in the Indian tradition in contrast to the Western notion of the division of mind (or soul) and body. But not all liberation is thus transcendental and metaphysically refined: there is dwelling with Visnu in his heaven; or in the Pure Land, this side of the portals of nirvana.

In the notion of a world of the ancestors we have a differing image of death from that of rebirth *per se*. The idea is, somewhat inconsistently, not absent from the Brahmanical tradition. But the vivid conception of a body of ancestors makes death more of a transition from one state of life to another. It adds one or two more stages to the career of the individual. So he or she will enter on to the state of being a member of the living dead. After that he or she may graduate to an obscure, limbo-ish state beyond, when their memories have faded in present society. In any case, if death be a line, it is a frontier crossed by society, which retains its intercourse with those who are newly dead and who may help society.

The Western religions have a certain ambivalence about the afterlife, since they incorporate both the idea of the eternal soul, destined (it is to be hoped) for heaven, and that of the resurrected person, who will rise to meet the final judgment. To some degree the image of rising from the dead has affected ritual, since on the whole cremation was not permitted in Orthodox or mainline Christian traditions. The body needs some sort of preservation if it is to be able to rise.

Despite my earlier image of going on living and living, putting off death as long as possible is also an aim, especially vital in the Chinese tradition. This is the basis of varying techniques, including alchemy, for the prolongation of life. It may be noted that the Indian term for medicine is Ayurveda, or the science of long life. Alchemical techniques are especially prominent in religious Taoism.

Death and sleep are for obvious reasons often paired. Yet sleep is also a potent cause of life, for it is the time when men and women have dreams, a source of knowledge about the gods. We shall return to this theme. Meanwhile something also about time needs discussion, namely God's time, or lack of it.

Time and God

We have already noted that sometimes the gods are depicted as timeless, in a *totum simul* manner. But often they are simply described as immortal, that is deathless and without end. From this perspective death is an evil, from which the God does not suffer. It is often considered the defining characteristic of a god. Here a god is not typically Creator, but a kind of rank. Gods are of course more powerful than humans – they embody great forces and entities, from sun and moon through thunder to rivers and the ocean. These aspects of nature are highly potent, so it is also reasonable to think of the gods as more powerful than puny individuals (though in these latter days they might have been greatly impressed by humans working together and letting off H-bombs). It is thus *hybris* for a person to claim to be the equal of a god. So death is the lot of humans but not of the gods (except of course in Buddhism, where the gods eventually peter out and are reborn). But the *totum simul* model, though liked by metaphysicians and theologians, looking on God as impassible, that is as incapable of suffering change, does not fit with the mythic model, which gives God's biography and so implies change. This is the main basis in modern times for those who want to see God as changing (most prominent in the so-called process theology, often linked to Whitehead's rather Buddhistic philosophy). It seems logical enough to suppose that God not only undergoes change but actually suffers too. In Christian terms this is because of love, and similar themes are found in other theisms (Jewish, Hindu, Islamic). The idea is especially vital in Christianity, because a main mythic theme is how God as Christ, out of love, suffers on the cross for the sake of human beings. If God loves, she surely suffers when loved ones suffer. There is little logic in a loving God who can experience no change, for suffering is itself a change (SMART and KONSTANTINE, 1993). Yet the concept of God being outside time also has its powerful reasons. If outside space then also outside time. One solution to the problem of the disjunction between the metaphysical outside-time God and the changing God of the mythic dimension is to hold, as various religions and philosophers do, that God has two aspects. One is non-personal timeless without qualities or *guṇas* and the other is Lord, personal, changeable and so forth. There is still a problem of the fissure between the two levels, which is one story above the fissure between the world and the metaphysical God. But it is a picture which is common enough and helps to reconcile various differing drives in the logic of religion.

To sleep: to dream

Time brought us to the thought of death, and death is sister of sleep, the milieu of dreams. We shall deal with this theme further in Chapter 4 on the experiential dimension. But it needs noting that dreams have important mythic and ritual meanings – partly because some narratives derive from dreams, since they are based on wide or prophetic dreamers' visionary interpretations, and partly because dreams are often part of a broadly ritual performance, where a shaman or initiate undergoes dreams within a ritually interpreted framework. Often dreams, even in early Christianity, are seen as a means of divine revelation. In this way they contribute to the story of God's dealings with humanity. To some of these themes we shall return.

Fire and light as connected with space

Another theme connected with space is that of fire. I have already remarked on the cliché that height is a symbol of superior (which is only Latin for 'higher') value. This is one reason why God is 'up there'. Another reason is that he (and I use the male pronoun here advisedly) is a sky or heavenly God, being male: he therefore controls the warmth and the wet, and so is a powerful fecundator from above. It is natural for many peoples therefore to identify the earth with the female, fecundated by the upper God: supplying the womb, the earth. The rain is like the sperm, falling on and into the earth, which brings forth, mysteriously, the crops and fruits. And so God generally is up there, not typically over there. This gives fire two properties which are greatly important in relation to the ritual of sacrifice. One property is to send things upwards. It is a means of transporting something in essence from this earthly realm upwards to the heavenly region where God is. But it also has the property of consuming what is being sacrificed. From this point of view its function is to render something tangible invisible, and so belonging to the realm of the gods. Substantially whatever is sacrificed is thus transformed and conveyed by the flames.

To complicate matters, fire is also light, and light too is the sun (less the moon). In many societies there is quite naturally a linkage between fire and light. So the myth of the sun can often intertwine and merge with that of fire. But light can also have quite a different thematic ambience, that of mysticism and gnosis. This is independent of its role in relation to sacrifice, or of its association with the thunderbolts of Indra or Zeus. The imagery of light in this mystical connection has much to do with the way light appears phenomenologically in the mystical, that is to say the inner meditational or contemplative process (CUMONT, 1987). It is a common symbol of intelligence, gnosis, insight: 'a *bright* person', 'I saw the light', 'the light of intelligence', 'he is enlightened', 'Lead me from the darkness into light', 'Lead, kindly light': there are so many phrases one could cite from the English language and from virtually all others too: *lux mundi, Aufklärung* and so on. Light is the nimbus round the saint's or the Buddha's head. Candles proclaim the glory of the divine and themselves become a form of prayer.

Further remarks on height

That flames fly upwards towards heaven is one of the significant features, as we have just noted, about fire. Height has its other natural embodiments. This is a main reason for the sacredness of mountains, which are like nature's ziggurats: ascent to the top is an approach to deity. It is also in shamanistic traditions a means of transformation and of revealing vision (ECK: ER). But some mountains can be approached only with the greatest caution, if at all, for the gods live there – especially stormy gods such as Zeus and Rudra.

A mountain as high and as central as Mount Neru could become the *axis mundi*, but it was an imaginary mountain, not itself known to pilgrims or known in a ritual context, except in so far as it came to be represented in ritual architecture (ELIADE, 1958a).

Mountains also display immutability and so were often symbols of divine everlastingness; thus in some general sense they transcend time. But modern geology has somewhat eroded this symbolism, as signs of their former molten and shifting state become more transparent to the understanding eye.

So far we have been considering themes which relate myths to the doctrinal dimension. Let us now turn to consider some which are at the interface with the ethical dimension. For here very often it is stories which help to vivify and inspire moral behaviour and attitudes.

Myth and the ethical

The root stories of a tradition concerning its founder or primary hero, if there is one, can have ethical implications either explicit or implicit. The former variety involve the setting forth in so many words of imperatives: such as the Ten Commandments or K'ung's ethical teachings. We shall be returning to consider such systematic teachings and the legal and ethical edifices built upon them later, in Chapter 5 on the ethical dimension. For the time being let us contemplate the implicit side of stories.

Some of these set forth a certain ethical ideal. For instance, the future of the Bodhisattva (DAYAL, 1970) in the Mahayana presents an ideal of self-sacrifice on behalf of others and of compassion (which becomes thus a central value among the four great virtues or *brahmavihāras*, of benevolence, compassion, equanimity and rejoicing in the joy of others). The way towards this ideal was of course already put forth in the *Jātaka* tales about previous lives of the Buddha. These often picture the Buddha as an animal, such as a hare or a lion, and draw upon Aesop-like folk material, narrating anecdotes which are explicitly seen as illustrating a certain virtue. The hare jumping on a fire and having himself roasted as a meal for a hungry holy person shows almost literally a case of self-sacrifice. Such moral tales take on mythic quality chiefly because they are linked to the figure of the Buddha himself. They also make use in an imaginative way of rebirth as a framework for moralizing (rebirth has a moral significance in itself because of the way karma and merit work across lives). In addition, the life of the historical Buddha offers ethical lessons – his concern with spiritual truth, his insight into others' condition, his serenity, all of which can give his followers an ideal of noble living. These nuanced attitudes are conveyed by Buddha statues, physical manifestations of spiritual states. The life of the Buddha has also given rise to modern biographies, themselves intended in part to generate spiritual uplift (HESSE, 1922). Perhaps in its day the most influential of such modern treatments was Sir Edwin Arnold's famous poem *The Light of Asia* (ARNOLD, 1880). Such accounts are matched by traditional accounts, like the *Buddhacarita*.

A central place in Christianity is held, of course, by the life of Christ. The Gospels are not biographical in anything but the loosest sense, though they do supply the materials for a whole strand of *imitatio Christi*. Various themes emerge: Jesus' self-emptying of his divine power and his willingness to experience life as a mere human – signs of humility. By contrast the chief human sin is pride (later to take first place among the seven deadly sins). Paradoxically Christ also appears as transfigured, as Creator, as numinous – in the icon of the Pantocrator, for intance. Recent interpretations of the Jesus story, in order in part to accommodate the findings of modernist researches, have swung more to the kenotic theme. God's death upon the cross became a tremendous theme in the early centuries of the church, when the theme of martyrdom flourished. The saints themselves became vehicles of revelation alongside the scriptures: they were, like the icons later, 'windows on heaven' (BROWN, 1967). From this it was not a long step to the use of lives of the saints as inspiring texts full of ethical meaning. The first major autobiography of Western civilization, Augustine's *Confessions*, became a narrative which was often formative of Latin Christian ideals.

To the lives of the saints we might wish to juxtapose examples in other traditions – such as the *Thera-* and *Therīgāthā* in Theravada Buddhism, and the accounts of Sufi holy persons in the Islamic tradition.

Thanks to the *hadīth* corpus, there are many more details of the Prophet Muhammad's life than of Christ's, and though the Prophet is vigorously stated to be human and in no way divine his status as an exemplar has paradoxically tended to be greater. It may in part be because Christ, being also divine, seems *too* exalted. At any rate, the Prophet's life in pragmatic terms is probably much more influential for ordinary Muslims than is Jesus'. An important aspect – indeed the most important aspect – of Christ's life, his saving work, cannot be imitated by Christians.

Confucius' life exhibits a special flavour which is highly typical of late Chinese culture (and no doubt was in part projected back on him). He is the sage. There developed the notion of the *ju*, the scholarly and gentlepersonly expression of wisdom. But just as K'ung himself did not claim to be an originator, but rather a preserver and interpreter of old tradition, so the ideal individual in China came to be seen as the transmitter rather than the creator. But the characteristics of the sage were much greater than those that would be attributed to the modern Western academic: he had insight, not just knowledge; and he upheld ancient ethical ideals. In short, the notion of the moral person, the well-cultivated and disciplined individual, was built into the very idea of the sage. So moral cultivation became central to the Chinese tradition.

There were some analogies with the Graeco-Roman world. There the philosopher could be the ideal. He was someone who not only loved wisdom but also found in it the reasons to be good and temperate. But one reason why Christianity found the unexpected favour it did in the Roman empire was that it seemed, as did Judaism in a more socially restricted way, to make a philosophical morality both possible and actual among ordinary people. From an ethical point of view it was a poor man's philosophy. In brief it was ethical wisdom more widely distributed.

Although the Confucians much detested the celibacy of Buddhism and its tendency to take young men and women out of society, Confucianism also had some of the properties of Christianity in the Western world: it made a good ethos possible among the lower classes ('lower', of course, because Confucianism, the wisdom of the *chüntzu*, was in essence elitist). However, to get back to our point of take-off here, the story of K'ung's life was an essential depiction of the moral ideal of the Confucian tradition. He thus became the paradigm of the sage and of sagely morality.

To a great degree in the Taoist tradition Lao-tzu played a similar role, even if more of his life is legendary. In fact he probably did not exist. His great work is more like an anthology. But as I once wrote (SMART, 1973), how appropriate it was that a person who founded a religion whose chief injunction was to act without acting should not have existed (one reviewer sternly told me off for self-contradiction). But whether he existed or not was irrelevant to the way in which his narrative could function to spell out certain ethical and political ideals.

In all this there happened in China on a larger scale something which compares to the complex and messy myths of Greece or India. The myths contradict one another, but they also exert a kind of complementary dialect. So in Chinese culture they learnt to live together with differing moral ideals from the diverse stories of the differing traditions.

In India there was the *iṣṭadevatā* or chosen deity concept. There is also in a sense, and by the same token, an *iṣṭadevatā* analogue, namely the 'chosen myth'. All this means that the stories of the ideal person, such as Krsna or Rama, express ideals for adoration and imitation. Hinduism is a religion by induction, growing from many differing roots, while a number of those we have been considering are religions by deduction, growing from a single source (though not without graftings from outside); the latter have a much clearer relationship between myth and ethics. Hinduism, however, growing like a reverse banyan, has many ethical ambiguities. It is pluralistic in regard both to the gods and to humans. Its very complex *jāti* system and its untouchable offshoots have been bound to create a plural ethos. Buddhism was much more homogeneous, in relation both to its social structure and to its ethics.

Pluralism, though, even if it can be confusing, breeds an ethic of its own, one of toleration. This state of harmony with certain ideals both of liberalism and empire had a strong effect on India, which has created within a generally Hindu ethos a remarkable new political and religious pluralism. So toleration has tried to become a central ethos.

The message of the Shinto tradition, which essentially dates from the present time but with projections going back to the deep past, has political as well as ethical implications. Politics is not at all absent from the traditions which we have been considering, and I shall return to it later. Meanwhile I shall move on to consider the Jewish tradition, and some others on a smaller scale.

The Jewish tradition follows the others in having its mainstream stories, most of which have a pragmatic correlate. The story of Moses and the children of Israel has a great ritual and existential impact on Jewish people. The Exodus story, after all, forms the core of what is the high point of the bumpy landscape of the Jewish year. It highlights a primary obligation, to support the welfare and survival of the Jewish people. At a Passover I attended not so long ago (as a Christian guest), great unease was expressed about God's treatment of the Egyptians. So there seemed to be some kind of tension between the ethics the objectors represented and that which they took to be the plain message of the Biblical text and the deliverance of their conscience. But rabbis interpret and find their way around awkward texts. This may illustrate a point I shall later make: the mutual interactions between myth and morals are by no means all one way. Why should they be – any more than the interactions between the doctrinal and the mythic dimensions are one way?

So far we have been looking at Biblical stories. What about the extra-scriptural but nevertheless canonical literature? The Talmud has a plethora of stories, many with ethical implications; so have the corpuses, both Sunni and Shi'i, of the life of the Prophet. In some societies the full 'revelation' incorporated within the texture of the ancient tradition is by no means everything. There are additional corpuses of sacred – yet not quite so sacred – texts, which function as a secondary source of myth. Perhaps most notable among such collections are the *smṛti* of the Hindu tradition and the oral Torah of Judaism.

Historical stories

Although narratives from the Talmud or the Bible may have an important historical content, it is above all in modern times that historicity has become an important sign of authenticity (BREISACH, 1983). This is first of all true in the way in which scholars have approached texts, above all Biblical ones – to see how many of them convey genuine history. Notorious is the famous quest of the historical Jesus (RICHARDSON, 1964). But more important is the institutionalization of history within the context of the nation-state. Historians are typically charged with recreating the country's story, and it is true that, as history as a social sicence has developed, its critical posture has grown in importance. There is usually thought to be a great deal of glory even in critical history, so it is important for citizens and in particular for high-school children to learn the nation's story, including biographies of its luminous figures, whether poets, generals, statesmen or whoever (DEUTSCH, 1966). Like other stories it is laden with messages, this story of the country. You should as a citizen be loyal to its glory; you should fight on its behalf; you should learn at school to make yourself useful and even creative. Anecdotes are woven which have lessons – Robert the Bruce and the spider, Washington and the truth, Nelson and the blind eye. Dates give history a ritual dimension: they become anniversaries – the Battle of the Boyne, the Fall of the Bastille, the 1918 Armistice, and so on (KOHN, 1955).

One great advantage of historical stories is that they are sanctified in two special ways, whose authority is difficult to gainsay. The first is by retrospective concept. This is after all (let us say) the history of *England* we are celebrating in our school. The country is defined in a clear way, even if when William I strode ashore the confines of the kingdom were unclear. The same applies even more egregiously to the Republic of India: there was really no such thing in the time of Akbar or Asoka or Clive or Ram Mohan Roy. But when people write histories of India they may deal with the India of Wavell or of Nehru; whichever model they choose, they are projecting a geographical and historical concept backwards in a mode which is unrealistic (SEN, 1973). But we accept the backward conceptuality. Second, the authority of the history is, as it were, guaranteed by the historical method. We might quarrel about details, but we tend to look upon the history as real. So we take the history of a nation as for the most part authoritatively true. This is the new mode of authority: we may quibble about the authority of the Gospels, but the history of our country is *true*.

Truth should be impartial and objective, but that is not how we look at it. Ideological flavours attach strongly to the narrative, because the nation turns out to be 'ours'. Already 'ours' produces huge valuations. In addition, there is a recognition of nationalism abroad, and the ideology of loyalty to the people is 'normal'. So history slides easily into people's thinking.

In addition it is very often reinforced by religious loyalty. The history of a given national culture may be soaked in a given religious tradition. Irish are largely Catholic; Serbs largely Orthodox; Sinhala largely Buddhist; the ethos of India tends to be Hindu; Indonesia is largely Islamic; and so on. It is not always thus, of course. The Swiss are bonded neither by language nor by religion, but they have their history; so with Singapore, Kenya and a lot of other nations. Nevertheless, religious cement often plays a highly important role (GEERTZ, 1963).

How religious myths turn into historical stories

As we move towards another century and into it, the divergence, considered phenomenologically, between the old myth and the new history tends to fade away. Legends of Moses and Krishna and the Buddha and Confucius tend to solidify. Since historicity is regarded as a plus, there is a trend towards thinking of the legendary as historically real. In any case, it becomes a problem to distinguish between the two. We notice it already in films. If a documentary (so regarded) portrays JFK very often, it is that JFK who sticks in the imagination. Between the reality and the portrayal fall many bits of hypothesis and many shadows, but we find it hard to keep those shadows vivid or to maintain the hypotheses as genuine possibilities. So gradually the mythic becomes 'historical' (just as history takes on the laden properties of myth).

A further factor in all this arises from the very nature of the task of acquainting people with the past: it is vital to simplify if you are to lay out the schema of the past. You have to make it simple in order that people may have a picture of the past which they can then perhaps analyze. A mess of data, a vast congeries of past events, a history which has little plot – these presentations are hard for people to grasp. The simplified picture, on the other hand, can in the future be criticized and certainly thought about. History becomes more than a flow of events – it becomes a pattern.

In all this, an identity is both postulated and forged. It is through this that history is grasped as being 'ours', while we are defined as those who have *this* history. Moreover, we often have an illusion of relationship. In our immediate circle we have family links, and we imagine that beyond that there are ever widening links. Though genetics gets lost in the mists, there is some feeling that the group defined by the story has intertwined roots.

Another factor to think about is how 'our' history is defined by the Other. A highly vital ingredient in loyalty arises from the battles fought against others. Not only is the enemy a dynamic character in the saga of the country, he also inflicts upon *us* death and destruction. Such losses, provided they do not wind up in some ultimate defeat, enhance the value of our story. The dead are sacrifices, to be celebrated in memory and to be immortalized in memorials. This is especially true of the modern period of nationalism. The commemoration of the numerous dead of the last two world wars is particularly important, and there is scarcely a village in France or Britain which does not contain such a memorial. The contemplation of the flesh and blood sacrificed enhances the poignancy and depth of the vast struggles.

These features of history underline an ethical lesson: that it is every citizen's duty to sacrifice himself or herself on behalf of the nation. This is part of that wider fabric of duty which is inculcated, it is to be supposed, in school and in the family. Generally speaking, it is highly effective. The passions of patriotism are deep and sincerely felt, reinforced by the various rituals of the state – the flying of the flag, the annual commemorations, the marchpasts and the like. If I have stressed this whole mode of historical stories as myths, it is because in our modern world the sacrifice of death is fuelled more by nationalism than by any of the more traditional religions.

Some other parallels to traditional myths

Just as history may forge identities, so some other narratives may provide lessons and reflections about the deeper and more existential aspects of life. Modern literature, both literary and dramatic, supplies stories and depictions of action which in some ways substitute for older spiritual texts. The transition from one mode to another was transparent in ancient Greece, from myth and ritual to dramatic presentation. In modern times we have had the evolution of the model and before that the drama. In fact, modern literature as it has emerged in schools is a kind of 'existential philosophy', in which literature provides the texts which bring young people towards a grappling with life's deeper issues. It is not philosophy as reason, but philosophy as feeling. Thus for many people (largely an elite), novels and plays are a substitute for Bibles and prayer-books. Beyond these lie more popular media which can play a similar role, namely films and television. These also teach an ethic and a mode of reflection. Of course they are designed merely as pastimes and entertainments, as literature often is too. But we should not neglect the fact that *Hamlet* and *Anna Karenina, Ghosts,* and *The Old Man and the Sea* have mythic roles in modern imagination (ABRAMS, 1971).

Here the myth takes a differing direction. It is not, like historical myth, meant to be literally true, but it is meant to be obliquely so, for the play and the novel are all or mostly fiction. It does not greatly matter whether the action is true or not. But it ought to be realistic (in general), since it should tell you about life. It is that veracity to life which gives it a religious edge, and an existential depth.

How does existential story relate to traditional myth?

Only some traditional myths really correspond to deep fiction. There are, we can have little doubt, some mythic themes which have depth – for instance, the story of Oedipus – and Greek dramatists showed long ago the way to make the stories of the gods and heroes strongly meaningful. But do aetiological myths often reverberate in human psyches? Does the story of the creation *per se* throw light on the human predicament? Do ethical tales often have psychological meaning? The *Jātaka* tales are good moral stories in part because they are good stories. And it should be noted that independently of the existential aspect of tales there is the sheer narrative dynamic: many stories are compelling in themselves. It is true that without any existential aspect they could not be good stories.

So I would argue that traditional myths are first of all to be defined as stories about the transcendent, or if you like about the divine or about the gods. They relate divine events to human ones. They have transcendental depth, but not necessarily psychological depth. Perhaps we are fascinated by them in the hope that we shall find the psyche in them. But generally they are the narrative of gods and men, and we shall glance shortly at the way they may relate to religious experience. The historical narrative corresponds to the stories of the divine because it contains the quasi-transcendental depth of the narrative of the nation or of the hero. We should not, however, confuse the narrative with deeper meanings, which really arise from differing sources: from religious themes (and we have looked at some of these in terms of such notions as height – a variation, it might be said, on ideas drawn from Eliade's corpus); then again from psychic rather than symbolic themes; and from ethical themes, which can often be plain. Moreover, many of these latter notions can be displayed through parables and aphorisms. The Good Samaritan parable or the Buddhist story of the mustard seed are not difficult to penetrate. Their meaning seems plain. The story of the kitten or the monkey in the Ramanuja tradition is easily illustrative of grace. The symbolism is transparent. It may be that psychological messages are less easy to unfold. On the whole, though traditional myth often deploys symbolism and gives out an ethical message, it does not need to be obscure. It is a narrative with depth, but that is something other (JASPERS, 1959).

Reflections on narrative

In summary, the present chapter has sketched out ways in which we can analyse narrative broadly, including those materials commonly called myths. We do not hold that there is anything especially mysterious in the mythic, though of course what are commonly called myths are stories of the gods or of the transcendent (and immanent). But even when common thoughts of the gods have faded there is a close analogue in the narratives of value-laden entities such as the nation. There are varied ways in which narratives may, as scripts, nest in ritual practice; and there are also ways in which they interface with the doctrinal dimension – already the notion of the transcendent or unseen has a philosophical air. Moreover, there are to be found various genres of stories which relate to the various dimensions. Thus many stories illustrate the ethical, and parables can illustrate doctrinal themes, such as that of grace. We note also how in modern times the existential aspect of stories has been strongly developed through literature and drama (and film, television and so on).

Narrative has no power without our intuitive clothing of its episodes in feeling: we are creatures of flesh and blood, and death, sex, cruelty, fear, love, pleasure and so forth animate the tales which we tell and hear. It is important for us therefore to link our myths with the emotional and experiential dimension of religion. Perhaps the easiest way might be to begin with that fundamental aspect of religious experience, the shaman's inward narrative. But for various reasons it may be best to work our way back to that, first taking note of some of the more telling and powerful religious experiences which have made themselves felt in the history of the major religions.

CHAPTER FOUR

The Experiential and Emotional Dimension

Some preliminary reflections on the role of the experience in modern thinking

Both during the period of the Enlightenment and much later there were two notable resorts to experience as a foundation on which to build up religious thought. It was vital in the scheme of Friedrich Schleiermacher, and later in the work of Rudolf Otto. But Schleiermacher's defence of Christian philosophy was, as a child of its time, not equipped to look broadly at religion and religions (REDEKER, 1973). Even Otto's attempt to be comparative was not entirely successful. His great book *The Idea of the Holy* has had a mixed reception since its publication in 1917. The resurgence of Christian neo-orthodoxy, above all in the writing of Karl Barth, obscured the importance of the cross-cultural and more impartial approach. In the 1980s there has been scepticism about the importance or even feasibility of appealing to the subjective. Nevertheless, even if there are those who feel that experience alone cannot be seen as a set of building blocks to construct religion, it seems to me absurd to ignore it. It is obvious that inaugural and inspirational experiences helped to shape the careers of Isaiah, Paul, Arjuna, Muhammad, the Buddha and many others in the history of religions. It is therefore right to consider experience as one of the formative dimensions of religious experience. It is also reasonable to think of the inner, emotional life as vivifying certain aspects of ritual, narrative and so forth.

Although they have some purchase on reality in the history of religions, both Schleiermacher's sense of dependence and Otto's sense of the numinous are ultimately too narrowly conceived. It is not easy to see the manifestation of a *mysterium tremendum et fascinans* as present in purely mystical experience, for instance in that of the Buddha attaining enlightenment. This seems a different phenomenon from the apprehension of a fearful Other such as one finds in the prophetic experience of Isaiah or Paul's vision on the Damascus Road. Putting the contrast rather crudely, the numinous experience as evocatively described by Otto is of an Other, while often mystical apprehension is delineated as non-dual, as if the subject–object duality disappears. The one is *tremendum*, to be shuddered at, and the other is supremely serene. Moreover, the one is often linked to the postulation of a creator, and the other need not be so at all (ALMOND, 1984).

A theory of religious experience

We may put forward a preliminary theory (to be modified anon): that there are two main poles of experience in religion. The first is precisely that depicted in Otto's famous *Das Heilige* – the numinous experience of the holy as a *mysterium tremendum et fascinans*, the Other. I have hinted at this theory in previous pages. The second is the contemplative or mystical experience which does not postulate an outside Other and which feels the disappearance of the subject –object distinction. It is true that so-called theistic mystics may hold that somehow there is an interpersonal mingling or union or communion within the self. But, where there is no concept of the Other beforehand, such a sensation does not seem to be present. Initially, therefore, I shall postulate a non-dual experience as inner feeling. There is a double initial contrast with the numinous: the latter experience is of an outside Other, the mystical of an inner non-other.

This polarity of two kinds of religious experience will turn out to be useful in an explanatory and diagnostic way. I wish later not just to refine this contrast but to link both sides to shamanism, which is another vitally important experiential phenomenon. Before moving on

I need to say something about the whole question of experiential context. There is dispute among scholars on the philosophical issues raised in all this.

Experience and context

In regard to mysticism – that is, the contemplative experience as briefly depicted above – there has been much debate on the degree to which diversities of context themselves dictate real differences of experience (WAINWRIGHT, 1981). Broadly, there are two major groups of scholars: those who hazard the guess that there is a kind of perennial mystical experience shared by the major traditions; and those who hold either that theistic experience is very different from non-theistic mysticism, or more strongly that every tradition has its particular diversities. The issues are difficult to decide. It is clear that often the language of different traditions is indeed very different. How does one disentangle the basic experience from the way in which it is described? Can one do this at all?

There are reasons why I think the particularist stance is unconvincing. First, extreme cross-cultural particularism is not in general altogether plausible, since human beings have many likenesses both physiological and psychological that lead one to expect overlaps of religiosity. One may add that this point implies that religion is a 'natural' product of humankind despite the great variations of particular religions. Second, one can begin to indicate reasons for variations in descriptions of inner events because such apprehensions are embedded in major contextual differences. Thus the mystic who approaches her inner 'target' from the perspective of a life of worship and theism is liable to have different feelings about it from a non-theistic mystic. It is natural to think of communion or union in the one case and not in the other. In short, context does affect phenomenology. But it does not follow from this that the phenomenology is utterly obscured by context. Consider the relations between two persons: George and Dolores may be in love, and the configurations of their faces, bodies and characters we suppose to be particular. But it does not follow that there is not a similarity between their love and that of Andrew and Deirdre. Theorists may have diverse axes to grind, as indeed I may have. But there are those who love particularities. They bolster their own particularity, and such particularity can easily be defensive.

There is a general method which I have used which has a certain plausibility. That is to contemplate those pieces of language which are less ramified compared to those which are more ramified and to count them as more directly descriptive of mystical experience. If a mystic says that she experiences a dazzling darkness, that seems more directly descriptive than if she says she beholds the birth of the Trinity in the soul. I am not saying that the latter description is without phenomenological purchase, but you have to take a lot for granted before you can begin to apply it to the experience. This is analogous to my saying I see a yacht floating near the further shore of the lake, a statement which takes more for granted than if I say I see a white sail over there. Or if I say I see a white figure on the balcony, this takes less for granted than if I say I see the Pope up there. So by using degrees of ramification one can begin to sort out the basic descriptions of mystical states. Thus I have published a detailed comparison between two very different contexts, namely the account of contemplation in Buddhaghosa and that in *The Cloud of Unknowing* (KATZ, 1993). I am fairly convinced by this example.

I do not want through such an instance to deny that there can be phenomenological variations between similar cases. In other words, context flavours phenomenology. So the claim that 'mysticism is often or everywhere the same' must not be taken too literally. There is a convenient analogue with sexual relations. The phenomenology of sex as experienced by a sailor in Milwaukee, by a newlywed in Ghana, by a tantric adept in the Himalayas, by a Communist Party official in Hanoi, and by the President of Turkey (let us say) is liable to differ. But do we doubt that the basic sensations are alike? They are not wholly determined culturally.

Consequently I conclude for the time being that one pole of religious experience is the mystical. Or perhaps we might use the term 'contemplative'. For we have to add one or two footnotes about the mystical. Some writers have used 'mystical' to cover at least one variety of experience which is covered by neither of our two poles.

Thus Zaehner (1957) has used the category of 'panenhenic' to refer to the experience of feeling absolutely at one with the world or cosmos, that is to feel a kind of eyes-open fusion with reality which lies about the person. Because of the fusion, it is not like the numinous experience, and, because it is not interior, it is not like the contemplative case. So far, then, we have three varieties of religious experience: the numinous; the panenhenic; the contemplative.

Some writers use the adjective 'mystical' to refer to all kinds of religious experience, and the noun 'mysticism' to refer to all phenomena of direct experience of the ultimate (HAPPOLD, 1970). Because the variations in usage are confusing, it seems better for us here just to give up the use of these terms and abandon 'mysticism' and 'mystical' altogether. Though I am using the above threefold classification, I do not necessarily want to prejudge issues, and I am willing therefore to divide the contemplative experience into two kinds, theistic and non-theistic. Whether that is an interpretive division or a more substantive one, I leave on one side. By this I mean that the phenomenological distinction may arise from contextuality and built-in interpretation, rather than from an inner basic distinction. As we have noted, making these distinctions is difficult. Some writers (KATZ, 1978) are inclined to say that all experiences are interpreted, which adds another twist to the debate. It may be reasonable, however, still to insist that there are relative degrees of interpretation.

I now return to the importance of my preliminary theory of the two poles. It helps to explain the types of doctrinal system, and I have already touched on the theory in Chapter 1 on the doctrinal dimension. Very roughly we can correlate the numinous experience with dualistic systems, and above all with the three major Western monotheisms, together with varieties of Asian theisms. We can correlate the contemplative experience with non-theisms, notably the Theravada. There is no question here of union with an ultimate. Similarly, the notion of 'emptiness', so crucial to the Mahayana, correlates with the non-dual contemplative state. Further, the non-dual experience ties in with concepts of union with the Other, with communion with the Trinity and the like. We can analyse the impersonal aspects of the description of the Divine as emerging from the contemplative path. Moreover, the numinous as 'softened' yields the stance of *bhakti*.

Let me repeat something already adumbrated in Chapter 1. While the more dramatic sensations of the numinous are frightening, and the fear of the Lord is supposedly the beginning of wisdom, the logic of the numinous is kindlier, since the one Holy is the source of holiness and so of salvation. It is easy to make the transition therefore from fear to love: you love God since God loves you – and you know she loves you because she conveys salvation to you. This being so, the connection between the numinous and devotionalism is transparent. And so religions of grace and devotion naturally abound out of holy dualisms. But without any trace of duality or of the numinous there cannot be *bhakti*. Yet *bhakti* emerges from the Great Vehicle as soon as Buddhas become objects of worship. It is almost a reverse evolution. By the time we get to Tibetan deities, the fierceness is manifest. It is like this: the contemplative experience; devotion to deity-like Buddhas; numinous apprehensions of the Other. By contrast, let us consider a schematized view of Islam: the numinous experience of the Prophet; devotion to the merciful God; the contemplative union with God (Sufism). We may note that a way of reconciling tensions between the numinous and the contemplative is to have a double-decker Divine: the impersonal ultimate, and manifesting from it the personal Lord. Such schemata are quite common in the history of religions: in Sufism; in Christian mysticism, for example Eckhart and some of the Eastern mystics; in Brahmanism, where the impersonal is reinforced by ritual concepts and possibly – according to Zaehner (1952) – by the panenhenic experience; in aspects of neo-Confucianism; and so forth.

Further thought about the two-pole theory

It is important to note how rituals go with the differing poles: we have already touched on this in Chapter 2. Obviously the numinous generates or matches feelings and attitudes such as fear, trembling, respect, humility, while the contemplative produces serenity, confidence, calm, happiness. Secondarily, as we have noted, the numinous creates *bhakti*, which generates devotion, love, a sense of grace, spontaneity. Secondarily, the contemplative life creates (and is itself reinforced by) self-awareness, a sense of wisdom, moderation and equanimity. These states of feeling and attitude help to produce a style or styles of ethic. The person of humility is supposed to repudiate pride; the person of equanimity rejects anger. Possibly there is not so much cross-over. The contemplative can become a guru and achieve arrogance and indeed pride, if he does not watch out, while the person devoted to the Mystery and the *tremendum* can catch the fear-making mode and take on what is supposedly divine anger. That is why the preacher, who in his ritual function stands as the mouthpiece of the Lord, can easily begin ranting.

While the two-pole theory helps to delineate diverse patterns in religiosity, it should not neglect the fact that the two poles are not exact opposites, since there are certain analogues between their twofold phenomenologies. That is, there are modes in which they have indirect resemblances, which enable them to some extent to combine plausibly. It is this set of analogues which helps to make the affinity between the poles look plausible. This in turn makes combined religions look true.

Combination of religions here means forms of piety where both types of experience are cultivated. Thus in various kinds of Mahayana Buddhism, *bhakti* directed towards Buddhas and Bodhisattvas and contemplation conducted as the higher form of spiritual life are both evident. We can see in Sankara's Non-Dualism both the higher *jñāna* based on yoga and the 'lower' *bhakti* directed towards the *īśvara* are evident (POTTER, 1981). Medieval Christianity both East and West saw sacramental piety combined with the contemplative life. In Taoism both the worship of the supreme gods and the life of harmonizing with the Tao were practised together. In such cases there is to be seen a certain analogy between the poles, which helps to keep them together, and so produces a sense of harmony despite the divergences of types of experience and so of types of practice. Before I get on to this, I ought to say a word about practice. Let me begin with *bhakti*, with an illustration from the Catholic tradition.

Christianity has traditionally encouraged ways of giving warm expression to the practice of worship. Loving worship involves well-known prayers, hymns, lighting candles, prostrations, approaching proximate entities such as the saints, and above all the Virgin Mary (DIX, 1945). The material dimension is usually geared up with much richness of texture to give the faithful a feeling of *bhakti*. Gold leaf, statues, altarpieces, glittering cloth, stained-glass windows, soaring arches, fine vestments, processions – all these produce in the faithful a sense of glory and a feeling of devotion to the Lord. Through such means the practice of *bhakti* is encouraged, and this surrounds the whole sense of the numinous. Other factors encourage the contemplative: the very appearance of grave monks and nuns who seem to exhibit in their lives a dedication to the contemplative life; retreats and teachings; books on self-awareness and humility; and the air of calm which can pervade the holy cloister.

So the nature of religious experience has to be seen through the mists and flavours of practice. Beyond practice, however, lie some of the important properties of more direct experiences. The analogies are as follows. First, the higher experience of the numinous seems to put us in touch with the everlasting. God is beyond time, somehow. Likewise the inner experience of (say) nirvana has its timeless aspect. So it is that the poet said 'I saw eternity the other night,' while nirvana is said to be the *amatam padam* or immortal place. Another feature which harmonizes is the transcendent. Nirvana lies beyond the changing and timely *saṃsāra* (or at least it does in the Theravadin cosmography: complications arise in the Great Vehicle). Third, both the numinous and the contemplative have ineffability, though perhaps for differing reasons. Hence the *mysterium* is beyond speech: higher than our words can soar. Hence too nirvana is ineffable, and has a certain deep inexplicability. Fourth, both nirvana and the numinous are literally invisible, and such invisibility symbolizes the transcendent. Fifth, neither the Divine nor nirvana is in space. Sixth, both are full of potential bliss, beyond ordinary joy. All these reasons converge in encouraging us to think that the differing experiences might apply to the same entity. In other words, perhaps nirvana and the Divine are one. It is not *de rigueur* to think this, but it is a possibility. This enables us to merge nirvana and the Dharmakaya, and the impersonal 'object' of mystical experience and the Divine target of numinous experience.

It is normal enough to think of identity statements in this way.

Typically you have diverse points of access to what is declared identical. For instance, if I say that John Paul II is the Pope, I have two points of access: one is through an individual identified by a particular name; the other is through someone identified as a functionary of a particularly organization. In brief, the analogies between the poles give a sort of plausibility to the claim that they both relate to the One. But they do not need to relate to the One.

In brief, the two-pole theory allows of three modes. You can have only the numinous; you can have only the contemplative; you can have both. Theoretically you can go further – having one dominant, the other dominant and both equal. In fact, I think this fivefold possibility is correct: one exclusively; the other exclusively; the one dominant; the other dominant; both equal. And if you like, for completion's sake, neither: the person or tradition that has no experience of the beyond is, after all, a vital possibility too. Let us look at the varieties through the lenses of the Indian tradition (ELIOT, 1957): there is numinous theism; there is Theravadin contemplation; there is dominantly numinous Visistadvaita (Ramanuja's theism) (CARMAN, 1974); there is dominantly contemplative Advaita (Sankara's partly theistic absolutism); there is equally balanced Bhedabhedavada (semi-personal theism) (RAD-HAKRISHNAN, 1960); there is atheism, without either the numinous or the contemplative. There is, moreover, a great merit in this more complex hypothesis.

The merit is that beginning with two poles, and allowing of their merger and absence, you have a very simple schema which offers great variety. It starts from simplicity and already begins to generate reasonable complexity. It is the simplest and most elegant way of generating correlations between types of doctrines and combinations (or non-combinations) of kinds of experience.

Does it have plausibility from a human point of view? One advantage of the two-pole theory over the postulation of a single core of religious experience is very obvious. If you believe like Otto that there is a single kind of experience at the core of all religions, it utterly fails to account for the varieties of religious belief and practice. You will have to account for the types by reference to certain strong cultural divergences, for instance by philosophical or ritual kinds of religiosity. But it seems quite plausible to suppose that there is more than one kind of major spiritual experience.

Further we have already reached beyond the two poles, to a third, by the addition of the panenhenic experience. I shall later wish to add the shamanic experience (though this may be a kind of ancient root of the two poles).

Let us now look on the two-pole theory from another point of view. Is it plausible in relation to human nature?

The two-pole theory and human nature

The typical account of the numinous experience describes the apprehension of an external power. Beginning with pre-theistic religion, the usual interplay between the individual and his environment relates to environmental forces. Consider the gods of the polymyth, such as gods of the sky and thunder, of the ocean, of rivers, of mountains, of fields, of the earth, of vegetative powers. We have already noted that humans evolved rituals which related human life to the various Others. Sacrificing to Neptune, for instance, meant entering into an elaborate transaction with that god. All this was a highly intelligible mode of operating, and it remains so in many countries. There is nothing greatly mysterious about religion. It is only that in many societies we do not carry on in this way. The arrival of monotheism and atheism has wiped away the particular gods and with them the rituals which supposedly kept them happy and benevolent. But there are still rituals to be operated towards the one God behind the whole cosmos. Anyway, pre-theistic rites, as I have called them, already surround the numinous with practice; and the same ultimately applies to monotheism (the same applied to Hindu-type refracted theism, which combines features of both theism and polytheism). Humans in such religious conditions have an apprehension of the invisible force behind their environment. It does not seem therefore out of place to think of the numinous as an intuition of what is 'out there'. Otto's theory seems to integrate with pre-theistic religions (GRIMAL, 1965).

The contemplative, by contrast, appears to have a very diverse provenance. The contemplative state lies within the individual. Human experience itself has a two-pole nature: there is what lies 'out there' and what it interacts with 'within here'. In fact, contemplative experience reaches back to the core of consciousness. It is a common claim of mystics to be delving into pure consciousness. Perhaps the Divine lies at the basis of the soul, but at any rate it is reasonable to think of the heart of contemplation as reflecting pure, and for that matter non-dual, consciousness. Perhaps that pure consciousness is the ultimate flower of evolution, that which helps to provide luminousness to perceptions and to give a kind of self-awareness to the cosmos itself. From this point of view the quest for the inner is also the search for the meaning of the universe. In brief, the two poles lead us both outward and inward in the cosmos. But I do not want to argue this directly here. It is not for us in a work like this to argue for the *validity* of the two modes of religious experience. It was wrong, in my view, for Otto to underpin his phenomenology with later Kantian paraphernalia. His philosophy of religion was totally irrelevant to the rightness or otherwise of his description of what he took to be the core of religious experience. The two should have been held quite separate.

Nonetheless it is reasonable to try to argue that the two types have a coherence with other aspects of human experience. It helps me to argue that it is good to think of at least two poles and so resist the notion of a single core. I have tried to see whether the two-poles theory is plausible not just in terms of the variety of types of religion, but also from the standpoint of human nature. I do not mean to say that there is some essential human nature; I merely claim that the tendencies which we humans exhibit and the characteristics with which we are endowed chime in with the first crude deliverances of religious phenomenology.

Experience and projection – some remarks

Projection theory, whether it be of Feuerbach (WARTOFSKY, 1977), Freud (RIEFF, 1979) or others, tends to be feeling-based. It rarely takes theoretically what is found more up front in notions like those of Otto or of perennialist adherents of the centrality of contemplative or mystical experience, such as Huxley or Guenon or Zaehner (in his modified way). If we took seriously a form of non-reductionist projection theory, we might look on the whole enterprise of religious studies differently. If we thought of God as a 'projection' of the numinous and of nirvana as a 'projection' of the contemplative, would we not think of religious experience as intrinsic to the explanation of religious belief – not as something deep down which arises simply out of human feeling, the human psyche and so forth? There is a difference if we take religious experience seriously. But what is it? In my view the answer is a very simple one: that core-type religious experiences are intrinsic to the human psyche in some way. They can flourish or not flourish in differing conditions. Hence you do not need to suppose that religion itself is an artificial or tangential creation. Moreover, you can begin to explain other phenomena through religion. Because of the Marxist and related influences in the intellectual life of the last hundred years or more, there has been a tendency to downplay religion in human life and history.

This has been deplorable for at least two reasons. First, it has exhibited ideological determinations of theories and judgments in history and the social sciences. I am proud to be involved in a profession, religious studies, which has taken seriously the phenomenological method, banning the ideological or theological determination of descriptive or historical truth. Such determination remains frequent in academe, which is sad. Of all the social sciences, the study of religions is the most consciously neutralist. Those who do not hold to this way of exploring the human world have a serious defect in their method, and are naive. Yet this fault is a frequent one, partly because many of our academics, alas, are Marxists (they are possibly now ex-Marxists, but the same faults are often evident). In brief, there is no more reason in the case of religion than anywhere else to adopt a reductionist or projectionist stance.

Second, religion in the UK (for example) has its own entrenchment. From this angle, you get the opposite to the downplaying of religion, yet in a way it has the same effect. It is easy, for instance, to overplay the role of official religion, partly because the analyst, having been raised in this milieu, can exaggerate the value in society of (say) the Church of England.

Experiences and emotions in religion and worldview

So far I have been writing mainly about experiences rather than emotions. Despite the more dramatic impact of the kinds of experiences which I have been delineating and classifying, there are modes of feeling which are highly relevant (for instance) in rituals. We have touched on these before, but it is worth reinforcing our observations at this point, since we are now venturing through the experiential dimension. In both the Christian and Hindu traditions the call to sing hymns has a strong emotional impact. How can we characterize some of the emotions of faith? These lie beyond the strongest sensations of faith as exhibited, for intance, in intense *bhakti*. It remains true that hymns create a sense of exaltation, a sublime sense of holiness, sorrow at the death of a saviour, a feeling of ethical commitment, loyalty to the tradition, and so forth. We need to recognize the power of words and music to fashion these feelings. It is an aspect of ritual which has depth and power. It is something which is a vital part of the phenomenology of religion, even if we find music hard to characterize or come to terms with. Similar effects are brought about by secular equivalents, such as national anthems and military music.

Experiences and experiencing as

Our two-pole theory can get a further extension if we look to the 'process' known as 'experiencing as' (HICK, 1983). The numinous experience provides a revelation of divinity, so to speak, and that putative revelation can be applied further to daily experience: we can see the divine handiwork in the world about us. John Hick has taken some work by John Wisdom on seeing as and recast it as experiencing as, and roughly speaking I follow his lead here. In other words, certain root concepts and their attendant feelings are applied continuously. Thus the presence of the Divine as Creator, in everything we encounter in life, helps to stimulate feelings of wonder and gratitude.

It is not implied that the process here is simply one of artificial superimposition. The perception of the divine in the beauties of nature, for example, has its evidential justification. This in no way amounts to a proof of the presence of God, but still it involves seeing signs of God's creative activity. We can perhaps divide the phenomenon into two forms, one dispositional and the other spontaneous. By this I mean that the way a person experiences the world may on the one hand be canalized into a disposition, rather like being in love. On the other hand, there is the point at which a kind of conversion occurs: she begins to see the world as the divine handiwork. This could happen because of the advent of the direct numinous experience, though this may not be necessary – something less may happen, the arising of the vision of the divine in the world. And so to schematize. First, you can have the numinous experience; second, you can have the vision of the divine; third, you can have the continuing disposition to see the divine in the world.

The distinction between what may be thought of as the prophetic numinous vision and coming-to-see something of the nature of the vision is a realistic one. For one thing, it reflects the role of preaching and the outpouring of prophetic vision. The task of the prophetic figure is to stir his audiences to see something of what he sees (ROBERTSON, 1978).

Similar remarks can be made in relation to the contemplative path. Even where there is no linking of contemplation with a Creator, which provides a framework for a luminous perception of the divine in everything, there can be a basis in the attainment of pure consciousness for a disposition to see the cosmos *sub specie aeternitatis*, as a network of linked events, for example in the vision of Hua-yen. There are in the *Theragāthā* and *Therīgāthā* of the Theravadin canon numerous instances where monks and nuns record their new visions. There is the Thera who on seeing a dancing girl in the village street, whither he has gone to beg, has a sudden and deep conviction of the misery of her condition, by contrast no doubt with the serenity and unshakeableness of the path of the one who is on the way to nirvana. There are other adepts who become 'converted' to the Buddha's vision through a variety of circumstances, including a sense of the connectedness of nature. And so we may wish to schematize the experience of the Theravadin in a threefold way which is analogous to that applied to the numinous. First, there is the high experience of nirvana, seen through the prism of pure consciousness; second, there is the coming-to-see the existential truth of the Buddha's analysis of the nature of the world; third, there is the continuing disposition to see the world under the aegis of that vision and that analysis.

It may be useful to give names to these phases of experience. The first, dramatic phase we can call the numinous experience, the second the divine conversion, the third the divine disposition. In the case of the contemplative triad, the first we can call the contemplative experience, the second the luminous conversion, the third the luminous disposition. I have chosen the slightly vague term 'luminous' partly because it makes a nice twin to 'numinous', but also because with the blending of the contemplative and the numinous paths more possibilities are opened up. The Christian mystic, for instance, may come to see the world about her not just as the handiwork of God, but as glowing with the network of mystical illumination.

The complications may arise partly because of the application of other concepts than those rooted in the numinous to the contemplative experience. For instance, Brahmanism in the *Upaniṣads* refers to *brahman*, not so much as a Divine Being (though that is present too) but as the magical ritual power implicit in the sacrifice and by extension in the whole cosmos. It is possible to combine this notion with the consequences of the inner yogic quest.

It is interesting also for us to return to the panenhenic experience. It may be that that was an influence (so Zaehner thinks) on Brahmanism; one might see its footprint in the *Lao-tzu*. There are affinities between it and the numinous experience, though the latter is usually expressed as being *of* a personal, rather than a cosmic, being.

Relations of experience to ritual

We may now take up from a somewhat different angle that which we touched on in Chapter 2 on ritual. It is clear not merely that ritual in a broad sense may nurture experience, but also that it functions as a response to it. Thus the architecture and art of mosques and churches, say, may help to cultivate a sense of the majesty of the divine, and this fertilizes impulses towards the numinous and what I have called both the divine conversion and disposition. The marvellous sounds of ritual – the call of the minaret, the chanting of the sacred scripture, the singing of monks, the wonderful hymns (IRWIN, 1983) – in diverse ways give power to feelings which chime in with the numinous and the sense of the divine. So it is that rites begin to trace out a spiritual path.

But there is more to it than that: the experience of conversion gives a vivid sense of the presence of the Lord (or Lady: let us not forget the many female representations of the deity). In so doing it creates the impulse to respond to the wonders of the world conferred on it by God, and that response is most naturally seen as worship. Worship is itself the normal response to the worshipful. It is the way of recognizing the divine, and this independently of any material blessings that the worshipper might expect. There is a deep, numinous element wrapped up in the cloudy being of Poseidon which is independent of the fact that sacrificing bullocks to him may somehow increase the chance of a safe and prosperous voyage (WILLIGER, 1922). This response to the numinous is even more evident if you are hailing the great Creator who controls the whole cosmos, whose body is the cosmos, whose power extends to all human and non-human affairs. In short, the numinous experience gives you access to a being in part defined by ritual: a God is a person whom you ought to worship, that is partake in appropriate ritual towards.

The process becomes a kind of spiral. The revelation of God in the numinous experience spurs worship, which in turn nurtures the disposition to see the wonders of God in the world, which in turn spurs worship, and so on. It is a process seen in what Brother Lawrence called *The Practice of the Presence of God*.

By contrast, the contemplative pole of experience finds its nurture in the contemplative life, which has different patterns of practice in differing cultures, but which centrally involves self-control of diverse kinds, including breathing exercises (Taoism, yoga, Hesychasm) and mental exercises (Buddhist yoga and self-awareness, Christian mysticism, Sufism and indeed all paths). These can be combined with numinously oriented practices and rituals: worship can easily combine with yoga, and so on. It is also possible to blend religious and secular practices, as with the Zen cultivation of martial arts or the tea ceremony. Since the contemplative conversion fits in with philosophy or doctrine, reflection upon the intellectual aspect of Buddhism can be cultivated as part of a differing spiral: meditation can bring one to an existential understanding of the philosophy, which in turn can help to stimulate deeper contemplation, and so on.

Relations of experience to the organizational

There is a tendency for the contemplative experience to be associated with asceticism, a tendency which has had some major effects on religious organization. Thus the large role played by contemplation in pre-Protestant Christianity and in Buddhism has in both cases generated monasticism, where celibate monks and nuns have lived together cultivating the holy life. Islam has renounced celibacy, but brotherhoods have nevertheless formed within the development of Sufism. Taoism came to follow the example of Buddhism. While in principle the Protestant spirit might have cultivated more contemplation than it did, its rejection of works and so of monasticism greatly weakened this pole of religious experience. Rather, Protestantism's inwardness largely turned into *bhakti*. Moreover, since it was so Biblical in the inspiration of its doctrine and life, it concentrated much less on the Neo-Platonic and contemplative themes which had had such a large influence upon classical Christianity. There was, as we have noted, a reinforcement in the later Roman empire of ascetic themes, given that with the adoption of the faith by the ruling power the motivations for softness were so much greater. The life of the desert and the monastery was a substitute for the older risks of martyrdom and persecution.

The contemplative life may encourage the coenobitical, but it also pushes the adept towards the hermit or lone status. This came to be the more marked presence of the ascetic in the Hindu tradition, and could live in symbiosis with Brahmin dominance, itself underlining the importance of the temple and the ritual cult, which came to enhance *bhakti* and theism in a refracted mode. By contrast Islam, coming after the heavy entrenchment of the priesthood in Christianity and the legal specialist in Judaism, turned in a more 'protestant' manner away from the former model. Its egalitarianism was promoted by the absence of a hierarchical sacred structure. Often it turns out that *bhakti* can cut through ritualism and emphasize a warm equality before God. There were a number of movements of *bhakti* in the Indian tradition which stressed, despite the underlying caste system, that all believers are equally beloved of God.

In theistic circumstances particularly the lone holy person acquires what may be called a numinous exterior. The *staretz* and the guru, the hermit and the Sufi sage, the Christian saint and the Buddhist holy person may take the contemplative path, and in many cases may empty themselves; but the populace comes to revere them, even worship them (NEVILLE, 1978). In short, their outsides are like those of gods, even if their inward consciousnesses lie at a different pole. They can thus get involved in strange paradoxes. The hermit becomes surrounded with visitors. The poor saint may become loaded with gifts. The humble holy man or woman may become treated like a king or queen. It is all unnecessarily distracting and indeed tempting. Poverty is as hard to achieve as wealth, perhaps, under holy circumstances. The ascetic is not his own master.

The creation of the monastic style of life belongs to differentiated societies. It is hardly discoverable in smaller groups. In such communities asceticism takes the form of the vision quest and of shamanism. I shall come to look at these phenomena in a little while. In general the smaller societies, many of them hunting and gathering, generate the numinous rather than the contemplative pole, except in so far as shamanism itself may be an ancestor of it.

It may be noted that a sort of worldly asceticism, though not directly related to the contemplative pole, can be achieved within the framework of *bhakti*. The tendency of the Calvinist, for example, is against religious experience. Nevertheless his disposition is numinous. The logic of Calvinism is embedded in the notion that God is the sole causer of liberation or salvation. It follows that God causes damnation. By playing out this scenario in time, Calvinism comes up with the doctrine of predetermination of both salvation and damnation. Such a philosophy flows from the eternity of God seen as temporal rather than atemporal. The logic is fine in its way, and issues from the dualism of the numinous and the subject human. The

Calvinist experiences God as cause of both salvation and damnation: he sees the divine working inexorably in the world. He acknowledges God, and trusts that he displays symptoms of the divine salvation. But, because he does not believe that he can gain worth in the eyes of God by works, he does not withdraw to the monastery or go on pilgrimage. Within the frame of the numinous he acts in the world in a secular way, which does not count as meritorious religious conduct. So his this-worldly life can be directed towards worship (but not service precisely) of God. It is a life, in this world, of worship. This mode brings the secular into play very strongly, and within limits it has its asceticism, because the ethos is derived from the New Testament and more generally from the Bible. Elements of Jewish law, such as keeping the Sabbath, which have a very different meaning from that presented to Jews, are seen as contributions to a sober and ascetic life, but in a public milieu, not a monastic or conventual existence.

Generally speaking, highly ritual systems generate hierarchies and elites. While experiential forms of religion may live alongside ritual systems (for instance Roman Catholicism, at least in the old days), they tend to break through the ritual mould. They give rites an emotional meaning, and they are often hospitable to loose and more emotional ways of conducting ritual. In such circumstances the hold of hierarchy becomes less strong.

There is, no doubt for other reasons than the desire to loosen up systems, a modern trend towards the experiential (HICK, 1982). In other words, much of religion as it develops into modern urban living, whether that be in Natal, Bombay or London, has a keen regard for direct encounters with the divine or ultimate. There is abroad a sort of philosophy of religion, not of course acknowledged under that title, which holds that truth is most easily grasped by an encounter. Scriptures compete and become mysteriously entangled, and may seem at a remove from reality. What lies behind them in any event is the experience of the divine. Doctrines often divide unnecessarily and are not easy to judge, especially in relation to experience. So there is a *nisus* towards the poles of experience – towards the divine, conversion, direct knowledge; or else towards inner truth, pure consciousness, awareness.

Ethics and experience

There are no unambiguous relations between ethical attitudes and the twin poles of experience. But we have noted that the contemplative pole typically involves asceticism and often celibacy. This itself may create tensions where religious traditions favour family life and social integration. Thus Judaism, Islam and the Hindu tradition in particular have attempted to maintain the fabric of marriage, so that ideally the celibate is someone who gradually gives up ordinary social existence after meeting the requirements of marriage, or combines spiritual practice with family obligations. There is a rather widespread correlation between the contemplative life and vegetarianism, in the Indian traditions and Eastern Orthodoxy. Since contemplation also involves a largely passive approach, it fits in well with a gentle and harmless attitude towards other living beings, and often with a pacifist style. This is not to overlook ways in which coenobitical groups may develop away from the contemplative life to other avocations. One can cite the monks of war in the Christian middle ages, especially the armed Templars and Teutonic knights, soldier monks in Tibet and Zen militants (FRIED, HARRIS and MURPHY, 1975).

The contemplative path stresses self-knowledge and serenity, and adopts techniques of calming and the gradual purification of consciousness. These point in a certain ethical direction. Since morality in any case requires self-control, there is a solidarity between the contemplative pole and the moral life. But in some ways it is hard to demonstrate exactly how ethics and asceticism coincide. For instance, while Theravadin meditation is deemed to presuppose compassion, critics of the path see a tension. For in so far as the pursuit of nirvana is the pursuit of liberation, it may be thought to have an ultimately selfish goal, and so is in tension with the great virtues of Buddhism, namely benevolence, compassion, joy in others' joy, and equanimity. The Mahayana solution to the problem via the ideal of the Bodhisattva is an ingenious and satisfying one.

Because the tendency for mysticism is towards withdrawal from the world, there are also problems about how to combine it with social action. Much therefore depends on the interface between the ascetic and the lay person. In differing cultures, as we have noted, the contemplative acquires a numinous exterior, or creates some other mode of generating merit among those who revere him. Since the notion of the numinous involves the idea of power – the power of the *mysterium tremendum* – it is a type of religion much easier to integrate with kingly rule and law. It is partly for this reason that Buddhism, though highly successful as a religion, borrowed features of Brahmanism in its social and, particularly, its political arrangements. Because of the presence of power it could easily suffuse hierarchical systems. Nonetheless, we have noted that *bhakti* has a certain egalitarian thrust. Partly this is because of its greater 'personalism'. That is, because the Divine interacts with the faithful as a personal being, she or he equally dispenses grace. Moreover, even its fearful nature may have an equalizing effect, since the sense of the individual's alienation translates itself into a sense of sin, and all can consider themselves to be equal sinners before the one Holy One.

From both poles there can emanate a sense of love. Because the numinous Holy One dispenses grace, he is seen as a loving God, and *bhakti* reciprocates as loving adoration. The images of love are widely dispersed throughout the theistic religions and among quasi-theistic forms of Buddhism. From Yahweh to Avalokitesvara and from Christ to Krishna, the figure ranges of the loving God – not just an agapeistic Being but one who is often depicted in terms of sexual love, an image of the most wonderful bond and loyalty. There can also of course be more than echoes of fertility in some of these images, since God is also a potent help to the human project of feeding the multitudes and engendering them. All this fits too with the duties of the king, himself a kind of god under God.

From the contemplative goal, the picture of love emanates as soon as it is linked with a numinous Being. Once the quest of the contemplative is seen as directed not just inwards into the depths of the soul but more deeply into the fabric of the Divine, the notion of union or communion becomes commonplace. And the image of sexual love becomes a normal way of depicting the soul's union with the Other or the relevant analogues in the case of Buddhism (NYGREN, 1982). It is not surprising that the contemplative religions of India and the Himalayas came to breed Tantrism, with its often frank imagery of the male–female sexual bond. Of course, there could also be tensions in view of the asceticism of much of the contemplative path.

Apart from the passionate appeal of love there was also the interpersonal meaning of it. This was strategically exploited in the Christian tradition, with its notion that the Trinity exhibits the perfect bond of Love, which itself was seen as the central value of Christian ethics.

But ethical and legal requirements in a tradition may have a more contingent relation to the kind of experience central to it. In both the Jewish and the Muslim religions there has traditionally been a large array of legal norms. These have a general connection to the numinous characters of these faiths, but not a particular set of connections. What I have in mind is that the concept of a covenant, for instance, between the one God and the people of Israel is intelligible enough in the dynamic of the numinous experience of that people's leadership, just as later the numinous character of the prophetic tradition could link into an ethical critique of the people's progress. But the particularities of the dietary laws, for example, have a somewhat adventitious relation to the numinous character of God. This, of course, makes loyalty the more poignant and meaningful: it is just because God has set the people apart in that way that they are supposed to exhibit their loyalty to him.

Something of the same spirit is evident in Islam, although the law in this case is much more up front as a scheme for a new society to be created under the leadership of God and of his Prophet (and his successors). The laws are divine but they are intended to be eminently practical in shaping a holy community. Not surprisingly, much learning and prestige have gone into the profession of jurist in the Islamic tradition.

While in the West there is a modern tendency to separate out the ethical from the juridical, it is obvious in the Islamic case and to a great degree in China and India too that ethics has to be seen in the light of the creation of a working society, laws and all.

Some more reflections on the ramifications of religious experience

In making my simplified polarity between the numinous and the contemplative I have sketched a theory which usefully begins to get a hold on the differing kinds of religion. But there are variations within each genre which need to be noted. The numinous I have associated with the gods, but actually the bearers of the numen have not always been strictly divine, though they may be thought of as emissaries of God. The visions which clothe numinous experience can be figures other than the Divine, most notably in the Christian tradition of the Virgin Mary. The propensity of the Virgin to recreate herself in various places leads to her polytopic character. How common is it to refer to Our Lady of Guadelupe or of the Soccorso? This compares with a dearth of polytopic ideas of Christ. It is as if the One God has only one locale to inhabit (though according to theology he is supposed to be multipresent, indeed omnipresent – but this is not quite the same as having many particular associations). In other cultures a Goddess or God may also have a polytopic visionary reality. It is interesting in the case of Christianity, one of the great monotheisms, that in its classic forms, before Protestantism, it could admit numinous experiences of those lesser beings whom it counted as saints. One would have to modify a little what I said earlier: that the natural and proper response to the numinous is worship. For, according to orthodoxy, saints are not to be worshipped. Even so, they are reverenced. The response is on the brink of worship and this is eminently true of the Virgin (WARNER, 1976).

We may note too that there are parallels to visions in the auditory sphere, as in the case of Augustine's famous experience of conversion. The combination of sound and vision, and even a sort of seeing of sound (CHIDESTER, 1992), can be recorded.

I shall come back to the question of visions in linking the numinous to the shamanic experience. But it is noteworthy that the luminous contemplative experience is often referred to as a kind of vision, as though we have an inner mystic eye. This on the whole is not taken literally, whereas the vision of the Virgin, say, is typically a literal one. The metaphor of seeing occurs frequently, as it is in the English use of 'see' in relation to the seeing of the solution to a problem or the point of a joke and so on. However, there are ways in mystic paths where techniques of visualizing are used, especially in Tantric Buddhism. Mandalas, for instance, are used as visual methods. Potent forces or gods are imagined in order to unite with their potency. There was a great deal of interest in the symbolism of such means in the work of Jung and Joseph Campbell. But it is in marked contrast to the emptying techniques of most contemplation, whichever tradition we are thinking of. The purification of consciousness entails the removal of all imaginings through heroic self-discipline.

The potency of dreams and their relation to visions

Most cultures have had views about the possible knowledge conveyed by dreams. This includes, for instance, early Christianity, up until the middle ages, and Islam. Supernatural knowledge could arise both from divinely sent dreams and from demonically derived ones. The ancient classical world generated various learned works on the classification of dreams, including one by Macrobius (fifth century CE), which was largely reflected in Christian writing on the subject. We shall be looking at dreams further in relation to shamanic experiences. But it is interesting to begin by considering the life of Isaiah Shembe, the Zulu Zionist prophet, since this brings out some relationship between dreams and visions (SUNDKLER, 1976). Macrobius and other classical writers used the term vision or *visio* for dream states (by contrast with *oraculum*, which is its auditory equivalent). Shembe heard a voice telling him to go up a mountain to a cave; while asleep there he received a vision with a rather unique 'out of body' experience, the spectacle of his own rotting corpse. He also became convinced that he had seen Jehovah (there is often an Old Testament influence on African prophets, partly no doubt because there were good correspondences between the life and ethos of the Old Testament and those of African society). This dream led him to believe that he had been set apart by God as his prophet. The following year he was drawn up the mountain Inhlangakazi, where he encountered mysterious and dark forces, and fought off their tempting potency, declaring his loyalty to Jehovah. In due course, angels came and looked after him with food and wine. He conceived himself as acquiring a new identity, and on his return to society discovered that he had the power of healing.

We may note that in his preparation as prophet and healer, both dreams and visions were intermingled. The dream state, like the vision, is far removed (as I have noted) from the purification of consciousness so typical of the contemplative life. It is true that one Christian theory was that by removing the visions of ordinary ruminative and dreaming consciousness it was possible to make way for direct visions from God. But generally the dream vision has affinity to the numinous because in a way it follows the same logic. The theistic and polytheistic milieux were ones in which the distinction between the natural world and the world beyond was well understood. Nevertheless, the boundaries were fluid ones, the barriers penetrable. And so a striking dream could take one through the frontier to the divine world beyond it. further, dreams have a remarkable property: the ordinary distinctions of time and space disappear. This is, if you like, the beginning of a philosophy of transcendence: God exists, that is, beyond ordinary space and time. Yet events occur within that 'beyondness'. It is therefore a mysterious time and place. As a strange and creative intermediary existence, it figures in the famous Australian Dream Time, a remarkable and systematic conception. We may see dream-visions and auditions as taking their place on a continuum with numinous encounters. They also form a link with shamanism (VON GRUNEBAUM and CAILLOIS, 1966).

Shamanism: a major form of religious experience and practice

Although the word 'shaman' may originate from *śramaṇa*, the word for an early Indian recluse, and although shamanism in its classical sense refers to the religion and practice of adepts in the region of North Asia (Siberia), there is every indication that in fact it is a very early phenomenon going back deep into prehistory. It is no surprise that it should be prevalent in the Americas, seeing that much if not all of the population of the Americas derived from North Asia. From one point of view shamanism is a loose federation of cosmologies or more broadly worldviews, and there are recurrent themes. The shaman, for instance, is supposed to receive initiation into the various gods and forces which he or she will encounter; there is the picture of the world as centring upon an *axis mundi*, a vast tree or tent-pole. The shaman is supposed to be capable of leaving his body, and that supplies the scenario of a number of magical and healing accomplishments. In some cultures he has a special relationship with the Lord of the Animals, and so he has special knowledge of the best times and places for hunting.

For our present purposes, the main interests are the initiatory rites and processes which the shaman goes through. Though he may inherit his shamanic function, he nevertheless has to undergo special experiences as well as traditional training. Ecstatic trances and visions often supervene after illness, possibly mental in character. But there is typically a strong element of asceticism, solitude and seeming death. Indeed the theme of death and resurrection is important; and during the time of his initiation the shaman ascends to heaven and descends to hell, as a way of getting him into the practice of saving souls from death, a major aspect of his healing power. He is in this a psychopomp. (There are a whole number of shamanistic themes in ancient Greek mythology, and one finds echoes of them in the story of Jesus.) One common visionary theme is for the adept to see himself being chopped up and then reconstituted. It is as a new person, having passed through death, that he is a healer, a new person endowed with great secrets. More particularly, however, the ascent to heaven and the descent to hell give him visions of spiritual powers, including those of his Lord.

There are hints of affinity in all this with the twin poles of religious experience I have previously sketched. At one end, the shaman sees numinous beings and the *mysterium tremendum* of which Otto wrote (he did not make much of shamanism, although some shamanic materials are woven into prophetic experience). At the other pole there are the practical preparations for inner vision, notably the solitude and asceticism. It is quite possible, one supposes, that the practice of yoga and its attendant ideology in ancient India were an offshoot and specialized adaptation of shamanic ecstasy and thought. The asceticism could have been channelled in a particular direction, while hunting motifs could have been sublimated into the protection of animals (hence the value of *ahiṁsā*). The mythic trappings of shamanism were largely left behind – though traces remain, for instance, in the ascent of the *jhānas* in Buddhism and the matching of the psychological levels to the various heavens. The cosmologies of both Jainism and Buddhism bear some traces of the *axis mundi* theme. It could, however, have been converse influence which depicts the ascending heavens and descending purgatories in modern shamanistic cosmologies. Nevertheless, the antiquity of shamanism is attested not just by early cave paintings but also by the very widespread occurrence of its themes, which therefore signify very early spread. From this vantage point we may perhaps conclude that shamanism is a vital early form of spiritual experience which may have helped to develop the twin poles of religious experience as I have described them. There are also other offshoots of shamanism: the practice of various kinds of magic, and more vitally the techniques of shamanistic healing, which remained in many societies a vivid form of pre-scientific medicine. Further, as Eliade remarks (ER: 13, 207), there are relations between shamanism and epic and lyric poetry: it is perhaps the mother of literary creativity. All this fits in well with the birth of drama out of religion. Perhaps, as we have hinted in our discussion of supposedly secular narrative and dramatic performance, drama has never really left the sphere of religion, but is merely treating the existential themes in a new guise.

Especially in the Americas there has over a long period been experimentation with psychedelic drugs, notably mescaline, and tobacco. Naturally early attitudes to such plants differ rather from modern ones. The visions could be attributed to the divine nature of the plants themselves. It is more 'modern' to think that their effects come from being windows, so to speak, of vision – as though the mind is already at some level in touch with transcendental powers to which drugs can clear a pathway (HUXLEY, 1954).

Healing as itself a form of religious experience

Shamanism, as we have seen, is among other things a milieu for healing. The discovery by adepts, such as Shembe and other prophets, of their power to heal parallels the shaman adepts' aquisition of these potencies. There can be no doubt that, for all the scepticism which much modern medicine may bring to bear upon ancient and miraculous forms of healing, up to a point they do work. For one thing, nobody would discover his power to heal if such methods never succeeded. Morale is important in illness and dramatic changes can occur under the influence of psychic procedures. For the person who is healed, the experience is often seen under a doctrinal rubric in which some dislocation of creation or of the world is redressed. The patient is under the influence of some malevolent power realized primordially during the period of creation; or perhaps she is victim of some sin which dislocates the environment. So cure is a drama which restores life in some vital connection. Very often healing is taken as a confirmation of the truth and divine licence of the prophet or teacher, or of the supernatural being through whom the cure is effected. Thus the Virgin's genuine presence and activity at Lourdes is confirmed to the pilgrims whenever there is a miraculous healing. While for many traditional cultures there is a fluidity in the world, and no sharp distinction between the natural and supernatural order, the Catholic church has taken an interesting turn: it has (in line with Aquinas's theology and philosophy) separated out the two orders and then seen the breakthrough of the supernatural into the natural order as definitive of a miracle.

Healing also helps to deal with the problem of possession as something which can derive from both the divine and the diabolical. Exorcists have the intuitive power to recognize an afflicting potency and drive it forth, perhaps to inhabit some other being. One thinks of Jesus and the Gadarene swine.

So the numinous experience can on occasion be a perception of the Evil One, not just the Good. Both visions and auditions can be demonic; there is such testimony to that effect from various prophetic figures (including Zarathustra, Christ and Gnostic sources), and the notion is woven into the whole shamanic corpus.

Secular shamanism?

If we look to the secular worldviews of Marxism and scientific humanism, we see there a repudiation of religious experience. There was a drift away from taking religious experience seriously during the Enlightenment, but Schleiermacher, Otto, Stace and Aldous Huxley attempted to restore credibility to it. Nevertheless, Freud and Jung, together with other adherents of psychoanalysis, have gone back to Macrobius and others in order to somehow provide a scientific status to the study of dreams and more generally to the evaluation of the human life of symbols. Freud was a long way from taking the numinous at face value. Nevertheless, some of the experiential ingredients of traditional religion do make a serious reappearance in his methods of healing. Mysteriously, there are echoes of shamanism. The psychoanalyst has to suffer through the course of analysis, going into his or her own hells in self-awareness. Various parts of the complex social phenomenon of psychoanalysis echo religious ideology. There is first a cosmology, but it is the cosmology of an inner universe – the ego, the id and the superego dance like planets within our depths. The psychoanalyst has his priestly and ritual authority. Even the fees perform a function: they are a sacrifice which indicates seriousness. Dreams are scrutinized as visions which reveal something of a subject's spiritual state. Freudianism also has its doctrines of other religions. What is healthy is set over against unhealthy guilt, and so forth. Jung and Joseph Campbell are more positive in interpreting the religions, trying to give them a new and yet secular validity (GUNTRIP, 1971).

It is, of course, possible to absorb such complexes of value into traditional religions. Both Jung and Freud in differing ways have been drawn into the interpretation of Christianity and Judaism; and there have been a number of attempts to align them with Buddhist and Hindu ideas.

Some summary remarks about the experiential dimension

It is important, first of all, to underline the point that feelings, emotions, are vital in much of religious ritual. It is true that there are rituals of a mechanical or one might say magical character which have to be correctly performed by priests, and it may not matter for these whether anyone feels anything. But generally in worshipping a god it is important to feel loyalty and awe; and though in some forms of mysticism equanimity is a goal, that is in itself a feeling of absence of feeling – in other words, it still matters what you feel. It is not the same as a careless indifference. So much of religious practice is soaked in emotions. Without them, the practice would be insincere, mechanical, merely external, not really worth undertaking. However, in this chapter I have concentrated more on those dramatic encounters which are sometimes signalled out more narrowly as religious experience.

We have noted three forms for the two poles: that is, the numinous experience, the divine conversion and the divine disposition on the one hand; and the contemplative experience, the luminous conversion and the luminous disposition on the other. They could be named, in a rather loaded way and in terms of Western, mainly Christian, language, as revelation, conversion and ongoing faith, and mystical experience, mystical conversion and mystical union. In addition I named panenhenic experience as a special sort of event. I argued that the two poles may perhaps develop out of a primordial shamanic experience. This schema helps to explain some patterns of belief and practice. I also noted that healing and the use of psychedelic drugs are relevant as phenomena alongside the main kinds of religious experience.

CHAPTER FIVE

The Ethical and Legal Dimension

Ethics, law, societies and sub-societies

While sociologists have generally taken up the classification of religious organizations into churches, denominations and sects, this tends to fit best Western and in particular Christian phenomena. In reality, the relation of traditions of one sort or another is more floating and complex. In classical China there emerged, for instance, a complex symbiosis between four or more traditions: religious Taoism, Confucianism, Buddhism and folk religion, which overlapped and blended (BERLING, 1980). Until the Meiji restoration in 1868 one could look to something similar in Japan (Shinto functioning as an aspect of the folk tradition) (ANESAKI, 1963). It has usually been the case in Asia that Buddhism has had an interface with peasant cults of a miscellany of gods and spirits, and has sometimes incorporated elements of Brahmanism in court ceremonial and the like (SPIRO, 1982). In the Ottoman empire and other phases and areas of Islamic rule there has been a defined Islamic place for Christianity and Judaism (COULSON, 1971). During the major part of European history Judaism was a similar sub-tradition with a defined but in this case Christian place in the scheme of things. Only in very modern times, roughly since the French and American revolutions, has the pluralism of denominations and sects come into being. Meanwhile India, with its emerging Hindu federation of religious manifestations, its lesser groups such as Parsees and Christians and its (over a long period) parallel Buddhist Sangha and laity, has tended to be a much more complicated congeries of traditions (BROCKINGTON, 1981).

All these cases contrast with those small-scale societies where religion and society are effectively coterminous. It is not surprising if in all this religious ethics plays diverse roles, and legal systems also have a differing purchase on reality.

It is difficult to disentangle ethical from legal requirements. But briefly we may look first on legal systems as embedding ethical values, though they also play differing roles in differing social circumstances. Thus in Buddhism the *vinaya* is essentially a means of regulating the daily life of the Sangha. But Buddhism is broader than the Sangha, for the Order, while including close lay disciples, is surrounded by a wide penumbra of supporters who may or may not make up the great majority of society, as circumstances dictate. The situation in classical Eastern cultures is more complex still. To simplify: the law relates mainly to the heart of the Buddhist organization. In the case of the Hindu tradition the law-books of Manu apply to all those who acknowledge Brahmanical *smṛti*, even though at any given time large numbers of tribals, Buddhists, Jains and outlying mainstream religious traditions may in practice not follow the *dharma*. In the case of Islamic Shari'a we have a set of varying but largely uniform systems which explicitly aim to regulate the whole of the community. The 'natural' condition of the Muslim is to be found in an Islamic society, not in a minority state. The aim of Islam is to be both the spiritual and temporal life-pattern. On the other hand, Judaism has nurtured a Law (or Teaching) which generally applies to the sub-society of Jews. This is for two reasons: rarely have Jews been in control of society at large; and the details of the oral Torah are to be applied particularly to Jews – they are not of widespread application to Gentiles. The first of these reasons was reinforced particularly in the main period of medieval and early modern Christian history in Europe by the segregation, persecution and exclusion of Jews from mainstream civil society.

Morality, religion and motivations to be good

While a certain autonomy of morals can be detected in a cross-cultural context, since there are notable similarities between different virtues and rules in traditionally unrelated societies, morals are integrated in differing ways into religious traditions (LITTLE and TWISS, 1978). This affects the content to some degree, but to a greater degree it affects the motivations given to ordinary people to be good and observant. It makes quite a bit of difference, for instance, whether you believe in reincarnation. In those traditions where this is taken for granted, ethical conduct can be a mode of generative personal merit or karma (these being somewhat differing concepts but having similar advantages), which helps you to a higher life next time. This brings about a more educational attitude to morality: that is, it is something learnt over more than one life. On the other hand, a single life ending in the judgment of a God, as in the Egyptian Book of the Dead and in Western theisms, gives being good or bad a more dramatic meaning. Even in Buddhism though, one of the Buddha's similes underlines how rare and privileged it is to be a human being, which injects a very serious note into the Buddha's exhortations to virtue. But reincarnation theory implies, conversely, that wickedness is not completely fatal: there is always hope, since hells are not permanent – in effect they are purgatories. Moreover, the gradualism of moral progress seems realistic to people. You do not need to be a saint straight off.

Although in the theisms the weight of God's demands may seem tremendous (reinforced by the highly numinous character of the Divine Being, a person who may be merciful but who also exhibits his or her wrath), there is some mitigation because of contervailing aspects of divine behaviour. There is in the Christian tradition, for instance, a tension between the divine anger and grace. God's loving nature leads him to forgive the sinner, if the sinner repents. There is also some problem of motivation when the believer does right in order to go to heaven rather than out of the true love of God, or if he does right simply to avoid hell.

In the Confucian tradition metaphysical rewards are unimportant, though self-esteem within society is important. There was debate about whether human beings are naturally good, and the prevalent view was that they are. So the inculcation of virtue turned into an educational project, bringing out the best in the individual and nurturing his good impulses. Though the Confucian tradition is from one point of view the least 'religious' of the classical traditions, it takes ritual very seriously, much more than some other traditions, such as Buddhism, which sees it largely in psychological terms. Confucian *li* or proper behaviour, into which is interwoven ritual etiquette, is crucial for the good life. But in addition ethics is clearly placed within a political frame: in this respect Confucianism appeals to people to follow the moral life in order to ensure stability and prosperity in society. The motive in this respect is this-worldly (FINGARETTE, 1972).

In many ways, the ethical stance of the Jewish tradition is the more interesting. The formation of Judaism in the early centuries CE, after the destruction and the collapse of the religion as practised in the land of Israel, created the vast learning which came to be applied to the Torah, in particular the oral Torah: very much the sphere of the rabbis. This had some interesting effects. One was to embed the main principles of morality, which had been summed up in the Ten Commandments, in a great web of correct ritual and moral behaviour, controlling all the details of daily life. This was a way of making ethics and law constant reminders of God's rule and presence. Somehow, rabbinic Judaism manages to combine a deep sense of the majesty of God with a sense of his familiarity. At the same time the Torah defined the people. The people were created not on the whole genetically but by loyalty to the Law. This gave ethics a personal quality, a quality of personal loyalty both to the people and to God. As the rules developed, life became more awkward to prosecute in wider society, but this helped to ensure the continuance of the community across bad patches of history. Moreover, important aspects of the law were not primarily ethical but ritual in content. The kosher food regulations forbade the eating of pork and shellfish, for instance. This was a question of impurity, and was adopted, like other rituals, out of obedience to God. Another interesting side to Jewish obedience was the enormous prestige which came to be given to study of the Torah and of the immense Talmuds, which encoded huge numbers of rabbinical decisions about the Law. This prestige in learning had an interesting spiritual quality. Thus the details of sacrifices and other rituals connected with the Temple were studied with great seriousness, even though they had no application and would not have any till the Last Things, when the Temple might be restored.

The effects of metaphysics on ethics

We have noted in the previous discussion some of the motivations for people to follow religious law in varying cultures. We have also noted that there is a great deal of overlap in the diverse traditions – it is typical to find prohibitions against murder, stealing, adultery, lying, for instance. Despite these similarities such bans are expressed in differing ways, and with different restrictions. In some cases the reasons have to do with general beliefs expressed in the religion or tradition in question. Similar variations apply to virtues. Let us begin with an obvious example. Buddhism's ban on killing in principle applies to all living beings. It would be wrong gratuitously to kill a lion or a fly. This attitude clearly stems from belief in rebirth. To put it colourfully the lion might be your deceased aunt. Or, to put it more soberly, the lion is your kin. In the Hindu tradition it is wrong to kill humans, and cows are sacred. But this prohibition on killing is applied within the context of the caste system: hence the penalties for killing a Brahmin or a cow are much more severe than those for killing an untouchable. In certain religions, including that of the *kṣatriya* within the Hindu context, you have a duty to kill in battle (hence the dilemma presented in the *Gītā*, especially as the slaughter in the upcoming battle involves kith and kin) (DUMÉZIL, 1970).

Then again there are differences regarding sexual aberrations. While Islam, Judaism and Christianity forbid adultery, in practice other sexual faults are treated as sins – though adultery itself is of course a function of marriage laws. Moreover conceptions of women's status affect the relevant punishments (ANDERSON, 1959). These differences are only fortuitously connected to the main metaphysical beliefs. There is no necessary connection between monotheism and polygyny, let us say. But monotheism with its attendant belief in revelation can freeze law in the consciousness of the faithful. Because of the relation between the Holy Book and the law, there is a strong entrenchment of the rules governing society.

There are also some variations depending on whether the emphasis is on the objective prevention of certain ills like killing or lying or on the intentions of the actor. For instance, there is a much broader definition of wrong speech in Buddhism than in the monotheisms (SADDHATISSA, 1970). The Buddhist is discouraged not merely from lying but from unnecessary, painful and malicious utterance. In fact all the five precepts in Buddhism are rather widely framed. This is not merely because of emphasis on intentions, but it chimes in with it. Moreover, in mainstream Buddhism, because ritual is looked on in a utilitarian way, there are no ritual taboos, and ritual itself is thought of as a means of cultivating character and good psychological dispositions. There is of course no Divine Person towards whom the individual has loyalty or obligation. (I shall return to the topic of taboo a little later.)

The belief that God wishes to create a whole spiritual society is perhaps more evident in Islam and Mormonism (SHIPPS, 1985). It is evident in the duty of the faithful to give alms, since this provides a thoroughgoing social service that helps to look after the poor and ailing. This is one aspect of religious attitudes to money, which in some instances betray a particular metaphysical outlook on finance. Thus over a long period classical Christianity frowned on the charging of interest, and this is still a principle in Islam (NEALE, 1976). It was a sign of Christian modernism when, under the impact of Protestantism, it came to recognize up-to-date finance.

Another important feature of certain religions is the strong belief in duties to ancestors. Although in some weak sense every society thinks of the dead as owed some duties (the honouring of wills, for example, and the need to tend graves), it is in societies where the dead are considered really to be living that a special ethos prevails. This is especially noteworthy in Far Eastern countries with their partly Chinese cultural heritage (HSU, 1948). Because writing has been known for so long in those regions, there is a deeply entrenched and effective way of recording the dead and so of maintaining contact with them. In Africa and other cultures where the concept of the living dead is vital, much the same attitude applies even if memory by itself is less effective than the use of writing (MBITI, 1969). Hence some of the dead may be thought of as genuinely living, while others have faded, because the last humans who can visualize those individuals 'over the horizon' are themselves gone from the scene and have passed over. The idea that the ancestors remain as members of society is important and makes a difference to the scope of ethical duties (which include duties to perform rites on behalf of the dead).

Another effect of metaphysics on ethics has to do with the spiritual or ritual constitution of society, even apart from the question of ancestors. We shall have more to say about the general patterns of social belief in Chapter 6 on the social dimension. But it is worth remarking here on the Indian caste system, which divides people into a hierarchy of ritually divided groups. It helps to make ritual duties pervasive and thus gives a ritual to the whole notion of morality. Thus marriage and its obligations are not viewed as merely ethical in flavour; the very junction between two people itself takes on a sacramental significance. But caste has another side to it: the law books prescribe diverse penalties for the killing of different casts, and parallel punishments for other offences against caste members. This makes the whole universe a kind of ethical hierarchy, with differing kinds of human beings in effect becoming different species. This is only slightly modified by the ability of living beings to wander up and down the human and living hierarchy. Buddhism, Jainism and the *nāstika* schools generally make a radical contrast, since they treat human beings as part of a single species.

We should note the behaviour of secular ideologies in this regard. Both fascism and nationalisms tend to treat other nationalities as belonging to inferior species, or at least species towards whom you do not have the same duties. The death of foreigners is not such a matter of sorrow and can in war be a cause of joy. While many nations maintain civilized relations and reserve humiliations for the football field, others permit cruel behaviour towards one another's citizens, as in the Yugoslav civil war. Nazi ideology drew a line within the human species, with sub-humans lying on the other side from the Aryans (LAQUEUR, 1976).

The clash between Buddhist and Hindu attitudes to untouchability was seen in the way many Harijans became Buddhists under the leadership of Ambedkar before the Second World War (KUBER, 1978). And of course from within the Hindu tradition came powerful impulses to reform, notably under the leadership of Gandhi. It is worth noting this as an example of moral differentiation within a tradition. While we have hitherto been discussing the metaphysical relationship to the ethical as if it is a monolithic one within traditions, this is something of a simplification. The Indian is such a complex federation of castes and sub-groups that many forms of behaviour become possible, sanctioned in one way or another: warfare, homosexuality, meat-eating, and so on. It is without doubt the most variegated society in the world.

Another aspect of ethical conduct and legal provisions concerns toleration of sub-groups. In Islamic societies provision is made for a limited toleration of Christians and Jews, who are granted a certain status in the wider society on the ground that they follow the line of prophets who preceded Muhammad, and have holy books recognized in the Muslim tradition. But similar toleration does not extend to pagans, that is idolaters.

The variations which occur in the world's religions regarding drugs and intoxicants derive in part from views of the mind. The Buddhist ban on intoxicants springs from the belief that the path to nirvana requires clarity of mind, in particular self-awareness. Not only are intoxicants liable to stimulate runaway feelings, they are also confusing. Hence the ethic related clearly to the claim that the hindrances to liberations are greed, hatred and delusion, above all delusion. The Qur'an's ban on alcohol has a somewhat differing basis, and it is interesting that the imagery of heaven includes the joys of alcohol. So its evil nature is provisional, although absolutely enjoined.

The effects of the Enlightenment and colonialism on religious ethics

In the foregoing we have glanced at some traditional attitudes. But during the modern period such secular worldviews as the nationalisms and reforming philosophies have had their effects upon the Christian tradition, just as other traditions were later challenged by colonialism and related developments. One of the main thrusts of

Enlightenment thinking was to discover a morality which was autonomous. The most influential was that of Kant (CASSIRER, 1981),
and after that nineteenth-century utilitarianism (REEDER and
OUTKA, 1973). These represented a challenge to most religious
traditions, which were not on the whole inclined to jettison what may
be called revealed morality. But in so far as they did they came to
adopt modernist positions. Buddhism had the least difficulty, since it
was not exactly a revealed religion, and the Buddha often used
consequentialist arguments. Confucianism could proudly stand in its
own right as an ethical philosophy which if necessary could be
secularized in a modern way (FUNG, 1953). The trouble in this case
was that it was embedded in an old-fashioned bureaucracy. Confucianism was too wedded to the old literary examination system
which had difficulty, to put it no more strongly, in absorbing modern
scientific attitudes if China were to be able to strengthen itself in the
struggle with the West. Japan by contrast saw clearly that modernization, including ethical modernization, could be achieved and that at
the same time nationalism could be promoted by adding Shinto
attitudes as an ingredient in the national curriculum and by turning to
a renewed imperial ritual.

Both Kantian and utilitarian versions of ethics were at odds with
nationalism, though they could be shrunk to fit within the nationalist
framework (KAMENKA, 1976). They provided materials which
could be blended with the rising liberal Protestantism that was providing a new Christian optimism in the latter part of the nineteenth
century. The new industrialism was held to require nationalism,
whose function was to provide large enough building blocks for the
modern world, together with the various infrastructures capitalism
demanded, such as education and railways. Since capitalism itself
was one of the engines of European empire it also helped to promote overseas nationalism by reaction to colonial domination and by
the very demands which had fuelled it in the first place.

These developments transformed religious cultures into nationalist, modernizing ones, at least among the relevant elites. This was
evident in Japan, and in a differing way in India, in Russia, in the
Islamic world and ultimately in Africa. The Americas had a somewhat
different form of nationalism, and the USA in particular combined

Enlightenment and Protestant values in a constitution which gave peculiar definition to the society. Islamic modernism and nationalism had a rather chequered career, since the Ottoman empire was slow to fall apart, and the post-Ottoman settlement, manufactured in the Middle East by Britain and France, broke up the Arab nation. Meanwhile, in Europe, the effects of the new transformations led to the emancipation of the Jews, and this – combined with emigration to the USA – created Reform and Conservative as well as Orthodox Judaism. Zionism took its own secular path. But the reforming movements in all the major religions led to some ethical changes, which I shall sketch here in part.

In the Hindu environment modernism created pressures to reform widow-burning and aspects of the caste system. This came to be the great crusade of Gandhi, though he combined this with elements of non-Enlightenment ethics, namely of the simplification of life and reliance on rural values. In some degree he was influenced by Tolstoy, who at the end of his life espoused a Slavophil Christianity (but not Orthodoxy), which likewise underlined simplicity of life. In actual fact, it was India's elite who adopted modernist morality, while paying lip-service to ruralism. Beneath the English-speaking elite the mass of *dharmic* complexity carried on. Swami Vivekananda created a viable national ideology based on Hindu values and drawing upon the classical Non-Dualist philosophy, but it was also an ideology that embraced all religions, thereby creating an important place for Muslim, Christian and other Indian nationalists (his philosophy came under challenge following the rise of the Bharata Janatha Party). It was compatible with utilitarianism, in that Vivekananda thought of the highest spiritual life as involving the attainment of happiness, though this was a deeper, more spiritual concept than the notions of the British utilitarians.

In the case of Buddhism in Ceylon and South-east Asia there was little cause to change Buddhist ethics, and the religion could represent itself, as I have hinted, as already modern. In Japan, we have noted the role played by State Shinto. The Meiji restoration saw the forcible division between Buddhist and Shinto shrines, and Shinto became a means of ensuring loyalty to the *kokutai* or national essence as incarnated by the Emperor. Nationalism was boosted ethically by a greater emphasis on warrior codes, namely Bushido and the more martial aspects of Zen (MISHIMA, 1978).

Unfortunately for China, its traditional religions were unable to supply relevant modernization. Confucianism was too much entangled in an increasingly outmoded imperial bureaucracy. Buddhism, in so far as it underwent reform, proceeded in the direction of a restoration of world-negating spirituality, which hardly matched the demands of nationalism. Taoism was too magical to blend easily with modern society, and its older philosophical values were pacifist. Folk religion did not have national standing. So China turned to foreign secular systems – above all, in the long run, Maoism, whose ferocity turned well to war but destroyed the ethical system of China during the Cultural Revolution.

Marxism was spuriously modern and imperfectly ethical. It was the former because it mistook the temper of modern science, better caught by Popper than by Lenin: suppression of views is not the way to pioneer creativity in scientific knowledge. Its ethical problems arose from both its totalitarian character and its new caste distinctions. The message of class warfare conflicted with respect for human rights, the basis of all modern ethics, while the attempt to obliterate religions struggled against the ethical values of traditional society. When Marxism collapsed in the Soviet Union and its satellites, it was partly because of a recognition of the moral void which it had created.

The Islamic world underwent more complicated evolutions. Apart from India, Egypt was the first major modernizing country within the Islamic sphere, and attempts were made to reform law and bring changes to such areas as marriage, the charging of interest and kinds of punishments. In the period after the First World War, secularism was established in Turkey under Kemal Atatürk, and after the Second World War it came to be the predominant ideology in Syria and Iraq, with a strong infusion of Arab nationalism (which was the case in Egypt too). A similar worldview commanded the Palestinian movement. But this was succeeded by a neo-Islamic resurgence, which made gains in Pakistan, Iran, Sudan, Algeria and elsewhere. At stake was the status of Shari'a.

Modernism's chief successes were in the West. Protestantism had its fundamentalist backlash, but the mainline churches and denominations saw an integration of the Christian ethic and liberal values, so that marriage was largely modified by divorce, abortion tended to be liberalized, the status of women was raised, sexual freedoms were enhanced, and so on. A major development was the reformation instituted by Vatican II in 1962–5. Although the official teachings of the Roman Catholic church remained conservative in some respects, not least over artificial means of birth control, the actual practice of Catholics in the United States, Italy and other Western countries tended to be as radical as that of secular and Protestant citizens.

In Africa, the situation was much more mixed. The translation of the Bible into numerous languages led many Africans to perceive a tension between the scriptures and the teaching of missionaries, notably in relation to family law and polygyny in particular. Attitudes to health in the Bible often echoed those of indigenous societies. The result of such tensions was the emergence of a large number of new African religious movements, under black leadership and manifesting new forms of Christian worship and teaching. These new movements were a major ingredient in the post-colonial era of Christianity in Africa (BARRETT, 1982).

Nationalism and religions

In the twentieth century the predominant ethos became that of national loyalty. To a considerable degree the religious traditions became subservient to the national ideal. This had already been greatly facilitated by the emergence of magisterial Protestantism in northern Europe, and it was further advanced by the adoption of particular forms of religion in the formation of new national identities in comparison with neighbouring countries, as with Orthodoxy in Romania and Catholicism in Poland. Such identifications as we have noted became vital in a number of Middle Eastern and Asian countries. The consequence was that debates over new ethical values, especially in regard to family values, became conducted pregnantly within national boundaries rather than on a transnational basis.

One of the most intriguing developments among the traditions was the emergence of Zionism as a distinctive strand in Jewish thought and aspiration. While in due course religious Zionism became a significant factor it was itself in its main impulse a secular nationalist movement. This led to a very different ethos in the state of Israel from that of much of the diaspora and certainly a quite different set of ideals from those of Orthodox or other religious forms of Judaism. But there remain ambiguities, because Orthodoxy is given special privileges in Israel over certain aspects of the law, for instance the observance of the Shabbat, and also because the definition of being Jewish is religious, both formally and informally. The heroic success in building a Hebrew-speaking state on democratic lines in circumstances that have been difficult, even perilous, infuses Israel with a spirit reminiscent of ancient times.

The way in which Judaism has divided into differing branches, even if the sense of Jewishness has not, is also striking: no other religion has been so affected by modernism. Reform Judaism, which no longer follows the Torah in detail, but which sees in modern morality a vindication of the ancient ethical monotheism of the Jews, has a very different shape from the traditional faith (BLAU, 1976). It is close in spirit to those more rationalist branches of Protestant Christianity, notably Unitarianism. There was a great contrast between this Enlightenment-soaked kind of Jewish faith, which had a big appeal in the modernizing climate of the New World, and Hasidic Judaism, which came to dominate much of the Orthodox scene. Here ethics was taken up into that mixed numinous and contemplative mystical disposition which could see sacred significance in every item of living and saw in ethical behaviour a mysterious mode of co-operating in God's continuing struggle to overcome the satanic powers.

Reflections on the virtues in various traditions

Earlier we discussed the effects of metaphysical values on the rules governing moral behaviour. It is also worth reflecting on the virtues, and the way other dimensions of religion are relevant to them. I will not try to be comprehensive here, but will just indicate some interesting connections in some of the major traditions. In some ways the easiest one to begin with is Buddhism. Here the large virtues are described as the holy abodes or *brahmavihāras*, which are four in number. They are benevolence or friendliness (*mettā*), compassion (*karuṇā*), joy in others' joy (*muditā*) and *upekkhā* or equanimity. We may begin with the last. *Upekkhā* seems so obviously to spring from the central place allotted to contemplation. Thus self-awareness or *sati*, which is an important instrument in the individual's struggle for self-control, is meant to be a continuous way of knowing your sensations and dispositions. This helps us to check such impulses as anger and greed. It is clear that the whole strategy is to calm ourselves, and the net result of all that will be to achieve equanimity. Nevertheless, this is not the same as indifference.

Equanimity is important, however, in stilling our impulses in ways which will help us to develop the three more 'positive' virtues. It is clear that two of these in particular go together: compassion and sympathetic joy. It is because one shows suffering at others' suffering and the other joy at their joy that they match. Underpinning them is the benevolence which comes at the head of the list. Because Buddhism's general analysis of the human condition centres on *dukkha* or illfare very often compassion is seen as the principal virtue, because it sympathizes with the sad state of the human condition. But even more dispassionately we might see the four divine abodes as equal. At any rate, it seems reasonable to deduce the flavour of the four virtues from the contemplative core of Buddhism. Yet we need to note that the contemplation does not work without the benevolence. If the individual does not display benevolence, he easily veers into selfishness. The *arhat* without compassion is after all no saint, because he selfishly pursues his own salvation without consideration for the fate of others. It is interesting that this vital truth in the Theravada is often neglected by commentators. This, of course, is the secret link between the Theravada and the Great Vehicle. In other words, the Bodhisattva was always there.

If we now turn to the Christian tradition, we can speculate on the relation between religious experience and the ethical dimension expressed in the virtues (not to mention the deadly sins). Let us begin with the classical theological virtues (so called), faith, hope and love. They are dubbed theological virtues, which indicates their close relationship to the metaphysical or doctrinal aspect of the faith. But we need at this point to step back a bit and note the way Christianity classically saw itself as exhibiting its full ritual and doctrinal complexity. For in being a Jewish offshoot and at the same time worshipping Christ and the Holy Spirit (celebrating the death and resurrection of the Master and the coming down of the Spirit at the time of the formation of the church – and so celebrating as it were two incarnations), Christianity necessarily involved itself in some version or other of the Trinity doctrine. This had implications for ethical conduct and attitude which I have already touched on: love ultimately had to be the central core of Christian ethics. But, apart from love, why the emphasis on faith and hope, and why should these somehow be virtues (BEACH and NIEBUHR, 1955)?

They connected, of course, with the narrative dimension of religion. Faith was a form of life which expressed loyalty to the past, while hope expressed loyalty to the future. Faith grasped the life, death and resurrection of Jesus as having profound meaning for the individual Christian, while hope grasped the future, the Last Things. The Christian was supposed to conduct his life in the light of both the past and the future. There were wider implications in these ideas. In following Jesus the Christian was committed to the ethical life, and in looking forward to the ultimate consummation of God's work he thought of his ethical life as working with God in the future of the divine kingdom and its success. In brief, in classical Christianity the ethical life was seen not as autonomous but as closely interwoven with the spiritual life.

Perhaps the virtue of hope was especially important in the early church. We can see in this the vitality of the eschatological aspect of the narrative dimension. In modern times this virtue has tended to get secularized. After all, a prominent feature of the nineteenth and early twentieth century was optimism about our secular societies. This was true in all three of the major branches of secularist thought. In nationalism it was hoped that liberation of the nation would lead to a special new future. This had been true of Italy in the nineteenth century, of India in the 1950s, of so many optimistic parts of the world. Among many Christians, however, hope has faded, save among evangelicals who retain a vivid sense of the second coming. For a long period Marxism retained its eschatology: the hope of a better society (a new kingdom of God or rather of humanity) was nurtured. During much of the nineteenth century and to some degree through the twentieth (despite Nazism, the Holocaust, Mao, Stalin and other vast tragedies), the secular humanists hoped that better things would supervene in the future, in the name of progress and out of an evolutionary sense of the way of the world. Yet among Christians, except for evangelicals, we hear less of the theology of hope.

If the theological virtues relate strongly to the mythic or narrative dimension, the impact of the experiential dimension is more ambiguous. The feeling for the numinous can be used both to reinforce hierarchy and to militate against it. It can be used to infuse levels of the church and of society in ways that add sacred power to vertical dimensions. Some of the imagery of religion, such as the idea of kingship, could reinforce the feudal system in medieval Europe. On the other hand, as with Islam, the very overwhelming power of God can render all men (or all men and women) equal, as with some of the emerging Protestant ideologies. Calvinism's terrifying predestinationism could be democratic in its effects. As for mysticism, its tie to monasticism led more or less to its disappearance in the Reformation aftermath. It had its own authoritarianism, in part because the fabric of monasticism followed some of the patterns of the feudal church, in part because the strong discipline required of the ascetic and contemplative life led to important patterns of obedience.

The church in its classical phase, that is, both East and West up to the time of the Reformation, inherited the ethics of Aristotle and the Greeks. Perhaps it is in this dimension in some ways that the blended character of Christianity is most clearly visible. The second half of the twentieth century has rediscovered this because Latin America, Africa, Asia and other parts of the Third World are beginning vigorously to challenge the European (and American) ethos of the faith (BARRETT, 1982). In philosophy and theology, in ethics, in social orientation, Christianity has for most of its life been highly Westernized. The challenges of other parts of the world have been multiple: bringing African values into social orientation, importing a special breed of Marxism into Latin American faith and politics, and incorporating Asian philosophies, both South Asian and Far Eastern, in the expression of Christian doctrine in Asia.

A third example of virtue can be derived from the Confucian tradition. Here some injection of the mythic dimension is important in so far as Confucius himself had a deep regard for history, as he saw it, going back to the legendary ancestry of the Chinese people. Moreover, as we noted earlier, the ritual dimension had a vital part to play in Confucius's worldview, so that *li* or proper behaviour was central. It had more of a social and moral meaning than a religious one. From the standpoint of the rival Taoist philosophy, at least in the ancient literature of Lao-tzu and Chuang-tzu, *li* was much too formal and lacked spontaneity, but it chimed in, of course, with K'ung's emphasis upon education and traditionalism. Nevertheless, the central virtue is the all-inclusive *jen*, humaneness or humanity. Nearly a tenth of the chapters of the Analects concern it. Basically it means love of human beings, but it is supposed also to include other good attitudes, such as sincerity, generosity and earnestness. Though *li* had its formality it also was controlled by *jen*, involving both respectfulness towards other people and sincerity. So propriety was not just a matter of good manners and proper behaviour, but involved a sense of sincere concern for others. Later, Mencius reinforced such attitudes with the affirmation of human beings' essential goodness.

Confucius's ethics were deeply linked with politics. His was a vision of superior leadership, and this remained a norm throughout Chinese history, for Confucianism came to be the ideology of the mandarinate, until that collapsed in 1905, with the abolition of the imperial civil service. The ideal was the superior person or *chün-tzu*, who is linked to heaven. While Confucius played down the personal nature of the Divine, he nevertheless regarded heaven as a moral force, governing the cosmos; and the gentleman or superior man understands the will or mandate of heaven, loves the people, is courageous and wise, is eager to follow what is morally right, and studies deeply. In general, Confucius looked on virtue as deriving from above, and as involving an ambition for the superior life. The inferior person is more interested in personal gain. All the qualities of the *chün-tzu* are relevant to rule, and hence the close link between ethical life and politics. Of all the philosophies of the ancient world, Confucianism most clearly exhibits the way in which political life should be governed by moral principles. In effect it is an ideology for the training of political leadership, predicated on a hierarchical society.

Moreover, in its dominant Neo-Confucianist form, based on the example of Chu Hsi, the twelfth-century influential Neo-Confucian philosophy, the ideology is predominantly rationalist, with a strong emphasis on formal ritual as having (or as having had) two functions – helping to sustain the workings of the state and the embellishment and self-cultivation of the human being (GARDNER, 1986). Given too that Confucianism is a worldview closely linked to a society which is hierarchically ordered, it is not surprising that a central place should be given to the virtue of filial piety or *hsiao*. That same attitude should inform the other relevant relations: that of the minister with the ruler, that of the wife with the husband, that of the younger sibling with the elder sibling, and so on. Conversely, there are vital relations of reciprocity, so that the father trains and nurtures his son. The hierarchy of obligation of junior to senior applies even if the parent does not fulfil his obligations. It is in addition a chain which constitutes the duties to forebears.

We have looked at three major exemplars of the virtues in differing religious traditions, broadly bracketed under the varying influences of the contemplative life, the narrative schema of salvation history and the cultivation of ritual behaviour.

Some concluding reflections about the ethical and legal

Naturally there is a very wide spread in all societies, especially the myriad smaller societies, of ethical injunctions. There are considerable overlaps arising from the need for a certain framework in creating a stable society. It is true that familial arrangements can undergo considerable variations, but there have to be limits upon killing, lying and so on. As we have noted, there are great differences in the atmospherics of virtue – for instance, in accordance with differing emphases upon dimensions and styles of religion.

Moreover, modern society is becoming increasingly plural, and this tends paradoxically towards a single framework within which diverse social groups can live together. In those countries which are predominantly of one religion – as it happens, today these are mostly Muslim – there is the possibility of the imposition of a single law (and such societies often employ migrant workers who have to conform to the overall law). There are often nations with a majority religion which manages to place some part of its own law on the statute books – for example, abortion law in Poland or Ireland – even if a broader imposition of tradition is no longer feasible. And small-scale societies which were at one time relatively independent are no longer so, because they find themselves absorbed in a larger polity, such as Uganda or Papua New Guinea, with a national legal and moral system.

Though these reflections suggest greater homogeneity, there are ways in which genuine divergences can live side by side. An outstanding case is vegetarianism, which has spread from some of the older traditions, such as South Asian religious movements, and obtained much greater influence in the West, as part of the wider New Age mentality and of a renewed sense of conscientiousness towards animals.

There are also tangles of ethical values arising out of the complexities of modern technology – birth control, abortion methods, prolongation of life, the determination of sex in babies before birth, transplants of organs and so forth – which are introducing more dilemmas into medical and biological ethics. Rarely are these easy to resolve. As with so many other legal and ethical issues there is room for traditional interpreters of religions to manoeuvre.

CHAPTER SIX

The Social Dimension

The social dimension: some preliminary points

For various reasons it is best for us to begin our contemplation of the
social dimension of religion by looking at the various key individuals.
Some of them we have touched on already, especially in discussing
the ritual side of religion and society in Chapter 2. They include the
priest, the prophet, the contemplative, the healer, the shaman, the
guru, the incarnation, the sage, the preacher, the rabbi, the jurist, the
imam, the king, the monk, the nun, the hermit, the theologian, the
philosopher, the saint, the martyr and the icon maker. These experts,
functionaries, charismatic figures and holy persons exhibit in their
differing ways many of the modes of religious expression. Alongside
them we might place some secular individuals.

After we have given a sketch of these figures we can move on to
larger-scale configurations of religious societies. Naturally we shall
draw on work in the sociology and anthropology of religion, but we
shall try to give a wider perspective than sometimes emerges from
these disciplines. For anthropology has often in the past paid too
much attention to small-scale societies and give an insufficiently
rounded view of the larger regions and literate traditions; sociology
has concentrated too much on home-grown, that is Western, developments. One day we shall with good fortune achieve a global perspective on religions and societies. But there is no doubt about the major
contributions of the social sciences during the last hundred years.

Some religious figures to begin with:
prophet, sage, guru, contemplative

The aim of this preliminary look at certain pre-eminent figures in religions is to exhibit something of a contrast between them. We also need to note that there can be overlaps between functions: a priest, for example, can be a prophet too. Even so, the shapes do differ (LEWIS, 1971).

We can begin with Hebrew prophecy. The principal figure is a variety of ecstatic who could foretell Yahweh's message. It is true (and here is the variation) that in the Hebrew Bible some so-called prophets or *navi'* were tied to cults which may have been more mechanical and inspired, for instance casting lots. A prophet might or might not have a close tie to ritual, and could thus have been an independent speaker of sacred things. The most important kind though was an ecstatic possessed by a vision or audition from God. In terms of our discussion of religious experience earlier, a prophet is one who, above all, has a numinous experience and then speaks in the name of the Divine.

Such a person appears not just in the Hebrew Bible of course; he features in the New Testament too, in the figure of Paul, and for that matter in the person of Jesus (though he was not *only* a prophet). The founders of other traditions, such as Zarathustra and Muhammad, were also prophets. Mani no doubt conformed to a similar pattern. There seem also to have been likenesses between certain prophets and founders of numinous movements in India and East Asia; we shall explore this point further somewhat later.

Very often the prophets of the Western line seem to have been social critics as well as conveyers of the divine message. In the Hebrew tradition from the eighth century they came to be literary figures, and indeed formers of books which came to be part of canonical scriptures (LINDBLOM, 1962).

Generally speaking the prophet is not treated as divine, but rather as the mouthpiece of the divine. The logic of the numinous maintains itself: the possessed figure is different from the god. Nevertheless the prophet may be utterly convinced that the message he has to offer comes from God and has unwavering truth.

The figure of the sage in the Far Eastern tradition is rather different. He is a literary figure, but not so much possessed as a person of wisdom, who combines both knowledge and deep self-control. He may be in contact with heaven or the Tao, and uses his knowledge to advise human beings. But he is not primarily a recipient of numinous messages or visions. The sage is a learned person. Thus in the Han era it was thought that, because literature is a long and arduous study, only the leisured and well-bred can study it effectively: only such a person can become a sage. In short, being a sage is a matter of deep education. Being a wise person the leader exhibits wisdom and restraint and sets an example to those he rules.

As a religious ideal, then, the sage is removed from the more ecstatic and often harshly critical messages of the prophet, and is embedded in rather a differing scene. There may be variants of course: the Taoist sage has a less formal aspect than the Confucian wise person. His harmony with the Way gives him a high status, rather than strictly learning. It is the Confucian sage, however, who came to predominate as the ideal until recent times.

The guru is chiefly evident in the Hindu tradition. As the name implies, he is a person of weight. He is a spiritual guide or preceptor, very often a single wanderer or a celibate teacher, or a Brahmin instructor, and commands absolute obedience. He is often, too, the leader of a group of disciples, and so in effect may command a small denomination, or even in successful cases a large one. He is to some extent analogous to both the prophet and the sage, but he is different from both of them. The analogy arises because he is a direct path to the divine and thus has revelatory power, but he does not share the typical prophet's experience of the numinous – he is more like an incarnation of the divine. On the other hand, like the sage he has knowledge, and may utter his teachings in the form of theology. He is above all authoritative. He is not expressing the wisdom of the literary and educated person; rather he is the exponent of his own system of belief. He derives his authoritative stature from his spiritual accomplishment – his progress, often, along the mystical or contemplative path. He can thus resemble the contemplative type. The guru's student is an absolute disciple. The student of the sage has more independence because the subject matter is more open and accessible. Moreover, the guru typically has a succession and so comes to form part of an authoritative chain.

The contemplative is the mystic, and is found easily in a number of religious traditions (UNDERHILL, 1911). While the prophet has a numinous message, the mystic's message is unitive. Such a person may also be a teacher (may indeed be a guru). He may also be a monk or she may be a nun. Mystics can be found in all traditions: Hasidim, Sufis, Eastern Orthodox mystics, followers of Sankara, Buddhists, Ch'an Buddhists, Taoists and so on (WOODS, 1980). The mystic or contemplative often differs to a considerable degree from the other kinds of teachers who abound in religion. But among great contemplatives we can mention such figures as Eckhart, Teresa, Catherine, Palamas, Rumi, Arabi, the Besht, Sankara, Gautama, Buddhaghosa, Bodhidharma, Honen and Milarepa. As a contrast we can provide a list of prophets: Isaiah, Ezekiel, Jeremiah, Zarathustra, Mani, Paul, Muhammad and so on. Perhaps some Easterners, as I have already indicated, such as Nichiren, Hung Hsiu-ch'üan (leader of the Taiping rebellion) and Caitanya.

The four types are dissimilar, though they can overlap. But I describe them partly because they tend to embed themselves in differing kinds of society. Often contemplatives embed themselves in orders, such as monastic ones, whether with Christianity, Buddhism, Taoism or Hinduism. Often prophets embed themselves in communities: so the Hebrew prophets spoke to the nation as they conceived it, though lesser communities are possible. Sages are relevant within a certain political and social order, for example that of China or of some part of it, or of neighbouring nations where a similar ethos reigned. Gurus are slightly different, since their sphere of influence is interestingly smaller; it is nevertheless dictatorial. Contemplatives may not be authoritative, though they can be, for instance as heads of orders. They are most often found in monastic or conventual groups or societies of practitioners.

Each of these four has a certain prestige bestowed upon him – the prophet for his or her numinous experience and ability to speak in the name of the divine; the sage for his wisdom and character; the guru for his impressive character and seeming authority; the contemplative for her or his capacity to meditate and so for her or his large reserves of inward expertise. To some degree, therefore, they all have charisma.

Preacher, pastor, priest, imam

The preacher is analogous to the prophet in so far as he speaks typically in the name of the Divine Being (BRUEGGEMANN, 1978). His aim is to arouse the faithful in relation to some message. His function will tend to be important if he has no rival, so the preacher is vital in much of scriptural Protestantism, but less important where his function is undertaken as a secondary role, for instance when he is primarily a priest. The preacher in a religion dominated by the notion of God and imbued with the feeling of the numinous should be endowed especially with rhetorical gifts, and in a tradition which relies on scriptural texts should be trained in those texts.

The emphasis of the role of the pastor is rather different, though it typically overlaps with the other two. He is a person assigned in a community to look after the faithful – tending the sheep, as the image has it. In the Christian tradition the role of the pastor is particularly emphasized in that of the bishop. On the other hand it is used as a common designation in certain Protestant denominations, including the Lutheran.

The conception of priesthood differs widely among traditions, since it is often conceived as a hereditary office (JAMES, 1955). In such religious traditions it becomes the duty of the priest to marry in order to ensure succession. In the case of the Brahmins, though it is a hereditary office it is by no means obligatory. Sometimes hereditary control of temples is also normal. The priest is supposed to be the one who is equipped either by heredity or by training to perform rituals, especially those of sacrifice. This was one reason why Protestants often rejected the idea of priesthood, since they did not look on the mass or liturgy or communion as sacrificial. On a somewhat different tack, the Levis or hereditary priests of the Jewish tradition (and others with priestly names such as Cohen and Katz) retain their recognition even though there are no sacrifices to perform, and have been none since the destruction of the Temple.

The priest has to be trained in ritual (SABOURIN, 1973). One may broadly see the distinction between priesthood and other forms of ministry as lying in the greater involvement of the former with ritual practice. There are many references in the literature to Buddhist monks as priests, but often the term is inappropriate (RAHULA, 1974). In highly ritualized circumstances, for instance in Parsee or Zoroastrian prayer (MODI, 1937), it is important for the priest to learn the proper pronunciation of the verbal formulae. But the priest usually has to learn much more than this. He should know the scriptures (which in any case he may need to use in the rites), very often he is trained in the lore and learning of the faith, which may require the setting up of academies, institutions and universities. Indeed, one should extend this observation beyond the priesthood to the pastorate, preachers and so on. It is one of the developing marks of a new religious movement that it begins to consolidate itself through such institutions. The spiritual bureaucracy becomes formalized.

Indeed, this has its effects far beyond the devotion of resources to this task. Because academies tend to bring something of a critical spirit, the sharp edges of new movements are easily worn off by the more sophisticated training offered to the pastorate. But higher studies have considerable prestige, even if, from the angle of orthodoxy, they appear dangerous.

Priests are organized in different ways in different churches, of course, but there is usually a hierarchy, such as gives the range of positions in the Roman Catholic, Orthodox and other churches within Christianity. We shall return to the question of ranks later. Let us just mention at this point that in the Catholic church the priesthood is celibate, while in Orthodoxy bishops and patriarchs are also, since they are drawn from the ranks of the monks; but ordinary priests are married. In most religions priests and other functionaries are masculine, but changes in Christianity have generated women pastors and preachers, and even bishops. This ties in with new thinking by feminist and other writers directed towards an opening up of the genders to the service of the church, together with the realization that male patriarchy and what is thought of as confused thinking has in the past led to a wrongly masculine view of God. We have already commented on all this in Chapter 1 but, to sum up, it seems not to make sense to think of God as having literally male or female characteristics.

Islam does not have a priesthood, but it has strong analogues to clergy, namely functionaries who lead in the ritual and most of all the daily prayers performed collectively (they can of course be performed individually if a person so wishes, though on a Friday congregational prayer is obligatory for those who live in reasonable proximity to a mosque). Usually a mosque has an officially appointed prayer leader. He may be appointed by the government, but control of mosques is not an easy task in politically divisive times (MARTIN, 1982).

The monk, the nun, the hermit, the contemplative, the wanderer

Religions divide according to whether they have established monastic and conventual systems. It is the most clearly demarcated aspect of Jainism and Buddhism. Both the performance of austerity and the contemplative life are held in these religions to be best undertaken within the discipline of the community. There are other faiths, notably Islam, Judaism and Confucianism, which do not take this path. The Hindu tradition resisted it, but not absolutely, partly because it undermined (so it was thought) family rituals and duties. Nevertheless monasticism came to be such a pervasive element in South Asian society that it was hard for Hindus to sustain their resistance (DUTT, 1962).

Of the three monotheisms of the Middle East, Christianity was the only one to adopt the monastic way of life (CHADWICK, 1958). At first, it seems there were lone individuals or small groups of men and women who lived as wandering recluses, but in due course monasticism took the form of communities living together. It spread rapidly as a custom in the fourth century, from Pachomius's order in Egypt (he died in 346) as far as Scotland in the settlement found by Ninian (*c.* 400). It helps to consolidate a certain blending of Neo-Platonism into Christianity spirituality (O'MEARA, 1981). At any rate, the monk and nun became key figures in the Christian life, and helped to found differing orders with diverse vocations. Analogous to the mainline monks and nuns were the wandering friars in the middle ages. The chief aim of the monastic was to cultivate the inner spiritual life. While monks and nuns are neither in Christianity nor in Buddhism or elsewhere strictly priestly, priests must be provided because the monastery has to be run on Christian lines, which means the regular performance of the ritual.

It is possible of course to perform relevant spiritual exercises without undergoing the discipline of celibacy, for this was done among both Muslim Sufis (TRIMINGHAM, 1971) and Jewish Qabbalists (SCHOLEM, 1961), but it was thought among Buddhists and Christians and other monastic religions to be very helpful (to put it no more strongly). In the Theravada new drives to meditation among lay persons have arisen, and it was relatively late in the Mahayana that married monks became acceptable – and then only under pressures from numinous and *bhakti*-oriented kinds of piety.

The existence of nuns and monks in a community had great advantages for discipline: they could gather together not just for rituals but also for meditation. Moreover, the practice was encouraged by the pious laity, who could feel that they acquired merit from feeding the monks and nuns. They could also learn moral lessons from them and have the benefit of their scriptural knowledge. The monastery itself could be a place of pilgrimage – indeed every visit to the temple could be seen in this way. In the case of Buddhism it could be a notable centre of piety precisely because there was little alternative. It could house a bo-tree, be a repository of images, have a temple to the gods for convenience, be a place of interface with holy men or women, and be a focus for sermons and processions.

Indeed, the monk or nun can become in both East and West a special kind of resource, a place of interface with merit for the lay person. In addition some of the holy persons could also be hermits, living near the monastery or on his or her own. The intensely holy hermit became a cultural resource.

In Orthodoxy especially the monk could be selected by lay persons as a particularly apt spiritual adviser on intimate matters, for instance on the progress of a family's marriage. The monk therefore becomes a pastor. The supposition is that the holy man gains from his practice of contemplation, and the depth of his self-understanding helps him to understand others.

These various kinds of humans, showing their charisma in the face of the laity, are all contemplatives. But they also have other gifts: in both East and West monks and nuns have knowledge of the scriptures and other holy books. Learning of this sort is also respected among the lay people.

Although we have concentrated largely in this section on nuns and monks, wanderers must also be considered as a general type. They happen to be particularly important in the Indian scene. From early times the *śramaṇas* were of great vitality, and rivals to the Brahmins.

The rabbi, the jurist, the theologian, the teacher

The most important period in the evolution, indeed the formation, of Judaism as we know it was the first four centuries or so of the Common Era, and it was during this time that the title 'rabbi' became usual for those who were learned in the oral Torah (ALON, 1980). They were important not just in interpreting the Law, but in fixing the scriptural canon and shaping the Jewish calendar. They replaced the ritual actions of the Temple period with the scholarship of the tradition, and with a web of practical Law which determined the daily rites and observances of the Jewish people.

The whole loosely conceived institution of the rabbinate maintained Jewish identity and self-knowledge during the early middle ages, within the realms of both Islam and Christendom. The rabbi became a particular kind of learned person, paralleling in some ways the *ācāryas* and other learned people of the Indian tradition, not to mention the sagely scholars of Chinese and more generally Far Eastern literary traditions. Yet he was also very different. On the whole the works he wielded, especially the Talmuds, were not overly theological, but had a legal and practical cast; nor were they literary like Chinese collections.

The rabbinate underwent something of a crisis in the aftermath of the Enlightenment and the emancipation of the European Jews (KLEIN, 1979). The relative uniformity of the earlier period has rather disappeared, with the split of the religion into Reform, Conservative and Orthodox branches (to cite only three). The criteria for assessing the worth of rabbis has become more subjective. Nevertheless they have carried on the great tradition of a certain sort of learning which has itself served as a kind of ritual.

In the major religious traditions there are or have been differing relations between religious and secular laws. On the whole the matter of interpreting the law ultimately went with kingship in the Indian tradition, though the existence of the law books of Manu within the semi-revealed or *smṛti* naturally laid bounds upon royal prerogative (DERRETT, 1957). The same was true of Buddhist kingdoms in both South Asia and South-east Asia which used the body of Hindu law with variations (on the principle that Manu had been taught and inspired by the Buddha) (HOOKER, 1978). There was also the fairly dense body of Vinaya, which controlled the operation of the Sangha. This defined the sphere of monastic activity and thus curbed the power of the monarch. Similar remarks can be made in respect of East Asia. In China too the formulated body of *li* or ritual and behavioural propriety helped from early days to set limits to kingly power (CH'U, 1961). In these Asian cases we can see something of a differentiation between earthly and spiritual rules. But the role of the jurist came to be most prominent in Islam. Here the creation of the classical schools of Islamic law brought the need for a body of persons who were trained in an expert way in the law. Such *faqīhs* or jurists came to acquire high standing in the community. They had knowledge of the law which allowed them to interpret it, but in theory they did not have the power to alter it: the community was a body governed of course not by them but by the Shari'a. Islam in this respect might be described as a nomocratic religion, that is a religion under the governance of God *through* the law (SCHACT, 1964). *Faqīhs* also came to be bound by what was called the closing of the door of *ijtihad* or interpretation: that is, decisions reached earlier and so nearer the time of the Prophet could not be reopened. In more modern times there is some confusion. Western education has led many Muslims to ignore the complexities and difficulties of medieval treatises. National governments have changed the scope of the community. Debates have occurred about new ways of reviving ancient law, for instance by going back to the sources, that is the scriptures and the traditions concerning the Prophet. Revolutionary new ideas about a modern Islam have been propounded and put into action by the Ayatollah Khomeini and others (ayatollahs being a rank of Shi'i jurist). Rigid divides between Shi'a and Sunni law have not been maintained, nor essentially those between Western and Islamic law. But the prestige of the *faqīh* has diminished, owing to the medieval anchorage of the jurists' work. Reform of Islam often means going back to the beginning.

Meanwhile in the West, the Reformation for the most part brought about the secularization of the law and the creation of nation-states which had full control over the legal structure (BERMAN, 1974). The separation of church and state in the United States led to a new prestige for the jurists of the Supreme Court, for instance, disentangled from post-medieval arrangements which could entwine ecclesiastical and other forms of law. They became important secular jurists. Not dissimilar moves occurred in the modernizing states of Europe (STONE, 1965).

Another kind of specialist is the theologian (*ācārya* in the Hindu tradition, philosopher in Buddhism, Confucian scholar and so on), one who is charged with formulating the doctrines or teachings of a tradition or sub-tradition. Of course, theology is more important in some religions or sub-religions than in others. For instance, a good deal less attention is paid to it in Judaism than in Christianity (at least traditionally), though it remains true that there have been very important people who have fulfilled the function, such as Maimonides, Mendelssohn, Buber. But there are reasons why the intellectual formulations of the faith have proved more important in the Christian tradition – for the person who became a Christian did not inherit a body of custom and law. That, however, was what Judaism was to do once it had recovered itself in a new form after the destruction of the Temple and begun its struggle against the wide-ranging and more successful Christian tradition. Belief itself became a badge of Christian belonging, especially after the exigencies of early loyalty and the perils of martyrdom and deprivation had slid away. Although theologians might be very rigorous in their strict adherence to the Biblical tradition, many came to absorb ideas and values from older philosophies. Consequently the growth of a new intellectual class of Christian thinkers, such as Augustine, the Church Fathers and medieval philosophers, had an effect in blending new categories into the modes of Christian thinking. To a great degree it was the work of theologians who brought in so much of the terminology and ambitions of Neo-Platonism, which helped to consolidate the thought of classical Christianity, both East and West. Typically a theologian has to be a member of the faith or sub-faith that he or she is expounding, but the church sometimes has difficulty, especially in the post-Reformation period, in controlling theology. Much effort was expended, for instance, trying to keep modernism in the Roman Catholic church at bay from about 1880 to 1960 – ultimately without success, since it was precisely a form of modernism which came to rule the hearts and minds of Vatican II. In Eastern Orthodoxy it has long been common for lay theologians to acquire importance, and there is a more relaxed view of ecclesiastical control over thought. In more recent times there has been an efflorescence of women theologians in Christianity and they have had a major impact upon the scene, in virtually all denominations.

There are only the beginnings of such a movement in Islam. Traditionally Muslims have paid careful attention to both philosophy and theology, and a number of vital schools arose, such as the Kharijites, Mu'tazilites and Ash'arites (WATT, 1973). Sufism itself brought forth some distinctive worldviews. In more modern times one may observe some of the same effects as prevail among jurists, because the injection of new (Western) thought in the arena has made some of the older methods of training in traditional schools seem obsolete; so new forms of Islamic theology have been canvassed. Nevertheless, one of the most important modernists, Muhammad 'Abduh, was traditionally trained (GIBB, 1947).

The scene is somewhat different in South and East Asia. The heterogeneity of the Hindu tradition is startlingly great compared even with the variations which can be encountered in Christianity and Islam. The trained *pandit* has a diversity of texts to contemplate, and will normally be trained in one school or another. The most important set of schools is that of the major Vedantin systems, which came to develop a spectrum of relationships between the world, souls and the

Divine Being, ranging from Non-Dualism to forms of Dualism. In addition, outside the more traditionally orthodox schools are other more peripheral ones, also commented on by Brahmins such as Kashmiri Saivism. In modern times there has arisen a new blend of Western thinking and traditionally Indian concepts: this tends to be called 'philosophy', but perhaps we might in English call it more appropriately 'religious philosophy'. I am thinking of the work of such as Swami Vivekananda, M. Gandhi and S. Radhakrishnan. In certain ways these people function as theologians (FARQUHAR, 1915).

It is awkward calling Buddhists theologians since mostly they do not believe in God: there is no theos to dialogue about. It is common to call people like Nagarjuna philosophers in English. It is a pity we do not have some appropriate term: some have used Buddhologians. I shall call them dharmologians for the time being, expressers of the *dharma* or truth – what is ultimate in the way that for the monotheist the theos is ultimate. Such learned persons have helped to encourage changes in both thinking and practice through creative reinterpretations of the *dharma*. We can note that though much of Mahayana development had a practical nature, both in ritual (Buddha-worship, for instance) and ethics (new prominence for the Bodhisattva ideal), it also had a theoretical side (identity of nirvana and *saṃsāra*, universal emptiness, and so on). Such dharmologians became important ingredients in Chinese, Korean, Japanese, Tibetan and Mongolian life.

As we have noted, East Asian Confucianism and Taoism favour the notion of the sage, an intellectual with moral calibre and wisdom. This figure serves in effect for the theologian. But in neither case does that title fit properly, as it does in the case of Buddhism. The *zheren* or sage-person is from a Chinese point of view the true philosopher.

It is worth saying a word about the philosopher in the West. What has happened is that philosophy has become something specialized, notably in the English-speaking world. It is often constricted much more closely than it has been in the past. Not all philosophers of the past belong to the canon of today's approved list. Would Plotinus get a job in the modern Western academy? Or Confucius? It is doubtful.

Nonetheless, there remains a suitable usage for the term as meaning anyone who helps systematically to formulate a worldview. On this usage the philosopher covers the theologian and others, including the dharmologian. But the theologian may be more closely constricted by the discipline of the church or religious movement to which he belongs.

Finally, there is the overlapping figure of the religious teacher: such a person ranges from the Russian holy man or *staretz* to the formal teacher appointed in some official religious academy, and from the *ācārya* who formulates a theological philosophy to the spiritual director.

The king and the dictator

Ranging through the varying figures of the religious firmament, it is useful to see the king or queen as a religious entity. Even where kingship no longer carried with it an ancient ideology of divine power there remained vestiges of divinity: the divine right of kings (FIGGIS, 1914), the sacrality surrounding the coronation ceremony, and so on. Most human societies have passed through a phase of kingship, often throughout the greater period of their history, and during that time the magico-symbolic power of their persons has usually been connected up with divinity, in a web of influences which binds together their person, their people, their land and the cosmos. Both in the ancient Near East and in the Americas kings were depicted in relation to the cosmos, so that their palaces reflected the cosmos (CARRASCO, 1982). The king was present in the cosmic tree, the *axis mundi*. In Asia a representation of this was the royal umbrella. Typically society was organized in a hierarchy, with priestly, military and productive forces represented in the differing main branches of society (TAMBIAH, 1976). The king was in relation to them all. Thus he had a priestly function as king, as head of the priesthood; he had a military function, as leader of the army; and he had a production function, as head of those who cultivate the land, make tools, and so on. In this last connection he was often conceived therefore as having vital magical powers, to enhance the fertility of the crops. Generally speaking, the king was expected to behave correctly in this regard. It is true that for varying reasons certain lay taboos did not apply to him (for intance, incest taboos in Egypt). In some circumstances the breaking of taboos might itself release power. But usually correctness and virtue were important, and for this reason he was often hedged about with ritual regulations which would greatly inhibit his activity. This was true for a period with both Chinese and Japanese emperors (CHANG, 1983).

There are variations in membership of the kingship, in the sense that there was a dyarchy of the king and his son, or of two brothers, or of the king and his mother (for example, in Peru, among the Aztecs and in Rwanda respectively). Sometimes a king might be forced to kill himself if he failed; or he might be ritually sacrificed if he began to lose his powers. Sometimes in a period of transition a mock substitute would be elevated to the throne for as long as the chaos lasted. The inhibition of royal powers mentioned above could lead to the substitution of different government, confining the king to ritual functions.

In any event it seems clear that over much of human history the religious and secular powers of the king were combined. With the rise of more secular government, emanating essentially out of the Europe of the Reformation, the whole ideology waned. Certain substitutes were made. While the king would in earlier times encapsulate both his own and divine power, including the mysterious forces of nature and of the cosmos, the notion of government was to a substantial degree detached from cosmology, save in so far as God rules over all the universe; and the ruler or ruling group, instead of expressing the forces of nature, would express the will of the people. With that notion was tied up the new ideology of the nation and the nation-state. Constitutional monarchy might carry on, but it was a very pale reflection of older, fuller-bodied ideas of kingship.

Nevertheless, newer corporate states under the aegis of a dictator took up some of the earlier notions. Stalin, Hitler, Mussolini and others could claim to represent in their own persons the popular will. Perhaps most successful in all this, with the best grasp of ritual and an intuitive understanding of symbolism, was Adolf Hitler (HAFFNER, 1979; CARR, 1978). There he was simultaneously transcendent and immanent within the ranks of the people: his simple uniform looked like that of a field marshal, but he wore no insignia of rank. He incorporated the military prowess of the nation. But he also in his early years miraculously (so it seemed) restored full employment. Somehow too he conveyed a sense, from on high, of providence looking upon him and the German people. Part of that illusion came from his ideology, which for all its crudity yet conveyed a strong sense of destiny. The people in following him faithfully as *der Führer* bonded themselves sacramentally to him, in the manner of an ancient people and their king. The imagery of the reign was that of supreme sacrifice, death and victory. There were thus many echoes of ancient, sacred kingship, transmogrified into ultra-modern times and imbued with a sense of future renewal. If Stalin was less intuitive, he nevertheless had the advantage of a much more theologically sophisticated worldview, to woo the people and give them eschatological hope (MCNEAL, 1988).

The complexity of the ideology of kingship helped to link together both priesthood and political rule. This inevitably made traditional worldviews powerful, and indeed often brought the notion of central power to the fore. But no less interesting was the Buddhist viewpoint. Buddhism held as its central idea the opposite of power, emptiness. Yet it was one thing for Buddhism to confine itself to the empty Sangha, and to consider itself centred upon contemplation; it was another thing to look on itself as a holistic vision of the world. As far as the latter was concerned, it certainly held to a vision of family and social life on the one hand and of political life on the other. It is striking how the accounts of the Buddha show his affinity with kings and ministers, as well as merchants. One could joke perhaps that emptiness mirrored the notion of empty multiplication, the merchants' mode: multiplying profit out of mere money, rather than out of the fertile modes of agriculture. At any rate, Buddhism could surely offer society something which promised prosperity and merit and which appealed both to those involved in this world and to those who wished to withdraw beyond the everyday round. It could also offer kingship something: for kings could learn from the new order of merchant life. Later, in Sri Lanka it could offer kings not just the merchant mode, but more importantly the engineering method. Hydraulic civilization, in other words, could move beyond earlier models (BECHERT, 1966–73).

Even so, there remained something of a paradox about Buddhist civilization. While Buddhism was otherworldly, it also seemed to wield power. How did power and otherworldliness go together? How did the sacred power of kingship (priestly, sacramental, glutinous in ritual) combine with the relative emptiness of the monastic ideal, not to mention the insubstantiality of Buddhist philosophy? Despite differences of religious philosophy, there was an interface with Brahmanic civilization. Throughout South Asia and South-east Asia Buddhist culture made use of the sacramentalism of the Brahmins in organizing much of the ceremonial of the court. It was possible to make use of traditional ritual, in shoring up a system which ran on Buddhist philosophy.

Incarnations, and variants on the theme

As an intermediate between the full-flown idea of incarnation and the much weaker notion of the Jaina and Buddhas, as expressions of what lies beyond, you have the *avatāra*, commonly translated as 'incarnation' too (PARRINDER, 1970). We shall use the expression *avatāra*, despite its weaknesses. Since the word 'incarnation' has a Western provenance, let us begin there. It has the disadvantage that from the Christian point of view it is all or nothing at all: an incarnation is usually a whole incarnation, as in the case of Christ. It is this which can make the Hindu approach seem too easygoing, as if there were so many degrees of incarnation, up and down the scale of intensity. The tradition of Visnu within the Hindu ambience has had a number of differing incarnations, a characteristic which tends to water down the very intensity of each divine presence.

As we have noted, an avatar is, in its literal sense, a divine descent into a special form of the God Visnu, typically for the purpose of restoring universal order. But an avatar can also occur outside this context, as the concept has loosened – for example, in the case of Devi and Siva. In addition it can simply be a means of bestowing the divine presence on the worshipper. It is a kind of living extension of the notion of a sacramental image. The God or Goddess is thought in the Hindu tradition to reside in the representation. Indeed, the representation is not really a reflection of the God so much as a mode of making him or her present. Even so, the incarnation is alive in a way an image is not. It becomes the living presence of the Deity.

The conception parallels that of the Buddha's various appearances on earth – what came to be called the *nirmāṇakāya* or transformation body (MURTI, 1980). However, in this case there is no Divine Being to be incarnated. At most one might say that the Buddha, for instance Gautama, is a living mode of the ultimate. But even here to call him the ultimate may be to put it too positively, since it is not a thing or an entity, but rather emptiness. Nevertheless, there is the notion that, like the Vaisnava avatar, he came to earth in order to restore the teaching of the *dharma*. It may well be that the Hindu doctrine was borrowed from Buddhism, and extended. A similar idea, possibly even more ancient, can be found embodied in the Jaina Tirthamkara, makers of the ford, including Mahavira and Parsva and their predecessors (JAIN and UPADHYE, 1974).

There is a not altogether dissimilar idea that Lao-tzu was reincarnated at different times to teach diverse rulers his message (SEIDEL, 1969). Indeed, the Taoists put about the doctrine that the Buddha was a Western incarnation of Lao-tzu. This had some slight plausibility in so far as the teachings of the two religions had a certain likeness of spirit.

In many cases, especially in modern India, the difference between the divine and the human is very fluid. Religious teachers are often accepted as incarnations of God, though not necessarily using the language of *avatāra*, and they may even be recipients of worship. While the line is not always as sharp as it should be in the Christian context, and saints sometimes appear to be worshipped, the theoretical distinction is nevertheless of the greatest importance. The worship ascribed to Christ is unique in being directed towards a human being as incarnation of the one God. To the Jew and the Muslim, the monotheism of the Christian tradition seems seriously compromised, even if the Christian thinks of the Trinity doctrine as a logical and mysterious way of safeguarding his monotheism. From the Christian perspective Christ perfectly fuses the divine and the human in his person, and also introduces into the ancient world a genuine humanism. Other cults of demigods and the like fail to produce a true meeting of the human and divine.

Healer, shaman, magician

Healing has long been integrated into religion, because many and especially smaller societies do not differentiate greatly between the functions or functionaries. Some skills, for instance bone-setting, may be regarded as technical in character and so acquired through material training. On the other hand, some religious figures become renowned for their ability to cure, and sometimes the very salvation on offer is itself seen as a kind of cure. This was true of the Buddha's Four Noble Truths, which were expressed in the form of a diagnosis and cure (what is the disease, what is the cause of the disease, can the cause be removed, and how? – the answer is, of course, through treading the Noble Eightfold Path). Jesus is likewise represented as a spiritual and physical physician. Something of the same analogy appears in the Hebrew Bible and in the Qur'an, as well as in the Zoroastrian scriptures, and there is a close relationship between liberation and medicine in Taoism. The figure of the saint or prophet as healer, therefore, is not an unusual one, and it also connects up with the notion of the magician. For the most part, religions had some positive and some negative views of the magical specialist.

One reason was that major religions have involved themselves in miraculous healing, and occasionally in other arts (BLACKER, 1975). Needless to say, it is difficult to distinguish absolutely between miracles and the magical. Early Christians were often accused of deploying magic, and there is evidence of anti-magical propaganda against Christ in the New Testament (GRANT, 1952). Though in the surrounding Hellenistic culture there was something like scientific medicine, it was not altogether clear what the criteria were for determining some procedures to be scientific and not others. It was not unreasonable to suppose that a person's charismatic power might effect a cure, especially given the uncertain relationship between bodily and mental manifestations of disease. In Islam, there is a distinction between miracles and sorcery. In the case of miracles, the intentions of the agent are good and he works with the help of God. But in Islamic as in other civilizations the line between the two is never quite clear, and a great deal of use was made of various magic entities including amulets, especially those bearing the ninety-nine beautiful names of God (GELLNER, 1981).

In the Asian traditions there are no exact equivalents to the word 'magic'. If there are parallels to magic-workers they are mainly Buddhist and other yogis who through the concentration of their mental powers can wield certain supernormal powers known as *iddhis* and so on (BEYER, 1973). These may have the capacity, for example, to travel, assume invisibility or remove obstacles. The *jīvanmukta* or liberated person is supposed also to be able to create transformations of his body, and has powers analogous to those of the shaman.

Such manifestations tie in with lesser powers such as the ability to know the thoughts of others and what we today might recognize as paranormal capabilities. There is a belief shared by a number of cultures that yogic practice can bring you such powers. They can certainly add to the charismatic reputation of mystics.

Some other figures in the religious repertoire of society

We have by no means covered all the types of individuals who in one way or another specialize in religion within society. We have not discussed ascetics. Often it is true that the ascetic is really in pursuit of something other than pure self-denial, such as contemplative experience. Self-torture is in this regard merely a means to an end. On the other hand, in the Jain tradition and in the margins of Hinduism the practice of *tapas* (ritual heat) or asceticism is itself of more direct value, helping to eliminate karma and bring release. Moreover, it is often thought that *tapas* generates power, so the mighty ascetic may even threaten the gods (KNIPE, 1975). In Christian Europe the ill-kempt hermit who half-starves himself could gain a great reputation for austerity, itself a sign of sanctity. The Jain monk or nun exhibited *tapas*; and, while the asceticism was by no means severe in the Buddhist Order, the monk or nun was at least a moderate ascetic. For the Jain, the height of perfection was achieved by dying, when the time came, by giving up food altogether.

Something analogous to asceticism, but not self-inflicted, was martyrdom (FREND, 1965). Both in the early centuries of the Christian church and in the Shi'a movement within Islam it had considerable importance. The martyr was literally a witness to the faith. In an important way the one who died for Christ was part of the Gospel: in the book of life and death others could read the truth of the Christian message. In modern times martyrdom has been used in a new context, namely dying in battle on behalf of the Shi'a state of Iran (SACHEDURA, 1981).

At a lesser but still significant level of asceticism is the practice of celibacy. In the Christian tradition for many centuries being a virgin for Christ was thought to be an honourable condition. By contrast, Judaism and Islam had very little regard for giving up sex, since it was thought of as a normal condition, not to say necessary for procreation. In the Indian tradition the restraint of sex could be considered especially potent.

Some reflections on the varieties of religious specialists

In this fairly extensive survey of types we have placed the different figures in niches and roles within the variegated religious societies of the world. It gives a starting point for our wider survey of the social dimension of society. In this as elsewhere we want to see some of the interactions between this dimension and the others. It will for instance be possible to perceive dynamic relations between religious experience and social organization, and between some doctrinal or philosophical formulations and modes of conceiving societies. We are indebted to much work in the sociology and anthropology of religion, but in certain respects we go beyond them into phenomenology.

Coterminous religions and their fate

The simplest pattern is where the religion is coterminous with a particular cultural and linguistic group on a relatively small scale. It is in these circumstances possible for an anthropologist to write a

monograph on the religion of the Kikuyu or of the Azande and so
forth. Some fine studies of this sort have been done. Nevertheless, as
times have wound on such projects have become all but impossible,
for the simple reason that outside influences, now pervasive across
our planet, have brought in alternative beliefs, most often Christian.
There are also the less tangible effects of modern communications
and agricultural and other technologies. All this has happened within
the colonial framework, and has stimulated in many areas new
religious movements, all across the 'tribal' world, ranging from cargo
cults in Papua New Guinea and elsewhere in Melanesia to new
independent churches in Africa (BARRETT, 1982). I shall return to
this phenomenon a little later, since it is a significant way in which
small-scale cultures have come to terms with the invading forces. The
overall result of the northern impact, as it might crudely be called,
since it is the effect of powerful northern cultures upon smaller
cultures often to the south, is to divide cultural groups into two or
more religious types. One type stays with the indigenous customs and
values of the group. Another joins, let us say, a Christian church (or
more than one). We can often postulate a mixed group. And perhaps
there is a new mingled religious movement. Even those who stay with
the old customs learn to do so in a new way. For one thing, when
tradition is effortlessly operative, it does not need decision, nor is it in
the nature of the case self-conscious: it is the way 'we' do things. But
once the split in a culture occurs there have to be reasons for staying
traditional. Moreover, in the conditions of modern life, questions of
education begin to come up, and if traditional values are to be taught
rudimentary textbooks may eventually be required. At the same time,
the whole phenomenon of literacy brings a great change. The old
language miraculously finds itself embedded on paper, liable to speak
thereby in a person's head. Words are used to translate the Bible, and
they begin to acquire new meanings: the old tradition thus appears in
a new perspective. For all these reasons, nothing quite stays the same
in the old values. Of course, similar things have happened before, by
way of conquest and trade in ancient times – and that is why the study
of today's new religious movements can throw light on the past. What
we find in much of the past to which we have access, however, is what
may be called a different and to some degree more inductive form of

coterminous religion, where the boundaries are more those of civilizational groups of a tighter or looser kind. Before we move on to that, let us say more on the subject of ancient monarchies, beyond what we have said already about the figure of the king.

Monarchies and civilizational areas

In ancient Mesopotamia there was a long transition period from the formation of city-states to the establishment of fully fledged kingship with imperial spheres of influence. In Egypt the change to a unified pharaonic system took place much earlier, in part because the unification of that region was more easily carried out. The polytheistic systems of belief in both these areas and elsewhere, such as among the Incas and in Mexico, helped to provide a flexible method of uniting imperial and local cults. These emerged in varying ways, partly through the established beliefs and practices of cities within the wider imperial domains, partly from the numinous features of land-scapes, partly from local myths of other kinds. There was in the unified organization of an empire a tendency towards unity at the top – a supreme Sun God or Sky God for example. These particular examples also have plausibility: while mountains and rivers are many, the sky and its light are one (by day at least). Generally speaking, the ideology of monarchies, in both the Old World and the New, and in East and West, gives a cosmic role to the king, as a divine intermed-iary between the pantheon or the supreme God and the people and the earth. Very often the emperor could, by ignoring powers at the periphery, look upon himself as a kind of *cakravartin* or universal ruler. On the whole (we shall come to exceptions) this implies a unification of the political–cultural area and the religion, even if such unification may be relatively loose, with cities and regions for instance having their own priesthoods and cults. In a way therefore a monarchical or imperial system turns out to be what I have called an area having a coterminous religion.

It is interesting that, although Israel acquired a monarchy, it had a rather different ideology. This was partly because it did not have a pantheon and partly because the king (no doubt for that reason, since sacramental mergings of kings and gods were not natural in these circumstances) was regarded primarily as the servant of Yahweh as supreme God (ALLBRIGHT, 1968). Given this relative lack of commitment to the surrounding kingly ideology, the king found himself in a dialectical prediament: he was liable to a critique from the mouthpieces of Yahweh – the prophets. In due course Israel not only lost its monarchy, but projected the return of David into the future, thus shaping its messianic worldviews (GASTER, 1969).

Although there are analogies with Buddhist monarchy, these need to be looked at separately on account of Buddhism's special features, its relation to Brahmanism and its lack of a genuine pantheon.

Intellectually kingship systems co-ordinated with a pantheon and integrated into military, socia .nd productive processes created the beginnings of a deep sense of the cosmos. The universe was seen as a functioning whole, not unlike an hourglass with the king at the centre: that is, he was the pivot upon which the whole system moved. Naturally ritual was an important mechanism for keeping it moving. In relation to Mesopotamian religions, Jacobsen (RE) especially emphasizes the role of the numinous in the formation of the gods; but it is also vital to note the role of various myths and their place in the festivals which animated the calendar and boosted the fertility of the region. In the Egyptian case the king is represented as having a different soul from that of commoners, fluttering therefore between heaven and earth.

It may also be noted that some commentators regard the ritual side of kingship as no more than ornamentation and so in need of explanation. This is a misunderstanding. It is as if we were to imagine that a President of the United States could assume power other than by getting elected. The rituals of election are part of his power. The king's role is his place in relation to the pantheon and the whole web therefore of rites through which he must pass. It is true that in times of economic or political disaster – of disorder – the rituals' power may disappear and the kingship itself may be destroyed, but that is another matter. In its functioning reality it exhibits sacred power in a high degree. Nothing is more startling than the way the Spaniards, so few of them, cut a path to the heart of the Aztec and Inca empires and tore their ritual nets to shreds, and the way these mighty fabrics simply collapsed.

In brief, then, the sacred kingship was attested in varying parts of the world, and constituted an effective civilizational model, at least up to a point. It was woven into pantheonic religions with a hierarchical structure and buttressed with myth and cosmology, which provided an integrated vision both of society and of the universe.

There are some variations on the rather rich and complex Middle Eastern model in the Far East. Though Chinese sacred kingship had strong similarities, its ideology differed somewhat. In the classical period beginning in the Ch'in and Han dynasties (the era from 221 B.C.E. to 220 C.E.), the emperor was given unique status, though not as a divine being. During his lifetime he was the surrogate or representative of heaven upon earth, and in that sense he was the son of heaven, but not in the sense of being a descendant of God. Possibly in the much earlier Shang dynasty the ruler was so regarded, but not according to the classical worldview. Nevertheless his function was very much that of the sacred kings of the Middle East. He was a link between heaven and earth. It was his responsibility to maintain the harmony within the cosmos through the balance of *yin* and *yang* by means of the imperial sacrificial cult. An important aspect of the ideology was the concept of the mandate of heaven. In bad circumstances heaven would simply withdraw its favour. This provided a way of registering something of the feeling of the ruling classes and more generally of the people (FUNG, 1953). If they removed their support this was a sign that heaven had withdrawn its mandate. This was not altogether different in idea from the symbolism of the Persian monarchy, where the king was servant of Ahura Mazdah, and his glory or fate was represented by a halo-like symbol which would fade or vanish if he turned out to be unworthy of his office.

Greece and Rome as differing systems

Although in ancient Greece and Crete in Mycenean and Minoan times there were monarchies probably after the same pattern as those of the ancient Middle East, they disappeared in the second half of the second millennium B.C.E., and were replaced over a long period by the system of *poleis* or city-states. In Rome there was initially a monarchy, at least legendarily, but it was replaced by a republic, and following the Roman conquests the constitution was modified to render it suitable for rule over the growing empire. In the case of Greece we can speak of (roughly) a single religion, but it was complicated by the variations of cults in differing cities, by the existence of pan-Hellenic festivals such as the Olympiad and the Pythian festival, by certain central institutions such as the Delphic oracle, and by a pantheon of generally recognized gods, namely the Olympian pantheon. There were also religious movements, for example Orphism, which spread more or less throughout Greece. Moreover, philosophies came to take on the character of religions, including Platonism, Pythagoreanism and Stoicism. There were also mystery religions, some based in particular places such as Eleusis, which could attract members from Greece and beyond. Certain cults, such as that of Isis, were of foreign provenance. With the coming together of the Greek and Roman empires, there were often identifications of gods, such as Poseidon and Neptune (NILSSON, 1948). There were similar variations in Italy to those experienced in the Greek world, from oracles such as Sibylla to the heterogeneity of local gods and the adaptation of philosophies as religious credos, including the development of Neo-Platonism (which was to have a powerful influence upon the Christian faith).

In all, these two cultural regions illustrate what might be called civilizational religions, spreading over an area of common culture and language. Nevertheless, they were in no real sense unified systems of ideas or practices. They were a very loosely tied together set of gods and values, with overlapping and sometimes federal characteristics. Although it is common for modern scholars to write about Greek and Roman religion, these religions should not be mistaken for systems. Such phenomena can be found in other parts of the world, as we shall see. Unfortunately we do not as yet possess an agreed name for these loose congeries, but we may note that they demonstrated the emergence of a partial analogy to the kingship religions which we have been discussing. For Alexander of Macedon took on himself some of the properties of a sacred king, as did his successors in the Hellenistic region. The analogy likewise tempted Roman emperors, who therefore became divine kings, though not with the same integration of ideology as was applied to the Middle Eastern monarchs.

It was not until the formation of the Byzantine monarchy that the full doctrinal apparatus was restored and to some extent enhanced. In certain ways, of course, the Christian theology of kingship was much more unified, because it was a monotheistic system. The king imitated the Divine Being, ruling over the lower aspects of the cosmos, which was as a whole a divine monarchy. The beautiful icons depicting Christ as ruler over all, or Pantokrator, gave a sense of the majesty of the Byzantine system. The reverence paid to the emperor mirrored the worship paid to the Trinity. This highly integrated system was far removed from the looseness and complexity of ancient Greek religion.

As I have said, there is no neat expression for this later kind of religion. I have referred to it as a civilizational religion, but perhaps this is not precise enough in that it could equally well refer to a more tightly organized phenomenon, as well as to the kingship type which we have been discussing. I suggest two terms: civilizational network religion and regional network religion. There can be cases where regions have their own characteristics within the wider whole. Meanwhile, to describe the other type I suggest cosmic royal religion. Such a term implies that there is an overall cosmology which at the same time has a centralized system. This itself indicates the heavy imprint of a certain social system on the shape of the religion, though we have to notice that the culture is extensively determined by the religion, including myth and ritual (BELLAH, 1965). The so-called Myth and Ritual School was greatly influenced by the ancient kingly world. Such a tight nexus between myths and calendrical festivals is hardly surprising. It is of course much less expected in a looser system, what I have called the civilizational network type (SHILS, 1981).

A variant in the case of Buddhism

Ancient India presents a differing pattern. We do not quite know what went on in the cities of the Indus Valley. The civilization had connections with and analogues to the ancient Mesopotamian. There is a hiatus in our knowledge, such as it is, until we come down to the period of the Buddha and Mahavira, not to mention the earlier *Upaniṣads*. But Buddhism, which was to become the major ideological and religious influence in so much of Greater India and beyond, essentially arose before the creation of empires and kingships in north and central India. Part of its worldview seems to have been republican, at least to judge from the constitution of the Sangha (though at the same time the Buddha was a sort of monarch of the Order, even if present by his absence). In any case, the main body of the religion, which was undoubtedly the Sangha, was surely designed to exist in parallel with secular paths of power. Hence out of the Buddha's message there came to exist a kind of dyarchy between kingship and Sangha. The model came to be the Buddhist emperor Asoka. There were certain paradoxes, however, in the alignment of monarchy and the Sangha. Exploring them is a useful way of uncovering the logic of Buddhist kingship. First, the Sangha is in principle otherworldly, wedded to the principles of non-violence, asceticism and meditation. But the monarchy is overtly in the business of imposing worldly order and using violence to do so, in regard to both internal and external enemies. Second, the monarchy represents itself typically as responsible for the *dharma*. In South-east Asian kingdoms, the ruler saw himself as *dhammarāja*. Responsible for spiritual and not just worldly order, the monarch has the duty of sorting out the Sangha when necessary, for instance when there are sectarian disputes. Third, while the king is at the fulcrum of the cosmos, within the cosmology of the Buddhist and, for that matter, the Hindu traditions, that cosmology in the Buddhist interpretation rests on emptiness and not on power. The king's energy seems shadowy and insubstantial.

There came to be ways of dealing with the paradoxes and tensions implicit in the foregoing dialectic. There is the legend of Asoka himself, who is first of all cruel and later repentant and righteous (THAPAR, 1961). He 'uses' his cruelty to widen his kingdom and then imposes upon it the peaceful values of the Buddha's message. Second, the monarchy and the Sangha are seen to have a mutual interplay. The Sangha at one level supplies merit to society and to the monarch; the monarch in return supplies order and sustenance to the

Sangha. The Order is, after all, dependent on the laity, whose prosperity is in principle assured by the king. Third, the monarch either in this life or in some previous existence has used asceticism to create his power. The old Indian notion that *tapas* generates power is used in this context to account for the co-ordination between emptiness and vigour. Hence all the symbolism of Mount Meru and the centrality of the monarch in the cosmos can be used in a dynamic way, despite the underlying emptiness and insubstantiality of the Buddhist cosmology.

There is a formal reason for the special status and nature of the Buddhist kingship system: it is that the Sangha exists as a formal organization alongside the monarchy. In the case of the Hindu monarchy things are rather different, since Hinduism does not have the clear-cut system of organization of an Order. No doubt the king has to respect Brahmins and various other aspects of the Indian social system, and whatever entrenched powers there may be. But the Buddhist monarch has to pay special attention to a formalized and orderly entity. In effect a Buddhist monarchy is a kind of dyarchy, with a visible and an invisible ruler: the king as *cakkavattin* and the Buddha as *cakkavattin*. They are, as it were, side by side. Buddhist mythology plays its special role here. The king may claim, as many of them did, that he is Metteya, the future Buddha. This does not make him an incarnation of the Buddha Gotama, but he is potentially an equal. The Buddhist pantheon is not a unitary hierarchy. By contrast, the Hindu monarch may represent himself as Siva or Visnu or some other, that is, as a manifestation of the Divine Being.

Although Buddhist monarchs were free to make use of Brahmin help in court ritual, this only meant very partially buying into Brahmin myth and doctrine. The general theory was Buddhist. Why then make use of such priests? It was chiefly because Buddhism did not breed its own ritual specialists. Monks and nuns were not ritualists, except in a fairly minor degree through such ceremonies as the *paritta*, the chanting of texts in order to ward off evils of one sort or another. Even though Buddhism makes ample provision for pilgrimages, high festivals, Buddha's birthdays and so forth, its chief functionaries are not trained in these matters. They are trained in scholarship, meditation, chanting. Their accomplishments are supposed to be intellectual and spiritual. Just as Brahmins may be used in court ritual, so lesser priests can be used on the side to tend the gods who exist rather peripherally in the temple complexes.

It is true that the Sangha has not necessarily been unitary in a given state, but it has had a fairly unified aspect nevertheless, with some leaders often imposed upon it by the monarchy. Over various periods, Buddhist states were not in existence, but the Sangha could still persist. Where Buddhist monarchy did occur, it automatically provided an area for the operation of the Sangha in co-ordination with the king. So the conditions for a kind of dyarchy existed wherever Buddhist monarchy came into existence (GOMBRICH, 1988).

In discussing kingship of a Buddhist character, we have been thinking of South Asia and South-east Asia primarily. Arrangements were different in East Asia, where typically the monarchies had an ideology independent of Buddhism, even if they may from time to time have patronized the religion. The so-called Godling institution in modern Tibet (better, the Bodhisattva–king institution) is a variant on the Buddhist variant.

Hinduism, on the other hand, tended not to have the relative unification implied by the foundation and expansion of the Sangha – whose actual unity I have perhaps, for simplicity, tended to exaggerate. We shall need to glance back at the institution a little later in order to sort out terminology about such divisions as have existed: most of the literature makes use of Western notions which apply much better to Christian phenomena.

Indian religions – in particular Hinduism

Although a number of scholars want to criticize the reification that seems to be implied by the very term Hinduism – and indeed to spread the message of desubstantialism far and wide through the religion – nevertheless many fewer are worried about discussing Buddhism. There was, too, an easy word for a Buddhist, a *bauddha*, in the old days. There was always a degree of untidiness in the Hindu scene.

One reason for this is that it looks as if Buddhism came out of the teaching of a particular historical person. That could never be said about Hinduism. The two traditions were formed in quite different ways. In a metaphor: one came by deduction, the other by induction. There are for that reason some uncertainties, to put it mildly, about when Hinduism was formed. Was it when the *Ṛgveda* was assembled in the trained memories of early Brahmins? Or was it when the *Upaniṣads* were formed? Or the great epics? Or when the caste system gelled? Or when Vedanta was devised? Or in the late nineteenth century under the pressures and challenges of the British?

The fact is that over much of Indian history India was a cultural area rather than a political unity (WOLPERT, 1993), and we probably need to define the area differently from the way we normally do. We are, of course, mesmerized by the modern period, and look backwards too often through the prism of modern political divisions. The cultural area could be said to have grown from north India and spread out in due course to include Sri Lanka and south India, and then to have stretched over a large part of South-east Asia into the Hindu and Buddhist kingdoms of the region. South-east Asia was an Indic civilization, no less so than, let us say, the Dravidian south. The literary and intellectual languages were Sanskrit and Pali, floating above a sea of non-Indic tongues.

In the period of the Buddha we see a transition from republics, city-states and miscellaneous political arrangements to kingdoms, such as Magadha, and eventually to empires such as that of Asoka. Similar developments at a later period took place in the south and overseas. In the formative period, which I have called the time of the Buddha, the situation was not altogether unlike that of ancient Greece and Italy. There were various cults, movements, new religions, philosophies, values held in common and so on. During this time, then, I would characterize the kind of spiritual *mélange* as constituting a civilizational network religion. Later on in various parts of India and beyond it would be possible to talk of various regional network religions. It was only by later projection that these could be seen as unified traditions, and that in a rather unreal way. To this degree the critics of Hinduism as a single -ism are justified. In fact I would describe the situation as continuing like this until relatively modern times. This is because over much of Indian history there was only partial unification, while the Muslim and Mughal period, dominating the second millennium saw Islamic but not Hindu unification. The presence of the Muslims and later of the British prevented the formation of lasting empires, except in parts of South-east Asia. So while Islamic polities had a relatively homogeneous religion, the Hindus had neither a unified nor a homogeneous system. It was therefore only in the nineteenth century, and very late at that, that there was anything like an integrated ideology, and it was one which made much of its pluralism (RUDOLPH and RUDOLPH, 1967).

Even today there are problems with talking about Hinduism. For one thing, the unified ideology which lies behind the constitution of India is no longer broadly agreed. There is a rift between the pluralists and the Hindu nationalists. Moreover, there is a real question about how we should regard the Harijans or untouchables. Are they really Hindus? Well, sometimes by dint of piety and the designation of their worship of Ram (or whoever) as Hindu they can be recognized. But they also exist in a limbo outside many definitions of orthodoxy. There are of course other small groups, such as the Jains and the Parsees and Sikhs, recognized in some general sense as belonging in Indian and Hindu society. But in the case of the Sikhs there is a deep split on the question whether they really belong. So the Hindu world in some ways is still a broad network rather than any kind of agreed entity.

Nevertheless, in the course of the present millennium the Indic states in Greater India, fluctuating and battling as they were, settled down into regions with Buddhist kingship systems, with their dual polities. A similar development occurred much earlier in Sri Lanka, which pioneered the shape of Theravadin kingdoms.

Here we need to add a footnote from the colonial period. Colonial rule turned out to have a benign influence in Hindu India, paving the way towards a new synthesis of Hindu values with tolerance towards Muslims and others and creating the opportunity for a Hindu-dominated India. But its effects were less constructive elsewhere in the region. The impact of the British and the French helped to destroy the old Buddhist monarchical system in Sri Lanka, Burma

(Myanmar), Cambodia and Laos, though in Thailand it flourished, thanks to the reforming initiative of Mongkut and Chulalongkorn. The new order after World War II has not functioned with much success, while to complicate matters in French Indo-China Marxist and Khmer Rouge totalitarianism has deeply damaged the Buddhist heritage.

Christendom and Islam as concepts

As Europe was transformed, following the spread of Christian values into the north and east and the detachment of the southern and eastern parts of the Roman empire by Islamic conquest, a sense of Christendom developed, encouraged by the Crusades and their identification of a single external enemy. But with this fragile complex there was a large number of regional powers. Meanwhile the Dar-al-Islam or sphere of Islam lost the cohesion imposed by the unitary Arab Empire and began to disintegrate too. Thus both Europe and Islam projected a theoretically unified religion masking a fragmentation of political power (in Europe this arrangement came to be loosely identified, despite the division, as the Holy Roman empire). These configurations are rather different from those we have looked at hitherto. Even so, the European model provided the foundations for the nationalism that spread across the world in the nineteenth and twentieth centuries. The relation between church and state, and more generally between religion and the state, underwent significant changes, to which I shall return shortly.

Islam's control over areas with sizeable Christian and Jewish populations led to the evolution of what was known under the Ottomans as the *millet* system. Providing a differing model for the symbiosis of religions, this gave the minority religions certain privileges of self-government under their church or community leadership, though their members were in effect second-class citizens (COULSON, 1971). It was an important form of cultural toleration, and individuals could even gain important advisory and political positions. But the political powers nonetheless resided with the Islamic community. The number of adherents to these minority religions inevitably declined in the wake of bans on proselytization, and extra taxes and the implicit loss of opportunities also had a discouraging effect.

During the medieval period, however, Christian opposition to the other groups was much more hostile. Jews were expelled from Spain (POLIAKOV, 1965–73), for instance, at the culmination of the Reconquest from Islam, and special measures (such as the Inquisition) were taken against heretics of all sorts. It was during the period of nationalism that some rethinking occurred in relation to toleration (VON GRUNEBAUM, 1962).

Modern regional networks: towards unification

Partly because the colonial experience brought them into a more intense self-awareness, certain large regions – previously disparate – are now considered as cultural networks. A prominent example is Africa, primarily south of the Sahara. Black Africa was an extensive region before the advent of the European powers and of Arab and Western slavers. Its cultural variety was immense, and its range of languages, political arrangements and economic levels was very considerable, from the Bushmen of the Kalahari to the metal-working kingdoms of West Africa, from the culture which created Zimbabwe to communities of Pygmies. During the fourteenth to sixteenth centuries kingdoms sprang up in a number of regions, a development which implied a certain degree of convergence, with similar ideas arising independently in different areas. Nevertheless, Africa as a region was perhaps closer to Bismarck's description of Italy: merely a geographical expression. But the notorious scramble for Africa in the latter part of the nineteenth century and the beginning of the twentieth was bound to create a sense of commonality and to generate pan-African identity and indeed nationalism. The colonial boundaries, though short-lived, lasted long enough to stay in place when independence was granted after the Second World War and create new predominantly artificial nationalisms, punctuated here and there by civil wars between ethnic groups, as in Nigeria and Ethiopia (versus Eritrea). Nevertheless, the bond of pan-Africanism remained important.

This was in some degree reinforced by the growth of African sentiment in the New World, in the various areas from North America through the Caribbean to Brazil which had been affected by the slave trade. There is a concept not just of Africa but also of Greater Africa. Scholars moreover are seeing greater bonds between some of the new religions of the Americas, such as Vodun and Santeria, and the cults and traditions of the Western African coast.

The effect of all this has been to create the notion of African religion, to promote attempts to treat the whole of Black Africa as a single cultural area. The variety of the material makes this a difficult task: it is not as though there is some single stratum of culture, such as Sanskrit-speaking Brahmins in India and Greater India, which spread over the whole area. At best there were overlaps and influences working as a sort of chain across the area, and perhaps one may look for family resemblances. Whether or not the task of giving a unified view of traditional African religion is at all possible, it is *becoming* more unified. For as developments occur, so do convergences. There are over 10,000 new African religious movements which betray many similarities (WILSON, 1973). Moreover, an African ideology (Negritude and so on) has been fashioned by African intellectuals and others, including Placide Tempels (TEMPELS, 1945) and Jean-Paul Sartre.

We may look on this as retrospective conceptualization. The very act of applying the words Africa and Africans to a whole area and set of peoples accords them unity of a kind. In short, the networks are used to create a degree of unification. We should be used to this, because retrospective modes of creating nations occur across the globe. If, retrospectively, the very different colonies and republics of Transvaal, Orange Free State, Cape and Natal, themselves formed out of complex tribal and national histories and diverse waves of conquest and exploitation, can now be perceived together as South Africa, worthy of a sense of national identity, much larger identities can also be fashioned (HOBSBAWM and RANGER, 1983).

What has happened by retrospective conceptualization in the case of Black Africa can even be extended to Africa as a geographical area, so that (let us say) ancient Egypt can be claimed for Africa, enabling the Xhosa in the Cape – by a strange kind of verbal and geographical

alchemy – to take some credit for the achievements of pharaonic
Egypt. We are doing this sort of thing all the time. As a Scot I am
proud of the achievements of the Scottish Enlightenment, even
though a lot of my blood is Highland and the two parts of Scotland
used to have very different blood, language and culture (and the
Enlightenment was chiefly a Lowland matter).

There are other regions where a similar alchemy has been taking
place. A notable case is what is now called Native American religion.
Again this embraces very different cultures, from the Inuit in the far
north to the Hopi town-dwellers, from the Iroquois to the Chumash.
The native cultures of Mexico and Central America, not to mention
those of South America, provide a broader example. There are
similarities within the diversity of religious practice and myth, but
there are profound differences too. It is the same phenomenon that
has begun in Africa. There is an ideology of Native Americanness, for
understandable reasons, and there is power to be had both in
formulating it and in gathering together the forces of the different
cultures.

A parallel process is under way in Melanesia and Polynesia with the
conception of the Pacific Way. Within Polynesian culture, there are
many more similarities among its constituent elements than is the
case in the African and Native American scenes, which are so much
more variegated and have developed in a much more complex way.
The astonishing success of Polynesian navigators overcame the dis-
unity implicit in their far-flung situation. Quite closely related groups
settled, admittedly at differing times, in different lands. Even so,
some of the same effects of retrospective conceptualization occur, not
least an increased consciousness of cultural and religious unity. But
very little is left of indigenous religion, since almost all of this vast
area has become Christian, mainly through conversion by Protestant
missions. The possibility of treating Polynesian religion itself as a
kind of Old Testament before the Christian New Testament is now
being explored.

Siberian religions, tribal religions in South-east Asia and so forth
may offer further examples of this process. The cases we have
considered can be dubbed retrospectively conceptualized regional
networks. Nevertheless, though they have modern ideological and

cultural significance, each nation or tribe (nomenclature in this regard is not easy, least of all in Africa) until the impact of modern or mostly modern missions, typically Christian and Islamic, had a coterminous religion as described earlier. Some of the new independent churches and new religious movements overlap tribal or ethnic identities. So we have a complex set-up: a coterminous religion, an overlapping new movement, a 'universal' religion or religions (TURNER, H. W., 1977). The coterminous religion itself may create its own new religious movement which is itself coterminous. But by this time we use the word 'coterminous' in a somewhat honorific way: not one of the religions on offer in the scenario I have depicted can any longer be characterized as coterminous. Still, the original ethnic religion was coterminous and is held in memory in that way.

The changes in social placement brought about by the rise of nationalism

The rise of modern nationalism linked with the bursting asunder of Christendom after the Protestant revolution has led to great changes in the dispositions of religions in societies. Protestantism walked hand in hand with the principle *cuius regio eius religio*: the religion of the ruler has to be that of the citizen. This notion spread across much of Europe – even, in many areas, before the nation-state was institutionalized. That is, though some nations (such as England and later the United Kingdom, Sweden, Spain and France) were well advanced in institutionalization, others like Germany and Italy were still fragmented into principalities. But in both cases the principle was upheld. In the American colonies there was a messy system, with some of them exhibiting English-style establishment and others entrenched nonconformist, that is non-Anglican, establishment. The concept, adopted for the sake of peace after disastrous religious wars, implied that the religious ideology of the prince or ruler was important for the nation or principality as a whole – in short, that religion was a form of ideology.

However, the very idea of a nation underwent change, as a result partly of Enlightenment political philosophy and partly of the

Romantic movement. It was deeply affected, moreover, by the events of the American and French revolutions, and to some extent before that of the English Revolution of 1688, itself an aftermath of the Civil War. All these called into question the role of the monarch in one way or another. At the same time the status of religion came under scrutiny (DAWSON, 1938).

The idea of the nation underwent change because it became defined in terms of the people themselves. That is, sovereign power shifted from on high (from God through the king) to the people, but it had to be defined in a certain way. In America it was defined through the constitution and through an eschatology. In European countries the criteria of history, language and religion were used. But the French Revolution removed traditional religion from the calculation. Moreover, in much of Europe there were impulses towards toleration, for instance of the Jews. With nationhood now being defined culturally rather than religiously, Jews would be eminently useful citizens. So Napoleon could assemble a Sanhedrin or Jewish assembly and ask its members whether they truly regarded themselves as French citizens. Of course they did. This was a major beginning in the prising apart of religious from civic ideology.

Nevertheless, many nations retained establishment, though with modifications. Some continued to show an insouciant disregard for toleration. Thus Russia, for all its changes – including emancipation of the serfs, industrialization (if only on a modest scale) and European-style higher education – kept to a solemn sense of the Orthodox destiny of the nation under the tsar, and permitted itself pogroms and other exercises in religious imperialism. Yet in the latter part of the nineteenth century it was ideologically divided between the Slavophiles and the Westernizers. By an irony, it was to be taken over by a Westernizing revolution which possessed many of the instincts of the Slavophiles.

The predominant ideology of nationalism as it developed during the nineteenth century came to be liberalism, because it was a philosophy that promoted capitalism, and one of the main functions of the modern nation-state was to facilitate industrialization, by being large enough to accommodate major industrial operations and by having the resources to provide the infrastructure of capitalist development – canals, railways, education, sanitation, housing and so forth. Liberalism was often in conflict with traditional religion, notably Catholicism and Orthodoxy. The consequence was a number of different patterns of church–state relations in the West, with consequences in Asia and elsewhere.

We shall come to look at these, but it is worth noting that differing compositions of religion in the population prevailed, and these proportions clearly made a difference. Thus in Europe certain prominent nations had populations of overwhelmingly one denomination (though in talking thus we are rather ignoring the fact that many such attachments were no more than nominal, especially in northern European countries). The Scandinavian countries, for example, were almost wholly Lutheran, Poland all but exclusively Catholic (though with a very substantial Jewish population and, up to the end of the First World War, divided between three empires). Germany was largely Protestant and Catholic, and had to make compromises between the two. The United Kingdom's divisions were not severe, but were nevertheless interesting. The four main countries comprising it each had a differing complexion of religion – Anglican, Presbyterian, Free Church and Catholic – but each with significant minorities of one or more of the other types. Switzerland had long made both religious and linguistic compromises. The Balkans had a complicated mixture of ethnic and religious divisions – Islam, Orthodoxy and Catholicism being prominent. The Austro-Hungarian empire likewise had substantial Catholic, Orthodox, Protestant and Jewish peoples. With the break-up of the Ottoman and Austro-Hungarian empires at the end of the First World War, there were to be explosive divisions on religious and other lines. These nationalisms and their religious conflicts were to foreshadow other problems, especially in Asia and Africa, for instance in the communal battles which saw the birth of India and Pakistan, religio-ethnic division in Sri Lanka and civil war in the Sudan. Meanwhile in the Americas different conditions prevailed. In Central and South America, the predominant religion was Catholicism, with minorities of indigenous religions and, in the Caribbean, patches of Protestantism. In North America by the twentieth century there was a mingling of mainly Protestants, Catholics and Jews (BARRETT, 1982).

The question of religion–state relations in the new nationalisms

The principle of *cuius regio eius religio* was considerably softened with the rise of nationalism. The unification of Germany naturally led to compromises between Protestant and Catholic establishments. In Britain toleration made the disadvantages of belonging to a religious minority largely disappear. Similar remarks applied to Scandinavia, France and elsewhere. In Iberia the question of minorities barely arose; the same was true of Italy, where the estrangement between liberal nationalists and the Catholic church gave a special and on the whole open complexion to political life. In Russia and other Orthodox countries such as Romania there was a solid connection between patriotism and Orthodoxy, with continuing persecution of Jews triggered by the rising pan-Slavic nationalism at the end of the century. This itself was a potent stimulus for a new Jewish secular nationalism, namely Zionism. There was a whole array of relations between religion and the state, and these can be set out in a number of models. It is useful in this to remind ourselves of a theoretical point about certain secular worldviews such as Marxism and fascism, which acted as religions in terms of the demands made upon citizens in relation to belief and practice. Marxism might represent itself as not a religion (for instance, in the constitutions of the USSR and East Germany), but its role was very similar to that of the older established religions Orthodoxy and Lutheranism. I shall therefore include secular ideologies of this kind in the list of models of differing systems.

Although the first model is in many ways least normal from the standpoint of total world history, it nevertheless has a lot of influence today. This is the United States model, which entails separation of church from state or, more generally, religion and ideology from state, except to the extent that such separation might itself be held to be an ideological item. Separated models of this kind are often described as 'secular' states, but this word should be used with care, since it has two quite differing senses, meaning pluralistic and anti-religious or non-religious. There is no implication of this latter sense in a 'separated' state. For instance, India looks on itself as a secular state, but it is a highly religious country. There is no anti-religious bias in the state apparatus itself: it is merely that it is supposed to treat each religion equally and fairly. (Whether it does so perfectly can be a matter of dispute, but the intention of the constitution is pretty clearly to do so.)

Another model may be called polite establishmentarianism, in which an older model is formally retained, but in which to all intents and purposes religious pluralism is maintained (VIDLER, 1961). This is the typical situation in modern European countries which still retain establishment, but in a rather minimal way, such as Britain, Sweden and Germany. In some of these the clergy are still paid by the state, and there are sometimes educational tensions in respect of new minorities, such as Muslims. The influx of guest-workers from the southern part of the Mediterranean and from Turkey, India and Pakistan has greatly increased significant minority religions in terms of classical European patterns.

Another pattern is more aggressively secularist (that is, anti-religious), of which a chief example is Turkey under the reforms of Kemal Atatürk, who abolished a number of Islamic institutions, including the caliphate, the use of Arabic script in education, the fez (this was not strictly Islamic but it was taken to be Muslim, symbolic-ally at least), the Sufi orders, the veiling of women and above all the Shari'a (LEWIS, 1965). For a substantial period Arab nationalist constitutions, such as those of the Ba'ath in Iraq and Syria, had a somewhat anti-Islamic or anti-traditionalist stance. Mexico too falls into this pattern.

Another model is pluralistically religious but not universally open. An example is Indonesia, which has a constitution requiring belief in one God, though within that rubric it allows a wide pattern of worship, covering everything from Islam to indigenous, coterminous religions of various tribes and peoples.

Still another model is frankly establishmentarian, such as Ireland and Greece, where the reigning church has various privileges and has a strong influence on certain aspects of the law (such as family and sexual law).

Somewhat stronger as a model of establishmentarianism is the pattern in which religious law is itself build into state law. This is found in a number of Muslim states, for example in Saudi Arabia (which has as its constitution the Qur'an), in the Sudan, in Pakistan. Not all these cases incorporate the full law, but they at least include family law. In the Sudan this model is a major cause of the continuing civil war, with Christian and indigenous religions in the south struggling against it. Another instance is the Islamic Republic of Iran.

A still more rigorous form of establishmentarianism is the Marxist mode (more rigorous because imposed by totalitarian methods), in which Marxist ideology is in effect the imposed state religion and behaviour is, or was classically, strictly prescribed. It is weakening during the 1990s in China, but is very severe and conformist in North Korea. There are some non-Marxist or semi-Marxist variants, for instance in Myanmar (Burma).

It is clear from all these cases that religious bodies will play differing roles in the various nations involved. Clearly, too, any typology of church and denomination, such as is derived from Weber's analysis, will require a variety of shadings to fit the diverse situations. In addition, it is interesting to note that there is a way in which differing churches are connected.

It became a feature of the Reformation that churches followed political units. In due course every official or established church became a national one. In this the magisterial Reformation followed the Eastern church, which had a series of national patriarchates. There were other churches, of the radical Reformation, which did not recognize the connection between citizenship and faith, seeing faith itself as a more personal, and adult, matter. While churches of the same persuasion maintained links with each other, their primary point of reference was typically national (even in the case of radical groups). On the other hand, Catholicism, while tending to conform to the national model, adhered to its transnational constitution. Similarly, the Jewish community, even if split in diverse ways as between Orthodox and Reform and Sephardic and Ashkenazic, maintained its transnational character, though paradoxically rooted after 1948 in the national entity of Israel. There are strong transnational characteristics in Islam, enhanced by the ideal of the community as a whole, and the constant reminders of unity expressed through the annual Hajj and the daily turning towards Mecca in prayer. There are transnational elements of course in Buddhism and in some other religions. Moreover, the situation in modern times, especially since the Second World War, has become more complex, because even nationally rooted religions such as the Hindu tradition have significant and increasingly influential diasporas. And so it is that there are transnational aspects to all religions, practically speaking.

Again, there are in the modern world some other ways in which the national identities of religions are becoming modified and expanded, namely through a variety of ecumenical movements. Since 1910, the progress of Christian unity has been greatly advanced (BROWN, 1967), and some Eastern traditions, notably Buddhism, have made similar moves towards co-operation. The diverse national types of other faiths, such as Islam, are likewise gaining some experience of co-operation as a result of the diaspora. Muslims from many different places and sub-traditions have to live together in the less friendly ambience of major Western cities such as Los Angeles and London.

However, our major concern in this section is with the differing kinds of establishmentarianism which exist. While there are modifications to national identity brought about by rapid communication and transfers of populations, it remains true that the major placement of religions in the modern world is in national environments.

Reflections on the relation of national myths to religious ones

The question of whether a religion is established or not, or what degree of establishment it may retain in a more secular or pluralistic environment, is obviously linked to the way it relates to the story of the nation. In other words, how is it looked on within the telling of the national myth? There may be tensions. It is obvious that Protestantism played a large part in the story of the emerging United States; yet it has no special privilege within the constitution. Again, the story of Catholicism and the Risorgimento contains tension, provoked by anti-Catholic strands within the process of liberation. But it is difficult for a religion to have embedded itself in the life of a people without acquiring a nationalist flavour in the telling of the people's story. It is notable that many of the heroes of a people are spiritual or saintly figures, going back perhaps to a legendary saint (such as

St George in England). To list a few is to make the point: in India, Asoka and Gandhi; in China, Confucius and other sages; in France, St Joan of Arc; in Germany, Luther; in the Czech Republic, Jan Hus; in Russia, Alexander Nevsky; and so forth.

However, religions do stand in diverse ways to the particular identities of differing peoples. Lutheranism does not differentiate the neighbouring Scandinavian states. On the other hand, Poles are conscious that they are flanked by peoples of differing faiths in Lutheranism and Eastern Orthodoxy. Sometimes national identity as expressed primarily in language has nevertheless been preserved by means of religion. Thus, Welsh in a dire period was preserved in the nonconformist chapels which constituted such a vibrant part of community life. Likewise it appears that both in the 'lost' medieval period and during the time of Ottoman incursions and rule the Romanian language was maintained by the Orthodox church (WARE, 1964). So there is an almost indissoluble bond between faith, language and national identity, a fact which does not make it easier for the Hungarian, German, Turkish and Gypsy minorities. In Sri Lanka the coincidence of being Sinhalese-speaking, especially in modern times, and being Buddhist, and the contrary coincidence of the Tamil and Hindu traditions, help to make the chronicles of Ceylon a vital part of the fabric of Sinhala nationalism (itself not easy always for Sinhalese to distinguish from Sri Lankan nationalism, not least given that the imagery of the island as a whole is the *dhammadvīpa* or island of the teaching).

Sometimes the way in which faith integrates into patriotism is most ambitious. It is so with Sri Lanka, but was also greatly so with Russia in times gone by and will be perhaps in times yet to come. The Russian reflection on Christian history is that neither Roman Catholicism nor Protestantism has been faithful to the insights of the early church or the teachings of Christ. Neither Byzantium nor Rome has been spiritually successful: it will become the turn of Moscow, the third Rome, which will deliver the message and example to save the world. There is something of this messianism about America, yet it is prevented from being sectarian. Rather America can be the moral and democratic exemplar for the whole world. Marxism sometimes wove itself into national history in a similar way, with Maoism as China's ultimate purifying revolutionary contribution to the whole world. Such a flavour was detectable in the hopes of Iran as the world's first modern Islamic republic.

An intellectual point about religion and nationalism

We shall return to our reflections on the relation between national histories and religious values shortly, but it is worth at this point making an important observation about the political worth of religious affiliation, and more generally about worldview. While the nation (as we have already noted) is analogous to a religion, as can be seen in the unfolding of the various dimensions, it is weak in one of them. It is strong in myth, it has impressive ritual, it generates strong emotion, it imposes a demanding ethic and web-like law, it has a strong institutionalization through its various arms and organs, it has a large material embodiment from its mountains to its monuments; but it does not have much of a philosophy – not by itself (SMITH, B., 1978). Scotland in itself does not display a philosophy, but it has to acquire a philosophy. A nation demands loyalty and often very severe sacrifices, ranging from wounds in war to onerous taxes. What justifies these? It is here that a religion or worldview makes its mark. It is psychically advantageous for a worldview – a doctrinal dimension – to weigh in on the scales of patriotism. This is one reason why it is good to have a national faith, a national saint and national philosophical as well as other kinds of heroes.

Since the nation-state is a rather modern invention, it is good for a state to have an up-to-date ideology, but this can be blended with religion. Moreover, in times of stress and warfare when sacrifices become everyday occurrences, it perhaps matters more to have the religion than the ideology. Or it could be that the ideology is a sort of fascism, which is a sort of extreme and slightly generalized patriotism, mixed with corporatism or socialism. However, religious values have a useful and universal ring, and, if a faith is associated with your country, your Madonna, your history, you can take advantage of its overarching values.

Often the worldview which constitutes the doctrinal dimension of your nation is a blend, for instance of democratic and Christian values. These were often appealed to in the world wars by the British. They were also, further back, an ideology that justified empire. The British were in the business of empire in order to spread Christianity and eventually democracy (but first the subject peoples needed a period of civilizing education and tutelage). At first the imperial spread was somehow natural: it happened as a result of this and that, including war with the French, a very natural thing. But later the imperialists became uneasy about such an unphilosophical stance. It was better to have a view which turned the imperial mission into something noble; and so Britain had its destiny. It was allegedly the mother of democracy, and it was a good Christian nation which had fought off evil powers, such as Spain, and had made a balance of decency on the continent of Europe. The blended philosophy could easily enough be woven into our history and inculcated in high-school textbooks and the like.

Nevertheless, it is a problem appealing to a universal ethic, blended or not, on behalf of a particular national identity. The doctrinal dimension of nationalism is always troublesome. Sooner or later the tensions become apparent. We have numerous instances in modern history: the tensions of the international communist made to toe Stalin's 'socialism in one country' line; the contradiction in supporting Chilean dictatorship on behalf of democratic values; the Christian duty of the German officer in the Second World War; the Israeli soldier made to shoot at Palestinians in the name of a shining state; and so on.

The attempt, therefore, to give a religious or ideological justification of the actions of a particularist state has eventually to break down. But it is nevertheless a phenomenon that universal myths and philosophies are in fact brought in to justify the sacrifices that we as citizens are from time to time compelled to make. I am not here wanting to form a judgment; but I am concerned rather to point to a phenomenon: the tensions that exist between the doctrinal and some other dimensions of the national entity.

A return to the question of religion and national myths

We have noted differing modes in which religion integrates into a national myth. It may be useful to categorize these in a more formal way. One can distinguish between the importance of a faith and its constitutive character, so that it may be a major factor in a country's history without being constitutive of national identity. Or it may be that no one religion is dominant. Or it may be that religion is constitutive without actually being dominant. We apply these notions also to 'secular' worldviews.

A case where a religion is both constitutive and dominant is Pakistan. It was a nation explicitly formed out of the Islamic provinces of the Indian sub-continent, over against the Hindu-dominated regions which came to be the Republic of India. India, however, was not constituted by Hinduism and was overtly formed as a secular state. Since 1990, though, there has been a national campaign by the Bharata Janatha Party to make India into a Hindu state, on the basis of so-called Hindutva (SMART AND THAKUR, 1993).

It could be argued that in the pre-communist period, Romania was both constituted and dominated by Romanian Orthodoxy, despite the existence of substantial minorities. On the other hand, Italy, though predominantly Catholic, has never been constituted as a Catholic state, having other ideologies to define it – liberalism, fascism and post-war anti-fascist pluralism. Japan under the Meiji constitution came to form itself as a nationalist state, defined by respect for Shinto rituals and values. But it was not in any real sense predominantly Shinto: most practice for most people was actually Buddhist. A similar situation, though arrived at from a different angle, obtains in Israel. The state is a Jewish state and Jews from all over the world have rights there. Ultimately that definition implies something about belonging to a religious tradition, even though most Israeli Jews do not practise the faith.

The transition from older systems, where a given religion was established, to a modern pluralistic democracy means that a given religion becomes no longer constitutive but at best predominant. Indeed, to be realistic one must often recognize that adherence to the faith is largely nominal, as are Lutheranism in Sweden and Presbyterianism in Scotland.

Naturally many of the judgments we make in respect of the mode in which a faith operates are sketchy. We might think that Marxism is the dominant religion in Cuba, but we do not know what people will actually say if and when the lid is taken off. If Marxism is disestablished in Cuba, we may discover that, as in Eastern Europe, most people do not believe in it and would not pay lip-service to it without coercion.

This raises a question about the real functions of religion and ideology in a society. I have cited Sweden as a case where the majority of the population have only a nominal respect for Lutheranism. Still, within the rubric of 'nominal respect' there can be differing functions. Thus people may still want a religious wedding and funeral. From this perspective there is a much wider worldview or set of values to which people adhere, and within that a small part is played by traditional religion, as a kind of solemn ornament at crucial passages in a person's life and in the life of the community. It is therefore worth repeating that in modern societies the trend is to have a blend of liberal ideas of varying kinds and traditional religious values with diverse weights. But this wider worldview goes beyond the older standpoint of faith. Values are not subordinated to an overarching religious cosmology and philosophy, but religion tends to be fitted in a complex metaphysics which embodies prominent ideas from science, views about how to run the state and values derived from the media and elsewhere. This is where the study of religion needs to branch out into worldview analysis (SMART, 1983).

Relations between religious patterns of organization and the dimensions

It may be useful at this juncture to sketch some of the admittedly rather hazy relations between a type of religion and the kind of polity in which it subsists. Some major cases I have referred to as cosmic royal religions. Jacobsen is probably right to see the influence of the numinous in such cases, but it is reinforced by ritual practice, given certain items of doctrine, inchoately set forth although integrated into a unified cosmology. The rituals of the kingship canalize powers, such as those of the earth and people involved in production, for the king is a conduit of heavenly forces down to earth. The numinous character of the divine beings is a sign of their inherent strength. The elements of doctrine refer to the way the cosmos operates and delineate the patterns of kingly power. The annual cycle is of obvious importance, and the festivals of the year mark important ritual applications of cosmic power.

In India a similar conception is not only reinforced by a more explicit philosophy, in which the relation between Creator and the world is set out more systematically, but other mythic concepts are brought in, most importantly the notion that asceticism can generate power. So it is that the king as manifestation of Siva can tap into the reserves of dynamism flowing both from *tapas* and from his numinous character.

On the other hand, the Buddhist model as we have seen rests on certain paradoxes chiefly arising from the fact that the faith is organized in order to promote the life of contemplation with its attendant world-withdrawal (Hinduism is much more thoroughly ambiguous). With the mystic life there goes a metaphysics of impermanence and emptiness. And so the ultimate, with is nirvana or emptiness, has an insubstantial, not a powerful, nature. At any rate, the dialectic between kingly power and the monkish life is reflected in a rather different role for religion as organized in a Buddhist kingdom. It is explicitly made into a systematic order, and the king reigns in parallel with it. There are elements of similar systems, differently patterned, in the Far East.

Moreover, because the Hindu religion was inductively rather than deductively arrived at, its theoretical unity was achieved rather late. But there were aspects, such as the Advaitin monastic system, which up to a point reflected the Buddhist pattern, and for the same reason: a well-patterned attempt to organize the contemplative life. Even so, the main structure of Hinduism, unlike that of Buddhism, was deeply ritual. Consequently, the central place was held by a hereditary priesthood which spread its taboos far and wide. Its very power rubbed off on sacred divisions in general. The other classes of society were fenced off by the rituals of the Brahmins, and then more narrowly the distinctions between *jātis* or castes proper took hold across the board. In fact the caste system, by its varied entrenchment of religious customs, wedding criteria, eating habits and so on, was a marvellous mechanism for ordering an anarchic society: centralization *per se* was not needed. Probably it was this glutinous character of the caste system which ultimately defeated Buddhism in India. Perhaps too it was no surprise that towards the end of its days in the region Buddhism succumbed to ritualistic methods as expressed in Tantra (MITRA, 1954).

Some of the features of contemplative Buddhism were to be found in classical Christianity. Although originally it had, not the Sanghic-style organization, but rather a network based essentially on ritual practice, with a numinous background of a single God, the coming into being of monastic practice created a relatively homogeneous organization (even if there were variations in the Celtic northwest, for instance). This helped to reinforce the systematic aspects of Christian diocesan structure, which in turn had its beginning in the hierarchy of the priesthood. What is striking is that a sacramental style of ritual conduces towards unification, while a less 'magical' kind of ritual allows of congregationalism. When later the Lutherans began to demolish the Roman structure it was the dismantling of the monastical and conventual system and the weakening of the sacramental ideology which began the move towards a break-up of the unity of the system. Of course, Roman Catholicism had another reinforcement of its homogeneity, and that was the emergence of a monarchic papacy. This naturally owed something to reflection on the imperial system.

Another factor in Christian organization was the need for doctrinal unity, both between East and West and then more particularly within each region. This need was prompted by two major factors. First was the way in which the empire was turning itself into a cosmic royal religion, successfully accomplished in the Byzantine empire. The notion of a unified cosmology with the king as the link between heaven and earth and a whole hierarchical system beneath him was a much more systematic worldview than even the ancient Egyptian. Its doctrinal side was more clearly and philosophically worked out. Its myth could embrace Roman imperial history as well as that of the Jewish tradition. Christianity was already embracing Neo-Platonist metaphysics as well as Neo-Platonist methods of contemplation. The whole system then was coherent and powerful, and it survived a long time – a millennium or more in the East; while in the West as a religious system, though not as a cosmic royal religion, it surmounted the disintegrating chaos of the late Roman empire. The second factor giving rise to the need for an important doctrinal dimension was that the new people of Israel was constituted, as we have seen, not by genes and descent, but rather by agreement in belief, as well as a sense of ritual community. The need to have a coherent and agreed set of doctrines led, of course, to the coming together of the councils of the church (DULLES, 1971), but the desire for credal unity helps to reinforce the position of the pope, in the West. An ecclesiastical monarch was after all a good substitute for a temporal one. It helped Western Catholicism to transcend the boundaries of the various kingdoms of northern Europe and the western Mediterranean.

We have not said much about the material dimension. It is a factor, however, in modes of governance. The cosmic royal mode and its variants create the need for glorious expression: the emperor or king is the juncture point between heaven and earth. His system is centralized. The great sacred edifices which royal patrons created are not just representations of the ideologies: they are part of them. They are huge expressions of the ritual practice which is part of the power of the cosmic ruler and of his servant or incarnation here on earth. In Byzantium there was a more or less unified system, and in the West a partial dyarchy as between the spiritual monarch presiding over the church and other emperors and monarchs ruling over earthly affairs. This found eloquent expression in the architecture of the middle ages. The wonderful cathedrals and abbeys on the one hand matched the palaces and castles on the other.

One can point to similar reflections of the divine–kingly interrelation in the Temple of Heaven in Beijing, and further manifestations in other Chinese capitals; and in cities such as Anuradhapura and Polonnaruwa in Sri Lanka. The very weight of such constructions both glorifies the monarchy which accomplishes them and helps to make the imperial power and riches necessary.

The diminution of ritual significance in a worldview owes something to a renewed emphasis on the experiential and ethical dimensions. For instance, the Roman church encouraged ritual works among the laity and others: this was not, of course, always without ethical significance, but it was ritually expressed. Confession, pilgrimage, attendance at mass, even indulgences had a ritual meaning – indulgences because the monetary payment let you off so many ritual acts. Part of Luther's revolution was to emphasize inwardness again. What was important was faith (not ritual works). To make the experiential dimension the most important was already to undermine, though it did not obliterate, rituals. This in turn was bound to weaken the role of the priest, to convert him more into a pastor and a preacher. Even more vital in some ways was Calvin's emphasis upon revelation, the Word and therefore preaching. This, too, was directed towards feeling, but it also had a lot to do with the mythic and doctrinal dimensions. Most significant perhaps of all the moves was the radical insistence of the Anabaptists upon adult baptism. The very notion of infant baptism included a collective idea of the family and more widely of the church, as if the community had its own organic substance. But if you insist that only the adult is aware enough to express his faith, you already have the makings of a future individualism. In turn this affected church governance: the radical Reformation movements – Anabaptists, Baptists, Congregationalists (or independents), Quakers – shifted away from hierarchical government to congregationalism. They were by that very move potent in creating a drive towards democracy in Protestant countries and overseas in parts of North America (AHLSTROM, 1972).

Moreover, such moves hit at the very formula of *cuius regio eius religio*. They represented a move against the older ideology of the divine or divinely licensed monarch. Religion, in going from bottom up rather than top down, tended to abandon a vision of a sacramental universe. These moves paved the way for a philosophy of the rights of the people over against kingly powers. So we note that a shift in the emphasis upon certain dimensions of religion had potent consequences. Church structures themselves were influenced by the weight put upon, or not put upon, sacramental ritual.

The Calvinist and other Protestant emphasis upon a kind of

inner-worldly asceticism, to use Weberian language, also enhanced the role of the ethical dimension. Rather than ritual works, upright practices were important in this new order. The fading of the more magical world of the old order led to the decline of spending on the material dimension. By and large, Protestants inherited great cathedrals but did not create new ones. One the whole their buildings were plainer. Paintings turned to the secular: to the landscape, the interior, the portrait. Great altarpieces were no longer in demand.

How far is it possible to trace effects in the opposite direction? How far did the material dimension have its effects on the spiritual path? There are some influences, which I can trace briefly here. The existence of monasteries, for instance, as a material aspect of the life of contemplation gives conquerors and governments a powerful grip upon religions. The destruction of monasteries in north India after the incursion of Turkish troops was part of the death knell sounded for Buddhism. In the Ottoman lands there were assaults on churches, and churches were even constructed on wheels, so that they could be hauled away in the face of enemy troops. By contrast, in communist times Baptist and other evangelical preachers could evade detection because of their lack of material possessions: no more than a Bible in the pocket.

The sociology of religion and the question of secularization

A major thesis among modern sociologists is that of increasing secularization (FENN, 1975). It is clear that something of a diminution of religious reasons for public action was bound to occur given the shift to a more pluralistic society. The switch to a modern nationalism involved the decay of the cosmic royal kingship system: the bringing of the substantial power from heaven to the people diminishes royal significance. The national idea brings about a new view of education, and with that some subtraction from religious myth and doctrine in the ideology being presented. Moreover, we may note highly significant social changes during the period of industrialization and the growth of capitalism, which themselves altered the logic of events. We can depict these in relation to the old Indo-European pattern of three classes (actually a pattern that is inevitable in complex societies and so not unique to the Indo-Europeans). The differing classes tended to split. At the lower level the agricultural labourers became differentiated from the urban workers; at another level, the priestly class, disproportionately influential among the intelligentsia, drifted apart from the new scholars of the Enlightenment period, who became dominant; and the ruling class, headed by the king, tended to drift into a military wing on the one hand and a more professional ruling class, embedded in parliament, on the other. Such alterations occurred throughout the new nationalist world, once it began to take shape. In differing countries and not just Christian ones the same pattern could be detected: the modernist intellectuals of Egypt or later Pakistan came to be much more influential than the traditionally trained religious experts (EISENSTADT, 1968). Because the church was organized in the past according to a system of parishes drawn along agricultural lines the urbanization implied by industrialization caused much disorientation. The removal of power from the king also diminished the use of religious symbolism and ideas.

With industrialization there was also a subtle shift of attitude. The urban environment was ineluctably artificial. Steel mills, canals, trains, mines, gas installations and so forth had the unmistakable nature of human creations. Men and women came to recognize their deep dependence on other humans. It was easy to think, therefore, that their well-being arose out of politics and economics. The older religions had spoken more of relationship to nature and the cosmos. The new age of the industrial nation beckoned more to ideologies, whether of free trade, or of fascism, or of Nazism, or of Marxism. The new saviours were more earthly than the old. They could be incarnations of the people and of the nation and of the forces which promised goods and prosperity. The ideology of kingship and fertility was no longer very relevant, nor were the prayers for rain and crops. Northern Europe, more rapidly industrialized, was to become secularized more quickly than the south. Catholicism for various reasons was better equipped to withstand some of these forces in any case. The north had seen the system dislocated through the Reformation, and often that revolution was a top-down affair, emanating from the new middle classes and backed by many rulers. So many of the workers were already alienated from the church in any case. But these events had not occurred in the south. Second, the complex and colourful rituals of the Catholic church could still appeal widely to all classes.

Oddly, the migration of large numbers of poor people from northern and eastern Europe to the Americas and especially to North America saw a pattern of re-Christianization abroad. In the United States German, Swedish and other migrants, who left their home countries with lukewarm feelings for the churches there, settled into church allegiance in Minnesota or Wisconsin or wherever. In fact the United States came to be substantially churchgoing. This was partly because church allegiance in the place of new settlement reinforced values which had been left behind, and at the same time expressed the hopes which the new land fostered (ALBANESE, 1981).

If we neglect areas where Marxism came to the fore – which in any case meant that in effect a new form of religion was implanted – the same secularizing process had only limited manifestation in colonial areas. For one thing, colonialism forced people back on their traditions, at the very time they wanted to modernize. What they wanted to do was to save the best of their past and their customs. In short, they were far removed from the secularized workers and intellectuals of northern Europe. Moreover, industrialization as such was slower in coming, except in Japan. In so far as the secular mode took a hold, it came from new blends of older traditions and modern worldviews. This naturally gave traditional religious ideas less prominence in political and economic decisions, and the shift to city life caused great dislocation. All these consequences of nationalism contributed, then, to secularization – that is, a drift away from traditional rituals and ideas.

The thesis of secularization was often presented as something inevitable. But this scarcely seems to be true, from varying points of view (MARTIN, 1978). The thesis never really held good in the US. After the Eisenhower period there was a certain falling away of church and synagogue attendance, but that period was itself a surprisingly religious period. The fluctuations in religiosity in America are not that great. And, while secularization in northern Europe has been marked, it has been less so in the south, though by certain indexes more evident there since Vatican II (1962–5). The situation in Islamic countries has a certain ambiguity. For instance, there has been a flourishing of so-called fundamentalism from the 1970s onwards, partly as a result of disillusion with secular Arab nationalism (ANTOUN AND HEGLAND, 1987). By a paradox, therefore, secularism is itself in some decline, and Islamic revival is evident in a number of countries, notably in Algeria, Tunisia, Egypt and Iran. There is some revival of religion both in Russia and in Islamic Central Asia, in the former USSR. It is hard to say what the future holds for China, where adherence to Maoism is declining, and there are at least some signs of the revival of Buddhism and Taoism. In short, the general thesis of secularization is open to question, and in the long run may or may not be valid.

Nevertheless, certain factors which relate to secularization should be taken into account, since they are important for the understanding of the development of global religion. First, there is some erosion of authority, since with the movement of peoples, better education, choices of religious allegiance and so on, people have a more open view of traditional claims. Second, the growth of individualism in Western countries particularly has led to an eclecticism in regard to religion. Such an attitude is sometimes referred to as New Age. This covers a variety of Eastern religious and other ideas forming a congeries of spiritual notions which may be adopted in their own right or drawn into traditions. In any event, individuals often make up their own religious systems, neglecting dogmas and traditional values, and do not feel the need to adhere to a broader system of values. It is not that such people regard themselves as being non-religious. But they are by no means traditionalists.

The situation in the former Marxist countries is confused, and in the early years after the demise of the Soviet Union it is perhaps too soon to work out how things will be. The long years of anti-religious education and inculcation in communist values have left their mark. The destruction of many churches and mosques has caused what might be called a void of ritual. But there is evident good will towards the reconstruction of religion, though one might expect a diminution in interest in sacramental ritual and a greater concern with the experiential dimension. Perhaps this is already evident in the penetration of evangelical missions in the former Soviet Union.

If we look at some of the dynamic countries of the world, the evidence on the whole is against the theory of increasing secularization. I would detect a growing concern with religion from 1980 in Pakistan, Bangladesh, India, Sri Lanka, Afghanistan, Russia, Ukraine, Belarus, Poland, Tunisia, Algeria, Malaysia, Indonesia, Sudan, Yemen, Iran . . . These countries alone provide a very sizeable chunk of the world population. We do not know what is going to happen in China; and the thesis of secularization does not hold up so far in Russia and other countries of the former USSR. Africa is a more enigmatic continent.

Perhaps the area where the thesis has the most plausibility, beyond northern Europe and its cultural offshoots (Australia and New Zealand, possibly Canada and the USA), is among the Chinese diaspora: Hong Kong, Taiwan, Singapore and perhaps ultimately China itself. The pragmatism of the Chinese may lead them beyond superstitions and so too much entanglement with their more traditional folk religion, Taoism and so on. Still, Buddhism may well retain its appeal, as in Japan and South Korea. Its easy way of merging with the scientific worldview may in due course stand it in good stead (SMART, 1993).

Latin America is a large cultural area which also needs to be examined in this connection. Its largely Catholic superstructure has been challenged in recent years from below by a fervent Protestantism, emphasizing most strongly the experiential dimension of religion – appealing to conversion, the sense of the numinous, a new *bhakti* or devotionalism, jettisoning the complexities of Catholic ritual and traditional forms of obedience: in other words, offering a sense of a new life. It is interesting too that since the early 1970s there has been a quasi-Marxist Catholic movement in Latin America, pioneered by Catholic priests writing in the so-called tradition of liberation theology. This also has a grassroots basis and challenges the older sacramental ritual and hierarchical character of the church. Above all it challenges traditional Catholic alliances with the ruling classes in the area. Both evangelical and liberation-theology forms of religion are in some degree secularizing, in so far as they move away from older forms. But they are nevertheless religious or spiritual in intent, and tap into other dimensions in exerting their dynamism: the evangelical tap into the narrative or Biblical dimension and the experiential dimension (emphasizing the experience of conversion and of the risen Christ); the impetus of liberation theology is towards tapping into the ethical dimension and a sense of the church's duty towards the poor, though it also makes use of intellectual theories which are of a doctrinal character far removed from traditional Catholic categories.

Sometimes the thesis of secularization has gained greater plausibility than it may have warranted because of two factors. First, it has been adopted by Western sociologists who have been more familiar with northern European and North American data, which might be thought to have favoured it more. Second, they have tended to neglect data from other continents where cultures have undergone a rather different experience that may have favoured traditional cultural ideas. But it is too soon to come to conclusions. The global nature of culture as it emerges may itself move in a direction more favourable to secularization.

The thesis of pluralization and of synthesis

What is, however, clearly plausible is the thesis that modern societies have by and large moved towards pluralization, that is, towards a situation in which religious minorities are offered greater toleration. The consequence is, as we have noted, that political arguments are not so often conducted according to particular religious or worldview assumptions. In this way religions adopt a blend or synthesis with liberal worldviews. Even those which represent an opposition to certain aspects of liberalism may do so only within certain limits. For instance, conservative Christianity in the United States does not adopt a generally anti-democratic stand. We shall return to this in later discussion of the political and economic significance of religions and religious values.

The exceptions to the thesis of pluralization lie primarily with the Marxist-controlled societies, such as the People's Republic of China (as evidenced most startlingly in its suppression of religious freedom in Tibet) and North Korea; but also important here are certain Islamic countries, including Saudi Arabia, Iran and the Sudan. Even countries which as yet did not have political freedom, such as South Africa and Malawi, tended to retain religious pluralism.

It could be argued that pluralization can lead to secularization, not merely in the style of argumentation used in public debate but in the diminution of fervour where less is at stake. It is true that the support for the Roman Catholic church in Poland was greater during the struggle against the communist regime, with its implications of Russian dominance (Soviet dominance masking Russian imperialism). For obvious reasons, religion could call more easily upon national sentiment. On the other hand in a country such as Albania, officially declared to be atheist, the throttling of overt expression of religion was replaced by a flowering of outward commitment to the religions of the country, so it is hard to judge relative commitments before and after the collapse of the Marxist regime.

A major aspect of the synthesis between religious and other values in a modern society is agreement on ways to settle disputed issues, that is via democratic voting process or by the law – for instance with issues such as abortion law and capital punishment. This agreement in one respect involves a climbdown by traditional religion, so in this respect it represents a weakening of older claims. This does signify a certain degree of secularization in the wake of pluralization. But there remain imponderables. Does willing adherence to a religious tradition perhaps count for more than a state-enforced or state-encouraged conformism? The mutual measurement of differing systems is difficult.

Reflections on the social dimension

I have brought out various features of the social dimension. First of all, I have sketched an inventory of the major kinds of religious figures. In this I have tried to keep realistic phenomenologically, and have departed somewhat from certain sociological categories, perhaps most strikingly not following the broad Weberian category of the prophet (his notion of the exemplary prophet applied to the Buddha is at fault). I then sketched out various of the religious social systems, ranging from coterminous religions in relatively small-scale societies through the various cosmic royal religions, but noting the variant of civilizational and regional network religions. I then traced the changes which occurred through the colonial period to the formation of a universal system of nationalism, and the effects of this on religions and worldviews, with the occasional substitution of secular (that is non-religious) worldviews. These secularisms actually functioned much more like traditional established religions than did the blended democratic systems, with a pluralistic cast. I then discussed issues about secularization and pluralization. From a global perspective the thesis of secularization is rather doubtful, except in so far as pluralization tends to make secular arguments more important in the settlement of disputes within a given national society.

I also noted ways in which the differing dimensions have effects upon social arrangements: for example, the way the social dimension of a religion is affected by its sacramental ritual or alternatively its devotion to the contemplative life, and the ways in which the inwardness of religious experience may contribute to the growth of individualism.

We shall return briefly to the political and economic scenes in Chapter 8, where I shall consider some political stances and the economic relevance of worldviews.

CHAPTER SEVEN

The Material Dimension

Some reflections on the ways religions reflect themselves materially

The gods are paradoxical. They are invisible, yet they express themselves in the world (KOSAMBI, 1962). They have a need to be identified, and so they are often represented as or by images. I say 'as' as well as 'by' because in many cultures images have a sacramental rather than just a symbolic significance. That is, the statue of Visnu in front of me, which has been duly consecrated, actually is Visnu, just as in classical Christianity the bread and wine, duly consecrated, actually are the body and blood of Christ. Of course, there are religions which look upon the use of sacramental or indeed any other kind of image as blasphemous, and this itself has profound effects on the material dimension of such a religion.

But before we get on to such matters, let us just remind ourselves of how the gods operate, for this will show us how there is a transition from nature to artefact in the treatment of the divine.

A god, say of the sea, manifests himself through the sea. The sea is his body. This means that the sea is more than a great object (which roughly is how we tend in a secularized mode to view it). It is a person which heaves and billows and tosses ships around yet is often flat and tranquil. It is a person with varying behaviour, which the worshipper hopes to influence, for instance by sacrifices. It is a person which can therefore be addressed, and which in suitable temples can be realized in statues. But it does not need statues, in so far as language can already reach him, with what Homer called 'winged words'. To build a temple, though, is a pleasing act, and is typically done by the shore, where indeed sacrifices tend to be made. So, briefly, a god has a double body: there is the ocean itself, and there is the special portrait which humans make.

Another aspect of the material side of the worship of Poseidon is the sacrifice made to him – the bullocks killed on the beach, to be consumed by both god and humans. The burning of the meat and more deeply the killing of the animals somehow convey their essence to the invisible realm of the god. The smoke goes upwards and away; the soul too flies into the beyond. So the sacrifice is like the winged words, conveying the goodness of the meat and animals to the god. We shall later have to note some of the economic effects of sacrifice, because it involves destruction and the use of wealth (NILSSON, 1948).

Certain aspects of our environment can be picked out as divine: a river, a mountain, the sea, the wind and so on. From this point of view, nature and its parts are portions of the material dimension of religions. In modern nationalism they still function rather like this. The body of the nation is its land, and this is often the object of national piety, through tourism. Poets celebrate the beauties of their country. To complicate matters, particularly sacred or beautiful places are decorated with buildings, such as the temple at Kanya-kumarin at the tip of India. So we have a blend between natural and artificial in the formation of material places or objects of reference.

Aniconic religions and natural objects

The strongest religion expressing itself in an aniconic way is Islam, but of course it draws its inspiration from the Jewish tradition. Christianity had a human God and so could never quite maintain its ban on representations of Christ. The notion that depictions of God are not to be allowed expresses an interesting position, which can be thought of in the following way. Religions which represent particular parts of the world as divine, such as the ocean, have a diminished view of God. If God is wholly beyond or behind the visible cosmos, he controls everything. In an important way, therefore, an aniconic religion signals the omnipotence of the Creator. It leaves symbolism to the spoken and written word: holy scriptures above all become the means of representing God.

This does not by itself diminish the importance of the material dimension. Mosques and synagogues may be elaborate and expensive, and important resources may be put into illuminated manuscripts (DAVIES, 1982).

Other aspects of the material

The material dimension comprises various aspects: buildings for worship and ritual, statuary and paintings, the dress and vestments of priests and so forth, books, amulets and the like, graves, burning-ghats and so on, and sacrificial animals and the like.

Secular worldviews also have their material entities, including the decoration of the capital city, statues of national or ideological heroes and the paintings which depict important scenes. Often there is a blend which reflects materially the mingling of sacred, traditional edifices and national monuments, such as the National Cathedral in Washington and such items as the Lincoln Memorial and the Vietnam Memorial.

The richest of religions are those which include both cosmic royal religions and the newer nationalisms. Because the cosmologies of the powerful traditional belief systems display themselves and attempt to show the glories of the rulers who link heaven and earth, they are liable to use up considerable resources. In the more modern religions there are typically parallel buildings which show off both the traditions and the newer palaces and parliaments of the new era. In the twentieth century there is a special predilection for elaborate displays of military might, with march-pasts, aerial displays, naval ceremonials and so on.

It will be useful for us to look at the differing patterns of temples, churches, mosques and so on. To some degree the differing patterns will help to underline some of the varieties of symbolisms and doctrine underlying the differing traditions. I shall begin with some animadversions on Egypt and the ancient Near East, before moving to

Buddhist and Hindu temples, and then to Far Eastern temples; after that I shall present certain features of Jewish, Christian and Islamic architecture.

Egyptian and other Mediterranean temples

The ancient temple was an enormous dwelling house of the gods, rising from the entrance to the innermost sanctuary. The god dwelt in the holy of holies and was there tended by the priests, who acted for the king. The god was treated (as in India much later) as if he were a human being, being looked after in his daily needs. On the walls typically were depictions of the ritual presided over by the king. These pictures helped to maintain the rites even if there were hiatuses in the priestly actions. From the innermost sanctuary the god was carried down to the crowd of attendants into the outer courtyard (LURKER, 1980).

In the Aegean, in the kingly palaces of Crete, shrine rooms evidently served sacrificial purposes, including probably human sacrifices. On the mainland Mycenaean practice seems to have followed Cretan custom, and representation of the goddess apparently helped in the protection of the sites. In general Greek and Roman temples were not large. Nevertheless, though they did not normally house many worshippers, the main festivals, with significant sacrifices, drew large congregations. Both the gods and humans witness the sacrifices. Very often temples served as storerooms for valuable givings, as well as houses for statues of the goddesses and gods. As a result of Alexander's conquests, the custom of building temples spread through the Middle East, though in Egypt the traditional pattern continued (PETERS, 1970). Roman temples were similar to Greek ones. The most spectacular was at Heliopolis in the Lebanon, which was dedicated to Jupiter.

Buddhist and Hindu temples in India and South-east Asia

Initially Buddhist shrines consisted of simple *stūpas* which housed relics of the Buddha or other saints. The mound shape of the *stūpa* was reminiscent of the cosmic egg, but the notion of creation was not important in the Buddhist doctrinal scheme. Later, *stūpas* were carved out inside caves. Initially there were no statues of the Buddha: at most, as at Sanci, there were bas-reliefs depicting scenes in the life of the Buddha, with the Buddha himself registered by his absence. This conception may have involved the notion that the Buddha was absent in nirvana. It was a way of depicting the Buddha as transcendental in some sense.

The influence of Greek statuary made itself felt after the establishment of Hellenistic kingdons in Central Asia and north-west India. The growth of *bhakti* from the first century BCE helped to encourage a more positive mode of representing the Buddha. The gradually more elaborate ways of worshipping celestial Buddhas, as well as the earthly Buddha, brought about a material way of representing Buddhahood, both in India and in Central Asia, as well as in Sri Lanka (SNELLGROVE, 1978).

Parallel with all these developments was the establishment of monastic dormitories and schools. Thus the typical monastery came to develop a complex structure of *stūpa*, shrine room and dormitory, with a pavilion for preaching sermons to the laity, and a bodhi tree. More than this, there were regal compounds which enshrined the dyarchic system of kingly rule, with its spiritual and earthly aspects. Perhaps the most glorious Buddhist shrine of all was the remarkable cosmological structure at Borobodur in Java (MUS, 1978).

From the fifth and sixth centuries C.E., Hindu temples began to take permanent form (KRAMRISCH, 1976). Small shrines, often of impermanent materials, preceded them. Generally the temple came to be conceived as a palace of the God and sometimes too as a fortress, which helped to ensure order in the cosmos. Typically there is a womb within to hold the main image of the God or Goddess, and a tower which represents a cosmic mountain, or indeed four mountains on each side. Access for the worshippers is, of course, important, and there is frequently a tank for them to bathe in. Temples come in diverse styles in Orissa, Tamil Nadu and elsewhere in India, but apart from the major constructions in cities there are thousands of examples in villages up and down India. A temple is not usually a focus for congregational worship, but is more a local pilgrimage place for the faithful. It is also for celebrating the calendar of festivals which mark the year.

While the South Asian Buddhist temple has an open aspect and a much less dense structure, being devoted to light rituals of pilgrimage and reverence, the Hindu temples on the whole have a closed and heavily ritual aspect and are guarded by a priestly class. The gods, like those of Egypt, are clothed and looked after as sacramental images. Access is not allowed to all. So the atmosphere of the Hindu temple is a numinous and daunting one, exuding power; the Buddhist compound, though not without a certain awesome quality, does not suggest ritual power of the same degree.

Far Eastern temples

Buddhist architecture became widespread in China from the third and fourth centuries C.E. and showed two variants from the main South Asian pattern. The image hall for the figure of Buddha was modelled on the Chinese palace. It reflected the strong *bhakti* aspect of the Mahayana which took hold in China. The other variant was the pagoda, derived from a form evolving in Central Asia as Buddhism travelled slowly to China along the Silk Route. It resembled a Chinese watchtower, but it probably struck many Chinese as peculiar since it dominated the low buildings of a typical Buddhist compound. Also fairly important in China were the cave temples, which dated from the fourth century and introduced a new motif into Chinese architecture.

Somewhat later than the spread of Buddhist architecture are the temples of the Taoist tradition, following much the same pattern, but housing deities of various kinds, including Lao-tzu, transcendent gods, local heroes and various mysterious beings (WILLIAMS, 1961).

The Confucian temple is a rather different sort of building from the Buddhist and Taoist structures. There is considerably less provision for the ritual of worship. Its central contents are not images as such, which help to warm *bhakti*, but rather tablets, though the statues of famous past officials and local sages give a sense of sagacity to the courtyards. The chief ceremonials celebrate K'ung's birthday. The symmetry of design and other factors give a sense of sobriety to the whole, and of *li* or ritual propriety coupled with an air of rationality. Every major city of China has such a temple – or had. The onslaught on Confucianism, during the Cultural Revolution particularly, had a devastating effect. Indeed, all three religions suffered considerably during the post-revolutionary period, especially so in the material sense.

On the whole the edifices of South and East Asia are not congregational buildings. By contrast, Jewish, Christian and Islamic buildings are just that.

Synagogues, churches, mosques

Early synagogues cannot be identified, no doubt because they were no different from secular buildings. From the third century C.E. they tended to have a pattern like that of a Roman basilica, without at first an apse for the Torah scroll, which later became a marked and later a universal feature. The separation of men and women does not seem to have been practised in these early times, though later a separate room for women and then a gallery were added. In Reform Judaism in America there is no need for such a feature, and innovatory architecture – for example by Frank Lloyd Wright – has been introduced. Some large synagogues exist, such as one in Amsterdam, but on the whole they never reached the scale of Christian churches and cathedrals (DAVIES, 1982).

Christian architecture includes not only houses of worship but also monasteries. Basically church buildings were late in emerging, because early Christians worshipped in synagogues and in the Temple, and for a long period in private houses. The earliest extant building which was altered for use by a Christian congregation dates from the first half of the third century C.E. But from the time of the conversion of Constantine Christianity as the emerging imperial religion came to need a quasi-official building, modelled on the basilica, and in due course the typical architecture of a Christian church emerged. It took the form of a building heading towards an apse and altar (the apse for the bishop's throne). Pagan temples were also converted to Christian use.

Eventually the middle ages saw the creation of spectacular cathedrals with high altars. Though the chair or *cathedra* of the bishop was a necessary feature, it was usually put on one side. The whole perspective was of a mounting or long nave, culminating in the altar. The Gothic style also gave a soaring view towards heaven. This was in the West; the design was somewhat different in the East. Instead of the tower and the spire, the East favoured the dome, a symbol of overarching heaven. It was used not only in churches but in the tombs of saints. A dome could be carried lightly on columns, and the effect is that it looks downwards like the sky. A further elaboration is the use of mosaics, if possible throughout. There also came to predominate the iconostasis, or screen decorated with icons, themselves seen as windows on to heaven, representing Christ, Mary and the saints. This custom started in Russia in the fourteenth century and spread across the Orthodox world. The revolution from secular house-churches to sacred spaces was complete in both East and West.

But the Protestant Reformation made a considerable difference. Before we come to this it is worth noting that in both East and West the structure of the monastery was important – not only of the buildings, typically comprising both living quarters and a church for the performance of the mass or the liturgy, but typically too of the land that went with them. The tag *laborare est orare* expressed the vocational approach to agriculture. The monasteries played a vital role in opening up agriculture in Europe.

The Reformation, however, had an ideological distrust of monasteries. They were perceived as attempting to buy salvation by works. This was partly because of the celibacy of the monks and nuns; it was also because of the hard work required by the contemplative life. Indeed there is a general contrast to be made between the prophetic and the mystical, between the numinous and the luminous, between conversion and the contemplative. The first of these pairs is highly spontaneous, while the latter tends towards practice. Of course, there may be some spontaneous aspects of the business of working at the inward path, but the general consensus about the path of yoga is that it has to be practised. So the move of the Protestant religion towards faith and the numinous experience, and towards the Biblical or narrative side of religion, and away from the more abstract aspect of doctrine, was itself a major factor in the dissolution of the monasteries. Of course, there also was the financial dimension of kingly decisions. The ideology suited kingly interests.

Meanwhile, differing things happened in relation to churches. The more traditional forms of magisterial Protestantism such as Anglicanism and Lutheranism simply took over the Catholic churches and cathedrals. This happened to some extent in Calvinism, though later on the Presbyterians were to build their own buildings – much plainer, with pews and pulpits dominant. The altar was in effect replaced by the pulpit, because the priest was replaced by the minister, learned and loquacious. Even plainer chapels and meeting houses were created by the radical reformers. In America these were often of a singular plain beauty. In general, the Reformation simplified the real estate (TURNER, 1979).

Beyond the Reformation there are various styles of religious building conceived by the new religious movements. The Mormons have created impressive temples, with access confined to believers. At the other end of the scale are the small meeting places of Jehovah's Witnesses. The Christian Scientists have impressive neo-classical buildings.

Islam has its characteristic spaces (GRABAR, 1973). Whereas most Christian buildings are in one way or another devoted to liturgical activities, whether of a complex ritual kind or devoted to the simpler setting of prayers, Bible readings and sermons, Muslim meeting places or mosques characteristically embrace both religious and secular activities. The courtyard can be used for political purposes, legal sessions and educational activities. Thus a mosque may house the precinct of a university. (Naming a professor's post as a chair derives from Muslim custom.) Since the mosque is the gathering place of the community as a whole the sermon often includes political, financial and other news. Among the accoutrements of a regular mosque is the *qiblah* wall, which is on the side facing Mecca, with its niche or *miḥrāb*. The wall is usually a very broad one, since it was thought that the side nearest Mecca was especially auspicous.

This gives mosques a different shape from the typical Christian church, with its long nave. Also in the mosque is a lectern for reading from the Qur'an, and a place for reading the sermon. The whole mosque is also secluded from the profane world, since it is for revelation, for the utterance of God's world and prayer to God himself. Similarly a prayer mat is a way of demarcating the space of one's individual sacred activity. There is also mounted on a mosque the location of the call to prayer, or minaret (PADADOPOULO, 1979).

Generally Islam has rejected decorations which directly depict human or animate objects. These are held to be blasphemous and to degrade prayerful activity. Consequently mosque architecture has been decorated in a much more abstract way, through geometric patterns and more richly through calligraphy drawn from the Qur'an itself. Mosques across the world vary in style, tending to reflect local and regional variations. The use of tiling and gilt on the dome is particularly striking and beautiful in Persia, while the Mughal architecture of India was a subtle blending of Central Asian and Hindu motifs and methods. In the Sudan and sub-Saharan Africa, different materials are often employed, with adobe surfaces and wooden beams pushing forth. In China and the Far East upward-sloping traditional Chinese-style roofs prevail.

There has been a considerable amount of mosque-building in modern times, in part becaues there have been extensive migrations of Muslims from countries traditionally Islamic into Western nations predominantly Christian. Thus there are grand mosques built in London, in Germany, in France and elsewhere.

Pilgrimage centres

Probably the most effective religion involving pilgrimage is Islam. The idea that the foundation place of the faith, primarily Mecca, and from a lesser point of view Medina (not to mention Jerusalem), should focus loyalty from all over the world is an effective one. In these latter days, with aerial transport so relatively cheap, there has been a massive increase in the Hajj. It is interesting that material acts such as going on pilgrimage acquire important material conditions. Thus the pilgrimage to Kataragama in Sri Lanka, near the south-east coast, has become much more popular since the coming of the motorbus and the car. One year I noted how bus tours of fourteen southern Indian temples had greatly expanded the attendance at these sites. The pilgrimage to Santiago de Compostela in north-eastern Spain has burgeoned. No doubt in all cases merits have multiplied. In general there is a globalization of the process of pilgrimage, with airports being prepared, more hostels and hotels created, more souvenirs sold and so forth. One can expect the revival of older itineraries, say to Canterbury, where they have long fallen into desuetude. Moreover, there are what might be describe as semi-pilgrimages, quasi-tourist trips which take travellers to holy shrines in which they might be interested even if they are not adherents of the religions in question, or even if they are Protestants who do not altogether believe in pilgrimages – one thinks of travels to Angkor Wat and Borobodur, and to Palestine, or Israel (VAN DER LEEUW, 1986).

The significance of holy books

New mechanical and other means of production obviously affect sacred consumption. The Bible during the middle ages was expensive to produce, partly because it was written on vellum and other expensive material, partly because of the considerable labour in-volved. This had an inhibiting effect on the circulation of Bibles, and helped to restrict much of the transmission of texts to ritual occasions. It also led to attempts to recite the Qur'an on a mass basis in the Islamic world. But the evolution of the printing press had an obvious effect on piety, giving rise to new genres of pious and polemical literature during the process of Reform. Gradually secular literature too could evolve – volumes of poetry, histories, books of philosophy, novels, journals, accounts of discovery, and so on, all of which tended to swamp sacred literature. The same developments could create dense possibilities of scholarly works such as commentaries on sacred texts.

The colonial period exploited these material developments. It saw the magical effects of printing being repeated in society after society, particularly in previously non-literate societies where the translation of the Bible into varied tongues brought about the miracle of speaking books. But even in previously literate societies the new techniques had impressive consequences. Such enterprises as the Pali Text Society saw the promulgation of the whole of the Theravadin canon, plus many commentaries, and helped to bring about a revival of Buddhist scholarship and self-knowledge. Similarly the new editions of the Sanskrit texts, particularly the *śruti* and *smṛti* of the Hindu corpus, added to the wave of new Orientalist scholarship. The matter was not just a material consequence, for the same waves helped with the propagation of new ideas of critical learning, thereby bringing the influence of modernism to bear on the traditions. Moreover, the ease of circulating printed works facilitated communication across worlds, not least in the Muslim learned world from Indonesia to Rabat and from Samarkand to Dar es Salaam. Perhaps these developments had impact in the Far East, given that China had long ago pioneered the printing press. And romanized script, so widely adopted in the rest of the world, had less impact on Chinese culture.

Other religions tended to take over some of the techniques of Christian missionaries, who used pamphlets and other publications to spread the Gospel. Even some religions such as Jainism, which were scarcely in the business of proselytizing, made use of these methods of polite propaganda, wishing to spread the word about their ancient and wonderful faith, even if they did not seek converts. Other religions, including Buddhism, were more in the business of persuasion and often made effective use of the new methods to persuade outsiders of the rationality of their faith. They also, as did other religions (among them Christianity), created series of books and booklets to persuade their own members, who they sometimes felt might fall victim to the argumentations of foreign missionaries.

In part because of the tremendous impact of translating the Bible into a native, previously non-literate language, Christian methods of missionizing seem to have been most successful among non-literate peoples, though they were not without effect in parts of India, Sri Lanka, Vietnam and Korea. Christians put a great deal of effort into education, and higher education especially had a marked impact throughout the colonial lands in creating new elites, themselves marked by at least some Christian influence (SHARPE, 1975).

Some thoughts about paintings and sculptures

We have noted that some traditions are aniconic and others partially so, but those traditions with a developed taste for painting and sculpture have burgeoned. At the same time religious factors have caused the arts to move in new directions. After the Reformation, art in Western Europe tended to take two forms. One was the very florid style of the post-Tridentine Catholic church. The other was a secularization which followed upon the aniconic tendencies of the Protestant traditions – the creation of Dutch interior art, still lifes, landscape painting and so on. The rich traditions of Catholic stained glass, sculpture and altarpieces, for example, supplied a way of illustrating the Bible, though they became less relevant as the production of books expanded. It provided too a broader teaching than was possible by illuminated manuscripts.

The Baroque thrust of Catholicism had its eventual effects on the Protestant art tradition, chiefly through the Anglo-Catholic movement, which did much to revive church building in Britain during the second half of the nineteenth century. It was not without its waves in Presbyterian Scotland, whose stern Calvinism gave in somewhat to Gothic revival. Similar influences abounded in mainline Protestantism in the United States (VIDLER, 1961).

Reflections on the material dimension

It is obvious that the richer the ritual and the stronger the demand for art works to decorate religious buildings, the greater the importance of wealth for rulers who patronize religion and the greater the need for contributions to sacred causes. It is an interesting irony that it was this demand which led to the unveiling of Catholic corruption which sparked off the Protestant revolt and with it the Reformation. It is also clear that the more impressive the demand for royal temples en-hancing the ritual links between heaven and earth, the stronger the ideology of cosmic kingship needs to be. The material dimension is a reinforcement of ritual, and with that a reinforcement of cosmology. The impressiveness of the institution is registered through vestments, relics, jewels, glittering divinities, glorious statues, soaring buildings. In effect the material dimension is both congealed ritual and concep-tual hardware.

CHAPTER EIGHT

The Political Effects of Religion

The globalization of the world and the phenomenology of religion

Much of this book has been relatively old-fashioned. We have been concerned with traditional categories and symbols of religion – not wholly, but substantially. Yet it is unwise to conduct too much of the study of religion as though it is ancient history. It is true that many of our noblest and most profound scholars are ancient historians, but if we are students of religion and worldview we need to consider what is available. We are never of course going to meet an ancient religion or an ancient religionist – no Buddha, no Jesus, no Moses, no Hillel, no Muhammad, no Sankara, no K'ung, no Meng, no Shinran. We are only going to meet a modern religion and a modern adherent. Our final analysis therefore will relate to contemporary global religion and worldview. It will have to deal with modern faith. It will be useless from this point of view to consider ancient history (ROSZAK, 1975).

In our era certain symbols have emerged that were not available before. It is hard to estimate the effect of the beautiful blue and brown pictures of the globe from far away in outer space. They convey a sense of the fragility and close compactedness of our planet, and it is out of this sense that the imagery of the 'spaceship earth' has grown. Nor should we underestimate the daily weather maps which hint to us the coming smallness of the earth we inhabit: even a large country like the United States seems crimped a little. There is another side to our human space exploits. We have become used to looking inward, not just downward, at ourselves. Perhaps we have the same cast as Dali's wonderful picture of God looking down at himself, following the sketch of San Juan de la Cruz (a picture exhibited in Glasgow's new museum of comparative religion, a new insight into ourselves and the first such building in the world).

Although it is very slow in coming, there is a chance that soon the human race will become used to looking at itself in a phenomeno-logical way or, if you like, in a comparative way. There tends to be very slow take-up of such a viewpoint in higher education. Marxists, relativists, deconstructionists and other such people tend to advance arguments which downplay phenomenology and interiority – downplaying what I have called 'informed empathy' and indeed downplaying modes of understanding the Other. Apart from this, there is a weight of media input across the world which is inimical to pluralism. But although the idea of mutual understanding is, as I say, slow in growing, it is surely coming. There are several reasons for this. First, it is obvious that we can and do understand one another across cultures; second, we note the dangers of not understanding one another – understanding is an antidote to nationalism and racism; third, notions of the incommensurability of cultures plainly founder on the availability of translations (most arguments against the trans-latability of cultures founder on perfectionist accounts of translation).

With the coming realization that there are themes and concepts which exist cross-culturally, there will no doubt be a tendency to think that no religion is in the bad sense unique, and that it is important for people of differing cultures and traditions to enter into serious dialogue (as the fashionable word is). Although it is ever unwise to be too optimistic about the human condition, we can at least hope that the position of dialogue and mutual understanding will help us to think of the globe in a more federal way. There are serious dangers in globalization of course, but we need to think of each other in an interrelated manner. Probably we ought also to mobilize our spiritual resources. It seems to me that the future of such institutions as the World Congress of Faiths is bright. I am not claiming that the differences between religions are unimportant or that it is wise to enter into easy agreements between faiths – as if human decisions about the convergence of mysticism or whatever can resolve disputes that exist at a deeper level, possibly at a divine level. Nevertheless, we may as a globe get more used to good and sensible discussions about resemblances and differences, and we may get used to a tolerant style of debate. I think, as I have said, that such convergences at least of the spirit of debate and thinking are in the long run inevitable. And I think too that the idea of the phenomenological also will spread and deepen. This is where it is reasonable to be optimistic. Persistent irrationality and the espousals of mutual unintelligibility are bound to wither, and many will look back on modern thinking with contempt and amazement.

Global matters and the options which exist for differing traditions

Globalization brings about the close juxtaposition of differing traditions and their exponents (WALLERSTEIN, 1974). There has never been such a period in world history. One could perhaps point to a period in Roman history, for example, which exhibited the interplay between a number of faiths – Zoroastrianism, its lesser Mithraism, Christianity, Judaism, Roman imperial religion, certain mainly Greek philosophies from Platonism to Stoicism, and so forth, as well as the cult of Eleusis, that of Isis, Orphism and a whole lot more. But although the Roman empire presented a pluralist fact not at all unlike that of the present era, with its multiple major traditions, that old model does not really look the same. For one thing the legion of the gods was fading, not just because Christianity was on the march and the gods did look a bit feeble, but because it never properly marshalled its ideology or worldview or philosophy: the theory of the gods was rather weak. Moreover, though there were forms of philosophy, notably Neo-Platonism, which had a strong spiritual side; philosophies did not always present the same side of life as did the gods, while the strong existential forces, namely the mystery religions, did not on the whole marshal philosophical breadth. The present era's rivals are more powerful. Not only that, they exhibit within themselves alternatives. With their flexibility and power they represent a formidable array. It is also becoming evident that people can be eclectic, perhaps in ways that were not so clearly open in the Roman world (BERGER, 1979).

There is the possibility too of a higher-level structure of faith which may embrace complementary worldviews. That is, while Christians or Muslims may remain such in their allegiance, they may become increasingly conscious that each organic faith system has its riches which honourable people can hold side by side. Such a recognition of a sort of dialogical faith at a higher level would in effect be an acceptance that we can agree to differ in religion. Already to see that would be to hold, in essence, a higher-order global religion which most humans could agree upon (HAMMOND, 1985).

Education and the sense of a global history

Although perhaps it is not yet evident to people, the collapse of the Soviet Union has indeed ushered in a new period of world history. We can probably assume that the remaining Marxist states will wither too. Probably China will create its own form of capitalism, assuming that the experiment of a dual system with Hong Kong is successful. The pervasiveness both of United Nations and of World Bank interference will lead to convergence. If so, no longer will the globe be bitterly divided by ideology. In these circumstances it will probably come about that world history will be taught in much the same way in different countries. Although national history will still play its ideological role in the differing states, one may hope that it will be seen against the background of a teaching of world history. In this new milieu the history of religions will have to play an important part. Out of this will emerge an appreciation of the great figures of the past not as national personages but as world figures. And with that will come about a new and universal cult of ancestors, in which we can all recognize each other's great women and men.

Probably the narrative dimension is the easiest to conceive in this global manner. If we can start with the great figures of religious history, it would also be possible to bring Max Weber up to date and see the contributions different worldviews can make to the economic and political development of world civilization (MIKERJI, 1983). The role of Protestantism in setting the scene of capitalism is already well recognized. But in the progress made in Asian countries since the

Second World War we can already perceive some of the contributions of the Confucian ethos to the creation of powerful new economies, partly because of its very heavy investment in education – a vital factor in the success of new economies – and partly because of its symbiosis with a largely rational tradition in Buddhism, which combines well with twentieth-century science.

So far, however, Western countries, which still tend to dominate academic life, are not particularly hospitable to world philosophies and tend to restrict the concept of philosophy to modern Western ideas. But no doubt the time will come when a genuine concern with the varieties of concepts and arguments created by the diverse cultures will animate conversations across cultural borders. At any rate, we may hope that global education, which ought to include the differing dimensional contents of religions and worldviews, will gradually shape a world consciousness. For along that direction lies a sense of humanity as the ultimate focus of ethical and spiritual loyalty, rather than the narrower focus of the ethnic group (SMITH, LITTLE AND SHACKLETON, 1981).

Political futures of religious traditions

Within the consciousness of humanity as a whole the political future of religions is worth pondering (LUHMANN, 1982). Traditional influence may have belonged to traditional heartlands, but it will shift, primarily as a result of demographic factors. Thus the heartlands of Christianity reside in Europe and America, but the numbers have already moved south. The majority of practising Christians live in Central and South America and in Africa. Sooner or later the influence of southern Christians will make itself felt, which will affect Christian thinking about poverty. This will coincide with a period of human crisis – the permeation of the North–South membrane. The startling success of capitalism in the last forty years has widened the gap between the rich and the poor nations of the globe. Meanwhile the globalization of transport and the media makes the gap obvious, and offers the hope that it may be possible to jump across it somehow. Though there are political and juridical barriers – what I call the membrane separating the North and South – it is in fact a permeable one. The northern countries are just beginning to feel the onslaught of illegal immigration from differing directions. No doubt Christianity will be one of the forces pressing for ways of reducing the gap in wealth, encouraged by its new lobby from the south.

Likewise, Islam has traditionally considered the Middle East as its fulcrum, yet overwhelmingly its population is Eastern (BENDA, 1958). The four largest Islamic countries all lie east of Iran. There has moreover opened up to the north an array of Muslim countries in the former Soviet Central Asia which are important areas of influence (perhaps mainly from secular Turkey). One of these regions, the Indian sub-continent, is religiously inflammable: the resurgence of a sort of Hindu radicalism may deeply disturb the Muslim minority in the Republic of India and bring about civil war, which would almost certainly suck in Pakistan (GHOSE, 1973). Nowhere is it more urgent to work out a means of symbiosis of the two great religions (JUERGENSMEYER, 1993). But, despite this crisis, the East of Islam has an important stake in Asian prosperity, and may have a more easygoing attitude than appears in the rhetoric of the rising Arab 'fundamentalists'.

Probably the most important thing for Islam collectively to work out has to do with law (VOLL, 1982). It will become clear as global consciousness develops that all religions are minority faiths. It is doubtful if any will ever become a majority tradition. As such the provision of a new way of looking at the Shari'a may be crucial, since if a nation is defined as the unit of ultimate concern, you can have the state setting Islamic law as its model; but if the globe is the unit of ultimate concern, then Islamic law becomes a minority option, and perhaps should be viewed in the same way as a Muslim has to look upon the law when residing in a non-Muslim state. In any event, more and more Muslims will be living as minorities across the globe, in such countries as America and Germany.

We have already noted that these diaspora situations will become increasingly influential. Already there are world newspapers concerned with Hinduism, and publications for Parsees, Sikhs, Mormons, Unificationists and so on. These diasporas reinforce the viability of smaller traditions. But they may also multiply ethnic conflicts, with diasporas funding insurgent movements at home. There are plenty of signs of this in relation to such groups as Kashmiris, Tamils, northern Cypriots and Tibetans. These conflicts often have a partly spiritual basis.

Unfortunately, too, the mutual images created among Christians (or Westerners) and Muslims have tended particularly since around 1970 to be negative (WAARDENBURG, 1969). Arab propaganda against Israel, the events of the Iranian revolution, the hijacking and destruction of aircraft, Western help for Israel, the Gulf War, support for modernist governments as in Egypt, and so on, have been factors stirring hostility. Islamic 'fundamentalism' has not been understood or appreciated in Western capitals, while Western colonialism, especially at the time of the carve-up of the Ottoman empire, still rankles. This mutual hostility may itself become an important political factor in the future (SAID, 1979).

Another religious factor to take into account is this: the smaller-scale faiths, such as the coterminous religions of ethnic groups, the thousands of new religious movements in Africa and the diasporas of lesser religious or ethnic groups in big cities, especially Western ones, when combined with one another, represent a significant slice of the global population. There are increasing signs of alliances between the oppressed and neglected. They may in due course be in a position to exert pressure for toleration, since it is in the interests of each group to promote the rights of the others. Religions have not at all had a good record in dealing with minorities among them, but in this case they may have a benign effect.

One of the general consequences of the open study of religion, as it exists now in many countries (especially in the West), is an increase in the demand for pluralism, as students of religions become advocates for their rights. This growth of a new attitude to the many and the Other is desirable in so far as we wish to promote a new world order.

A reflection on the experiential dimension

When we survey the whole global pattern of spiritual life, we note that the combination of strands of religious experience has an attraction. That is, while the numinous experience helps to account for some of the patterns of revelation in the diverse traditions, and while the contemplative experience helps to account for others, world history as a whole signals the drift of religions into both modes (SMART, 1982). Both Islam and Christianity, which started out of numinous backgrounds, came to absorb contemplation as a major feature. It was the combination of the two which made up classical Christianity and the rich creativity of the Sufi movement. At the other end of the bipolar scale, Buddhism seems to have begun without significant *bhakti*, but in the course of the evolution of the Great Vehicle it developed foci of worship in such figures as Amitabha and Avalokitesvara. Putting it simply: Buddhism made the opposite transition from that of Islam. It so happens that in the current Islamic revival, Sufism has a bad name: it is accused of being superstitious and in some real sense responsible for the corruption of Islam, itself a cause of its demise under the crushing weight of colonialism. Modern revivalism wants, so to speak, to cut out the middle ages, to go back to some sort of pristine purity. We may respect the motivation of such a move. Nevertheless, it seems attractive to applaud those religious movements which combine both strands of experience (not to mention other variants such as shamanism and the panenhenic experience). There is another reason for going along this path: both Sufism and Mahayana philosophy, as well as analogous combinations in the Hindu tradition and in Judaism, have a more open view both of other religious traditions and of scientific and humanistic knowledge. If we wish to have profound dialogue, these kinds of religion seem most promising.

This is not at all to espouse the notion of the perennial philosophy. It is not to say that the core of all religions is the mystical (that is to say, the contemplative). That thesis cannot easily stand up, either empirically or philosophically. But it is to count the contemplative strand as a crucial element in spirituality. It may be that such mystical religion will come as the second wave of dialogue, after the discussion which should take place between the earthier religious radicals of different faiths has brought about an understanding of the immediate world order. If we are searching, down the road, for a deeper global ethos which combines, in a complementary way, the values of religions, then some guidance from Sufism and the like will be in order.

In any case, if we take seriously world figures in religion we need to take seriously a swathe of contemplatives: I am thinking of Plotinus, al-Hallaj, al-Ghazzali, ibn ʿArabi, Śankara, Bhaskara, Ramakṛṣṇa, Gautama, Nāgārjuna, Shinran, Wang Yang-ming, Teresa of Avila, Catherine of Siena and many others. So the two projects fit will together: mysticism and ancestor worship or global narrative.

Moreover, the contemplative path tends to be softer. The ethics of the yogi are quietist. Now, while quietism is not altogether realistic, it is a good emphasis. The most terrible threat hanging over us is that of nuclear war. Its coming is not at all inconceivable: there are various parts of the world where it could flare – Israel, the Ukraine, India, North Korea, to start with. We have only just seen the beginnings of nuclear proliferation. As the world becomes more sophisticated, more and more nations will be capable of making the big bombs. Terrorism becomes a greater risk too. We need to think more clearly about the admissibility of warfare. Probably the right solution to the dilemmas which we face in this matter is to argue for the minimization of violence. This is the mid-point between pacifism and the outright condoning of warfare. Since, strange to say, our human instincts so often turn towards warfare, we need the counterpoise of the pacifist side of religion – and this is often supplied by the mystic (SMART AND KONSTANTINE, 1993).

A conclusion

These last remarks are forward-looking, and I feel that the futures of religions are likely to be rich, perhaps richer than the past. Yet we can learn much from the past. The phenomenology of religion seeks to draw out varying patterns, and these are important. What I have tried to do in this volume is to use a dimensional shape to exhibit these patterns, but I recognize that there are other ways of going about the task. Moreover, I have not always been as detailed in dealing with all dimensions. But I hope that, if others feel the need for a different approach, they will not be hesitant in trying it out. It happens that we have rather too few general studies of religion and worldviews, and a great richness of monographs. I consider that the task of understanding patterns in religion is not at all an easy one. But we can all benefit from grasping some of the major themes in what has, after all, been a pervasive feature of human history and life. By reflecting on the past of the human race we may gain better insight into our present and future. We may also, in having a clearer picture of human patterns of symbols and of the taxonomy of the sacred, clarify what the major concerns are in the differing cultures of the human race.

Some aspects of the sacred are flourishing, others fading. The ritual dimension, though pervasively important in human life, is fading somewhat because attempts to bend the powers of the world by such means no longer hold out their old promise. But others are burgeoning: the experiential grows in importance as men and women search their inner lives for greater meaning. While we do not sacrifice to Poseidon and are not so afraid of the ocean, there remains the poetry of the waves and the bitter taste of salt.

REFERENCES

ABRAMS, M. H. *Natural Supernaturalism* (New York, 1971).

AHLSTROM, SYDNEY E. *A Religious History of the American People* (New Haven, 1972).

ALBANESE, CATHERINE L. *America: Religions and Religion* (Belmont, CA, 1981)

ALLBRIGHT, WILLIAM F. *Yahweh and the Gods of Canaan* (London, 1968)

ALMOND, PHILIP C. *Rudolf Otto: An Introduction to His Philosophical Theology* (Chapel Hill, 1984)

ALON, GEDALIAH *The Jews in Their Land in the Talmudic Age 70–640 CE* (Jerusalem, 1980)

ANDERSON, J. N. D. *Islamic Law in the Modern World* (New York, 1959)

ANESAKI, MASAHARU *History of Japanese Religion* (Rutland, VT, 1963)

ANTORUS, RICHARD T. and MARY ELAINE HEGLAND, eds *Religious Resurgence* (Syracuse, NY, 1987)

ARNOLD, EDWIN *The Light of Asia* (Boston, 1880)

AUSTIN, J. L. *How to Do Things with Words* (Cambridge, MA 1975)

BABB, LAWRENCE A. *The Divine Hierarchy: Popular Hinduism in Central India* (New York, 1975)

BAILEY, GREGORY *The Mythology of Brahma* (New York, 1983)

BANTON, MICHAEL, ed. *Anthropological Approaches to the Study of Religion* (London, 1966)

BARRETT, DAVID B., ed. *World Christian Encyclopedia* (New York, 1982)

BEACH, WALDO and H. RICHARD NIEBUHR, eds. *Christian Ethics: Sources of the Living Tradition* (New York, 1955)

BECHERT, HEINZ *Buddhismus, Staat und Gesellschaft in den Landern Theravada–Buddhismus* (Frankfurt, 1966–73), 3 vols

BELLAH, ROBERT *Beyond Belief: Essays on Religion in a Post-Traditional World* (New York, 1970)

—— , ed. *Religion and Progress in Modern Asia* (New York, 1965)

—— and HAMMOND, PHILLIP, eds *Varieties of Civil Religion* (San Francisco, 1980)

BENDA, HARRY J. *The Crescent and the Rising Sun* (The Hague, 1958)

BERGER, PETER *The Heretical Imperative* (Garden City, NJ, 1979)

BERLING, JUDITH *The Syncretic Religion of Lin Chao-en* (New York, 1980)

BERMAN, HAROLD J. *The Interaction of Law and Religion* (Nashville, 1974)

—— *Law and Revolution: The Formation of the Western Legal Tradition* (Cambridge, MA 1983)

BEYER, STEPHAN *The Cult of Tara: Magic and Ritual in Tibet* (Berkeley, 1973)

BIANCHI, UGO *Probleme der Religionsgeschichte* (Göttingen, 1964)

BLACKER, CARMEN *The Catalpa Bow* (London, 1975)

BLAU, JOSEPH *Judaism in America* (Chicago, 1976)

BOLLE, KEES *The Freedom of Man in Myth* (Nashville, 1968)

BOMAN, THORLEIF *Hebrew Thought Compared with Greek* (Philadelphia, 1960)

BRANDON, S. G. F. *Man and His Destiny in the Great Religions* (Manchester, 1963)

—— *The Judgement of the Dead* (London, 1967)

—— , ed. *The Savior God* (Westport, CT, 1980)

BREISACH, ERNST *Historiography: Ancient, Medieval and Modern* (Chicago, 1983)

BROCKINGTON, JOHN *The Sacred Thread: Hinduism in Its Continuity and Diversity* (New York, 1981)

BROWN, ROBERT MCAFEE *The Ecumenical Revolution* (Garden City, NY, 1967)

BRUCE, F. F. and RUPP, E. G. *Holy Book and Holy Tradition* (Grand Rapids, MI, 1968)

BRUEGGEMANN, WALTER *The Nature of the Prophetic* (Philadelphia, 1978)

BUDDHAGHOSA, tr. Nyanamoli *The Path of Purification* (Ceylon, 1964)

BUTLER, EDWARD C. *Benedictine Monachism* (New York, 1961)

CARMAN, JOHN B. *The Theology of Ramanuja* (New Haven, 1974)

CARR, WILLIAM *Hitler: A Study in Personality and Politics* (London, 1978)

CARRASCO, DAVID *Quetzalcoatl and the Irony of Empire* (Chicago, 1982)

CASSIRER, ERNST *Kant's Life and Thought* (New Haven, 1981)

CAVENDISH, RICHARD *Visions of Heaven and Hell* (London, 1977)

CHADWICK, OWEN, ed. *Western Asceticism* (London, 1958)

CHANG, KWANG-CHIH *Art Myth and Ritual: The Path to Political Authority in Ancient China* (Cambridge, MA, 1983)

CHENU, M. D. *Toward Understanding Saint Thomas Aquinas* (Chicago, 1964)

CHIDESTER, DAVID *Patterns of Power: Religion and Ethics in a Comparative Perspective* (Belmont, CA, 1987)

—— *Religions of South Africa* (London, 1992)

CHRISTIAN, WILLIAM *Oppositions of Religious Doctrines* (New York, 1972)

CH'U, T'UNG-TSU *Law and Society in Traditional China* (Paris, 1961)

COLLINS, STEVEN *Selfless Persons: Imagery and Thought in Theravada Buddhism* (Cambridge, 1982)

CONZE, EDWARD *Buddhist Thought in India* (London, 1962)

COOK, FRANK H. *Hua-yen Buddhism* (University Park, PA, 1977)

COPLESTON, FREDERICK C. *Aquinas* (Baltimore, 1961)

COULSON, NOEL, J. *A History of Islamic Law* (Edinburgh, 1971)

COWARD, HAROLD G. *Pluralism: Challenge to World Religions* (Maryknoll, NY, 1985)

CRAWFORD, CROMWELL, ed. *In Search of Hinduism* (New York, 1986)

CUMONT, FRANZ *Afterlife in Roman Paganism* (New York, 1959)

—— *Lux Perpetua* (New York, 1987)

DARWIN, CHARLES *The Origin of Species* (London, 1859)

DASGUPTA, SHASHIBHUSAN *Obscure Religious Cults* (Calcutta, 1969)

DASGUPTA, S. N. *A History of Indian Philosophy* (Delhi, 1975), 5 vols

DAVIES, J. G. *Temples, Churches and Mosques* (New York, 1982)

DAWSON, CHRISTOPHER *Religion and the Modern State* (New York, 1938)

DAYAL, HAR *The Bodhisattva Doctrine in Buddhist Sanskrit Literature* (Delhi, 1970)

DE CHARDIN, TEILHARD *The Phenomenon of Man* (London, 1955)

DENNY, F. N. and TAYLOR, R. L., eds *The Holy Book in Comparative Perspective* (Columbia, SC, 1985)

DERRETT, J. D. M. *Hindu Law Past and Present* (Calcutta, 1957)

DE SILVA, LYNN *Buddhism: Beliefs and Practices in Sri Lanka* (Colombo, 1980)

DE SILVA, PADMASIRI *Tangles and Webs* (Colombo, 1974)

DETIENNE, MARCEL and VERANT, JEAN-PIERRE *Cunning Intelligence in Greek Culture and Society* (Atlantic Highlands, NJ, 1978)

DEUTSCH, K. *Nationalism and Social Communication* (New York, 1966)

DHAVAMONY, MARIASUSAI *The Love of God According to Saiva Siddhanta* (Oxford, 1971)

DIMMITT, CORNELIA and VAN BUITENEN, J. A. B., eds *Classical Hindu Mythology: A Reader in the Sanskrit Puranas* (Philadelphia, 1978)

DIX, GREGORY *The Shape of the Liturgy* (London, 1945)

DONIGER, WENDY *Asceticism and Eroticism in the Mythology of Siva* (London, 1973)
DOUGLAS, ANN *The Feminization of American Culture* (New York, 1977)
DOUGLAS, MARY *Purity and Danger* (New York, 1966)
—— *Natural Symbols* (New York, 1970)
DULLES, AVERY *The Survival of Dogma* (New York, 1971)
DUMEZIL, GEORGES *The Destiny of the Warrior* (Chicago, 1970)
DUMONT, LOUIS *Homo Hierarchicus* (Chicago, 1980)
DUNDES, ALAN, ed. *Sacred Narrative* (Berkeley, 1984
DURKHEIM, EMILE *The Elementary Forms of the Religious Life* (New York, 1965)
DUTT, SUKUMAR *Buddhist Monks and Monasteries of India* (London, 1962)
EARHART, BYRON *Japanese Religion* (Belmont, CA, 1982)
EDSMAN, CARL-MARTIN, ed. *Studies in Shamanism* (Turku, Finland, 1962)
EDWARDS, PAUL, ed. *Encylopedia of Philosophy* (New York, 1967)
EISENSTADT, S. N., ed. *The Protestant Ethic and Modernization: A Comparative View* (New York, 1968)
ELIADE, MIRCEA *Patterns in Comparative Religion* (New York, 1958a)
—— *Yoga: Immortality and Freedom* (Chicago, 1958b)
—— *Cosmos and History* (New York, 1959a)
—— *The Sacred and the Profane* (New York, 1959b)
—— *Shamanism* (Princeton, 1964)
—— *The Quest* (Chicago, 1969)
—— *Australian Religions: An Introduction* (Ithaca, 1973)
—— *Occultism, Witchcraft and Cultural Fashions* (Chicago, 1976)
ELIOT, CHARLES *Hinduism and Buddhism: An Historical Sketch* (London, 1957), 3 vols
ER = *Encyclopedia of Religion*, ed. M. Eliade, 16 vols (New York, 1987)
EVANS-PRITCHARD, E. E. *Witchcraft, Oracles and Magic Among the Azande* (Oxford, 1958)
—— *Theories of Primitive Religion* (Oxford, 1965)
FARQUHAR, J. N. *Modern Religious Movements in India* (New York, 1915)
FENN, RICHARD K. *Toward a Theory of Secularization* (Storrs, CT, 1975)
FIGGIS, JOHN BEVILLE *The Divine Right of Kings* (Cambridge, 1914)
FINDLAY, J. N. *Language, Mind and Value* (New York, 1961)
FINGARETTE, HERBERT *Confucius: The Secular as Sacred* (New York, 1972)

FREND, W. H. C. *Martyrdom and Persecution in the Early Church* (Oxford, 1965)

FREUD, SIGMUND *The Future of an Illusion* (London 1927/1961)

—— *Moses and Monotheism* (London, 1939/1960)

FRIED, NORTON, HARRIS, MARVIN and MURPHY, ROBERT *War: The Anthropology of Armed Conflict and Aggression* (Washington, 1975)

FUNG YU LAN *History of Chinese Philosophy* (Princeton, 1953), 2 vols

GARDNER, DANIEL K. *Chu Hsi and the Ta Hsueh* (Cambridge, MA 1986)

GASTER, THEODOR H. *Myth, Legend and Custom in the Old Testament* (New York, 1969)

GEERTZ, CLIFFORD *The Interpretation of Cultures* (New York, 1973)

—— ed. *Societies and New States* (New York, 1963)

GELLNER, ERNST *Muslim Society* (Cambridge, 1981)

—— *Nations and Nationalism* (Oxford, 1983)

GENNEP, ARNOLD VAN *The Rites of Passage* (Chicago, 1980)

GHOSE, SANKAR *Socialism, Democracy, and Nationalism in India* (Bombay, 1973)

GIBB, H. A. R. *Modern Trends in Islam* (Chicago, 1947)

GINZBURG, LOUIS *Students, Scholars and Saints* (Philadelphia, 1928)

GIRARD, RENÉ *Violence and the Sacred* (Baltimore, 1977)

GOMBRICH, RICHARD F. *Precept and Practice* (Oxford, 1971)

—— *Theravada Buddhism* (London, 1988)

GONDA, JAN *Aspects of Early Visnuism* (Utrecht, 1954)

—— *Die Religionen Indiens* (Stuttgart, 1960) vol. 1

—— *Change and Continuity in Indian Religion* (The Hague, 1965)

—— *Visnuism and Sivaism* (London, 1970)

GRABAR, OLEG *The Formation of Islamic Art* (New Haven, 1973)

GRANT, ROBERT, M. *Miracle and Natural Law in Graeco–Roman and Early Christianity* (Amsterdam, 1952)

GREEN, ARTHUR ed. *Jewish Spirituality* (New York, 1986–7)

—— *History of Jewish Spirituality* (New York, 1986)

GRIMAL, PIERRE, ed. *Larousse World Mythology* (New York, 1965)

GRIMES, RONALD L. *Beginnings in Ritual Studies* (Washington, DC, 1982)

GROF, CHRISTIAN and GROF, STANISLAV *Beyond Death* (New York, 1980)

GUNTRIP, HARRY, J. S. *Psychoanalytic Theory, Therapy and the Self* (New York, 1971)

GUSDORF, GEORGES *Mythe et métaphysique* (Paris, 1953)

GUTHRIE, W. K. C. *The Greeks and Their Gods* (London, 1950)

GUTTMAN, JULIUS *Philosophies of Judaism* (New York, 1964)

HAFFNER, SEBASTIAN *The Meaning of Hitler* (London, 1979)

HAIGHT, ROGER *The Experience and Language of Grace* (New York, 1979)

HAMMOND, PHILLIP *The Sacred in a Secular Age* (Berkeley, 1985)

HAPPOLD, F. G. *Mysticism: A Study and an Anthology* (Harmondsworth, 1970)

HARAKA, STANLEY S. *Towards Transfigured Life* (Minneapolis, 1983)

HARDY, FRIEDHELM *Viraha Bhakti* (Oxford, 1983)

HARMAN, DAVID *Maimonides: Torah and Philosophic Quest* (Philadelphia, 1976)

HARNER, MICHAEL J. *The Way of the Shaman* (New York, 1982)

HAZRA, KANAI LAL *History of Theravada Buddhism in South-East Asia* (New Delhi, 1982)

HERMEREN, GORAN *Representation and Meaning in the Visual Arts* (Stockholm, 1969)

HESSE, HERMANN *Siddharta* (Berlin, 1922)

HICK, JOHN *Faith and Knowledge* (Ithaca, 1966)

—— *Death and Eternal Life* (London 1976)

—— *God Has Many Names* (Philadelphia, 1982)

—— *Philosophy of Religion* (Englewood Cliffs, NJ, 1983)

—— *An Interpretation of Religion* (New Haven, 1989)

HOBSBAWM, E. J. and RANGER, T. O., eds *The Invention of Tradition* (New York, 1983)

HOLCK, FREDERICK H., ed. *Death and Eastern Thought* (Nashville, 1974)

HOMANS, PETER *Jung in Context: Modernity and the Making of a Psychology* (Chicago, 1979)

HOOKE, S. H., ed. *Myth and Ritual* (London, 1933)

HOOKER, M. B. *A Concise Legal History of South-East Asia* (Oxford, 1978)

HOPKINS, JEFFREY *Meditation on Emptiness* (London, 1983)

HORTON, ROBIN and FINNEGAN, RUTH, eds *Modes of Thought* (London, 1973)

HSU, FRANCIS L. K. *Under the Ancestors' Shadow* (New York, 1948)

HULTKRANTZ, AKE 'A Definition of Shamanism', *Temenos* 9 (1973)

HUBERT HENRI and MAUSS MARCEL, *A General Theory of Magic* (London, 1972)

HUNTINGTON, RICHARD and METCALF, PETER *Celebrations of Death: The Anthropology of Mortuary Ritual* (Cambridge, 1979)

HUXLEY, ALDOUS *The Doors of Perception* (New York, 1954)

IRWIN, JOYCE, ed. *Sacred Sound: Music in Religious Thought and Practice* (Chico, CA, 1983)

JAIN, HIRALAL and UPADHYE, A. N. *Mahavira: His Times and His Philosophy of Life* (New Delhi, 1974)

JAINI, PADMANABH *The Jaina Path of Purification* (Berkeley, 1979)

JAMES, E. O. *Christian Myth and Ritual* (London 1933)

—— *The Concept of Deity* (London, 1950)

—— *The Nature and Function of Priesthood* (London, 1955)

JASPERS, KARL *Truth and Symbol* (New York, 1959)

JONES, CHESLYN, WAINWRIGHT, GEOFFREY and YARNOLD, EDWARD, eds *The Study of Liturgy* (London, 1978)

JORDAN, LOUIS HENRY *Comparative Religion: Its Genesis and Growth* (Edinburgh, 1905)

JUERGENSMEYER, MARK *The New Cold War: Religious Nationalism Confronts the Secular State* (Berkeley, 1993)

JUNG, C. G. and KERENYI, KARL *Essays on a Science of Mythology* (Princeton, 1969)

KALUPAHANA, DAVID *A History of Buddhist Philosophy* (Honolulu, 1992)

KAMAL, AHMAD *The Sacred Journey* (New York, 1961)

KAMENKA, E., ed. *Nationalism* (New York, 1976)

KATZ, STEVEN T., ed. *Mysticism and Philosophical Analysis* (New York, 1978)

—— ed. *Mysticism and Language* (Oxford, 1993)

KING, URSULA 'Historical and Phenomenological Approaches', in F. WHALING, ed. *Contemporary Approaches to the Study of Religion* (New York, 1984), 2 vols

KING, WINSTON *In the Hope of Nibbana* (La Salle, IL, 1964)

KISHIMOTO, HIDEO, ed. *Japanese Religion in the Meiji Era* (Tokyo, 1956)

KITAGAWA, JOSEPH M. and LONG, CHARLES, eds *Myths and Symbols* (Chicago, 1969)

KLEIN, ISAAC *A Guide to Jewish Religious Practice* (New York, 1979)

KNIPE, DAVID *In the Image of Fire: Vedic Experiences of Heat* (Delhi, 1975)

KOHN, HANS *Nationalism, Its Meaning and History* (Princeton, 1955)

KOSAMBI, D. D. *Myth and Reality* (Bombay, 1962)

KRAEMER, HENDRIK *The Christian Message in a Non-Christian World* (New York, 1938)

KRAMRISCH, STELLA *The Hindu Temple* (Delhi, 1976)

KRISTENSEN, BREDE *The Meaning of Religion* (The Hague, 1960)

KUBER, W. N. *B. R. Ambedkar* (New Delhi, 1978)

LANG, PAUL *Music in Western Civilization* (New York, 1941)

LANGER, SUZANNE *Philosophy in a New Key* (Cambridge, MA, 1957)

LANTERNARI, VITTORIO *The Religions of the Oppressed* (New York, 1963)

LAQUEUR, WALTER, ed. *Fascism* (Berkeley, 1976)

LARSON, GERALD J. *Classical Samkhya* (Santa Barbara, 1979)

LAU, D. C. tr. *Tao Te Ching* (Hong Kong, 1982)

LÉVY-BRUHL, LUCIEN *How Natives Think* (London, 1926)

LÉVY-STRAUSS, CLAUDE *Mythologiques* (Paris, 1964)

—— *The Savage Mind* (London, 1966)

LEWIS, BERNARD *The Emergence of Modern Turkey* (London, 1965)

LEWIS, I. M. *Ecstatic Religion* (Harmondsworth, 1971)

LINDBLOM, HOHANNES *Prophecy in Ancient Israel* (Philadelphia, 1962)

LING, TREVOR O. *Buddhism and the Mythology of Evil* (London, 1962)

LITTLE, DAVID and TWISS, SUMNER B., JR *Comparative Religious Ethics* (New York, 1978)

LONG, EUGENE T., ed. *Experience, Reason and God* (Washington, 1980)

LOTT, ERIC J. *God and the Universe in the Vedantic Theology of Ramanuja* (Madras, 1976)

LUHMANN, NIKLAS *Funktion der Religion* (Frankfurt, 1982)

LURKER, MANFRED *The Gods and Symbols of Ancient Egypt* (London, 1980)

MCINTIRE, C. T., ed. *God, History and Historians: An Anthology of Modern Christian Views of History* (New York, 1977)

MCNEAL, ROBERT H. *Stalin: Man and Ruler* (New York, 1988)

MACQUARRIE, JOHN *Twentieth Century Religious Thought* (New York, 1981)

MARANDA, PIERRE, ed. *Mythology* (Baltimore, 1972)

MARASINGHE, M. M. J. *Gods in Early Buddhism* (Ceylon, 1974)

MARINGER, JOHANNES *The Gods of Prehistoric Man* (New York, 1960)

MARTIN, DAVID *A General Theory of Secularization* (New York, 1978)

MARTIN, RICHARD C. *Islam: A Cultural Perspective* (Englewood Cliffs, NJ, 1982)

MAUSS, MARCEL *A General Theory of Magic* (London, 1972)

MBITI, JOHN S. *African Religions and Philosophy* (New York, 1969)

MERKL, PETER and SMART, NINIAN, eds *Religion and Politics in the Modern World* (New York, 1983)

MESLIN, MICHEL *Pour une science des religions* (Paris, 1973)

MIKERJI, CHANDRA *From Graven Images: Patterns of Modern Materialism* (New York, 1983)

MISHIMA, YUKIO *Hagakure: The Samurai Ethic in Modern Japan* (Tokyo, 1978)

MITRA, R. C. *The Decline of Buddhism in India* (Calcutta, 1954)

MODI, JIVANJI J. *The Religious Ceremonies and Customs of the Parsees* (Bombay, 1937)

MOORE, SALLY and MEYERHOFF, BARBARA, eds *Secular Ritual* (Assen, 1977)

MOREWEDGE, PARVIZ *The Metaphysica of Avicenna (ibn Sina)* (New York, 1973)

MUDIMBE, V. Y. *The Invention of Africa* (Bloomington, 1988)

MUELLER, F. MAX *Introduction to the Science of Religion* (Oxford, 1873)

MURTI, T. R. V. *The Central Philosophy of Buddhism* (London, 1980)

MUS, PAUL *Barabudur* (New York, 1978)

NAKAMURA HAJIME *Indian Buddhism* (Tokyo, 1977)

NASR, HOSSEIN *Sufi Essays* (London, 1972)

NEALE, WALTER C. *Monies in Societies* (San Francisco, 1976)

NEUSNER, JACOB *Early Rabbinic Judaism* (Leiden, 1975)

NEVILLE, ROBERT *Soldier, Sage, Saint* (New York, 1978)

NEWELL, WILLIAM H. ed. *Ancestors* (The Hague, 1976)

NICKELSBURG, GEORGE, *Resurrection, Immortality and Eternal Life in Inter-Testamental Judaism* (Cambridge, MA, 1972)

NILSSON, MARTIN P. *Greek Piety* (Oxford, 1948)

NYGREN, ANDERS *Agape and Eros* (Chicago, 1982)

OBERMAN, HEIKO A. *The Roots of Anti-Semitism* (Philadelphia, 1984)

OCHSHORN, JUDITH *The Female Experience and the Nature of the Divine* (Bloomington, IN, 1981)

O'MEARA, DOMINIC J., ed. *Neoplatonism and Christian Thought* (Albany, 1981)

OTTO, RUDOLF *Das Heilige; The Idea of the Holy* (Breslau, 1917; Oxford, 1923)

Oxford Dictionary of the Christian Church (Oxford, 1983)

PADADOPOULO, ALEXANDRE *Islam and Muslim Art* (New York, 1979)

PAKENHAM, THOMAS *The Scramble for Africa* (London, 1991)

Pali Text Society Translation Series (London, 1901–)

PARRINDER, GEOFFREY *Avatar and Incarnation* (New York, 1970)

PAUL, LESLIE *Nature into History* (London, 1962)

PENUMAN, T. K. *A Hundred Years of Anthropology* (New York, 1974)

PETERS, F. E. *The Harvest of Hellenism* (New York, 1970)

PETTAZZONI, RAFFAELE *Miti e Leggende* (Torino, 1948–59)

—— *Essays on the History of Religions* (Leiden, 1954)

POLIAKOV, LEON *The History of Anti-Semitism* (New York, 1965–73), 2 vols

POTTER, KARL *The Encyclopedia of India's Philosophies*, vol. 3 (Delhi, 1981)

PYE, MICHAEL *Comparative Religion* (New York, 1972)

RADHARKRISHNAN, SARVEPALLI *The Principal Upanisads* (New York, 1953)
—— *The Brahma Sutra* (New York, 1960)
RAHMAN, FAZLUR *Islam* (Chicago, 1979)
RAHULA, WALPOLA *What the Buddha Taught* (New York, 1962)
—— *The Heritage of the Bhikkhu* (New York, 1974)
RAMSEY, IAN T. *Religious Language* (London, 1957)
RANGER, T. O. and KIMAMBO, ISARIA N., eds *The Historical Study of African Religion* (Berkeley, 1972)
REDEKER, MARTIN *Schleiermacher: Life and Thought* (Philadelphia, 1973)
REEDER, JOHN P., JR and OUTKA, GENE H. *Religion and Morality: A Collection of Essays* (New York, 1973)
RICHARDSON, ALAN *History Sacred and Profane* (Philadelphia, 1964)
RIEFF, PHILIP *Freud: The Mind of the Moralist* (Chicago, 1979)
ROBERTSON, ROLAND *The Sociological Interpretation of Religion* (New York, 1970)
—— *Meaning and Change* (Oxford, 1978)
ROBINSON, JOHN A. T. *Honest to God* (London, 1963)
RODO, JOSE ENRIQUE *Ariel* (Austin, TX, 1988)
ROSZAK, THEODORE *Unfinished Animal* (New York, 1975)
RUDOLPH, KURT *Die Relionsgeschichte an der Leipziger Universität und die Entwicklung der Religionswissenschaft* (Berlin, 1962)
RUDOLPH, LLOYD I. and RUDOLPH, SUSANNE HOEBER *The Modernity of Tradition: Political Development in India* (Chicago, 1967)
SABOURIN, LEOPOLD *Priesthood: A Comparative Study* (Leiden, 1973)
SACHEDURA, ABDULAZIZ ABDELHUSSEIN *Islamic Messianism: The Idea of Mahdi in Twelver Shi-ism* (Albany, NY, 1981)
SADDHATISSA, H. *Buddhist Ethics: Essence of Buddhism* (London, 1970)
SAID, EDWARD *Orientalism* (New York, 1978)
SCHACHT, JOSEPH *An Introduction to Islamic Law* (Oxford, 1964)
SCHIMMEL, ANNEMARIE *Mystical Dimensions of Islamic Law* (Oxford, 1964)
SCHIPPER, KRESTOFER *Le corps taoiste* (Paris, 1982)
SCHOLEM, GERSHON *Major Trends in Jewish Mysticism* (New York, 1961)
SCOTT, NATHAN, JR *The Poetics of Belief* (Chapel Hill, 1985)
SEARLE, JOHN *Speech Acts* (London, 1969)
SEIDEL, ANNA K. *La divinisation de Lau tseu dans la taoisme des Han* (Paris, 1969)
SEN, SIBA PADA, ed. *Historians and Historiography in Modern India* (Calcutta, 1973)

SHARMA, B. N. K. *A History of the Dvaita School of Vedanta and Its Literature* (Bombay, 1981), 2 vols

SHARPE, ERIC J. *Comparative Religion: A History* (London, 1975)

SHILS, EDWARD *Tradition* (Chicago, 1981)

SHIPPS, JAN *Mormonism: The Story of a New Religious Tradition* (Urbana, IL, 1985)

SKORUPSKY, JOHN *Symbol and Theory* (Cambridge, 1976)

SMART, NINIAN *Reasons and Faiths* (London, 1958)

—— *Secular Education and the Logic of Religion* (London, 1968)

—— *The Religious Experience* (New York, 1969)

—— *The Science of Religion and the Sociology of Knowledge* (Princeton, 1973)

—— *Beyond Ideology* (San Francisco, 1982)

—— *Worldviews* (New York, 1983)

—— *The World's Religions* (Cambridge, 1989)

—— *Doctrine and Argument in Indian Philosophy* (The Hague, 1993)

—— and KONSTANTINE, S. *Christian Systematic Theology in a World Context* (London, 1993)

—— and THAKUR, SHIVESH, eds *Ethical and Political Dilemmas of Modern India* (London, 1993)

SMITH, BARDWELL *Religion and Legitimation of Power in Sri Lanka* (Chambersburg, PA, 1978)

SMITH, D. HOWARD *Chinese Religions* (New York, 1968)

SMITH, JANE I. and HADDAD, YVONNE *The Islamic Understanding of Death and Resurrection* (Albany, NY, 1981)

SMITH, JONATHAN Z. *Map Is Not Territory* (Leiden, 1978)

SMITH, M., LITTLE R., and SHACKLETON, M., eds *Perspectives on World Politics* (London, 1981)

SNELLGROVE, DAVID L., ed. *The Image of the Buddha* (Paris, 1978)

SODERBLOM, NATHAN *The Living God* (London, 1933)

SPIEGELBURG, HERBERT *The Phenomenological Movement* (The Hague, 1960), 2 vols

SPIRO, MELFORD *Buddhism and Society: A Great Tradition and Its Burmese Vicissitudes* (Berkeley, 1982)

STAAL, FRITS *The Vedic Ritual of the Fire Altar* (Berkeley, 1983), 2 vols

STEINER, FRANZ *Taboo* (New York, 1956)

STRENG, FREDERICK J. *Emptiness* (Nashville, 1967)

STRENSKI, IVAN *Four Theories of Myth in Twentieth Century History: Cassier, Eliade, Lévi-Strauss and Malinowski* (Iowa City, 1987)

—— *Religion in Relation: Method, Application and Moral Location* (Columbia, SC, 1993)

STRUNK, ORLO, ed. *The Psychology of Religion: Historical and Interpretative Readings* (Nashville, 1971)

SUNDKLER, BENGT *Zulu Zion and Some Swazi Zionists* (London, 1976)

SWINBURNE, RICHARD *The Coherence of Theism* (Oxford, 1977)

TAKEUCHI, YOSHINORI *The Heart of Buddhism* (New York, 1983)

TAMBIAH, STANLEY J. *World Conqueror and World Renouncer* (Cambridge, 1976)

TAYLOR, CHARLES *Hegel* (New York, 1975)

TEMPELS, PLACIDE *La philosophie bantoue* (Elizabethville, 1945)

THAPAR, ROMILA *Asoka and the Decline of the Mauryas* (Oxford, 1961)

TILLICH, PAUL *The Courage to Be* (New Haven, 1952)

—— *What Is Religion?* (New York, 1969)

TRIMINGHAM, SPENCER J. *The Sufi Orders in Islam* (New York, 1971)

TURNER, H. W. *Bibliography of New Religious Movements in Primal Societies*, vol. 1: *Black Africa* (Boston, 1977)

—— *From Temple to Meeting House* (The Hague, 1979)

TURNER, VICTOR *Dramas, Fields and Metaphors* (Ithaca, NY, 1974)

—— *The Ritual Process* (Chicago, 1969)

—— and TURNER, EDITH *Image and Pilgrimage in Christian Culture* (New York, 1978)

UNDERHILL, EVELYN *Mysticism* (New York, 1911)

VAN DER LEEUW, GERARDUS *Religion in Essence and Manifestation* (Princeton, 1986)

VIDLER, ALEC *The Church in an Age of Revolution* (Baltimore, 1961)

VIVEKANANDA, SWAMI *Complete Works* (Calcutta, 1964), 8 vols

VOLL, JOHN O. *Islam: Continuity and Change in the Modern World* (Boulder, CO, 1982)

VON GLASENAPP, HELMUTH *Buddhism: A Non-Theistic Religion* (New York, 1966)

VON GRUNEBAUM, G. E. *Modern Islam: The Search for Cultural Identity* (Berkeley, 1962)

—— and CAILLOIS, ROGER, eds *The Dream and Human Societies* (Berkeley, 1966)

VRIES, JAN DE *Perspectives in the History of Religions* (Berkeley, 1977)

WAARDENBURG, JACQUES *L'Islam dans le miroir de l'Occident* (Paris, 1969)

—— *Classical Approaches to the Study of Religion*, vol. 1 (The Hague, 1973)

WACH, JOACHIM *Sociology of Religion* (Chicago, 1964)

WAINWRIGHT, WILLIAM J. *Mysticism: A Study of Its Nature, Cognitive Value and Moral Implications* (Madison, WI, 1981)

WALLERSTEIN, IMMANUEL *The Modern World-System* (New York, 1974)

WALPIN, NISSON, ed. *Seasons of the Soul* (New York, 1981)

WARE, TIMOTHY (Kallistos) *The Orthodox Church* (Baltimore, 1964)

WARNER, MARINA *Alone of All Her Sex* (London, 1976)

WARTOFSKY, MARX W. *Feuerbach* (New York, 1977)

WATT, MONTGOMERY *The Formative Period of Islamic Thought*
(Edinburgh, 1973)

WELBON, GUY R. *The Buddhist Nirvana and Its Western Interpreters*
(Chicago, 1968)

WHEATON, PAUL *The Pivot of the Four Quarters* (Chicago, 1971)

WILLIAMS, C. A. S. *Encyclopedia of Chinese Symbolism and Art Motives*
(New York, 1961)

WILLIGER, EDWARD *Hagios* (Giessen, 1922)

WILSON, BRYAN R. *Magic and the Millennium* (New York, 1973)

WOLPERT, STANLEY *A New History of India* (New York, 1993)

WOODS, RICHARD, ed. *Understanding Mysticism* (Garden City, NJ, 1980)

YINGER, MILTON *The Scientific Study of Religion* (New York, 1970)

ZAEHNER, R. C. *Mysticism, Sacred and Profane* (Oxford, 1957)

—— *At Sundry Times* (London, 1958)

—— *Hinduism* (London, 1966)

ZIMMER, HEINRICH *Myths and Symbols in Indian Art and Civilization*
(Princeton, 1972)

INDEX

INDEX 315

sciousness in 47; cosmology of 33, 51,
52–3, 142, 149, 192, 242–3; death in
149–50; creation in 46; degeneration in
147–8; and *dharma* 44–5, 50, 197, 232;
doctrinal dimension 10, 44, 45, 56, 57,
67; ecumenical movement 257;
ethical/legal dimension 11, 197, 198,
201, 203, 224; exchange in 21; and folk
religions 196; formation of 242, 245;
gods in 28, 30, 33–4, 35, 38, 39, 152;
holy persons 99–100; human and
non-human beings 53–4, 200, 202; in
India 27, 264, 267; in Japan 23, 27, 68,
102, 147, 271; kingship in 238, 241–4,
263; and magic 234; material dimension
278–80; meditation in 16, 29, 48, 67, 76,
140, 182, 218, 263; missions 286; and
modernism 59, 110, 204, 205, 206;
monasticism 66, 120, 132, 220, 221–2,
234, 243, 263, 279; mythical dimension
10, 29, 243; non-identity theory 61, 62,
81–2; non-theism of 27–8, 31–2; pilgrimage in 86–7, 89; ritual dimension
201, 231, 243, 264; scriptures 125; and
shamanism 192; social dimension of 186,
230–1, 241–4, 263; temples 278–80; and
theology 227; transnationalism of 256;
virtues (*brahmaviharas*) 11, 103–4, 155,
185, 209; *see also* Mahayana Buddhism;
Theravada Buddhism
burial 12, 120
Burma 5, 28, 246, 256
Bushido 206
Butler, Edward C. 98
Byzantine Empire 241, 264, 265

calendar, religious 147, 280
in cosmic royal religions 238, 241, 263; and
myths 12, 126, 129; Reformation and
124; and ritual 83–4
Calvinism 97, 121
asceticism in 183–4; ethical dimension
121–2; experiential dimension 11, 266;
material dimension 283, 287; predestination in 42, 62, 122, 183–4, 211
Cambodia 28, 247
Campbell, Joseph 189, 194
capitalism 292
and nationalism 252–3, 267; and Protestantism 21, 204, 293
cargo cults 236
Caribbean 253
Carman, John B. 174
Carr, William 229
Carrasco, David 228
Cassirer, Ernst 204
caste system 55, 183, 245

and *brahman* 82; and ethics 200; and modernism 205; and ritual 113–14, 202; and
social organization 264
cathedrals 282
Catholicism 253
dimensional analysis of 12–13; doctrinal
dimension 10, 265; experiential dimension 184; and liberation theology 271–2;
material dimension 173, 287; miracles in
193; and modernism 23, 124, 207, 226;
and nationalism 207, 254, 256, 257,
268–9; papacy 66, 264, 265; pilgrimage
in 86, 87; priesthood 220; responsive
function in 58; ritual dimension 266;
social dimension 265; transsubstantiation in 120–1; worship in 89, 172–3
Cavendish, Richard 63
celibacy 235
in Buddhism 157; of contemplative 185; in
monasticism 98, 182, 222, 282; of priesthood 119, 220
centrality 53, 141
ceremonial 71, 107, 116, 120
Chadwick, Owen 221
Ch'an 68, 218
Chang, Kwang-chih Art 229
Chenu, M.D. 64
Ch'i 63
Chidester, David 18, 137, 188
China:
ancestors in 201; architecture in 265, 280,
284; death in 151; doctrine and community in 66; law in 187, 224; leadership
of 212, 229, 239; Maoism in 23, 58,
85–6, 206, 256, 258, 272, 292; and
modernism 206; myths in 158; pilgrimage in 85, 87; religions of 16, 23, 39, 63,
196; response to missions 57; sage in
227, 258; and secularization 270, 271
Chinese Buddhism 68, 102
bhakti in 94; degeneration in 147; nirvana
in 62;
and Taoism 57, 196
Christ:
Crucifixion of 138, 152; and Eucharist 9,
91; as exemplar 156–7; as healer 233;
incarnation of 7, 232; as prophet 216;
story of 10, 50, 68
Christendom 247–8
Christian, William 56, 66
Christian Scientists 283
Christianity 3–4, 291
abstractification of 60; architecture 281–3;
contemplation in 12, 16, 98, 172, 296; as
cosmic royal religion 264–5; demography
of 293–4; dimensional analysis 12–13;
doctrinal dimension 12, 264–5; dreams

in 153; ecumenical movements 257;
emergence of 98; ethical dimension 198,
200, 201, 210, 211; grace in 92; histories
of 8; hostility to Islam 295; human and
non-human beings 53–4; kingship
theology 241; martyrdom in 235;
material dimension 281–3; and modernism 23, 59; monasticism 13, 98–9,
221–2, 264; mysticism 96, 171, 180, 181,
182; mythical dimension 10, 12, 43–4,
50, 138, 156, 265; optimism of
148; orthodoxy in 56, 57; as personalistic
theism 40, 49; pilgrimage in 86, 88;
ritual in 121, 151, 178; self-sacrifice in
101; social dimension 247–8, 264; and
theology 225–6; virtue in 209–10; worship in 8, 90–1, 94, 172–3
Ch'u, T'ung-tsu 224
Chu Hsi 213
Chuang-tzu 212
Church of England see Anglicanism
churches 281–3
circumcision 118
civilizational religion 240–1, 245, 274
class system 268
    see also caste system
collective past 132
colonialism 3, 22, 57, 60, 236, 246, 274, 295
    and ethics 203–7; missionary 5; and na-
    tionalism 248, 269; and printing 286
combined religions 172
communication:
    and devic causation 108; through ritual
    77–9, 93, 112
communion see Eucharist; mass
Communism 14, 76, 267, 270
    see also Marxism
communitas 88
community, and doctrine 66–7
comparative religion 5–6, 136
compassion 103, 155, 185, 209
    see also love
conformity, religious 67
Confucianism 196, 221
    abstractification of 61; architecture 280–1;
    and economics 21, 293; ethical dimen-
    sion 11, 198–9, 212; gods in 9; li 125,
    127, 129, 199, 212; and modernism 204,
    206; Neo-Confucianism 61, 171, 213;
    and orthodoxy 57; responsive function in
    57; ritual in 199, 212; sages 66, 125, 217,
    227; as state ideology 21; virtue in
    212–13
Confucius (K'ung) 136, 258, 281
    ethical teaching of 155; as exemplar 156–7;
    and virtue 212
congregationalism 264, 266, 281

of pilgrimage 87, 88
Congregationalists 266
consciousness, pure 51, 67, 121, 123, 128,
    176, 179, 185, 189
    as impersonal god 43; and liberation 47; in
    Sufism 104; in Theravada Buddhism 29,
    97
consecration 72, 119–22
contemplation:
    and asceticism 182, 185; Buddhist 16, 29,
    48, 67, 140, 172, 263; Christian 12, 16,
    98, 172; and ethical dimension 185; and
    experiencing as 179–80; globalization of
    296; and impersonal god 43; and
    material dimension 282; Neo-Platonist
    45, 121; non-theistic nature of 49, 95; as
    pole of experience 167, 169–71, 173–4,
    188, 195; patterns of practice 181;
    provenance of 175–6; and ritual 96–9,
    111, 128, 181; and self-awareness 172,
    209; and shamanism 191; and social di-
    mension 263–4; as union 96, 103, 186;
    and worship 97–9, 101; see also medita-
    tion; mysticism
contemplative 218, 297
    monastic 12, 121, 173, 211, 218, 221–3
context:
    in cross-cultural studies 6, 7, 20
    experiential 168–71
conversion 181, 182
divine and luminous 179–80, 195
Conze, Edward 27, 130
Cook, Frank H. 46
Copleston, Frederick C. 64
coronation 103, 116
cosmic royal religions 241, 262–5, 267, 274,
    277, 288
cosmology 268
    Buddhist 33, 51, 52–3, 141–2, 149, 192,
    242–3; Eliadean 30; God in 38–9, 75;
    and heaven 51–2, 141; Jain 32, 192; and
    kingship 228–9, 237–9, 242; and
    material dimension 277, 288; in psy-
    choanalysis 194; shamanic 192; Ther-
    avadin 40; time and space in 52–3; and
    transcendance 142–3; see also
    creation
coterminous religions 66, 235–7, 251, 273,
    295
Coulson, Noel J. 196, 247
covenant 44, 187
Crawford, Cromwell 23, 78
creation 7, 45, 46–8
    and myth 133; and nearness of God 145;
    and numinous experience 167, 178–9,
    181; sacrificial model of 81–2; in theism
    41; in Theravada Buddhism 30–1; and

BAKER & TAYLOR